Ukraine

Sarah Johnstone

Contents

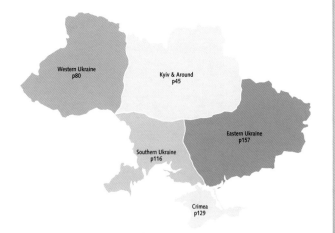

Western Ukraine p80

Kyiv & Around p45

Eastern Ukraine p157

Southern Ukraine p116

Crimea p129

Destination Ukraine

At some point, every guidebook to Ukraine trots out the fact that the country's name means 'borderland'. However we prefer the equally valid translation 'on the edge'. On the eastern frontier of the EU, on the point of decisive social change, and on the verge of discovery by Western travellers, today's Ukraine is an edgy, interesting place to be.

Not that it's risky. When this vast Slavic nation made a global splash in 2004 with the Orange Revolution against a corrupt government, news correspondents were astounded that a people so bitterly divided were also so peaceable. Instead, it's stepping into a rich, fascinating but largely unknown culture that creates the sense of daring here.

Locals joke that theirs is a land of churches, cafés and petrol stations, and it's true the golden domes of myriad Orthodox cathedrals leave a dazzling impression. But so does the monumental architecture of Kyiv, the slatternly neoclassical charm of seaside Odesa and the cosy Central European atmosphere of Lviv. Plus there's the breathtaking beauty of Crimea, where sheer cliffs tower above a winding Mediterranean-like coast.

It would be underselling this one-time region of the USSR to make too many comparisons with Russia because Ukraine draws on numerous other historical influences, including Byzantine, Polish, Cossack and Tatar. But it does share its northern cousin's penchant for tragicomedy, improvisation, and genuine human warmth mixed with occasionally surly Soviet-style bureaucracy. It puts the foreign back into European travel and acts as an antidote to an increasingly overexplored, identikit world. Think you've been there, done that? Not if you ain't been here.

CHORNOBYL (p75)
Sign up for the world's most bizarre day trip to the infamous nuclear reactor

LVIV (p83)
Take in the green Florentine domes, Central European charm and Père Lachaise-like cemetery

KAMYANETS-PODILSKY (p105)
Be awestruck by this medieval town marooned atop a tall rock island

ODESA (p118)
Relive film history on the Potemkin Steps and dance till dawn in open-air seaside clubs

VYLKOVO (p128)
Punt around the waterways of this 'Ukrainian Venice' in the beautiful Danube Biosphere

ELEVATION

1800m
1500m
1200m
900m
600m
300m
0

Poland
Belarus
Slovakia
Hungary
Moldova
Romania

Lomza
Bialystok
Baranavicy
Babrujsk
Homel
Novy Yarylovychy
Chernihiv
Siedlce
Biala Podlaska
Brest
Pinsk
Pulawy
Lublin
Chelm
Kovel
Ovruch
Chornobyl
Kyivske Reservoir
Korosten
Rzeszow
Chervonohrad
Lutsk
Novohrad-Volynsky
Korets
Kyiv
Borysp
Przemysl
Lviv
Dubno
Rivne
Shepetivka
Zhytomyr
Berdychiv
Bila Tserkva
Shehyn
Kremenets
Ternopil
Khmelnytsky
Drohobych
Stry
Kalush
Chortkiv
Vinnytsya
Nemyriv
Uman
Ivano-Frankivsk
Kamyanets-Podilsky
Mogyliv-Podilsky
Uzhhorod
Chop
Mukacheve
Carpathian National Nature Park Mt Hoverla (2061m)
Kolomyya
Chernivtsi
Briceni
Yampil
Pervomaysk
Satu Mare
Botosani
Edinec
Berezivka
Baia Mare
Balti
Chisinau
Ode
Illichiv
Cluj-Napoca
Iasi
Tiraspol
Pervomaisc
Bilgorod-Dnistrovsky
Dnistrovsky Estuary
Turda
Piatra-Neamt
Cimislia
Tirgu Mures
Medias
Birlad
Sebes
Sibiu
Bolhrad
Lake Sasyk
Hunedoara
Danube Biosphere Reserve
Brasov
Galati
Izmayil
Vylkovo
Buzau
Braila
Tulcea
Pitesti
Ploiesti
Bucuresti
Constanta

KYIV (p45)
Be dazzled by glittering church domes, wide boulevards and glamorous nightlife

Russia

Russia

0 ——— 80 km
0 ——— 40 miles

Brjansk

Orel

Lipeck

Novhorod-Siversky

Shostka

Krolevets

Kursk

Voronez

Mena

Konotop

Nizhnyn

Sumy

Romny

Belgorod

Pryluky

Pyryatyn

Lubny

Kharkiv

Kupyansk

Starobilsk

Cherkasy

Smila

Poltava

Krasnohrad

Izyum

Rubizhne

Lysychansk

Kremenchuk

Svitlovodsk

Slovyansk

Kramatorsk

Luhansk

Znamyanka

Oleksandriya

Novomoskovsk

Pavlohrad

Kostyantynivka

Horlivka

Bryanka

Krasnodon

Kirovohrad

Pyatykhatky

Zhovti Vody

Dniprodzerzhynsk

Dnipropetrovsk

Krasnoarmiysk

Makiyivka

Krasny Luch

Sverdlovsk

Kryvy Rih

Zaporizhzhya

DONETSK

Shakhtarsk

Novoşahtinsk

Nikopol

Vasylivka

Dovzhansky

Rostov-on-Don

Mariupol

Taganrog

Mykolayiv

Melitopol

Berdyansk

Nova Kahovka

Kherson

Ochakiv

Novooleksiyivka

Russia

Sea of Azov

KARA-DAH (p155)
Marvel at the sci-fi volcanic landscape and odd-shaped rocks of this protected reserve

Krasnoperekopsk

Dzhankoy

Kerch

Ekaterinodar

Black Sea

Yevpatoriya

Feodosiya
Kara-Dah
Nature Reserve

Anapa

Novorossisk

BAKHCHYSARAY (p136)
Learn about Tatar culture at the Khans' Palace, then explore the cave city of Chufut-Kale

Simferopol

Bakhchysaray

Sudak

SUDAK (p154)
Follow the crenulated walls of a historic Silk Road fortress to the isolated top tower

Alushta

Sevastopol

Yalta

Balaklava

Tuapse

SEVASTOPOL & BALAKLAVA (p140)
Delve into Crimean and Cold War history beside the blue waters of these two towns

YALTA (p145)
Revel in post-Soviet kitsch, drop in at Chekhovs' and tour historic palaces

Highlights Ukraine

Chill out with a glass of local champagne on the shores of Novy Svit (p154)

Dancers in traditional central Ukrainian dress help keep the folk traditions alive

PHOTOBANK.KIEV.UA/ALEXANDR IVANOV

PETER WILLIAM THORNTON

Relax at an outdoor café on Lviv's charming market square (p85)

OTHER HIGHLIGHTS

- Wander among the weird volcanic shapes of the Kara-Dah Nature Reserve (p155)
- Scan the horizon from Hoverla (p97), the highest Ukrainian peak
- Walk along the fortress at Sudak (p154), which is like a mini-wall of China
- Enjoy a gondola ride with a difference down the canal streets of Vylkovo (p128)

DENYS SAVCHENKO / ALAMY

Contemplate the mournful beauty of Lviv's Lychakivsky Cemetery (p87)

Visit Livadia Palace (p150), where the great powers shaped the face of postwar Europe

JONATHAN SMITH

Get down with religious pilgrims and subterranean mummified saints at Kyiv's Caves Monastery (p56)

PHOTOBANK.KIEV.UA/OKSANA TSEATSURA

Catch up on Tatar history at the Khans'
Palace (p136), Bakhchysaray

Explore the hidden nooks and crannies of the cave
city of Chufut-Kale (p137), Bakhchysaray

Orange revolutionaries celebrate their victory at Kyiv's Independence Square (p53)

Getting Started

As a largely non-English speaking region of the former Soviet Union, Ukraine still welcomes mostly package tourists. So, contrary to the following itineraries (p13), the most common route is actually down the Dnipro River on an expensive cruise.

Independent travellers backpacking around the country will rarely find their needs directly catered for. Precious few tourist information offices exist, 90% of signage is in Cyrillic only and accommodation that is simultaneously cheap and decent is scarce. Buses are like those in the developing world. Trains are also painfully slow – although they do run on time and usually provide a fun journey. In that respect, this is a destination for more adventurous souls. But, on the other hand, Kyiv is a vibrant, cosmopolitan capital just waiting to be discovered as an exciting city break. English is more widely spoken here, as it is in the two other Ukrainian cities most welcoming to tourists – Lviv and Odesa.

WHEN TO GO

Spring (late April to early June) is the best time to visit, when perfumed chestnut trees bloom and people the country over rejoice in throwing off heavy winter coats. The Orthodox rituals surrounding Easter are fabulous, plus there's a sense of reawakening as cafés begin to set out pavement seating again and hikers retake the heights of the Carpathian and Crimean Mountains.

For climate information see p174.

During the sometimes stiflingly hot summer, things get relatively busy as locals head en masse for Crimea, the Black Sea Coast and the Carpathians. Everything is focused on the great outdoors in July and August, and most theatres close.

Autumn (Fall) is almost as inviting as spring, as the crowds dissipate and the mercury drops to a more comfortable level. In December and January it's bitingly cold inland, particularly in the east. But this is a good time to head to the Carpathian Mountains, Ukraine's skiing district.

It's wise to book ahead during the public holidays in the first weeks of January and May (see p178).

DON'T LEAVE HOME WITHOUT...

- Valid travel insurance (see p178)
- Checking whether you need a visa (see p182)
- A phrasebook, if you don't speak the language and are venturing further than Kyiv
- Ensuring your vaccinations are up to date (see p194)
- A basic first-aid kit, possibly including sterile syringes and eye drops – smog in some places can get to you and some local brands sting
- A torch, for the many unlit streets
- An airline mask to block out the light in hotel rooms with frequently thin curtains
- A scarf and below-knee skirt, for women visiting Orthodox churches
- A sense of humour and flexibility

COSTS & MONEY

While Ukrainians grapple with the question of how European or Russian their national identity is, travel costs in the country definitely resemble Russia more than, say, the Czech Republic – although, unlike in Russia, foreigners and locals are charged the same prices (except by taxi drivers!). Public transport is dirt cheap, as are museums and eating, at least outside the larger cities. However, accommodation is sometimes wildly overpriced and restaurant prices in Kyiv and Odesa are approaching those in Western Europe.

A decent Western-standard hotel room in Kyiv (single or double) will generally cost at least $80 and is more likely to kick off at $145. (Renting an apartment is the answer, see p172.) A basic meal in a reasonable restaurant in the capital can easily cost 100uah to 150uah ($20 to $30) per person.

However, if you choose cafeteria-style eateries or spend more time in the countryside, meals can set you back as little as 10uah ($2). Furthermore, if you're prepared to stay in unappetising former-Soviet hotels, and share a communal bathroom, you can get away with paying $10 to $20 a night. Decent hotels in the countryside usually range from $30 to $40 a night.

Museum entrance is a bargain at 3uah to 15uah (60¢ to $3) and public transport is even cheaper at 50 kopecks (10¢) to 3uah (60¢). A train ride across the entire country will set you back no more than 50uah to 75uah ($10 to $14).

On the other hand, those who would never usually consider hiring a guide or going on an organised day trip might find themselves doing so briefly in Ukraine to reach out-of-the-way places. This will cost a sizable $60 to $100 per day.

HOW MUCH?

Kyiv metro ride
50 kopecks

Bottle of Hetman vodka
(0.7L) 16-26uah

Cup of brewed coffee
7-14uah

Ticket to opera in Kyiv
20uah

Ticket to football game
at Dynamo Stadium in
Kyiv 15uah

**LONELY PLANET
INDEX**

Litre of petrol 3.10uah

Litre of bottled water
2.50-3.50uah

Half-litre bottle of Obolon
beer 3.50uah

Souvenir T-shirt 25-30uah

Street snack (perepichka –
meat roll) 2.50uah

TRAVEL LITERATURE

Not many authors – of fiction or nonfiction – have made their way across Ukraine. So take your diary – there's a gap in the market here. Anna Reid's *Borderland* (see p19) functions as much as a travelogue as a history book.

Everything is Illuminated by Jonathan Safran Foer follows a Jewish American searching for the Ukrainian woman who saved his grandfather during WWII. Letters between him and his language-mangling translator and guide build up a wacky, almost stream-of-consciousness novel. Brilliant.

In *Long Way Round,* actor Ewan McGregor and friend Charley Boorman cross Europe, including Ukraine, on their motorbikes. But they're not writers and devote at least as much space to their practical tribulations as to the countries. *Riders to the Midnight Sun* by Marc Llewellyn chronicles an earlier trip, this time by pedal power from Sevastopol to Murmansk, Russia. As countless Ukrainians welcome the author and his girlfriend into their homes, it offers greater local insight.

Innocents Abroad by Mark Twain recounts the great 19th-century American journalist's second trip through Europe, taking him en route to Sevastopol and Odesa. Then in ruins, the first city didn't impress. The second did.

INTERNET RESOURCES

Ukrainian websites come and go faster than the norm. However, the following sites have endured many years. You can find news and links at the website of **Lonely Planet** (www.lonelyplanet.com), where there are a couple

TOP TENS
Monasteries & Churches
Even the most confirmed atheist will be impressed by the plethora of ornate churches that sprout like mushrooms across Ukraine, particularly in Kyiv. Inside are ancient frescoes and remarkable iconostases. The larger monasteries also contain mummified monks and 'miracle-working' icons.

- Caves Monastery, Kyiv (p56)
- Pochayiv Monastery, Pochayiv (p110)
- Khrestovozdvyzhensky Monastery, Poltava (p164)
- Uspensky Monastery, Bakhchysaray (p137)
- St Sophia's Cathedral, Kyiv (p55)
- St Andrew's Church, Kyiv (p55)
- St Volodymyr's Cathedral, Kyiv (p60)
- St Michael's Monastery, Kyiv (p56)
- Transfiguration Church, Lviv (p85)
- St Nicholas 'Drunken' Cathedral, Chernivitsi (p102)

Museums
Many Ukrainian museums are starved of cash and some are downright musty. However, the country also has some stunning exceptions that have lashings of ancient gold, are of global historical significance, or offer intriguing insights into Ukrainian history or folk culture.

- Historical Treasures Museum, Kyiv (p59)
- Livadia Palace, Crimea (p150)
- Chekhov House-Museum, Yalta (p147)
- Pyrohovo Museum of Folk Architecture, Kyiv (p62)
- Museum of Microminiature, Kyiv (p58)
- Museum of the Great Patriotic War, Kyiv (p60)
- Pysanky Museum, Kolomyya (p100)
- Museum of Hutsul Folk Art, Kolomyya (p100)
- Chornobyl Museum, Kyiv (p56)
- Bulgakov Museum, Kyiv (p61)

Our Favourite Adventures
Ukraine is a land of the unconventional and the quirky, which surprises with everything from stunning landscapes to ancient pagan rituals and Cold War history.

- Clambering over the cave cities of Crimea (p137)
- Bungee jumping in (or just wandering around) Kamyanets-Podilsky (p105)
- Hiking in the Kara-Dah Nature Reserve (p155), Crimea
- Making like a pagan during the Ivan Kupalo festival (p28)
- Climbing the highest Ukrainian mountain, Hoverla (p96)
- Visiting the Chornobyl exclusion zone (p75), around Kyiv
- Jumping into the freezing Dnipro or being splashed with icy water during Epiphany (p65)
- Scuba-diving into Balaklava's secret nuclear submarine factory (p144)
- Exploring the catacombs of Sevastopol (p142) or Odesa (p123)
- Boating around the Venice-like Vylkovo and the surrounding Danube Biosphere Reserve (p128)

of enthusiastic posters on Ukraine in the Eastern European section of the Thorn Tree bulletin board.

Art Ukraine (www.artukraine.com) A broad range of articles on Ukraine are compiled here. They focus on culture but also include travel.

Brama (www.brama.com) Run by US Ukrainians, this comprehensive site ranges from links to news on Ukraine to a few online maps, and has a great travel bulletin board.

CIA World Factbook – Ukraine (http://cia.gov/cia/publications/factbook/geos/up.html) Frequently updated statistics and other information on demographic, social and economic basics.

Infoukes (www.infoukes.com) Visa information, frequently asked questions, books to buy about Ukraine, online maps and tips on where to visit are all offered on these Canadian-Ukrainian pages.

Ukrainian Government Portal (www.kmu.gov.ua/control/en) Go to the Press Center to catch up on all the latest government policies and reforms, including potential changes to visa regulations.

Itineraries

CLASSIC ROUTES

THROUGH THE CENTRE

Two Weeks

Set the ball rolling in colossal **Kyiv** (p45). You'll need three to four days to take in the mix of gold-domed Orthodox churches, monumental Stalinist architecture and leafy parks, plus the **Caves Monastery** (p56) and a few museums. Don't forget to sample the myriad eating and drinking opportunities, too. Wrenching yourself away, head south via Uman, the home of **Sofiyivka Park** (p77), the Ukrainian Versailles. Now head down to **Odesa** (p118). If you land in this Black Sea port on a weekend, more's the better, as this hedonistic city is renowned for its restaurants and nightclubs. In any case, spend a few days tripping down the world-famous **Potemkin Steps** (p119), admiring the neoclassical architecture and just generally drinking in the beguiling southern magic, before catching the overnight train to Simferopol and travelling straight through to the principal Crimean resort of **Yalta** (p145).

For the next few days, base yourself in Yalta while making side trips to the **Livadia** (p150) and **Alupka palaces** (p152), **Mt Ay-Petri** (p152) and whatever else takes your fancy. On the way home, stop in **Simferopol** (p132), from where it's an easy day trip to the Khans' Palace and cave city in the Tatar capital of **Bakhchysaray** (p136). If travelling by train, leave a full day to get back to Kyiv – or simply hop on a Simferopol–Kyiv flight.

From dynamic Kyiv, plunge straight into the quintessential Ukrainian experience. This 2000km journey takes you through sybaritic Odesa, before landing you in striking Crimea, with its historic palaces, Tatar culture and kitschy post-Soviet chic.

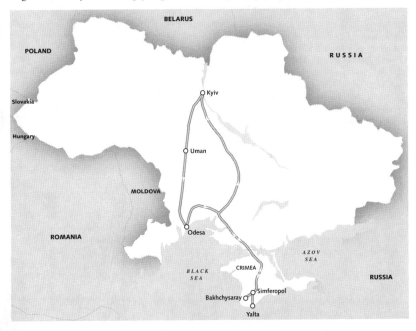

CARPATHIAN CAPER   Two Weeks

Once again the kick-off point is **Kyiv** (p45). However, this time, after three to four days of exploring the capital, your destination is the most patriotically 'Ukrainian' region of the country. The first port of call is the enchanting Galician capital of **Lviv** (p83). If you wish to travel here in style, book yourself a berth on the luxury **Grand Tour train carriage** (p92). Allow two to three days to get to know Lviv, interspersing visits to its ornate Ukrainian Catholic churches, Italianate buildings, Gothic cemetery and panoramic castle hill with long coffee breaks in the city's many Austrian-style cafés.

Head for the hills on this 1650km trek through the rustic west. After the Central European charm of Lviv, you'll reach the highest Ukrainian peak and take in some native Hutsul culture before exploring the fortresses around Kamyanets-Podilsky.

Thus stuffed full of cake and caffeine, head south towards the **Carpathian National Nature Park** (p95). Stop briefly in **Ivano-Frankivsk** (p93), or proceed straight to **Yaremcha** (p98). Spend a few days hiking to the highest Ukrainian mountain, **Hoverla** (p96) and in Yaremcha's immediate vicinity. Afterwards, turn your attentions east towards tidy **Kolomyya** (p100) and its two unusual museums. One showcases the country's largest collection of *pysanky* (painted Easter eggs); the other has a wide variety of folk art produced by Hutsuls, the native people of the Carpathian region. After a brief stopover to view the university building in **Chernivtsi** (p101), be sure not to miss the absolutely stunning landscape of **Kamyanets-Podilsky** (p105), where the medieval Old Town perches atop a tall rock in the middle of a river loop. Also remember that **Khotyn fortress** (p109) is an easy day trip from here. Overnight trains run daily from Kamyanets-Podilsky to Kyiv, arriving in the capital in the early morning.

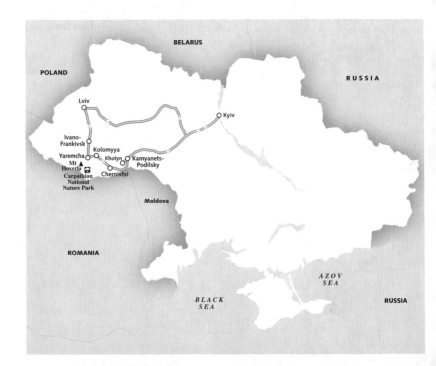

ROADS LESS TRAVELLED

BLACK SEA MAGIC   Three Weeks

By starting in **Odesa** (p118), which has direct international flights, you'll have more time to explore Ukraine's Mediterranean-like coast. Using larger towns as a base for side trips, as we frequently suggest, cuts down on the awkward process of carrying luggage on cramped *marshrutky* (minibuses).

Spend two to three days exploring Odesa, then embark a two-day side trip to **Vylkovo** (p128) and the surrounding Danube Biosphere Reserve. If visiting in June, July or August – when you should book accommodation ahead – you can catch a catamaran (p189) around the picture-postcard coast to **Sevastopol** (p140). Outside these months, take the train instead and change at Simferopol for the regular *elektrychka* (electric) commuter service. In Sevastopol set aside one day to explore this formerly closed military base, one to visit the Tatar capital **Bakhchysaray** (p136) and another to see **Balaklava** (p143). From here, take a scenic *marshrutka* ride to **Yalta** (p145), and use this happy-go-lucky resort as a launch pad to surrounding attractions.

Now you're venturing where few foreign tourists do, into the Crimean peninsula's even more stunning east. Catch a bus from Yalta to **Sudak** (p154), visit the fortress here and make a day trip to the beach of **Novy Svit** (p154). And don't forget to pick up a bottle of champagne while here. Plunge on to **Feodosiya** (p155), which is mainly worth visiting as a gateway to the **Kara-Dah Nature Reserve** (p155), with its eerily shaped volcanic rocks. From Feodosiya, take a bus back to Simferopol and make your way by train to Odesa.

Want a seaside holiday with a real difference? This relaxed 2200km route gives you a warm feeling by combining beaches, clubs and cheap champagne with strikingly unique landscapes, fascinating history and loads of culture to boot.

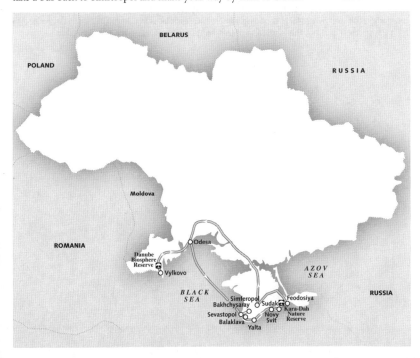

The Author

SARAH JOHNSTONE

Sarah had her first brush with the USSR and Russian lessons at the age of eight in the bizarre setting of a Soviet cruise ship sailing from her native Australia. However, she was a latecomer to independent Ukraine, venturing there for the first time as a journalist at the end of the 1990s. The place got her hooked – the wacky stories, the irreverent characters, the beguiling architecture and scenery. She had to come back and did repeatedly, most recently to write this guide. Before signing with Lonely Planet, 10 books ago in 2002, London-based Sarah worked at Reuters, Business Traveller and for too many other publications to bore readers with here.

My Favourite Trip

Any overnight train journey in Ukraine I find thrilling. Buying provisions beforehand, having a cast-iron excuse to laze around for hours and all the old-fashioned rituals take me right back to childhood. Plus, trains here are always great, boozy communal meeting places, so if the carriages finally pull into a favourite station, well, that's the icing on the cake. I've always been captivated by Odesa (p118), one of those places that just 'has something'. Friendly Lviv (p83) is a wonderfully charming Central European city, the 'rock island' of Kamyanets-Podilsky (p105)

is unforgettable and Kyiv (p45) is engagingly energetic. Few places in Crimea (p129) can be reached by train (rather than bus) but the landscape of that entire peninsula is pretty damn amazing.

Snapshot

'I'm disappointed to be translating these lies,' Natalya Dymytruk signed to TV channel UT-1's deaf viewers on 25 November 2004, during the most disputed presidential election in Ukrainian history. 'Don't believe the results they have announced,' she continued, referring to government candidate Viktor Yanukovych's 'win'. And with that, the humble sign-language interpreter did her bit to help usher in a new era.

During Ukraine's 'Orange Revolution' that freezing month, hundreds of thousands did the same, taking to Kyiv's streets to protest corruption and vote rigging. Normally state media restrictions would have meant viewers getting a one-sided story. But after Dymytruk told them what she'd done, her colleagues followed. Suddenly, reports discussing electoral fraud were on air and Kyiv's chants of 'Yu-shchenka' in support of the opposition candidate were broadcast countrywide.

Today, with one election rerun and several Supreme Court battles far behind them, Ukrainians are trying to mend their broken society. Finally elected president, Viktor Yushchenko promised big things. 'If this country is governed by honest people and the government can survive, people will feel the effects…within a year,' he told Polish TV – his once-handsome face disfigured by a poisoning attempt on his life during the campaign. But, even with plans for closer European links, the challenges are huge.

Ten years under president Leonid Kuchma left an enormous gap between rich and poor. Ukraine, which has plentiful resources and potential for wealth, became one of the world's most corrupt countries. Between 1994 and 2004, controversial privatisations placed lucrative companies in the hands of the president's cronies, at a fraction of the market value. Other scandals included the murder in 2000 of opposition journalist Grygory Gongadze (see p27), where audio tapes pointed to the alleged involvement of Kuchma. Outrageously, while the economy was growing by 9% in 2004, nearly a third of Ukrainians continued to live in poverty.

So Yushchenko's government must raise living standards over the next few years. At the same time, it has to build bridges with the pro-Russian, pro-Yanukovych eastern Ukraine and keep the country stable. Another priority is good relations with Russia, Ukraine's biggest trade partner, which also backed Yanukovych. Such Herculean tasks put the new administration under an intense spotlight. Yushchenko – a former banker and prime minister (1999–2001) – is believed honest and has a good economic track record. But being poisoned with dioxin has cast a shadow over his health, and his political lieutenants are held in lesser esteem. Some even view the wealthy Yuliya Tymoshenko – the new prime minister – and Petro Poroshenko just as new oligarchs to replace the old.

Still, despite the potential pitfalls awaiting them, many Ukrainians remain optimistic, surprised by their revolution's success and excited by the very possibility of change. Indeed, if a global mobile phone giant hadn't beaten them to it, their cry might be: 'The future's bright, the future's orange'. Cripes. Life might imitate art sometimes, but how often does it imitate advertising?

FAST FACTS

Area: 603,700 sq km, just smaller than Texas

Population: 47.1 million

GDP per capita: $5400 (2004)

Inflation: 5.2% (2004)

Registered unemployment: 3.7% (believed much higher)

Job sectors: services 44%, industry 32%, farming 24%

Life expectancy: women 72.3 years, men 61.3 years

Vodka consumption: 350 million litres a year (Canadean, 2003)

Railways: 22,473km of track

National anthem: Ukraine Has Not Yet Died

History

Although their northern neighbours disparagingly refer to Ukrainians as 'little Russians', it was Ukraine that was home to the first Eastern Slavic state. So historically Ukraine is the birthplace of Russia rather than vice versa. Another irony is that this initial state, Kyivan Rus, was founded in the 9th century by neither Russians nor Ukrainians, but by Vikings – an indication of just how much foreigners have meddled in the region's convoluted history.

CIMMERIANS TO KHAZARS

Before Kyivan Rus, Ukraine's prehistory is tribal. First came the Cimmerians in the 12th century BC. Then, fierce warrior Scythians from Central Asia settled the steppe in the 7th century BC, while Greeks from western Asia Minor established city-states around the Black Sea. The two groups formed a symbiotic relationship. The famous gold work found in Scythian tombs is believed commissioned from Greek artisans; a fine collection is found in Kyiv's Caves Monastery (p56).

Successive waves of nomadic invaders – Samaritans from the east, Germanic Ostrogoths from northern Poland and Huns from Mongolia – continued to sweep into Ukraine. The Slavs, thought to originate from a region near the borders of present-day Poland, Belarus and northwestern Ukraine, remained untouched by these invasions. Turkic/Iranian Khazars from the Caucasus were probably the first to bring the Slavs under subjugation, in the 8th century AD.

KYIVAN RUS

Meanwhile, Scandinavians – known as Varangians or Rus to the Slavs – had been exploring, trading and setting up small states east of the Baltic since the 6th century. Travelling south from the Rus power centre of Novgorod (near modern-day St Petersburg) in 878, King Oleh stopped and declared himself ruler of Kyiv. The city handily lay between Novgorod and Constantinople on the Dnipro River, and under Oleh's urging it became capital of a huge, unified Rus state. At its largest – under the 978–1015 rule of Volodymyr the Great – this empire stretched from the Volga to the Danube and to the Baltic, its prosperity based on trade along the Dnipro. Despite Nordic rule, the territory's underlying culture remained essentially Slavic.

As well as consolidating Rus territory, Volodymyr firmly established Orthodox Christianity as the preeminent religion. By accepting baptism in 989 and marrying the Byzantine emperor's daughter (at Chersonesus outside Sevastopol, see p140), he opened the door to Byzantine artistic influences and cast Kyivan Rus as a European, rather than Islamic Asian, state. St Sofia's Cathedral in Kyiv (p55) is still testament to Kyivan Rus' greatness and the importance of Orthodox Christianity within the state.

By the 11th and 12th centuries the empire had begun to disintegrate, dividing into some 10 rival princedoms, and when Mongol warriors sacked Kyiv in 1240, it largely ceased to exist. According to Russian and Western historians, who believe that present-day Russia, Ukraine and Belarus all

c470	878
Legendary Slavic brothers Ky, Shchek and Khoriv and sister Lybid found Kyiv	Nordic King Oleh becomes ruler of Kyiv and the first Eastern Slavic state, Kyivan Rus

stem from Kyivan Rus, the centres of power then simply shifted north and
west, with Russia evolving from the northern princedoms of Novgorod
and Vladimir-Suzdal. Some Ukrainian historians, however, prefer to
treat Russia as a distinct civilisation – emanating from and returning to
Novgorod.

MONGOLS, TATARS & TURKS
The Mongol invasion that destroyed Kyivan Rus in 1240 was led by
Genghis Khan's grandson Batu. As a result of his handiwork, a large
swathe of the Rus empire was subsumed into the so-called Golden Horde
(horde meaning region) of the Mongol empire. This encompassed much
of eastern and southern Ukraine, along with parts of European Russia
and Siberia, with the city of Sarai, on the Volga, as its capital.

Over time, Mongol leaders were gradually replaced by Tatar overlords,
and when the horde began to disintegrate in the 15th century, it divided
into several smaller khanates. One – the Crimean Khanate – became a client state of the Constantinople-based Ottoman Turk Empire, after the fall
of Byzantium in 1453. The Crimean Tatars, as the people of the khanate
were known, made frequent slave raids into Ukrainian, Russian and Polish
sides until the 18th century. When Russia overran Crimea in 1783, the
Tatars suffered dreadfully and have ever since. However, remnants of their
once-powerful civilisation can still be seen in Bakhchysaray (p136).

Anna Reid's acces-
sible *Borderland* skilfully
weaves her observa-
tions of Ukraine during
the early 1990s as an
Economist correspondent
into a journey through
Ukrainian history. Recent
events, however, have
derailed some of its
predictions.

GALICIA-VOLYNIA
Meanwhile, from 1197 under the rule of Prince Roman Mstyslavych,
the region of Galicia-Volynia (most of present-day western, central and
northern Ukraine, plus parts of northeastern Poland and southern Belarus) became one of the most powerful within Kyivan Rus. This enclave's
geography differentiated it from the rest of the empire. It was far enough
west to avoid conquest by eastern invaders like the Mongols, and more
likely to fall prey to its Catholic neighbours Hungary and Poland – or later
Lithuania. More densely populated than any other part of Kyivan Rus, it
developed a rich, agricultural society.

Until 1340 Galicia-Volynia enjoyed independent rule under Roman,
his son Danylo, grandson Lev and descendants, who kept the Mongols
at bay and helped Lviv and other cities to flourish. Political control was
wrested from this local dynasty by the Poles and Lithuanians in the 1340s,
who split the kingdom between them and used it as a base to expand
eastwards into other areas of Ukraine, including Kyiv. However, its brief
period of early self-determination seems to have left Galicia-Volynia with
a particularly strong taste for Ukrainian nationalism, which is still evident
in the region today.

COSSACKS
Later lionised – perhaps overoptimistically – by nationalist writers such
as Taras Shevchenko and Ivan Franko, the Cossacks are central to the
country's identity. They arose out of the steppe in the country's sparsely
populated midsouth. In the mid-15th century, it was a kind of no-man's-
land separating the Polish-Lithuanian settlements in the northwest from
the Tatars in Crimea.

989	1240
Volodymyr the Great organises a mass baptism into Orthodox Christianity in the Dnipro River	Mongols sack Kyiv; Kyivan Rus crumbles and its east is absorbed into the Golden Horde

However, the steppe offered abundant natural wealth, and poorer individuals in Polish-Lithuanian society began making longer forays south to hunt or forage for food. The area also attracted runaway serfs, criminals, bandits and Orthodox refugees. Along with a few semi-independent Tatar bands, the hard-drinking inhabitants formed self-governing militaristic communities and became known as *kozaky* (Cossacks in English), from a Turkic word meaning 'outlaw, adventurer or free person'. The people elected the ruling chieftain (hetman). The most famous group of Cossacks was based below the rapids *(za porozhy)* on the lower Dnipro, in a fortified island community called Zaporizhsky Sich (see p166).

Cossacks eventually united to form the Cossack Hetmanate, which reasserted the concept of Ukrainian self-determination to a degree, although it officially came under Polish rule after military defeat in 1569. At the height of their power, the Cossacks waged a number of successful campaigns against the Turks, sacking the Black Sea cities of Varna and Kafa and twice assaulting Istanbul (in 1615 and 1620). While millions of peasants in the Polish-Lithuanian state joined the Uniate Church after 1596 (see p26), the Cossacks remained fully Orthodox.

Polish monarchs were often at odds with the Cossacks, even though they used them as mercenaries. In the 17th century there were Cossack-led uprisings to try to win greater autonomy. However, while initially successful, ultimately they only led to a change of overlord – from Polish to Russian (see the boxed text, below).

The website www.info ukes.com/history has links to most periods of Ukrainian history, with an emphasis on the last two centuries.

RUSSIAN CONTROL

Without Ukraine and its abundant natural wealth, Russia never would have been such a powerful player. It also offered access to the Black Sea, so

PARADISE LOST

To avoid offending Ukrainians, one should never say out loud that one of the country's greatest heroes ultimately led it to defeat. Unfortunately, it is at least partly true. The hero in question is the Cossack Hetman Bohdan Khmelnytsky, who led a huge rebellion against the Poles in 1648. Aided by Tatar cavalry, the Cossacks destroyed the Polish army at the Battle of Pyliavtsi (near present-day Khmelnytsky). Storming past Lviv, Khmelnytsky was poised for an invasion of Poland, but decided to accept an armistice and returned triumphantly to Kyiv. The following year, at another battle against Polish King Casimir, near Zboriv, Khmelnytsky was betrayed by his Tatar allies and forced to sign an armistice. A further forced armistice in 1651 made Khmelnytsky finally realise that foreign support was necessary for a decisive victory over the Poles. He signed a military alliance with Russia in 1654, which eventually also betrayed him.

Instead of supporting the Cossacks, Russia went into battle against Poland in 1660 for control of Ukraine. In 1667 and 1668 the two signed treaties carving up the country between them. Russia got control over Kyiv and northern Ukraine east of the Dnipro.

The Poles kept territory to the west of the river. Hetman Ivan Mazepa, aiming to unite Polish- and Russian-dominated Ukraine, allied with Sweden against Russia's Peter the Great but was beaten at Poltava (1709). Following victories against the Ottomans, Catherine the Great destroyed the Cossack Sich in 1775.

Bohdan Khmelnytsky, though, is still revered for his initial storming victory against the Poles. He's remembered not as a man who hesitated, but one who was fatally betrayed.

1349	1648
Poland overruns Galicia and, with Lithuania, inches further eastwards into Ukraine	Local Cossacks rebel against Polish rulers, but end up with Russian masters instead

after a series of wars with the Turks in the 18th century, Russia was keen to expand into southern Ukraine. Catherine the Great led the charge to colonise and 'Russify'. In 1775, the same year she destroyed the Zaporizhsky Sich, she annexed the region to the imperial province of 'New Russia' and charged governor Grygory Potemkin with attracting settlers and founding new cities. Potemkin had a hand in establishing today's Dnipropetrovsk, Sevastopol and Simferopol, but died before Odesa was completed.

In 1772 powerful Prussia, Austria and Russia decided to carve up Poland. Under the resulting 'Partitions of Poland' (1772–95), most of western Ukraine was handed to Russia – although the far west around Lviv went to the Austrian Habsburg empire. The Ukrainian nationalist movement was born in Kyiv in the 1840s, but when the tsarist authorities there banned the Ukrainian language from official use in 1876, the movement's focus shifted to Austrian-controlled Lviv.

Although a novel, Mikhail Bulgakov's *The White Guard* vividly brings to life the confusion that reigned in Kyiv during the 1918 Civil War – and provides a clearer explanation of all the competing factions than most history books.

CIVIL WAR

Following WWI and the collapse of the Tsarist monarchy, Ukraine had a shot at independence, but the international community was unsupportive, and none of the bewildering array of factions could win decisive backing. In Kyiv, the autonomous Ukrainian National Republic (UNR) was proclaimed in 1918 under president Mykhailo Hrushevsky. Meanwhile, Russian Bolsheviks set up a rival Congress of Soviets in Kharkiv. Civil war broke out, with five different armies – Red (Bolshevik), White, Polish, Ukrainian and Allied – vying for power, while various anarchist bands of Cossacks (the most famous led by Nestor Makhno) roamed the land. Author Mikhail Bulgakov estimated that Kyiv changed hands 14 times in 18 months.

Just as any UNR victories in Kyiv proved short lived, so too did the West Ukrainian National Republic (ZUNR) in Lviv. Proclaimed in October 1918, it was overrun by Polish troops the following summer. Under both the 1919 Treaty of Versailles negotiated after WWI and the following Treaty of Riga in 1921, Poland, Romania and Czechoslovakia took portions of western Ukraine, while Soviet forces were given control of the rest. Nationalist leader Semyon Petlyura set up a government in exile, but was assassinated in Paris in 1926.

DID YOU KNOW?

Ukrainians in North America have been lobbying to get *New York Times*' journalist Walter Durranty's Pulitzer Prize posthumously withdrawn, citing his complicity in covering up the 1930s Soviet famine.

SOVIET POWER

Thus handed to the Soviets, Ukraine was at the founding of the USSR in 1922. Behind Russia, it was the second largest and second most powerful republic in the union, but despite – or perhaps because of – that 'little brother' status, it came in for some particularly harsh bullying from the top. When Stalin took power in 1927, he looked upon Ukraine as a laboratory for testing Soviet restructuring while stamping out 'harmful' nationalism. In 1932–33 he engineered a famine (see the boxed text, p22). Executions and deportations of intellectuals and political 'dissidents' followed, along with the destruction of numerous Ukrainian palaces, churches and cemeteries. During the following great purges of 1937–39, an estimated one million people in the USSR were executed and a further three to 12 million (the numbers difficult to quantify) sent to labour camps, a high proportion of them from Ukraine.

1775	1918
Russian empress Catherine the Great destroys the Cossack settlement at Zaporizhzhya	Early attempt at independence fails and Ukraine comes under Soviet control

EUROPE'S HIDDEN HOLOCAUST

Between 1932 and 1933, more than five million citizens of Ukraine – 'Europe's breadbasket' – died of starvation while surrounded by fields of wheat and locked government storehouses filled to the brim with food. How? Stalin collectivised Soviet farms and ordered the production of unrealistic quotas of grain, which was then confiscated.

This man-made famine was part of the Soviet leadership's larger plan to solve the 'nationality problem' within several troublesome republics, especially Ukraine. A total of seven to 13 million people died throughout the USSR. (It's difficult to quantify, partly because those who took the next census were immediately ordered shot by Stalin.) Yet this genocide has never been fully recognised in the West.

Having fought a war of independence from 1917 to 1921, Ukraine continued to subtly resist Soviet rule during the 1920s. Moscow was unwilling to lose its richest colony and resorted to heavy-handed tactics. There were purges against the church and intelligentsia, both of which backed the nationalist cause. From early 1930, wealthier peasants (kulaks, or *kurkuli* in Ukrainian) who resisted collectivisation were deported and the remainder starved into submission.

Undoubtedly, there was an ideological basis to Soviet collectivisation, in which farmers gave up their land, animals and tools to work as mere labourers on huge state-run communes (kolkhozes, or *kolhospy* in Ukrainian). However, the setting of unattainable agricultural quotas had nothing to do with socialism, nor was it bureaucratic error; it was an instrument of control. Victor Kravchenko in *I Chose Freedom* quotes one communist apparatchik as saying: 'It took a famine to show them who is master here.'

By 1932, with Communist Party activists continuing to seize as much grain and other produce as possible from the collectives, the 'Great Hunger' ensued. Authorities conducted house-to-house searches for hidden grain. Watchtowers were erected above fields. Anyone caught stealing was executed or deported. Internal passports were issued to prevent desperate people running off in search of food. As entire villages died of starvation, people committed suicide and resorted to eating anything they could find. 'People cut up and cooked corpses; they killed their own children and ate them,' wrote Vassily Grossman in his book *Forever Flowing*. Photos of victims since published resemble those from a Nazi concentration camp.

At the time, however, Soviet authorities denied the famine's existence and few foreign correspondents, apart from the *Manchester Guardian's* Malcolm Muggeridge and freelancer Gareth Jones, were willing to risk reporting otherwise. The *New York Times'* Walter Durranty (a controversial Pulitzer Prize winner) swept the story under the carpet. And, despite new studies in the 1980s and 1990s reaching an academic audience, that's where one of the worst famines in history has largely remained.

WWII

Even by the standards of Ukrainian history, WWII was a particularly bloody and fratricidal period. Caught between Soviet Russia, Nazi Germany and an ongoing struggle for independence, some six million Ukrainians, 2.5 million of them Jews, were killed. Entire cities were ruined. The Red Army rolled into Polish Ukraine in September 1939; the Germans attacked in 1941 and occupied most of the country for more than two years. Two million Ukrainians were conscripted into the Soviet army and fought on the Russian side. However, some nationalists hoped the Nazis would back Ukrainian independence and collaborated with Germany. This was a source of much postwar recrimination, but many partisans in the Ukrainian Insurgent Army (UPA) fought both German

1932–33	1939–44
More than five million Ukrainians die in a famine engineered by Stalin	The country is laid to waste when becomes a battleground for Nazi, Soviet and nationalist forces; some six million Ukrainians die

and Russian troops in a bid for an independent state. The catacombs just outside Odesa (p123) sheltered a celebrated group of partisans.

In the end, the Soviet army prevailed. In 1943 it retook Kharkiv and Kyiv, before launching a massive offensive in early 1944 that pushed back German forces, obliterating Ukraine in the process. After the war the USSR kept the territory it had taken from Poland in 1939. A Ukrainian army under a government in exile led by Stepan Bandera (assassinated in Munich in 1959) continued a guerrilla existence well into the 1950s – mainly in Galicia – while millions of Ukrainians were deported or sent to Siberia for suspected 'disloyalty or collaboration'. These included the entire population of Crimean Tatars, who started to return to the peninsula in the mid-1990s (see the boxed text, p138).

NEW NATIONALISM

As far as some Ukrainians are concerned, the next 'war' after WWII was the nuclear disaster at the power plant Chornobyl (Chernobyl in Russian, see p34) on 26 April 1986. Many Ukrainians feel they came under attack not just from the radioactive material spewed over their countryside, but also from the authorities, who attempted to cover up the accident. The first Kremlin announcement wasn't made until two days after the event – and only then at the prompting of Swedish authorities, which detected abnormal radiation levels over their own country.

As more information came to light, discontent over Moscow's handling of the Chornobyl disaster revived nationalist feeling. Ukrainian independence had become a minority interest, mainly confined to the country's west, but slowly, the hard-core in Galicia started to take the rest of Ukraine along with them. In 1988 marches rocked Lviv, and the Uniate Church, banned by Stalin in 1946, emerged from the underground as a proindependence lobby. In 1989 the opposition movement Rukh (Ukrainian People's Movement for Restructuring) was established. By 1990 protest marches and hunger strikes had spread to Kyiv.

INDEPENDENT UKRAINE

With the nationalist movement bubbling up and the USSR disintegrating, many politicians within the Communist Party of Ukraine (CPU) saw the writing on the wall. After the Soviet counter-coup in Moscow in August 1991 failed, they decided that if they didn't take their country to independence, the opposition would. So, on 24 August 1991, the Verkhovna Rada (Parliament) met, with speaker Stanyslav Hurenko's wonderfully pithy announcement recorded by the *Economist* for posterity: 'Today we will vote for Ukrainian independence, because if we don't we're in the shit.' In December some 84% of the population voted in a referendum to back that pragmatic decision, and former CPU chairman Leonid Kravchuk was elected president.

As the new republic found its feet, there were more than the usual separation traumas from Russia. Disagreements and tensions arose, particularly over ownership of the Black Sea Fleet harboured in the Crimean port of Sevastopol. These were only resolved in 1999 by offering Russia a 20-year lease.

Published in 1986, leading historian Robert Conquest's *Harvest of Sorrow* was the first book to bring the 1932–33 Soviet famine to the attention of the West. Well researched and detailed, it still makes for shocking reading today.

DID YOU KNOW?

Nationalist leader Stepan Bandera's murderer, a KGB agent, was paid a new camera for his troubles. Bandera was a controversial figure, whose enemies linked him to Nazi Germany.

DID YOU KNOW?

Schoolchildren are taught the Ukrainian flag's bands of azure and yellow represent grain fields beneath a blue sky. However, the flag might actually come from ancient heraldry.

1986	1991
Nuclear reactor at Chornobyl power plant explodes, spewing out radioactive pollution	Ukraine's parliament votes for independence 'because if we don't, we're in the shit'

Orest Subtelny's 700-
page *Ukraine, A History*
is widely tipped as the
definitive work on
the subject, narrowly
edging out Paul Mago-
sci's similarly excellent
doorstopper *History of
Ukraine*. Both go from
prehistory to the 1990s.

Economic crisis forced Kravchuk's government to resign in September 1992. President Leonid Kuchma, a pro-Russian reformer, came to power in July 1994 and stayed for 10 years.

During Kuchma's terms in office, the economy did improve. Today's relatively stable hryvnia was introduced and inflation was brought down from a spiralling 10,000% in 1993 to 5.2% in 2004, by which time GDP was growing at a rate of 9%. However, much of the credit for this improvement is arguably due to Kuchma's prime ministers, including, from 1999 to 2001, Viktor Yushchenko.

Kuchma's tenure is likely to be remembered as a time of cronyism. Foreign investors complained that companies being privatised were frequently sold off to Ukrainian ventures with connections to the president, sometimes for well under market value, and international watchdog Transparency International named Ukraine the third most corrupt country in the world.

The biggest scandal surrounded the death of campaigning journalist Grygory Gongadze, whose beheaded corpse was found outside Kyiv in early 2000. A tape emerged in which a voice very similar to Kuchma's was heard to ask that something 'be done' about Gongadze. Despite massive street protests then, Kuchma never heeded calls from the public to resign, and an investigation into the murder stalled.

The website www.brama
.com/ukraine/history
offers a chronological
table of events from the
9th to the 20th century.

However in 2004, Viktor Yushchenko – the reformist prime minister that parliamentary communists and oligarchs conspired to sack in 2001 – reemerged as a strong contender for the presidency. After a disputed election, during which Yushchenko was poisoned but survived to win, Kuchma and his favoured presidential candidate, Viktor Yanukovych, were finally forced to listen to the message coming from the streets. The 'Orange Revolution' had arrived (see p17 for more details).

2000	2004
Unproved allegations surface linking President Leonid Kuchma to a journalist's murder	Opposition candidate Viktor Yushchenko is poisoned during a controversial presidential election; he lives to win

The Culture

THE NATIONAL PSYCHE

The Orange Revolution of 2004 consigned one shibboleth of Ukrainian identity to history. It's been said that people here are stoic, willing to accept what fate dishes up. Thousands of pro-opposition protestors camping out for a month in sub-zero temperatures suggest such passivity isn't completely true. The peacefulness of the demonstrations did confirm that Ukrainians aren't impetuous or hot tempered. As both these recent events and the 1991 move to independence showed, it takes something important to mobilise locals. But once mobilised, they dig in their heels. On the other hand, as commentators noted during the latest upheaval, Ukrainians have had such a divisive past, they're reluctant today to spill each other's blood.

Locals are nothing if not survivors; they've had to be. But what else constitutes 'Ukrainian' is up for grabs now. Culturally, many patriots can unite behind a vague sense of Cossack culture and the national poet Taras Shevchenko (see the boxed text, p30). This is a religious society, a superstitious society and one in which strong family and community ties still bind. It's a culture where people are friendly and often more generous (including to you) than they can really afford. Paradoxically, it's also one in which a certain Soviet mentality – of unofficial unhelpfulness and suspicion of saying too much – remains. For several reasons, *ya ne znayu* (I don't know) is a much overused phrase. But how long things stay like this is another question.

In recent years, a Kyiv ad agency ran an eye-catching campaign proclaiming 'I'm Ukrainian' and featuring everything from a city girl doing a Hutsul dance to a guy with a Ukrainian *tryzub* symbol tattooed on his tongue. That such adverts were considered necessary – and surprising – indicates how delicate the new sense of nationhood is. But, as the campaign's different characters showed, there are now so many possibilities.

LIFESTYLE

With an average national wage of 550uah a month ($105), life's a struggle for many Ukrainian households. Not that you'd particularly notice among the middle classes, who have ways of making do. It's usual for people outside big cities to grow food in their back garden and common for extended families to divvy up domestic duties. *Baba* (grandma) is frequently a respected household member. People hold down several jobs or pursue a number of money-making schemes simultaneously, while networks of neighbours and friends look out for each other. At least now, as opposed to in the early 1990s, most workers are paid regularly.

Things are better for professionals, particularly in wealthy Kyiv. There the average monthly wage is 900uah ($180), although realistically one would need $300 to $500 per month to live in the capital. The country's oligarchs and 'new Ukrainian' businesspeople have even become enormously rich. They're the ones you see driving the black Mercedes SUVs and shopping in Kyiv's designer boutiques.

At the other end of the scale, nearly one in three Ukrainians live below the poverty line. The plight of elderly people without family is particularly heartbreaking, and these are mainly women, thanks to WWII. With

It's tradition for newly-wed Ukrainian couples to have their photo taken alongside leading local monuments. So on summer days you'll see brides in white wedding gowns – and their entourage – traipsing all over towns and cities.

According to one leading local superstition, women should never sit down on steps, walls or anything concrete, lest their ovaries freeze and they become unable to bear children. Remember this when tired from sightseeing!

IS SHE REALLY GOING OUT WITH HIM?

You'll see a lot of oddly matched couples in Ukraine, as myriad dating agencies have sprung up to introduce overseas men to famously beautiful – but poverty-stricken – Ukrainian women. Many 'rich' male expats also hook up with much better-looking partners than they could hope to attract back home.

Of course, none of the resulting relationships are forged on a level playing field or unaffected by the partners' economic disparity. And it's worth noting that, with the sex trafficking of Ukrainian women and girls now a serious problem, many dating and marriage agencies advertised over the internet are also operated by criminal syndicates.

Victor Malarek, author of *The Natashas: The New Global Sex Trade,* contends: 'These agencies… are usually nothing more than online brothels.'

---

a monthly pension of 170uah ($32), they often sell their home-grown produce to make ends meet. The even less fortunate can be seen begging or rummaging through bins for empty bottles (to collect the deposits). They have no alternative.

POPULATION

Ukraine's population has fallen dramatically since independence, from 52 million in 1993 to today's 47.1 million or less. That's mainly because people have emigrated in search of a better life. Birth rates and life expectancy have also dropped.

The remaining population clings to the west around the Carpathians and to the industrial east, while the centre and south lie largely vacant. Some 15% live in big cities like Kyiv, Kharkiv, Dnipropetrovsk, Lviv, Luhansk, Odesa and Donetsk. The rest live in smaller towns or on the land.

Ethnically, 78% are Ukrainian and another 17% are Russian, mainly concentrated in the east. Other minorities include, in order of size, Belarusians, Moldovans, Tatars, Bulgarians, Hungarians, Romanians, Poles and Jews. Almost all of the country's 250,000 Tatars live in Crimea.

There are around 2.5 million expatriate Ukrainians, many of them in North America (particularly Canada).

For the low-down from Tatars themselves on their historic culture and contemporary socio-political issues, visit www.tatar.net, which links to such excellent sites as www.iccrimea.org and www.euronet.nl/users/sota/krimtatar.html.

RELIGION

As the sheer number of churches in Ukraine attests, religion is pivotal. It's provided comfort during many hard times and even shaped Ukrainian identity. By accepting Orthodox Christianity in 989, Volodymyr the Great cast Kyivan Rus as a European, rather than Islamic Asian, state. But this also created a cultural divide between it and Catholic neighbour Poland.

In the 17th century, when Ukraine came under Russian rule, so did its Orthodox Church. However, since 1990 the church in Ukraine has been re-established as the Ukrainian Autocephalous Orthodox Church (UAOC). In fact, in post-Soviet Ukraine there are three Orthodox churches with a total of 10 million adherents. Besides the UAOC, there's the breakaway Ukrainian Orthodox Church of Kyiv and All-Ukraine, and the Ukrainian Orthodox Church (UOC). The last is the former Ukrainian section of the Russian Orthodox Church and pays allegiance to the Moscow patriarch, while the earlier two have their own patriarch in Kyiv.

Territorial disputes still exist between those paying allegiance to Kyiv and the slightly larger number adhering to Moscow. The Ukrainian government's 1995 refusal to allow Kyiv Patriarch Volodymyr Romanyuk

(1925–95) to be buried inside Kyiv's St Sophia's Cathedral, for fear of reprisals from Moscow, is a perfect example.

To complicate matters, another five million Ukrainians follow another brand of Christianity entirely. In 1596 the Union of Brest established the Uniate Church (often called the Ukrainian Catholic or Greek Catholic Church). Mixing Orthodox Christian practices with allegiance to the pope, this church was – and is – popular in the western part of the country, bordering Catholic Poland.

Such religious distinctions are intensely political. Moscow patriarch Orthodoxy favours close ties with Russia. Ukrainian Catholicism – and to a lesser extent Kyiv patriarch Orthodoxy – welcomes greater Western ties. Indeed, banned by Stalin in 1946, Ukrainian Catholicism reemerged in the late 1980s as a major mover behind independence.

Minority faiths include Roman Catholicism, Judaism and, among Crimean Tatars, Islam.

SPORT

Football (soccer) is the leading spectator sport in Ukraine. The capital's resident team, Dynamo Kyiv, is known throughout Europe, and Ukrainian footballer Andriy Shevchenko has overtaken his namesake Taras Shevchenko, the Ukrainian national poet, on the world stage. The AC Milan player is a recent European Footballer of the Year.

Ukraine also enjoys ice hockey, and has an international presence in boxing with the brothers Vitaliy and Volodymyr Klychko. Vitaliy ('Dr Ironfist'), in particular, has gained prominence as the world heavyweight champion.

For popular participation sports, see p172.

MULTICULTURALISM

The 'ethnic' divisions between western and eastern Ukraine were under the spotlight during the most recent presidential election, with serious fears the country might split. True, with Russian immigration into Ukrainian territory from the late 17th century, some Russian Ukrainians still feel their allegiance lies more with Moscow than with Kyiv. But the divisions aren't as intractable as some politicians suggested.

Patriotic western Ukrainians often liken the difference between them and Russians to that between Canadians and Americans. (Other comparisons include the Spanish and the Portuguese or, perhaps most accurate historically, the British and Irish.) However, in public, the division is principally played out in religion and language. Russian dominates in the east and the south. Ukrainian is spoken in western Ukraine. However, people in the west are not quite so prickly about hearing Russian as they were just after independence, while even patriotically 'Ukrainian' Kyiv speaks Russian.

A different tension exists in Crimea, where more than 250,000 Tatars have resettled in the past decade. After early clashes, 14 Tatar seats were granted in the Crimean parliament and the situation quietened down. Disturbingly. however, there have been recent attacks by skinhead 'Cossack paramilitary' groups on Tatars and their property.

MEDIA

Press freedom is new to Ukraine. Under President Leonid Kuchma, opposition newspapers were closed for spurious reasons and independent journalists harassed, while the government issued others with daily *temniki* (themes) to cover in the news.

Dynamo Kyiv's official website at www.fcdynamo.kiev.ua is in Ukrainian and Russian only. If you don't read either, you can catch up with the popular football team's exploits at www.uefa.com/Competitions/UCL/Clubs.

One of the few Black faces regularly on the Ukrainian small screen, handsome Nigerian-Ukrainian presenter Miroslav Kuyaldin is known for his flamboyant dress sense. You can catch him on M1, the local equivalent of MTV.

The Tatars of the Crimea: Return to the Homeland by Edward Allworth is a thoughtful examination of 250 years of ill treatment of the Tatars, from the Russian annexation of Crimea and Stalin's mass 1944 deportation to contemporary racism.

'Ukrainians are looking forward to a continuing free press'

Some 18 journalists mysteriously died in the line of duty, the biggest scandal involving Georgiy Gongazde, editor of online *Ukrainsky Pravda* (Ukrainian Truth). Gongazde's decapitated body was discovered in 2000, soon after the 31-year-old started reporting on government corruption. A tape was found in which Kuchma was heard telling someone to 'deal with' Gongazde. The president admitted the voice was his, but he said the tape had been doctored so his words were taken out of context. After mass protests and EU intervention, a parliamentary committee was established to investigate the killing. In 2004 it suggested Kuchma be impeached but was ignored. Soon after the Yushchenko government came to power it made several arrests over the murder. The investigation suffered an early setback with the death (apparently by suicide) of former interior minister Yuriy Kravchenko but was set to continue.

During 2004's Orange Revolution, brave journalists began to throw off government reporting restrictions to report fairly on events. Ukrainians are now looking forward to a continuing free press.

ARTS
Folk Dance
Ukrainian folk dance falls into two broad categories: Hutsul and Cossack. Both originally emanate from calendar feasts in peasant life – winter *(koliada)*, spring *(vesnianky)*, summer *(kupalo)* and autumn or harvest *(obzhynky)* – as well as rituals attending birth, marriage and death. The *hahilky*, performed by girls during Easter, combined the rituals of prayer with the celebration of spring.

However, Hutsul dances include a minimum of circular movement. Largely they rely on stamping feet, and jumping up and down. (Some say this has to do with the Hutsuls' hillside lifestyle, which made this less awkward.) By contrast, Cossack dancers frequently link arms and twirl around in a circle. Such dances developed via the drunken celebrations that followed the Cossacks' successful military campaigns, and include movements like the 'duck-kick'.

A MIDSUMMER'S NIGHT DREAM

It involves fire, water, dancing, fortune-telling, and strong overtones of sex. So is it any wonder the Soviets tried to quash the festival of Ivan Kupalo, a pagan midsummer's celebration? Indeed, leaders since the middle ages – including Cossack hetmans – have tried to outlaw it, but all without success. The festival is still marked across Ukraine and beyond.

To ancient pre-Christians, Kupalo was the god of love and fertility, and young people would choose a marriage partner on this eve. Today's rituals vary, but typically begin with folk singing and a maypole-style dance performed by young women wearing white gowns and flower wreaths in their hair. After this, the women float their wreaths (symbolising virginity) down the requisite nearby river or other body of water. A wreath that sinks indicates bad fortune in love for its owner.

Later, a bonfire is lit, around which young couples dance. Couples will also jump over small fires, holding hands, to test whether – if they maintain their grip – their love will last. In ancient times, the young men would go off into the woods to seek a special 'magical' fern before dawn.

After Kyivan Rus adopted Christianity, the festival became mixed up with the birthday of John the Baptist. This not only means the festival has largely been shifted from the summer solstice on 22 June to 7 July, it sometimes means people walk in the fire or jump in the river as a 'cleansing' act. Check Kyiv listings magazines for events by the Dnipro or head to the countryside for more traditional celebrations.

Music
FOLK: BLIND KOBZARY & HUGE BANDURAS
Ukrainian folk music developed as a form of storytelling. *Bylyny* were epic narrative poems relating the courageous deeds of the heroes of Kyivan Rus. *Dumy* were lyrical ballads glorifying the exploits of the Cossacks and were performed by wandering minstrel-like bards called *kobzary*.

As the guardians of Ukrainian folklore, *kobzary* were highly respected (see the boxed text, p30). Traditionally, minstrels were required to be blind. The instrument they initially used to accompany their historical narratives was the lutelike *kobza*.

In the 18th century the *kobza* was replaced by the remarkable *bandura*, a larger instrument with up to 65 strings. Popular *bandura* choirs accompanied Ukrainian national songs and folk dances and this unparalleled instrument soon became a national symbol.

The Ukrainian Bandura Chorus (www.bandura.org) was founded in Kyiv in 1918 and still performs worldwide today. To find a *bandura* concert in Ukraine, check current listings. The National Philharmonic in Kyiv (p72) is a reasonable bet.

Ukrainian Minstrels: And the Blind Shall Sing by Natalie Kononenko sheds light on the fascinating lives of *kobzary* and related *lirniky*, with their distinctive professional requirements (including blindness), pecking order, training and extensive repertoire of songs.

CLASSICAL MUSIC & OPERA
The most notable local composer remains Mykola Lysenko (1842–1912). The 'father of Ukrainian national music' applied the logic of Ukrainian folk songs to piano-based classical music. Ukrainian operettas combine more acting and dancing than typical operas.

ROCK MUSIC
Listening to Ukrainian radio, you'll usually have your ear bent with Russian pop. However, the country has a whole roster of its own national stars. The only one that Westerners are likely to have heard of is Ruslana (www.ruslana.com.ua), a Eurovision song contest winner (see p97). Other names to keep an ear out for are chart-topping pop-rock group Okean Elzy, rockers VV, semiacoustic duo 5'nizza and Ivano-Frankivsk rap group Grinjolly (Sleds). Grinjolly's song *Razom nas bahato* (Together We Are Many) became the Orange Revolution's anthem and, after some controversially preferential treatment, Ukraine's 2005 Eurovision entry.

Get to grips with the Ukrainian music scene and buy CDs – from contemporary stars such as Ruslana or traditional Ukrainian folk artists – at www.umka.com.ua.

Literature
Taras Shevchenko (see the boxed text, p30) is the figure towering over all Ukrainian literature. However, two other writers rate a mention. Ivan Franko (1856–1916) is another respected hero, whose work ranged from philosophical debate to children's stories. For daring to discuss the issues plaguing Ukrainian society, he was arrested and temporarily imprisoned. His better-known writings include *The Turnip Farmer, The Converted Sinner* and *During Work*, while some of his poems can be found at www.franko.lviv.ua/ifranko/franko_eng.html.

Equally distinguished was Larysa Kosach (1871–1913), known by her pen name, Lesia Ukrainka. Her frail health inspired her to compose deeply moving poetry expressing inner strength and inspiration – symbolic beatitudes for the Ukrainian people. Her *Forest Song* inspired a ballet, an opera and a film.

There are several other proudly Ukrainian authors, but none translated into English. On the other hand, two internationally renowned authors usually claimed by Russia are Ukrainian-born. Mikhail Bulgakov's

---

ALL HAIL THE NATIONAL POET!

Taras. Shevchenko. Etch that name on your memory; you'll be hearing it a lot in Ukraine. In fact, statues of its owner now stand on pedestals vacated by Lenin across the entire west of the country. Shevchenko (1814–61) is *the* Ukrainian writer. He embodied and stirred the national consciousness, while achieving literary respectability for a Ukrainian language then suppressed under tsarist Russian rule. Born a serf and orphaned as a teenager, Shevchenko studied painting at the Academy of Arts in St Petersburg, where in 1840 he published his first work, *Kobzar* (The Bard), a book of eight romantic poems. It was a great success and his epic poem *Haidamaky* (1841) and ballad *Hamaliia* (1844) followed soon afterwards. Later works, such as *Son* (The Dream), *Kavkas* (Caucasus) and *Velyky i Lokh* (The Great Dungeon) were not immediately published, but are now held in great affection.

Through Shevchenko's prolific work, Ukrainian was elevated from a peasant tongue to a vehicle of eloquent and poetic expression. Combining vernacular expressions and colloquial dialects with Church Slavonic, he formed a unique voice. He passionately preached social justice, in universal terms as well as to the downtrodden peasant and to the Ukrainian nation, referring to 'this land of ours that is not our own'. A staunch anti-tsarist, the poet was banished to Siberia for 10 years, which led to his premature death in 1861. In 1876 Tsar Alexander II banned all Ukrainian books and publishing, but Shevchenko's message remained. He was a Ukrainian hero.

Some of Shevchenko's works – namely *Kobzar* – have been translated widely, but unfortunately English translations are either out of print or collector's editions costing $100 to $250. A brief autobiography and 14 poems are found in English at www.infoukes.com/shevchenkomuseum.

The Raspberry Huta and Other Ukrainian Folk Tales Retold in English by Canadian Danny Evanishen (www.ethnic.bc.ca) is the first of an extensive series of delightful children's books drawing on specifically Ukrainian stories.

(1891–1940) first novel *The White Guard* is set in his native Kyiv. Nikolai Gogol's (1809–52) novel *Dead Souls* and short story 'Taras Bulba' (about a Cossack hero and included in the collection *Mirgorad, Myrhorad* in Ukrainian) both have links to his country of birth.

Odesa-born Issac Babel (1894–1939) was the most famous chronicler of that city (see p124). Kyiv-based author Andriy Kurkov (1961–) has been called the Bulgakov's heir. That might be taking things a bit far but Kurkov's *Death and the Penguin* and *Penguin Lost* do at least indulge in the same flights of fancy as Bulgakov's classic *The Master and Margarita*.

Architecture

In Death and the Penguin by Andriy Kurkov, would-be novelist Viktor is eking out a miserable existence with his pet penguin Misha, when suddenly he gets a great gig writing stock obituaries for still living prominent people. Then suddenly, one by one, they all start dying…

Church design has wrought a vast influence on Ukrainian architecture. Byzantine layout has at various times been merged with traditional wooden Hutsul churches (colonnaded porches and free-standing belfries) and 17th-century baroque to produce unique styles. 'Ukrainian baroque', with its trademark green helmet-shaped dome, is typified by St Andrew's Church (p55) in Kyiv.

Otherwise various styles have come in and out of vogue. After St Petersburg proved such a success in Russia, its planned layout and neoclassical architecture was copied in Odesa and the Kruhla ploshcha (Round Square) in Poltava (p164). In the 19th century there were revivals of Byzantine design (as seen in St Volodymyr's Cathedral in Kyiv, p60) and Renaissance style merged with baroque – for example in the opera houses in Kyiv (p72), Odesa (p122) and Lviv (p86). A modern Ukrainian style based on Art Nouveau featured in the Regional Museum (p164) in Poltava and the eclectic Metropolitan Palace (p102) in Chernivtsi.

The Soviets had a penchant for pompous 'monumental classicism', with enormous templelike state edifices. Kyiv is full of such buildings.

Visual Arts

ICONS

Icons are small holy images painted on a lime-wood panel with a mix of tempera, egg yolk and hot wax. Brought to Ukraine by Volodymyr the Great from Constantinople in the 10th century and remaining the key religious art until the 17th century, icons were attributed healing and spiritual powers. Icon painters – mostly monks – rarely signed works, and depicted only Christ, the Virgin, angels and saints. Church murals, mosaics and frescoes, as well as manuscript illuminations, developed at the same time. Some of the oldest frescoes are found in Kyiv's St Sophia's Cathedral (p55).

For information, pictures and links about painted Ukrainian Easter eggs, start with either www .ukrainianmuseum .org/pysanky.html or www.4uth.gov.ua /pisanka_eng.htm.

PYSANKY

Painted Easter eggs, or *pysanky,* are an ancient Slavonic art. Designs are drawn in wax on the eggshell (these days hollowed out beforehand), the egg is dyed one colour and the process continually repeated until a complex pattern is built up. Different symbols represent varying natural forces – a circle with a dot in the middle, the sun, and so on – but each Ukrainian region has its own traditions. The country's largest collection of *pysanky* is found at Kolomyya's Pysanky Museum (p100).

ROMANTICISM

The first break from religious art occurred during the Cossack Hetmanate. A secular, romantic trend of folk painting slowly developed, common themes being the *Kozak Mamay* (a Cossack playing a *bandura* or *kobza),* country life and folk traditions. Most of these paintings remained unknown, but Ukrainian-born Ilya Repin gained international fame. His famous *Zaporizhsky Cossacks Writing a Letter to the Turkish Sultan* and other Romantic paintings are found in the Art Museum in Kharkiv (p161). The art museums in Kyiv (p62) and Odesa (p123) also display typical Romantic art.

BARE-ARSED IN SNOWY KHARKIV

He paid one homeless Kharkiv woman to pose for his camera in the snow, with her knickers pushed to her knees and her blouse above her breasts and scarred stomach. In another picture, a naked woman with a large cancerous growth jutting from her stomach tends a flower bush. And in a third a semiclothed drunk is carried by friends across snow like a crucified man. Yet Ukrainian photographer Boris Mikhailov wasn't censured or censored for such shocking images. He was awarded the prestigious Citibank Photography Award 2000. That same year, he also won the Hasselblad Photography Award for a career in which he has continually challenged viewers.

Mikhailov has said his aesthetics are about the 'dissolution of beauty' and his award-winning *Case History* – 450 photos of Kharkiv's *bomzhy* (homeless) – is certainly that. Going into professional photography in the 1970s, after the KGB found some nude amateur shots of his wife and had him fired from his engineering job, Mikhailov originally satirised Soviet realism. Since the demise of the USSR, however, he has documented the unravelling of society in Ukraine. Rebutting claims of voyeurism, he says homelessness didn't exist in the Soviet Union, and it's better to bear witness to the suffering of these people than to wish it away. He pays his subjects, believing it immoral not to, but also admits that such payments reflect the new capitalist realities.

His work is always compelling and ironically often beautiful. In his *Red Series* and *Private Series* Mikhailov photographed Soviet iconography as a backdrop to boring, everyday life. In *Salt Lake,* his sepia-tone pictures captured bathers in an effluent polluted lake.

Ivan Ayvazosky is regarded as one of the world's best painters of seascapes. Ethnically Armenian, he was born and lived in Feodosiya, Crimea, where hundreds of his works are found in the Ayvazosky Museum (p156).

SOVIET ERA & BEYOND

Socialist realism propagated Soviet ideals – the industrialised peasant, the muscular worker and the heroic soldier. Take, as an example, the sculptural reliefs near Kyiv's Museum of the Great Patriotic War (p60). Ukrainian nationalism asserted itself through the age-old tradition of folk art, leading the Soviet authorities to ban folk embroidery.

Since independence, Ukrainian art has enjoyed a reawakening, with the Academy of Fine Arts in both Kyiv and Lviv producing new young artists and style revivals. One of the most important artists to emerge from the former Soviet Union is Ukrainian photographer Boris Mikhailov. Born in Kharkiv in 1938, he now divides his time between there and Germany (see the boxed text, p31).

Israeli prime minister Golda Meir and film star Milla Jovovich were born in Kyiv; Bolshevik Leon Trotsky hailed from outside Odesa. Dustin Hoffman and Sylvester Stallone both have Ukrainian roots, while Jack Palance is fiercely proud of his ancestry.

Cinema

Ukrainian cinema is inextricably linked to the USSR and Russia. Ukrainian actors have appeared in Russian films – and still do. A Georgian-Armenian made one of the most celebrated Ukrainian-language movies under the reluctant auspices of the USSR, and one of the world's greatest silent films was shot in Ukrainian territory. But apart from producing, among others, 1964's *Shadows of Forgotten Ancestors* (by Georgian-Armenian director Sergiy Paradzhanov; see p100) and 1925's *Battleship Potemkin* (filmed in Odesa; see p122), Ukraine has also been the site of influential film studios in Kyiv and Odesa.

Recent films using Ukraine as a backdrop include the French East-West (2001), a Cold War thriller starring Catherine Deneuve and set in Kyiv. The slow-moving Russian Koktebel (2004) is a father-son road movie set in Crimea.

Those in Odesa (1916) are the country's oldest. The Alexander Dovzhenko National Film Studio in Kyiv (established in 1928 as the Film Institute) is one of the largest in Eastern Europe and still operates today. Its name comes from one of the true greats of Ukrainian cinema, whose silent epics *Earth* (*Zemlya*), about life, death and collective farming, and *Arsenal* are considered cinematic milestones and have been recently rereleased on DVD.

During the Soviet era Ukrainian cinema all but disappeared. However émigré Slavko Novytsky made two lauded documentaries: *Pysanka: The Ukrainian Easter Egg* (1975) and *The Harvest of Despair* (1972) about the 1932–33 famine.

Independent Ukraine's film industry is still finding its feet. Recent Cossack-style epics, such as Yuri Ilyenko's *A Prayer for Hetman Mazepa* (2002) and Oles Sanin's *Mamay* (2003) haven't fared well internationally. *A Friend of the Deceased* (1997, Vyacheslav Krishtofovich) was better received, even with a derivative plot about a Kyiv man who hires a hitman to kill him, but then changes his mind and can't contact his hired gun.

A Driver for Vera (a 2004 Russian/Ukrainian production featuring Ukrainian star Bohdan Stupka and shot in Crimea) has drawn favourable comparison to the Oscar-winning Russian film *Burnt by the Sun* (also worth viewing before visiting Ukraine).

Environment

THE LAND

Almost unknown to the outside world until recently, Ukraine surprises many people with its size. It's the largest country wholly within Europe, so how can something this big have ever been overlooked? Stretching some 2000km east to west and 1000km north to south, Ukraine outdoes both France and Germany in area and is only dwarfed by Russia, which stretches into Asia.

Vast, open steppe – flat plains and gently rolling grasslands – covers the heart of the country. You'll really appreciate this if travelling by day from Kyiv to Odesa, for example, where the plain stretches interminably in all directions and makes one feel very small. A small belt of forested highland interrupts this unending horizon in the northwest near Lutsk, while in the southeast there are river gorges and ravines near the Dnipro River.

The partially wooded area between the Ukrainian forest and steppe has a special name in Ukrainian: *liso-step* (forest-steppe).

Of four rivers crossing the country, the Dnipro is the biggest and most revered. Some 980 of its 2201 kilometres flow through Ukraine from north to south. It's the main transportation artery, with enormous hydroelectric dams harnessing its power at Kremenchuk, Dnipropetrovsk and Zaporizhzhya. The last of those has even swallowed the legendary waterfalls that existed in Cossack times. The Dnister, to the west, is the secondary river.

The only serious mountains are a short stretch of the Carpathians in the west and the Crimean Mountains in the far south. Even these are modest by world standards, with the highest peaks being the Carpathians' Hoverla (2061m) and Crimea's Roman Kosh (1543m).

Its rich natural assets make Ukraine's economic poverty heartbreaking and frustrating. A central belt of deep, thick, humus-rich soil *(chornozem)* covers almost two-thirds of Ukraine, constituting one of the world's most fertile regions.

Coal and iron are mined in the far eastern and south-central regions.

WILDLIFE
Animals

According to the World Wide Fund for Nature (WWF), the Carpathian Mountains – whose eastern section falls in Ukraine – are home to one of the planet's most diverse populations of mountain-dwelling animal and plant species. The mountains could be Europe's last refuge for large mammals like the brown bear, wolf and lynx. A relatively pure breed of the European wildcat *(Felis silvestris)*, a grey-brown animal, with bushy, blunt-ended tails and black stripes, is found here and the European bison was reintroduced in recent years. According to a WWF spokesman, all of these animals should be found on Ukrainian territory. However, organising wildlife-watching for English-speakers in Ukraine is still a niche pursuit. In the Carpathians, ask at the office of

---

WORLD HERITAGE SITES

There are only two World Heritage Sites in Ukraine – Kyiv's Caves Monastery (p56) and Lviv (p85). However, the Carpathian Biosphere Reserve (p98) and the Dunaysky/Danube Biosphere Reserve (p128) are both part of Unesco's global network of biosphere reserves. The authorities in Kamyanets-Podilsky (p105) have applied for World Heritage listing for the remarkable Smotrych River canyon, which forms a natural moat around the town.

the **Carpathian National Nature Park** (☎ 211 57; cnnp@jar.if.ua; room 20, 1st fl, vul Stussa 6, Yaremcha; ⏲ 8am-5pm Mon-Fri).

Bird-watching is best near the mouth of the Danube River in the southwest. The estuary here is home to more than 300 species of bird, including the largest population of pelicans in Europe, pygmy cormorants, red-breasted geese, the rare white-tailed eagle, osprey and kingfishers.

Plants

Ukraine is a tree-lover's paradise. Two areas are most heavily wooded. The north of the country in the Volyn district has mixed forests of pine (sosna), fir (yalyna), beech (buk), oak (dub) and spruce (kanadska ihlytsya). The Carpathians also have oak and beech at lower elevations, with

---

CHORNOBYL: 'A MONSTER WHICH IS ALWAYS NEAR'

In perhaps the blackest of ironies ever known to history, the world's worst nuclear disaster was the result of an unnecessary safety test. On the night of 25 April 1986, reactor No 4 at the electricity-producing Chornobyl power plant in northern Ukraine was due to be shut down for regular maintenance. Workers decided to use the opportunity to see if, in the event of a shutdown, enough electricity remained in the grid to power the systems that cooled the reactor core, and turned off the emergency cooling system. For various reasons, including a design flaw in the type of RBMK reactor at Chornobyl, operational errors and flouted safety procedures, the result of the test was a power surge, a steam explosion and a full-blown nuclear explosion. At 1.26am on the morning of 26 April 1986, the reactor blew its 500-tonne top and spewed nearly nine tonnes of radioactive material into the sky in a fireball. More than 90 times as much as radioactive material as in the Hiroshima bomb was blown north and west in the next few days. Fallout dropped mainly over Belarus, but also over Ukraine, Russia, Poland and the Baltic region. Some material also wafted over Sweden, whose scientists were the first to alert the world.

The Soviets initially remained silent while the emergency unfolded on their doorstep. Two people died in the explosion and another 29 firemen – sent in to clean up without proper radiation protection – died in the following weeks. Some 135,000 people were evacuated from the satellite town of Prypyat and a 30km radius around the plant, but were told it was only 'temporary'. And six days after the disaster, with radioactive clouds blowing over Kyiv, May Day parades in the blissfully ignorant city went ahead.

Today the long-term effects of the disaster are still being felt and assessed. The most obvious impact has been an upsurge of thyroid cancer in children, with nearly 2000 cases reported. Studies suggest that of the 600,000 'liquidators' brought in to clean up the site, more than 4000 have died from exposure and 170,000 suffer fatal diseases. In addition, some 35,000 sq km of forest has been contaminated, where meat, milk, vegetables and fruit produced have higher than normal levels of radioactivity. Silt carried down the Dnipro is radioactive – although the extent is still not fully known. Birth defects, suicides and deaths from heart disease and alcoholism are also unusually high in the region. By 2015 it's estimated the disaster will have cost the economy $200 billion.

The last working reactor at Chornobyl, number three, was finally shut down in 2000. However, reactor number four is still 'a monster, a monster which is always near', according to one of the 8000 scientific staff and monitors who travel to the site daily from the new town of Slavutych. After the accident, the damaged reactor and 180 tonnes of radioactive mess were hastily enclosed in a concrete-and-steel sarcophagus. That sarcophagus is crumbling, and work is due to start on a better, overarching casing in 2005, with international assistance.

Two 'exclusion zones' around Chornobyl remain, at 10km and 30km, but 350 of the 1500 residents who initially snuck back in after the accident still live within these restricted areas today. It's even possible to visit on a tour (see p75). Western medical and governmental sources agree that the risk to short-term visitors to Ukraine is insignificant.

pines and alpine meadows on higher ground. However, even Ukrainian cities are incredibly leafy; most have boulevards lined with chestnut trees (*kashtany;* the official symbol of Kyiv).

Oak and willow *(verba)* grow along the rivers, and both are well used. Willow is traditionally used for baskets, fences and household appliances, while larger constructions are made from oak. The legendary Cossack stronghold of the Zaporizhsky Sich was once built entirely from oak timbers.

The yew tree *(tysove derevo)*, Carpathian rhododendron *(Karpatsky rododendron)* and edelweiss *(edelveys)* are protected species. Other well-represented varieties include:

Cherry *(vyshnya)* Immortalised in Slavic literature by Anton Chekhov when he wrote *The Cherry Orchard* in Crimea.

Guelder Rose *(kalina)* This deciduous bush has clusters of white flowers and red berries and has been immortalised by Taras Shevchenko and other poets as a national symbol. Its fruit is used for making healthy juice and preserves.

Juniper *(mozhevelnyk)* The aromatic scent of this wood wafts all over Crimea and is sold as souvenirs. Some Ukrainians believe juniper attracts love, others that it protects against theft.

Linden *(lipa)* This lines country lanes, and its fragrant flowers are used to make a sweet tea.

Ukrainian babushkas (olde women) are great believers in herbal remedies. Their favourite is wormwood (*hirky polyn* in Ukrainian), which is thought to help with toothache, coughs, fever, kidney and liver ailments, and even memory.

As the former 'bread basket of the Soviet Union', Ukraine is unsurprisingly covered in fields of grain, ranging from wheat through to barley. It also grows enormous quantities of sugar beets. A narrow strip of Mediterranean vegetation runs along the southern coast of Crimea, where grapes and red onions are in abundance. Vineyards also thrive in Transcarpathia.

In the centre of the country, large tracts are set aside as grazing land, and in spring they explode into brilliant, swaying seas of red poppies *(maky)*, sunflowers *(sonyashnyky)* and golden-coloured mustard *(hirchytsya)*. There are scores of wildflowers, while dozens of varieties are cultivated for nectar and honey *(med)* production.

NATIONAL PARKS

Soon after Viktor Yushchenko kicked off his campaign for the historic 2004 presidential election, he made a highly symbolic gesture. He led a group of his supporters to the Carpathian National Nature Park

UKRAINE'S NATIONAL PARKS

Listed here is a selection of parks Western tourists will most likely visit. For a full list and location map, visit http://enrin.grida.no/biodiv/biodiv/national/ukraine/prt/res.htm.

If you do visit a national park, be aware that lighting fires is not allowed or only allowed in dedicated campsites; try to find out what the situation is where you are.

Park	Features	Activities	Best time to visit	Page
Askaniya Nova Reserve	bison, ostrich, flamingos, zebra	sightseeing safari	May–Nov	p128
Carpathian National Natural Park	rolling mountains, pristine lakes, bears	skiing, hiking	year round	p95
Carpathian Biosphere Reserve	Europe's only virgin beech forest	hiking (controlled access)	May–Sep	p98
Dunaysky/Danube Biosphere Reserve	Europe's largest wetlands, pelicans, cormorants	bird-watching	Mar–Nov	p128
Kara-Dah Nature Reserve	volcanic rocks, flowers, mineral crystals	guided hikes	May–Sep	p155

and climbed the country's highest peak, Hoverla (2061m), to clean up all the litter. Ukraine's national parks need politicians like this. The country's four biosphere reserves, 16 nature reserves and 10 national parks still only cover 4% of the national territory, and very few of these reserves are entirely or properly protected anyway. Logging, both legal and illegal, occurs in the Carpathian National Nature Park, for example. Under former president Kuchma, Ukraine even provoked international outrage by deepening a canal for shipping near the protected Danube Biosphere Reserve. Despite such official disdain for environmental protection, some parks are surviving well – sometimes simply because they are so remote.

It's Russian tradition to tie a ribbon to a tree in an area to which you wish to return, hence the 'littering' of tree branches with weather-washed ribbons in Crimea. In the Carpathians, it's the sign of a Hutsul wedding.

ENVIRONMENTAL ISSUES

The site of the Chornobyl accident, the world's worst nuclear disaster, Ukraine has a poor environmental record. The disaster was a wake-up call, when the country's green movement can be said to have started. However, today's 500 environmental NGOs still have many issues to contend with.

Besides recognising the horrors of Chornobyl (see the boxed text, p34), a major conference in Kyiv in 2003 concluded that water pollution, illegal logging in the Carpathians, a loss of soil fertility from intensive agriculture, the use of old, Soviet-era pesticides and low environmental awareness among the general public were all big challenges confronting Ukraine.

Biodiversity and government disinterest in sustainable development were also discussed. During Soviet rule, the drive to industrialise was ruthless, with nary a second thought given to environmental degradation. In 2003 the World Bank – having committed US$1.4 billion to regional environmental problems – still saw fit to criticise the Ukrainian government for failing to make companies comply with pollution limits and for frequently exempting politically influential companies from emission limits. Many rivers have been polluted by waste runoff from industry and agriculture because of such lax restrictions.

Some doomsayers say 'Chornobyl' means 'wormwood' and the accident was foretold in the Book of Revelations (8:10-11). Hmmm. In any case, *chornobyl* (black grass) is the different, if related, mugwort.

While air pollution remains a problem in cities, particularly in the industrialised east around Donbas and Zaporizhzhya, it has been reduced since the time of the Soviet Union, simply because so much heavy industry has collapsed.

No environmental organisations really offer regular tours to Ukraine for English-speakers yet, although you might want to search on the internet for special tours.

Food & Drink

'*Borshch* and bread – that's our food.' With this national saying, Ukrainians themselves admit theirs is a cuisine of comfort – hearty and mild dishes designed for fierce winters – rather than one of gastronomic zing. And yet, while it's suffered from negative stereotypes of Soviet-style beetroot slop and chicken Kyiv, Ukrainian cooking is on the up these days. Chefs have been rediscovering the wholesome appeal of the national cuisine, with an emphasis on old favourites cooked in new ways with fresh herbs and ingredients.

Meanwhile, Ukrainian theme restaurants are all the rage. This means there's more chance for overseas visitors to sample *kruchenyky* (beef roulades with prunes, bacon and spinach), *varenyky* (stuffed, ravioli-like dumplings), elaborately stuffed fish dishes or red-caviar pancakes washed down with chilled vodka or fresh-pressed cranberry juice. The *borshch* soup you encounter in these flash new restaurants is just as likely to be the aromatic green variety, based on sorrel, as the typical Ukrainian *borshch*, using beetroot.

Kyiv is the culinary capital, although Odesa is catching up and there are two interesting regional sidelines. The Hutsul people of the Carpathians favour river fish, berries and mushrooms, plus their own speciality cheese *brynza* (a cross between cottage cheese and feta) and polenta-style *banush* or *mammalyha* (see p97). Turkish-leaning Tatar cuisine spices up the menus in Crimea, with specialities like *shashlyk* (shish kebab), *chebureky* (a pastry filled with meat) and baklava (pastry with honey).

STAPLES & SPECIALITIES

Many of the country's specialities stem from down-to-earth peasant dishes, based on grains and staple vegetables like potatoes, cabbage, beets or mushrooms, then seasoned with garlic, dill and vinegar.

Borshch Locals would have you know that *borshch* (борщ) is Ukrainian. Not Russian, not Polish, but Ukrainian, and there's nothing better than a steaming bowlful in winter. A typical version of the national soup is based on beetroot, salted pork fat and herbs, but regional chefs might toss in ingredients like sausages, marrows or marinated apples.

Holubtsi Cabbage rolls (*holubtsi*; голубці) are stuffed with seasoned rice, meat or buckwheat, and topped with a tomato-based sauce.

Kasha A grain-based gruel, *kasha* (каша) is served as a side dish or a breakfast porridge, or used as stuffing. More strongly flavoured than you'd expect, it's an acquired taste.

Pancakes Three types of pancake might land on your plate. *Deruny* (деруни) are potato pancakes, and are served with a cream sauce and vegetable or meat. *Nalysnyky* (налисники) are thin crepes; *mlyntsi* (млинці) are thicker and smaller, like Russian blini.

FISHY BUSINESS

Ukraine breeds and manages its sturgeon population reasonably carefully, so it's probably OK to select any domestic varieties off the menu. However, any very expensive sturgeon is likely to come from the Caspian region, where the fish is endangered and should be avoided for environmental reasons. Eating red salmon caviar is uncontroversial but black beluga caviar comes from endangered Caspian breeds. Always ask about a fish's origins if it's not listed on the menu and if in any doubt, skip it. Be aware that there are international laws governing how much sturgeon caviar you can take out of the country. Anything over 250g will be confiscated.

TAKE YOUR TASTEBUDS TRAVELLING

Some Ukrainians seem more attached to *salo* (сало) than they are to sex. *Salo* sees them through cold winter nights and *salo* is always guaranteed to give them a thrill. They love this pure, un-adulterated pig fat; it's a centuries-old tradition that runs deep and thick, literally, in the Ukrainian blood. Despite ample artery-furring evidence to the contrary, Ukrainians argue that *salo* is good for them and keeps them slim. Songs and poems are even dedicated to it.

During times when meat has been unavailable or prohibitively expensive, *salo* has been the faithful alternative – and still is. Stored in vats, it needs no refrigeration and has the longevity of fine wine.

If you wish to sample this lardy 'delicacy', it's usually available everywhere, flavoured with garlic and salt, and spread on thick bread. The really adventurous gourmand might even try the 'Ukrainian Snickers bar' – *salo* in chocolate. It's found in Kyiv at the restaurant Tsarke Selo (p68).

Adventurous gourmands should also watch out for the charcoal-grilled sheep and bull's testicles sold at some Tatar roadside stalls and restaurants in Crimea.

Varenyky Similar to Polish *pierogies*, *varenyky* (вареники) are to Ukraine what dim sum is to China and filled pasta is to Italy. These small half-moon shaped dumplings have more than 50 different traditional fillings, ranging from vegetarian to meat. They're usually served with sour cream and a greaselike sauce.

DRINKS

Ukrainians have a sweet tooth, and it shows in their drinks, which range from delicious fruit juices such as cranberry *mors* (морс) or *uzvar* (узвар) to more sickly bottled confections such as *zhubzuk* (жубзук), a herbal lemonade similar to Austria's Almdudler. Even the wines and champagnes – produced in Crimea and Odesa but sold everywhere – are very sugary. Indeed, most Crimean wines are halfway to being sherry. If you're looking for something drier, try the Inkerman label.

On street corners in summer, you'll see small drinks' tankers selling *kvas* (квас), a gingery, beerlike soft drink; look for the big vats touting a hose-pipe attachment. However, the drink is proffered in a mug or cup that everyone shares, so you might want to bring your own glass.

Ukrainian beer isn't as fabulous as, say, Czech beer, but it's not bad tasting and it is fantastically cheap. The most popular brands are Obolon (Оболонь), Slavutych (Славутич) and Chernihivsky (Чернігівський).

One Ukrainian drink definitely worth souveniring is vodka, which is delicious, very reasonably priced and comes in attractive bottles.

CELEBRATIONS

Whole books have been written on the role of food in Ukrainian celebrations, which meld Christian and pagan rituals and are hence unparalleled. Marta Pisetska Farley's *Festive Ukrainian Cooking* (1990) will give you chapter, verse and recipes.

Christmas, celebrated in early January rather than December, involves a 12-course *Svyata Vecherya* (Holy Supper), which is traditionally prepared without meat or dairy products. Devout Orthodox Christians will still abstain from eating meat for 40 days beforehand, although fish is often not counted as meat.

At Easter certain foods are taken to church in a covered basket to be blessed. These usually include the 'official' Easter bread of *paska* (decorated and shaped into a cross), *babka* (a sweet egg bread), hard-boiled eggs and baked cheese.

Ukrainians also have a range of special wedding breads, including the tall, cylindrical *korovay*.

DID YOU KNOW?

Clinking glasses during a toast originated in Ukraine – or so poisoned president Viktor Yushchenko has claimed. By doing this, drops from one glass could spill into the other, he smiled at 2005's World Economic Forum, 'then nobody would poison you'.

WHERE TO EAT & DRINK

Restaurant (ресторан) and café (кафе) sound similar in English and Ukrainian. A *varenychna* (варенична) serves only *varenyky*, and a *stolova* (столова) is a Russian-style self-service canteen.

Visiting Ukraine, you should probably swallow any dislike of theme restaurants, as they're not only everywhere but also often have the highest standards and best Ukrainian food. Most restaurants are open from 11am or noon to 11pm or midnight, serving food constantly throughout. Cafés and canteens often open earlier, at 8am, but frequently stay open late too.

Eating out is still a special treat for many locals – nouveau riche Ukrainians excepted. So, outside Kyiv, restaurants are often empty. Finding yourselves the only guest/s is often a boon, however, as staff have less excuse to ignore you and will be more attentive to your accented Ukrainian, Russian or gesturing.

When eating in restaurants, be aware that many meat and fish dishes are listed on the menu by weight. For example, that *shashlyk* that looks good value at 10uah, might actually be 10uah per 100g, so read the menu carefully and if in doubt, ask. Bread and condiments are never complimentary, but they cost very little.

Tips aren't obligatory, but they are increasingly expected in the more cosmopolitan centres such as Kyiv, Odesa and Yalta, especially from foreigners. Around 10% will usually do.

A series of updated and adapted traditional recipes from American-Ukrainian homes is brought together in *Ukrainian Recipes*, edited by Joanne Asala. Daily staples and festive fare are both included.

Quick Eats

Food kiosks sprout on every spare inch of pavement in Ukraine, proffering drinks and snacks, especially around train and bus stations. Mostly they deal in cigarettes, sweets and the ever-present chewing gum. The bottles on the shelves range from water and soft drinks to beer, which is also considered a soft drink in Ukraine and is legal to imbibe on the streets.

Other stalls do sell pastries or warm snacks, including hamburgers, hot dogs, *shashlyky* and *perepichky* (frankfurters deep-fried in dough, fairground-style). It's not as if you would ordinarily need triple-strength health insurance to eat at these; however, if you do have a delicate stomach, give them a wide berth.

If you're self-catering, the local market *(rynok)* always provides a colourful experience. Old-style food stores *(gastronomy)* tend to be reminiscent of the USSR, but plenty of modern supermarkets now exist.

DID YOU KNOW?

In 2004 guests at a Simferopol food festival set a record by eating a 9-sq-metre sandwich containing 40kg of *salo*. Before the kick-off, the sandwich was guarded by police.

VEGETARIANS & VEGANS

While most Ukrainians are carnivores by nature, vegetarians won't find things too trying, especially in the larger cities where pizza joints and ethnic restaurants abound. Even Ukrainian cuisine can be meat-free if you

---

UKRAINE'S TOP FIVE

- **Za Dvoma Zaytsamy, Kyiv** (p68) Homy food and décor harking back to a cult Soviet film
- **Kozak Mamay, Kyiv** (p68) Traditional Ukrainian cuisine served up in a Cossack 'hut'
- **Kupol, Lviv** (p90) Delicious Polish and Austrian dishes in a chintzy 1930s room
- **Khutorok, Odesa** (p125) Fine dining in a huge, reed-thatched cottage on the beach
- **Rybatsky Stan, Sevastopol** (p142) Fresh, grilled seafood on the harbour front

---

FOODS THAT GLOW IN THE DARK?

Because mushroom and berries – two Ukrainian staples – tend to absorb more radiation than other foods, it's best to avoid them if you think they could have come from the woods around Chornobyl, the site of the world's worst nuclear accident in 1986.

You don't need to worry too much, however. Most mushrooms served in restaurants are champignons, which aren't grown locally, and some berries are also imported. To play it very safe, you should avoid home-grown berries sold on the street in Kyiv, but there should be no concerns in the Carpathians.

You can learn how to cook everything from different types of *borshch* to delicious honey cakes (*medovyky*) with Hippocrene's *Best of Ukrainian Cuisine* (1998) by Bohdan Zahny.

stick to a fairly bland diet of *deruny* or potato-and-mushroom *varenyky*. However, it's always a good idea to specify that you want a meat-free salad and *borshch* is, sadly, best avoided if you're strict about your diet. Even 'vegetarian' versions often use beef stock.

Vegans are much worse off. In a land that adores *smetana* (sour cream) and slathers its salads in mayonnaise, dining out will prove a trial. The best thing is to stay in apartments and visit the colourful local markets for cooking ingredients. Alternatively, come for Christmas (see p38).

WHINING & DINING

You might have other concerns about bringing children to Ukraine (see p173), but dining out should never be one. Kids are a common sight in restaurants, and staff are usually very solicitous, rustling up high chairs if they can. As it's not very spicy, the national cuisine is gentle on young palates; few young children will turn down well-cooked *varenyky*. Ukrainians have an extremely sweet collective tooth, so treats won't be hard to find, either.

HABITS & CUSTOMS

Lunch is traditionally the main meal of the day, although changing lifestyles mean many workers now eat on the run. Breakfast (sni-*da*-nok) is usually very similar to lunch (o-*bid*) or dinner (ve-*che*-rya); you'll rarely see muesli or toast.

DID YOU KNOW?

Borshch is imbued with all kinds of magical powers, including the ability to melt the hardest heart.

The best Ukrainian food is home-cooked and if you get invited to someone's house for a meal you're in for a treat. Ukrainian hospitality is legendary and having guests around turns the meal into a drawn-out, celebratory banquet, with plenty of courses and toasts.

EAT YOUR WORDS

In Kyiv and other major cities, it's always worth asking if there's an English-language menu. Sometimes one exists, even when the waiters don't speak a word. (You simply point.) Mostly, however, you will be faced with Cyrillic script – a good incentive to learn.

For pronunciation guidelines see p198.

Useful Phrases

Do you have any free tables?	У Вас є вільні столи?	u vas ye *vil'*·ni *sto*·ly?
Can I/we see the menu?	Можна подивитися на меню?	*mo*·zhna po·dy·*vy*·ty·sya na me·*nyu*?
Do you have a menu in English?	У Вас є меню англійською мовою?	u vas ye me·*nyu* an·*hliys'*·ko·yu *mo*·vo·yu?
I am a vegetarian.	Я вегетаріанець/ вегетаріанка.	ya ve·he·ta·ri·*a*·nets'/ ve·he·ta·ri·*an*·ka (male/female).
What do you recommend?	Що Ви порадите?	shcho vy po·*ra*·dy·te?
What is this/that?	Що це?	shcho tse?

I would like...	Я візьму…	ya viz'·mu…
	Я б хотів/хотіла…	ya b kho·*tiv*/kho·*ti*·la… (m/f)
I've been waiting for a long time.	Я вже давно чекаю.	ya vzhe da·*vno* che·*ka*·yu.
Bon appetit!	Смачного!	smach·*no*·ho!
Cheers!	Будьмо!	*bud*'·mo!
Thanks, I'm full.	Дякую, я наївся/	*dya*·ku·yu, ya na·*yi*·wsya/
	наїлася.	na·*yi*·la·sya (m/f).
I don't drink (alcohol).	Я не п'ю.	ya ne pyu.
The doctor doesn't allow me to eat/drink that.	Мені не дозволяє лікар їсти/пити.	me·*ni* ne do·zvo·*lya*·ye *li*·kar yisty/pyty.
Could we have the bill?	Можна рахунок?	*mo*·zhna ra·*khu*·nok?
Could I have a receipt please?	Дайте квитанцію, будь ласка?	*Da*·yte kvy·*tan*·tsiyu bud *la*·ska?
Thank you.	Дякую.	*dya*·ku·yu.
The meal was delicious!	Було дуже смачно!	bu·*lo duz*·he *smach*·no!
Compliments to the chef!	Передайте подяку кухареві!	pe·re·*day*·te po·*dya*·ku *ku*·kha·re·vi!

Menu Decoder

асорті овочеве (a·*sor*·*ti* o·vo·*che*·ve) – mixed vegetables
бануш (ba·*nush*) – cornmeal-based dish, like wet polenta
біфштекс пяний (bif·*shteks pya*·ny) – 'tipsy' beefsteak, cooked in alcohol and flambéed
блинчики (*blyn*·chy·ky) – oft-used Russian name for pancakes/pikelets
борщ зелений (borshch ze·*le*·ny) – green *borshch*, made with sorrel
борщ з пампушками та часниковою підливою (borshch z pam·*push*·ka·my ta chas·ny·*ko*·vo·yu pid·*ly*·vo·yu) – *borshch* with dumplings and garlic sauce
борщ Український (borshch uk·ra·*yin*·sky) – Ukrainian *borshch*, made with beetroot
вареники з картоплею та грибами (va·*re*·ny·ky z kar·*top*·le·yu ta hry·*ba*·my) – ravioli/dumplings with mashed potato and mushrooms
вареники з квашеною капустою (va·*re*·ny·ky z *kva*·she·no·yu ka·*pus*·to·yu) – ravioli/dumplings with sauerkraut
вареники з мясом (va·*re*·ny·ky z *mya*·som) – ravioli/dumplings with meat
відбивна (vid·byv·*na*) – steak
відбивна із лосося з креветками (vid·byv·*na* iz lo·*so*·sya z kre·*vet*·ka·my) – salmon steak and prawns
голубці з грибами (ho·lub·*tsi* z hry·*ba*·my) – cabbage rolls stuffed with mushrooms
деруни з грибами та сметаною (de·ru·*ny* z hry·*ba*·my ta sme·*ta*·no·yu) – potato pancakes with mushrooms and sour cream

---

DOS & DON'TS

- Do bring a small gift if you've been invited to lunch or dinner.
- Do inform your hosts beforehand of any dietary needs; refusing food can be rude.
- Do take off your shoes on entering your hosts' house.
- Do say *'smachnoho'* (bon appetit) before starting to eat.
- Do drain your shot glass of vodka in one gulp when drinking a toast.
- Don't bring an odd number of flowers; that's for funerals.
- Don't shake hands across the threshold, as it's bad luck.
- Don't refuse a drink without a 'proper' excuse, ie for religious or health reasons.
- Don't leave an empty bottle on the table during a meal; it's bad luck.
- Don't expect to keep up with Ukrainians making toasts – they can outdrink all comers!

FIRST AID FOR CAFFEINE ADDICTS

Coffee is a sore subject in Ukraine. Generally, only instant coffee was available in the Soviet Union and locals still haven't developed a taste for the real thing. Where else but in the former Soviet Union would a chain of coffee shops run by Nescafé be considered trendy? Where else are the 'espressos' so watery? Where else when ordering coffee will your server ask you to choose between Nescafé, Jacobs or MacCoffee, instead of latte, mocha or cappuccino?

But before your search for 'natural' (brewed) coffee gets you all misty-eyed for Starbucks – yes, things are that dire – try the following few places. Although most of them also have an excellent vibe, the scores here aren't for atmosphere, just the pure brew.

■ **Klara Bara, Odesa** (p125) Top marks for the Turkish coffee.

■ **Kaffa, Kyiv** (p71) Suddenly you're spoilt for choice is this African-themed outlet.

■ **Hotel Ukraine, Sevastopol** (p142) The only heart-pumping coffee in Ukraine that is possibly too strong.

■ **On the Corner, Kolomyya** (p101) With the Italian espresso-maker constantly on the boil, this hyper B&B runs on caffeine.

запечені баклажанчики (za·*pe*·che·ni ba·kla·*zha*·ny) – baked aubergine/eggplant dish
картопля відварна (kar·*top*·lya vid·var·*na*) – boiled potatoes
картопля запечена (kar·*top*·lya za·*pe*·che·na) – baked potatoes
картопля фри (kar·*top*·lya fri) – french fries
ковбаса (kov·ba·*sa*) – smoked ham sausage
котлета по-київськи (kot·*le*·ta po *ky*·yiv·sky) – chicken Kyiv, a crumbed chicken fillet, filled with butter and deep fried
кров'яночка (kro·*vya*·noch·ka) – blood sausage filled with buckwheat, bacon and calf's liver
крученики (kru·*che*·ny·ky) – beef roulades stuffed with prunes, bacon and spinach, served with red-wine sauce
курина грудинка з курагою та миндалем (ku·ry·na hru·*dyu*·ka z kura·*ho*·yu ta myn·*da*·lem) – chicken breast with dried apricots and almonds
лососина в шампанському (lo·so·sy·na v sham·*pan*·sko·mu) – salmon in champagne
мамалига (ma·ma·*ly*·ha) – cornmeal-based dish, like firm polenta
млинці з медом та маслом (mlyn·*tsi* z *me*·dom ta *mas*·lom) – pancakes with honey and butter
налисники з червоною ікрою (na·*lus*·ny·ky z cher·*vo*·no·yu ik·*ro*·yu) – crepes with red caviar
налисники з чорною ікрою (na·*lus*·ny·ky z *chor*·no·yu ik·ro·yu) – crepes with black caviar
овочі гриль or овочевий шашлик (o·vo·chi hryl/o·vo·*che*·vy sha·shlyk) – vegetable *shashlyk*
омлет (om·let) – omelette
пельмені (pel·*me*·ni) – Russian dim sum, akin to *varenyky*
печеня домашня (pe·*che*·nya do·*mash*·nya) – home-style roast beef
плов (plov) – dish of rice, meat and grilled vegetables, often served with a spicy sauce
пюре картопляне (pyu·*re* kar·*top*·lya·ne)– mashed potatoes
салат (sa·*lat*) – salad; looks like 'салам' when handwritten
свина ребрина в медовому соусі (svy·*na* reb·*ry*·na v me·*do*·vo·mu *so*·u·si) – pork ribs in honey sauce
солянка (so·*lyan*·ka) – slightly sour-tasting soup made with olives and salted cucumbers, plus meat or fish
шашлик із осетрини (sha·*shlyk* iz o·se·*try*·ny) – sturgeon *shashlyk*
шашлик із сома (sha·*shlyk* iz *so*·ma) – cat-fish *shashlyk*
шашлик із свинини (sha·*shlyk* iz svy·ny·ny) – pork *shashlyk*
шуба or оселедець під шубою (*shu*·ba/o·se·*le*·dets pid *shy*·bo·yu) – herrings under a layered salad of carrot, beetroot and mayonnaise
холодець or Студень (kho·lo·*dets*/*stu*·den) – meat, usually pork, in jelly
чебуреки (che·bu·*re*·ky) – pastry pocket filled with meat or cheese, like a Turkish *burek*
юшка (*yu*·shka) – thin soup or gruel

Food Glossary
BASICS

khlib	хліб	bread
...*chor*·ny	чорний	black
...*bi*·ly	білий	white
med	мед	honey
pe·rets	перець	pepper
sil'	сіль	salt
tsu·kor	цукор	sugar
va·*ryen*·nya	варення	jam
yay·tse	яйце	egg

DAIRY PRODUCE МОЛОЧНІ ПРОДУКТИ

ke·*fir*	кефір	drinking yogurt
ma·slo	масло	butter
mo·lo·*ko*	молоко	milk
sme·*ta*·na	сметана	sour cream

FRUIT ФРУКТИ

a·pel'·*syn*/po·ma·*ran*·cha	апельсин/помаранча	orange
ba·*nan*	банан	banana
hra·*nat*	гранат	pomegranate
ka·*vun*	кавун	watermelon
ki·vi	ківі	kiwi fruit
ma·*ly*·na	малина	raspberry
vy·no·*hrad*	виноград	grapes
ya·blu·ko	яблуко	apple

VEGETABLES ОВОЧІ

bu·*ryak*	буряк	beetroot
hryb	гриб	mushroom
ka·*pu*·sta	капуста	cabbage
kar·*to*·plya	картопля	potato
mor·kva	морква	carrot
tsy·*bu*·lya	цибуля	onion

MEAT М'ЯСО

ba·*ra*·ny·na	баранина	lamb
in·*dyk*/in·dy·*cha*·ty·na	індик/индичатина	turkey
kach·ka/u·*tya*·ty·na/hu·*sya*·ty·na	качка/утятина/гусятина	duck
ku·*rya*·ty·na/*kur*·ka	курятина/курка	chicken
svy·*ny*·na	свинина	pork
te·*lya*·ty·na	телятина	veal
ya·lo·vy·chy·na	яловичина	beef

SEAFOOD РИБНІ СТРАВИ

i·*kra*	ікра	caviar
...che·*rvo*·na	червона	red
...chor·*na*	чорна	black
fo·*rel*	форель	trout
ko·rop	короп	carp
kra·by	краби	crabs
lo·*sos*'/lo·so·sy·na	лосось/лососина	salmon
o·se·*le*·dets'	оселедець	herring

| o·se·*try*·na | осетрина | sturgeon |
| su·*dak* | судак | pike-perch (Rus) |

CONDIMENTS

	ПРИПРАВИ	
hir·*chu*·tsya	гірчиця	mustard
ket·chup	кетчуп	ketchup/tomato sauce
ma·yo·*nez*	майонез	mayonnaise
o·*li*·ya	олія	oil
o·*tset*	оцет	vinegar
so·us ta·*tar*·sky	соус татарський	tatar sauce
khrin	хрін	horseradish

PIZZA TOPPINGS

	НАЧИНКА ДЛЯ ПІЦЦИ	
a·na·*nas*	ананас	pineapple
ku·ku·*ru*·za	кукурудза	sweetcorn
ku·*rya*·ty·na/*kur*·ka	курятина/курка	chicken
o·*lyv*·ky/ma·*sly*·ny	оливки/маслини	olives
o·*sno*·va	основа	base (often used to refer to a margherita)
pe·pe·*ro*·ni	пепероні	pepperoni
pe·rets	перець	peppers/capsicum
po·mi·*dor*·i/pe·che·*ry*·tsi	помідори/печериці	tomatoes/tomato paste
sa·*lya*·mi	салямі	salami
shyn·ka	шинка	ham
syr	сир	cheese
tu·*nets*	тунець	tuna

SNACKS & SWEETS

	ЗАКУСКИ ТА СОЛОДОЩИ	
cheep·si	чіпси	chips/crisps
mo·*ro*·zy·vo	морозиво	ice cream
pe·*chen*·nya	печення	biscuits
sho·ko·*lad*	шоколад	chocolate
tort	торт	cake
zhee·*val*·na re·zyn·ka/ zhu·*vach*·ka	жувальна резинка/ жувачка	chewing gum

DRINKS

	НАРОЇ	
chay	чай	tea
...z ly·*mo*·nom	з лимоном	with lemon
ho·*ril*·ka/*vot*·ka	горілка/водка	vodka (Ukr/Rus)
ka·va/ko·fe	кава/кофе	coffee (Ukr/Rus)
...z mo·lo·*kom*	з молоком	with milk
...z *tsuk*·rom	з цукром	with sugar
mi·ne·*ral'*·na vo·*da*	мінеральна вода	mineral water
...bez *ha*·zu/ ne ha·*zo*·va·na	без газу/ не газована	still
...z *ha*·zu/ha·*zo*·va·na	з газу/газована	sparkling
py·vo	пиво	beer
sik/sok	сік/сок	juice (Ukr/Rus)
...fruk·*to*·vy	фруктовий	fruit
...a·*pel'*·syn	апельсин	orange
...a·pel·sy·no·vy	апельсиновий	freshly squeezed orange
vy·*no*	вино	wine
...*bi*·le	біле	white
...cher·*vo*·ne	червоне	red

Kyiv Київ

CONTENTS

Watching the disproportionate number of black SUVs and Mercedes with tinted windows barrel down wide boulevards lined with Stalinist concrete monoliths, visitors soon appreciate Kyiv's defining characteristics: it's flashy, fast and monumental.

From a historical perspective this might be the much-vaunted 'mother of all eastern Slavic peoples' but face-lifted modern Kyiv stands more as the apotheosis of 'new Ukrainian' conspicuous consumption. Like Moscow or London, this is a capital that attracts most of the country's wealth and its best talent, and the political classes and beautiful fashionistas all enjoy rubbing designer-clad shoulders here. While it's probably blasphemy to say so, even the trademark golden domes of its ring of Orthodox churches add to the overall impression of awesome showiness and glitz.

Of course, that's all a bit superficial. On the cobbled pavements above huge underground shopping malls, old ladies make ends meet by selling berries, corncobs, potatoes and other home-grown produce. Behind the glamorous, cosmopolitan façade everyone knows someone who knows someone else and it's just a big village really.

Above all, Kyiv (Kiev in Russian) is engaging and energetic; the local football team, Dynamo, couldn't be better named. By all means do the typical tourist stuff: pay your respects to the mummified monks of the Caves Monastery or visit the charming street of Andriyivsky uzviz. But also leave time to join the ever-present local crowds simply drinking in the atmosphere. Wander through hilltop parkland overlooking the Dnipro River and Soviet-built suburbs on the far bank and catch the funicular down the hill to the cosy European district of Podil. Or, in summer, set out your towel on the city beaches of Hydropark… Listen to talented classical musicians busking, stroll along the main street of Khreshchatyk, eat well, have a beer, go clubbing – that's when this whirlwind of a city really sweeps you off your feet.

HIGHLIGHTS

- See mummified monks by candlelight in the **Caves Monastery's** (p56) underground passages
- Catch the **funicular** (p56) down to **Podil**, then walk up Andriyivsky uzviz in the shadow of the magnificent **St Andrew's Church** (p53)
- Visit the **Chornobyl Museum** (p56) or even the damaged reactor itself (p75)
- Inspect the interior of **St Sophia's Cathedral** (p55) and any other major church that takes your fancy
- Get up close to **Rodina Mat** (p60), the Defence of the Motherland Monument – just because
- Take a stroll along **Khreshchatyk** (p63) and the leafy parks lining the river
- Sample the best sort of Ukrainian cuisine in the city's many excellent **restaurants** (p68)
- Enjoy a day in the 'countryside' at the excellent **Pyrohovo Museum of Folk Architecture** (p62)

★ Chornobyl Museum
St Sophia's ★   ★ Podil
Cathedral ★
★ Khreshchatyk

★ Caves Monastery
★ Rodina Mat

★
Pyrohovo Museum of
Folk Architecture

| ▪ TELEPHONE CODE: 044 | ▪ POPULATION: 2.5 MILLION | ▪ HIGHEST POINT: 179M |

HISTORY

Legend has it that three Slavic brothers and their sister founded Kyiv. The eldest, Ky, gave the city its name. The names of brothers Shchek, Khoriv and sister Lybid, now appear in its topography. An iconic statue (Map pp50–1) of the four siblings – the Foundation of Kyiv Monument – stands on the banks of the Dnipro River.

Four hundred years later the city really started to prosper, after Vikings from Novgorod took control. In 878 Scandinavian King Oleh had sent two emissaries, Askold and Dir, to Kyiv to strike a deal with the ruling Maygars. But, wanting greater control himself, Oleh journeyed to Kyiv in 882, dispatched his emissaries and declared himself ruler. This was the beginning of Kyivan Rus ('Rus' being the Slavic name for the red-haired Scandinavians). The city thrived on river trade, sending furs, honey and slaves to pay for luxury goods from Constantinople. Within 100 years its empire stretched from the Volga to the Danube and to Novgorod.

In 989 Kyivan ruler Volodymyr decided to forge a closer alliance with Constantinople, marrying the emperor's daughter and adopting Orthodox Christianity. Kyiv's pagan idols were destroyed and its people driven into the Dnipro for a mass baptism – an event still commemorated during Epiphany (see p63).

Under Volodymyr's son, Yaroslav the Wise (1017–54), Kyiv became a cultural and political centre in the Byzantine mould. St Sophia's Cathedral (p55) was built to proclaim the glory of both God and city. However, by the 12th century, Kyiv's economic prowess had begun to wane, with power shifting successively to several breakaway principalities.

In 1240 Mongol raiders sacked Kyiv. Citizens fled or took refuge wherever they could, including the roof of the Desyatynna Church, which collapsed under the weight (see p55).

The city shrank to the riverside district of Podil, which remained its centre for centuries. Only when Ukraine formally passed into Russian hands at the end of the 18th century did Kyiv again grow in importance, as tsarist policies encouraged Russian immigration. The city went through an enormous boom at the turn of the 20th century because of an upsurge in nearby sugar milling. Many new mansions were erected at this time, including the remarkable Chimera Building (p60).

During the chaos following the Bolshevik Revolution, Kyiv was the site of frequent battles between Red and White Ukrainian forces. Acclaimed author Mikhail Bulgakov captured the era's uncertainty in his first novel *The White Guard,* and the home in which he wrote this book is now a museum (see p61).

In August 1941 German troops captured Kyiv and more than half a million Soviet soldiers were caught or killed. The entire city suffered terribly. Germans massacred about 100,000 at Babyn Yar (see p61) and 80% of the city's inhabitants were homeless by the time the Red Army retook Kyiv on 6 November 1943.

The postwar years saw rapid industrialisation and the construction of unsightly suburbs. During the late 1980s nationalistic and democratic movements from western Ukraine began to catch on in the capital. Throughout the presidency of Leonid Kuchma, Kyiv and its young population increasingly became a base of opposition politics. During the Orange Revolution of 2004, activists from around Ukraine poured into the capital to

---

FIVE KYIV SURVIVAL TIPS

- Watch the traffic – at all times, even on pavements, where cars sometimes drive.
- Exercise caution entering the metro – those swinging glass doors pack a punch.
- Learn to hold your place in queues – people will try to butt in at all times, everywhere. Be firm without being too pushy.
- Be patient about addresses – sometimes what you're looking for is at the far end of a huge Soviet block bearing one street number. Many places are also hidden in courtyards. If in doubt, ask *'Gdye…'* or *'De…'* (Where is…).
- Ask to see the ID of any purported transport inspectors – many shakedown artists try to 'fine' foreigners for not having the right ticket.

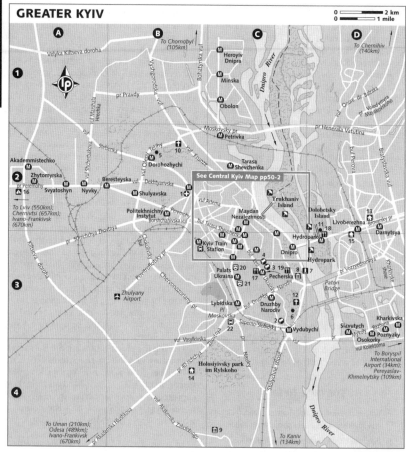

GREATER KYIV

demonstrate in Independence Square and outside the parliament building.

ORIENTATION

Kyiv's modern centre and old city are on the west bank – confusingly called the right bank – of the Dnipro River. This area alone is divided into three major districts.

Firstly, there's the Upper Town, on the hills above the Dnipro. This includes the old town, around the northern end of vul Volodymyrska, near St Sophia's Cathedral. Behind this is Kyiv's main commercial zone, where the main street, vul Khreshchatyk, runs north along a valley from pl Bessarabska towards maydan Nezalezhnosti (Independence Square).

Secondly, the area north of the Old Town from around St Andrew's Church to Kontraktova pl is called Podil, or Lower Town. This is the historic merchants' quarter and river port and sits below the rest of the city, on the river plain.

From the northern end of Khreshchatyk, vul Hrushevskoho runs southeast along a ridge past the Dynamo Kyiv stadium and the parliament building to a third district known as Pechersk. This is the historic ecclesiastical centre and site of the Caves Monastery. Woods and parks cover most of the west bank's slopes.

Midriver there's a cluster of islands with city beaches and parkland. On the east (left) bank lie grey housing blocks.

Maps

Souvenir stalls on maydan Nezalezhnosti sell street plans, and these can also be bought abroad. In the UK, for example, try Stanfords (p178). Hotels can often supply maps, too.

INFORMATION
Bookshops

Baboon Book Coffee Shop (Map pp50-1; ☎ 235 5980; vul Bohdana Khmelnytskoho 39; 🕙 9am-2am; M Universytet) A funky, boho bookshop-restaurant that has maps and a separate room full of second-hand English books.
Bukva (Map pp50-1; ☎ 234 8197; vul Lva Tolstoho 11/61; 🕙 9am-10pm; M pl Lva Tolstoho) Also has a well-stocked outlet in the Globus mall at central maydan Nezalezhnosti.

Emergency

American Medical Center (emergency ☎ 461 9595) Offers a 24-hour emergency service. See right for the centre's other medical services.

Internet Access

Cyber Kafe (Map pp50-1; ☎ 228 0548; www.cyber cafe.com.ua; vul Prorizna 21; per hr 8uah; 🕙 24hr; M Zolotoi Vorota)

Internet Centre (Map pp50-1; ☎ 230 499; vul Khreshchatyk 48; per hr 10uah; 🕙 24hr; M Teatralna) Also offers cheap calls to the US and Canada.
Orbita Computer Club (Map pp50-1; ☎ 234 1693; 2nd fl, vul Khreshchatyk 29; per hr 6uah; 🕙 8am-1am; M Teatralna) Bustling, often noisy centre.

Internet Resources

Go2Kiev (www.go2kiev.com) Friendly, reliable and usually up-to-date site, presenting just the right amount of information – and doing it well.

Medical Services

American Medical Center (Map p48; ☎ 490 7600; vul Berdychivska 1; 🕙 24hr; M Lukyanivska) Western-run medical centre, with English-speaking doctors.
Avanto (Map pp50-1; ☎ 531 3797; Room 239, 2nd fl, vul Konstyantynivska 19/17; M Kontraktova pl) English-speaking dentists.
Gormonalnykh Preparatory (Map pp50-1; ☎ 235 4035; bul Tarasa Shevchenka 36A; 🕙 8am-9pm; M Universytet) English-speaking pharmacist.

Money

Both ATMs and exchange booths signposted 'обмін валюти' *(obmin valyuty)* are ubiquitous. Rates offered by exchange booths in hotels are not necessarily worse. Larger banks will cash travellers cheques and give cash advances on credit cards.

Post

Central post office (Map pp50-1; ☎ 230 0838; vul Khreshchatyk 22; M maydan Nezalezhnosti) Includes post (🕙 8am-9pm, to 7pm Sun), fax (🕙 8am-9pm, to 7pm Sun) and internet (🕙 24hr). The entrance is on maydan Nezalezhnosti.
DHL International (Map pp50-1; ☎ 490 2600, 238 6985; www.dhl.com.ua; vul Ivana Franka 40b; M Universytet) One of many DHL express centres in town. Another is at the Hotel Rus (p67).

Telephone

Central telephone centre (Map pp50-1; vul Khreshchatyk 22; 🕙 24hr; M maydan Nezalezhnosti) You can make international calls here or buy phone cards.
Telephone centre (Map pp50-1; vul Bohdana Khmelnytskoho 32; 🕙 8am-8pm; M Universytet) Smaller and usually less crowded than the central telephone centre.
Telephone centre (Map pp50-1; ground fl, south terminal, Kyiv train station; 🕙 8am-11pm; M Vokzalna)

Tourist Information

Kyiv lacks a tourist office but many hotels have an information bureau.

CENTRAL KYIV

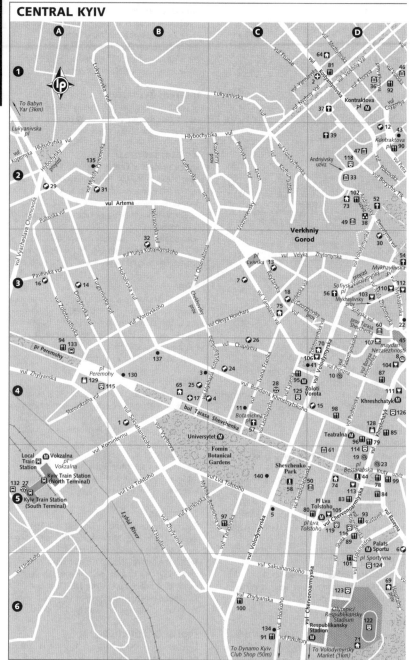

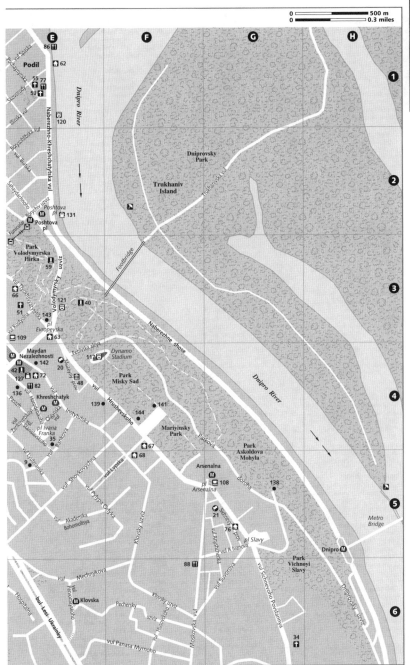

KYIV IN...

Two days

Enjoy a sumptuous breakfast in the 18th-floor **Empire** (p69) restaurant or cheap, delicious pastries at nearby **Puzata Khata** (p68). Wander up Khreshchatyk to **Independence Square** (maydan Nezalezhnosti; below). Cut through to **St Sophia's Cathedral** (p55) and **St Michael's Monastery** (p56). Catch the funicular down to Podil, visit the **Chornobyl Museum** (p56) and then walk up **Andriyivsky uzviz** (below). Choose a good **Ukrainian restaurant** (p68) for dinner.

Arrive early on the second day at the **Caves Monastery** (p56), before visiting **Rodina Mat** and the **Museum of the Great Patriotic War** (p60). On the way back, visit the **Parliament**, **Mariyinsky Palace** and **Dynamo Stadium** (p63). Spend your evening sampling one of the many **bars** (p70) or **clubs** (p71).

Four days

Follow the two-day itinerary, and on the third day visit the **Pyrohovo Museum of Folk Architecture** (p62). After this, explore a few more churches and buildings. Perhaps visit **Babyn Yar** (p61) or in summer head to the **beach** (p63).

Travel Agencies

Chervona Ruta (Map pp50-1; ☎ /fax 253 9247, 293 6909, 253 5236; www.ruta-cruise.com; vul Lyuteranska 24; Ⓜ Teatralna) This Dnipro River and Black Sea cruise specialist also offers bus tours of Ukraine.

Mandrivnyk (Map pp50-1; ☎ 490 6632; office@mandrivnyk.com.ua; Poshtova pl 3; Ⓜ Poshtova pl) Located at the river boat terminal, Mandrivnyk offer tours throughout Ukraine and boat information. They will also let you take the controls of a MiG fighter plane (for a huge fee).

New Logic (Map pp50-1; ☎ 206 3322; www.newlogic.com.ua; vul Mykhaylivska 6A; Ⓜ maydan Nezalezhnosti) All the usual packages, tickets and hotel bookings, plus trips to Chornobyl. Office is in a courtyard off the street.

Sam (Map pp50-1; ☎ 238 6959; www.sam.ua; vul Ivana Franka 40B; Ⓜ Universytet) The leading inbound operator organises sightseeing excursions, Dnipro cruises, visa support, hotel bookings and trips to Chernihiv, Chornobyl and Uman.

SoloEast Travel (☎ /fax 985 3115, 0-50 381 8656; www.tourkiev.com) Ukrainian-husband-and-Canadian-wife team offering tickets, apartments and tours, including to Chornobyl. Probably the most helpful, friendly travel service in Kyiv, with B&B accommodation just outside the city.

SIGHTS

Some of Kyiv's main attractions are half-day or all-day adventures in themselves and not always terribly central. So, rather than plunging right in, it's highly recommended to warm-up with an initial stroll. The walking tour on p63 provides a quick introduction to the city.

Independence Square   Map pp50–1

Fountain-filled **maydan Nezalezhnosti** is the city's most popular meeting place. This was plainly seen on worldwide TV at the end of 2004 when the square became ground zero for Ukraine's Orange Revolution (p17) and makeshift tent city. But, revolution or no revolution, the place is always busy. Vendors sell food and souvenirs, while teenagers carouse under the watchful gaze of winged angel statues, including the tall Independence Monument. In the evening, drinkers frequently watch live bands, while the late-night shopping malls keeps the tills ringing.

Maydan Nezalezhnosti lies on **Khreshchatyk**, Kyiv's broad, 1.5km-long main street. During WWII, the retreating Soviet army mined the buildings here, turning them into deadly booby traps for any German soldiers setting foot inside. Most places did explode or catch fire, which is why the rebuilt boulevard is in such an imposing Stalinist style. However, a few façades are reminiscent of the earlier cosmopolitan street. Khreshchatyk is at its best on weekends, when it's closed to traffic and becomes a giant pedestrian zone.

In case you're wondering, the dull metal parabola you can see from the northern end of Khreshchatyk is part of the **Friendship of Nations Monument**. For more details, see p63.

Andriyivsky uzviz   Map pp50–1

It says a lot for **Andriyivsky uzviz** (Andrew's Descent) that the souvenir stalls now overflowing on its cobblestones haven't stopped it

KYIV

KYIV METRO

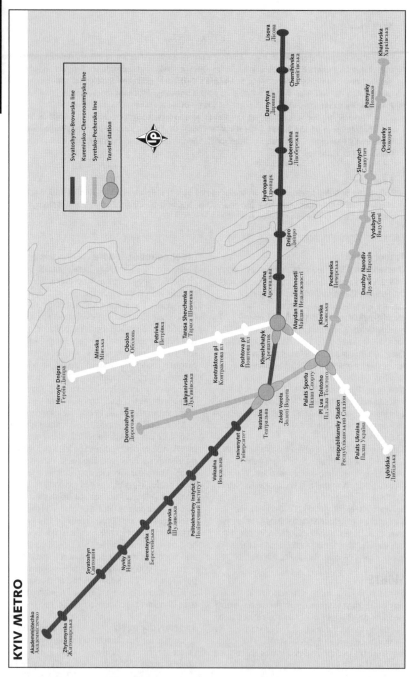

Svyatoshyno-Brovarska line
Kurenivsko-Chervonoarmiyska line
Syretsko-Pecherska line
Transfer station

Akademmistechko
Академмістечко

Zhytomyrska
Житомирська

Svyatoshyn
Святошин

Nyvky
Нивки

Beresteyska
Берестейська

Shulyavska
Шулявська

Politekhnichny Instytut
Політехнічний Інститут

Vokzalna
Вокзальна

Universytet
Університет

Teatralna
Театральна

Zoloti Vorota
Золоті Ворота

Dorohozhychi
Дорогожичі

Lukyanivska
Лук'янівська

Kontraktova pl
Контрактова пл

Poshtova pl
Поштова пл

Khreshchatyk
Хрещатик

Palats Sportu
Палац Спорту

Pl Lva Tolstoho
Пл Льва Толстого

Resp Ublikansky Stadion
Республіканський Стадіон

Palats Ukraina
Палац Україна

Lybidska
Либідська

Heroyiv Dnipra
Героїв Дніпра

Minska
Мінська

Obolon
Оболонь

Petrivka
Петрівка

Tarasa Shevchenka
Тараса Шевченка

Arsenalna
Арсенальна

Hydropark
Гідропарк

Dnipro
Дніпро

Maydan Nezalezhnosti
Майдан Незалежності

Klovska
Кловська

Pecherska
Печерська

Livoberezhna
Лівобережна

Darnytsya
Дарниця

Chernihivska
Чернігівська

Lisova
Лісова

Drazhby Narodiv
Дружби Народів

Vydubychi
Видубичі

Slavutych
Славутич

Osokorky
Осокорки

Pozniaky
Позняки

Kharkivska
Харківська

being one of Kyiv's most beloved and charming streets. Historically, this curving incline linked the high ground of the administrative centre, or Upper Town, to the arty district of riverside Podil. Nowadays it's frequented by purveyors of Ukrainian crafts, Soviet memorabilia, Osama bin Laden *matryoshky* (stacking dolls), Yuri Gagarin T-shirts and the occasional stunning photo of Kyiv. Yet the quaint houses and crooked pavements still give the place atmosphere.

The street is called Andrew's Descent after Kyiv's first Christian preacher, Andrivy (Andrew in English), who is said to have climbed the hill here, affixed a cross to its summit and returned via this path.

In many ways, for the modern visitor it's preferable to head uphill, past the **Museum of One Street** (p61) and the **Bulgakov Museum** (p61). This way you get the densest crowds last and arguably get a better view of the magnificent **St Andrew's Church** (☎ 228 5861; admission 4uah; ☒ 10am-6pm Thu-Tue), at the top of the hill. Built in 1754 by Italian architect Bartelomeo Rastrelli, who also designed the Winter Palace in St Petersburg, this is a magnificent baroque interpretation of the traditional Ukrainian five-domed, cross-shaped church. The fine figure its blue, white, gold and green exterior cuts against the skyline more than makes up for its disappointing interior.

The small bronze statue behind St Andrew's Church is of characters from the film *Za Dvoma Zaytsamty* (see p68). Meanwhile, across from the church, up a flight of stairs, and on the grounds before the **National Museum of Ukrainian History** (☎ 228 2924; vul Volodymyrska 2; adult/child 10/5uah; ☒ 10am-5pm Thu-Tue) are the **Desyatynna Church ruins**. Prince Volodymyr ordered the church built in 989 and devoted 10% of his income to it, hence the name (*desyatyn* means 'one-tenth'). The church came to an end in 1240, when it collapsed under the weight of the people who took refuge on its roof during the Mongol sacking of Kyiv. The museum has exhibits of archaeological and recent historical interest, including books and currencies.

St Sophia's Cathedral   Map pp50–1

The interior is the most astounding aspect of Kyiv's oldest standing church, **Sofiysky Sobor** (☎ 228 6152; Sofiyska pl; grounds 1uah; cathedral adult/child 11/4uah; bell tower 3uah; ☒ 10am-6pm Fri-Tue,

to 5pm Wed, grounds 8.30am-8pm daily). Many of the mosaics and frescoes are original, dating back to 1017–31, when the cathedral was built to celebrate Prince Yaroslav's victory in protecting Kyiv from the Pechenegs, tribal raiders.

While equally attractive, the building's gold domes and 76m-tall wedding-cake bell tower are 18th-century baroque additions.

Named after the great Hagia Sofia (Holy Wisdom) Cathedral in Istanbul, St Sophia's Byzantine architecture announced the new religious and political authority of Kyiv. It was a centre of learning and culture, housing the first school and library in Kyivan Rus. Adjacent to the Royal Palace, it was also where coronations and other royal ceremonies were staged, treaties signed and foreign dignitaries received. Prince Yaroslav himself is buried here.

Each mosaic and fresco had its allotted position according to Byzantine decorative schemes, turning the church into a giant three-dimensional symbol of the Orthodox world order. There are explanations in English of individual mosaics, but the one that immediately strikes you is 6m-high **Virgin Orans** dominating the central apse. The Virgin Orans is a peculiarly Orthodox concept of the Virgin as a symbol of the earthly church interceding for the salvation of humanity and, having survived this long, this particular Orans is now thought indestructible by Orthodox believers. (Unesco was slightly less certain, adding the cathedral to its protective World Heritage list in 1990.)

Less obvious, but worth seeking out, are fragments in the central nave and the north stairwell of two group portraits of Yaroslav and family. The prince's tomb is found on the ground floor, in the far left corner from the main entrance.

Visitors need to pay to enter the grounds, before heading to the ticket booth inside the entrance to buy a joint ticket to the cathedral, refectory and consistory. Only the cathedral is worth visiting. Entrance to the bell tower is separate, but also worth it for the view.

In front of the cathedral complex on Sofiyska pl is a statue of Cossack hero Bohdan Khmelnytsky. Just before the bell tower lies the ornate tomb of Kyiv Patriarch Volodymyr Romanyuk. Religious disputes prevented him from being buried within the complex; see p26 for details.

Trolleybus No 16 or 18, departing from the back of maydan Nezalezhnosti, will drop you off a block north of the cathedral, on vul Volodymyrska.

St Michael's Monastery & Around
Map pp50–1

Looking from St Sophia's past the Bohdan Khmelnytsky statue it's impossible to ignore the gold-domed blue church at the other end of proyizd Volodymyrska. This is **Mykhaylivska Zolotoverkhyi Monasterya** (St Michael's Gold-Domed Monastery; admission free; 8am-8pm), named after Kyiv's patron saint. The monastery's style is medieval/baroque, but the shininess of its seven cupolas gives it away: it's a modern copy. The original St Michael's (1108) was torn down by the Soviets in 1936 and this reconstruction was only opened in 2001. Those keen to learn more can visit the monastery **museum** (☎ 228 6268; adult/child 2/1uah; 10am-6pm Tue-Sun, ticket office to 5pm).

Left of the entrance to St Michael's is a moving **monument to the victims of the great famine**. Unfortunately, the accompanying small exhibition is difficult to appreciate unless you understand Ukrainian or are 2m tall! The English signs are posted well above any average person's head, so see p22 instead.

On the surrounding square, Mykhaylivska pl, are four statues of great Slavs: ruler Princess Olha, St Cyril and St Methodius (the founders of the Slavic alphabet and literacy), plus Apostle Andriy (Kyiv's first Christian preacher).

Heading around the left of the church to the rear, you'll find the quaint **funicular** (50 kopecks; 6.30am-11pm) that runs down a steep hillside to the river terminal and the former artisans' district of Podil. Although trees partially obscure your view as you ride down to the river, this is still the most fun public-transport ride in town. Slot a 50-kopeck piece directly into the barriers or, if you don't have the correct change, pay the attendants. Sometimes they'll accept your money and other times they'll just give you 50-kopeck pieces.

Chornobyl Museum & Podil
Map pp50–1

It's hard to convey the full horror of the world's worst nuclear accident, but the **Chornobyl Museum** (☎ 470 5422; prov Khoryva; admission 5uah; 10am-6pm Mon-Fri, to 5pm Sat, closed last Mon of month) makes a valiant attempt. Displaying the identity cards and photos of those killed in the aftermath of the explosion of Chornobyl power plant reactor No 4 on 26 April 1986, it's a permanent shrine to their heroism. The photos of the area afterwards and graphs of radiation contamination stand as a terrible reminder and stark warning: 'Never again'.

Guided tours in Russian or Ukrainian are available, but for English speakers there are two compelling segments. It's hard not to well up with emotion watching the grainy video of the brave but not fully informed 'bio-robots' who immediately started cleaning up the deadly radioactive debris protected only with flimsy lead aprons. These firemen died within weeks. There are also distressing photos, on the far right-hand wall of the largest hall, of the sorts of deformities – in animals and humans – the accident caused.

The signs above the stairs as you enter represent the 'ghost' cities in the area of the disaster. These were evacuated after the explosion and no longer exist. If you wish to see for yourself, it's possible to take a tour to the Chornobyl exclusion zone (see p75).

The Chornobyl Museum is located in the mercantile quarter of **Podil**, the river plain below Kyiv's row of hills. Dating back to the earliest settlements, the area grew quickly around the port. Podil was last rebuilt in 1811 after a devastating fire and, having survived WWII, retains a small-scale, 19th-century street grid. Today it's a buzzing restaurant district.

Kontraktova pl is the hub. Andriyivsky uzviz leads off this, and here you'll also find the prestigious **Kyiv-Mohyla Akademy**, the first higher education institution in Ukraine, established in 1615. When talking about this academy, Ukrainians use the same reverent tones the French reserve for the Sorbonne.

Caves Monastery
Map p58

Tourists and Orthodox pilgrims alike flock to the **Kyiv-Pecherska Lavra** (☎ 290 3071; vul Sichnevoho Povstannya 21; admission upper lavra 10uah, lower lavra free; upper lavra 9.30am-6pm, lower lavra sunrise-sunset, caves 8.30am-4.30pm). It's easy to see why the tourists come. Set on 28 hectares of grassy hills above the Dnipro River, the monastery's tight cluster of gold-domed churches is a feast for the eyes, the hoard of Scythian gold rivals that of the Hermitage in St Petersburg, and the underground labyrinths lined with mummified monks are exotic and intriguing.

For pilgrims, the rationale is much simpler. To them, this is holy ground – the holiest in the country.

A *lavra* is a senior monastery, while *pecherska* means 'of the caves'. The Greek St Antoniy founded this *lavra* in 1051, after Orthodoxy was adopted as Kyivan Rus' official religion.

He and his follower Feodosiy progressively dug out a series of caves, where they and other reclusive monks worshipped, studied and lived. When they died, their bodies were naturally preserved, without embalming, by the caves' cool temperature and dry atmosphere. The mummies survive even today, confirmation for believers that these were true holy men.

The monastery didn't just prosper below ground, however; it grew above it as well. The Dormition Cathedral was built in 1073–89 as Kyiv's second great Byzantine-inspired church, and the monastery became Kyivan Rus' intellectual centre, producing chronicles and icons and training builders and artists. The influential historian Nestor is believed to have written his *Chronicle of Bygone Years* here.

Wrecked by the Tatars in 1240, the *lavra* went through a series of revivals and disastrous fires before being mostly rebuilt. It was made a museum in 1926, but partly returned to the Orthodox Church (Moscow patriarch) in 1988.

The complex is divided into the upper *lavra* (owned by the government) and the lower *lavra* (which belongs to the church and contains the caves).

VISITING THE MONASTERY
As this is the city's single most fascinating and extensive tourist site, you will need at least half a day, and probably more, to get a decent introduction. It's also a waste to come this far out without having a closer look at **Rodina Mat** (p60) next door.

Try to avoid the monastery on weekends, when it gets extremely busy. If you must go then, visit very early and head for the caves first.

Admission allows access to churches, but some buildings levy additional fees. Those

worth visiting are the Historical Treasures Museum, the Museum of Microminiature and the Great Bell Tower (see later for details). Unless you have a burning interest in a particular subject – such as Ukrainian books or decorative folk art – you can forget the other museums.

Fees are also charged at the main entrance to the upper *lavra* for still (12uah) and video (20uah) photography.

Unofficial guides inside the upper *lavra* will offer to show you around and explain things in English for about 50uah. The **excursion bureau** (☎ 291 3171), just to the left past the main entrance to the upper *lavra*, sells three-hour guided tours in a wide range of languages for 200uah per group (including admission fees). These need to be booked beforehand.

If you only want to visit the caves, you can legitimately do so without paying anything but the price of a candle (1uah to 3uah). The caves are a site of religious pilgrimage, where it would be difficult for the authorities to charge an entrance fee. Simply use the gate direct from the street to the lower *lavra*, rather than going via the church-filled upper *lavra*.

To enter the caves, women must wear a headscarf and either a skirt which extends below their knees or, at a pinch, trousers. (Trousers are officially forbidden, but nowadays a blind eye is frequently turned to these.) Men are obliged to remove their hats, and wearing shorts and T-shirts is forbidden. Men and women will also feel more comfortable donning scarfs and doffing hats in the monastery's churches.

UPPER LAVRA
The main entrance to the Caves Monastery is through the striking **Trinity Gate Church**, a rather well-preserved piece of early-12th-century Rus architecture. Rebuilt in the 18th century, it once doubled as a watchtower and as part of the monastery fortifications. It now features interesting murals on all sides.

Monks' dormitories dating from the 18th century stretch out from the Gate Church. Just north of Trinity Gate Church is the small, late-17th-century **St Nicholas' Church**, with its blue dome adorned with golden stars. Inside is a temporary exhibit hall. Further around is the **Museum of Theatre, Music**

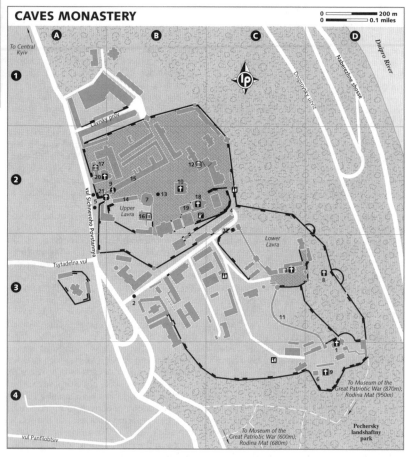

CAVES MONASTERY

0 ————— 200 m
0 ————— 0.1 miles

& **Cinematic Art**. Dramatic theatre was first introduced in Kyiv during the 17th century by Caves Monastery students.

The seven gold domes of the Orthodox **Dormition Cathedral** gleam even brighter than normal. That's because this is a modern replica of the building erected in 1077. The original was destroyed in WWII when the retreating Soviet army mined many of Kyiv's buildings. Today's intricate exterior was unveiled in 2000, but at the time of writing the cathedral's interior remained off limits to the public.

To the right, just before you reach the cathedral, towers the 96.5m-tall **Great Bell Tower** (admission 4uah; ☺ 10am-5pm). From the top of its 174 steps you have a 360-degree

panorama over not only the complex, but large parts of Kyiv.

The **Museum of Microminiature** (admission 5uah; ☺ 10am-5pm) provides something even for atheists within this holiest of holies – and, boy, is it popular, too! Possibly the most orderly queues in unruly Kyiv form in front of Russian artist N Siadristy's tiny creations. The world's smallest book (with some verses of Shevchenko), a chess set on the head of a nail, a 3.5mm frigate, a balalaika with strings 1/40th the width of a human hair and a flea fitted with golden horseshoes are just some of his works of whimsy. Each is so small that microscopes are needed to view them, but you can occupy yourself with the brief English explanations while you wait. On the wall just before the exit is a portrait of Lenin composed of 125,000 letters of his writings.

Directly south of Dormition Cathedral are the refectory and the **Refectory Church of St Antoniy & Feodosiy**, sporting the monastery's most famous gold-striped dome (1885–1905). Now a working church, the main domed space is slightly reminiscent of Istanbul's Hagia Sophia, with its ring of small narrow windows along the base of the drum. The interior is beautifully painted with biblical scenes, saints and Art Nouveau patterns.

Refurbished in 2004, the **Historical Treasures Museum** (admission 6uah; 10am-5pm) behind the Dormition Cathedral is devoted to historic items and precious stones and metal found or made in Ukraine. The highlight is the fabulous hoard of gold jewellery worked for the Scythians by Greek Black Sea colonists, much of which comes from two, 4th-century BC burial mounds – the Tolstaya grave in the Dnipropetrovsk region and the Gaimana grave in the Zaporizhzhya region. The jewellery is unbelievably well crafted, especially considering its age (around 2500 years old). From the Tolstaya grave comes possibly the most magnificent Scythian piece of all – a large mid-4th-century BC gold pectoral (a sort of large necklace) covered with superbly detailed animals and everyday scenes. Next to it is a detailed golden scabbard. Downstairs, past the 12th-century model of Kyiv, are exhibits of richly ornamented goblets, crosses, chalices and icons, crafted by Ukrainian, Russian, Polish and Lithuanian masters.

LOWER LAVRA
The entrance to the **Nearer Caves** (admission free; 8.30am-4.30pm) is inside the **Church of the Raising of the Cross** (1700). Before the stairs head downwards, there's a table selling candles (1uah to 3uah), and it's *de rigueur* to buy at least one to carry with you throughout the passages. Cameras must not be used at all inside either set of caves.

Underground, the mummified monks' bodies are clothed and you only see the occasional protruding toe or finger. Glass-topped coffins now protect the bodies from the attentions of, and humidity created by, so many visitors. The coffins are arranged in niches in the tunnels, underground dining hall and three **subterranean churches**. Antoniy, the monastery's founder, and Nestor the Chronicler are just two of the 123 bodies down here.

Tourists are only allowed into the first section of the caves, as many areas are cordoned off for Orthodox pilgrims and clergy. Monks frequently guard the entrance to restricted tunnels and are very good at spotting foreigners and nonbelievers.

Visiting the caves when they're not crowded can be a very moving experience. However, their low, narrow passageways are not for the seriously claustrophobic. And if you visit on a busy day it's total chaos down there. The monks' bodies are believed to have healing powers and pilgrims will bow to kiss the feet of one, before quickly diving to the other side of the tunnel to kiss the hand of another. Lost in religious ecstasy or sheer novelty, people wave their lit candles dangerously near to your back and face. Particularly if you're a woman wearing a flammable headscarf you will, frankly, feel more vulnerable than in the mosh pit of a huge punk rock concert. It's an experience you will never forget, but if you like to take things calmly, chose a weekday visit. Really.

KYIV

The **Farther Caves** (admission free; 8.30am-4.30pm) were the original caves built by Antoniy and Feodosiy. Their entrance is in the **Church of the Conception of St Ann** (1679), from where you wend you way through a shorter but even tighter stretch of tunnels. This cave system is also lined with ornamented mummified monks and contains three underground churches. Uphill from the Church of the Conception of St Ann is the seven-domed **Church of the Nativity of the Virgin** (1696). Rising to the right is the unusual high-baroque **Bell Tower of Farther Caves** (1761).

GETTING THERE & AWAY

The quickest route here is via the metro to Arsenalna, and then pick up a bus, *marshrutka* or trolleybus heading south down vul Sichnevoho Povstannya. Bus No 20 and *marshrutka* No 163 are just two of the services going in that direction.

Rodina Mat & Museum of the Great Patriotic War
Map p48

There's not much to say about **Rodina Mat** (literally Nation's Mother, but formally called the Defence of the Motherland Monument). However, from certain parts of Kyiv it's highly visible and so it requires a fittingly high-profile explanation. Especially when you're journeying in from the left (or east) bank, this 62m-tall statue of a female warrior is liable to loom up on the horizon and make you wonder, 'What the hell is that?'

What the hell, indeed. It's the icing on top of the **Museum of the Great Patriotic War** (☎ 295 9452; www.warmuseum.kiev.ua; vul Sichnevoho Povstannya 44; adult/child 4/1uah; 10am-5pm Tue-Sun). The statue has been nicknamed 'the Iron Maiden' and 'Tin Tits'. Even if you don't like such Soviet pomposity, don't say too much; you'd be taking on a titanium woman carrying 12 tonnes of shield and sword. She's rumoured to be not so steady on her feet these days, but looked to be holding up perfectly well at the time of research.

While the museum was built belatedly in 1981 to honour Kyiv's defenders during the 'great patriotic war' of WWII, you wouldn't know it. It seems straight out of the 1950s, with gloomy lighting and huge display halls covered in creaky parquet flooring. This is a sombre and sometimes even macabre ex-

hibition, such as in Hall No 6 where you find yourself looking at a pair of gloves made from human skin.

The overall effect is as moving as it is shocking. Westerners often don't appreciate how much Ukraine suffered as Nazi troops moved eastwards towards Moscow. Here you get a better idea.

In the grounds – besides Rodina Mat – there's also an elevated walkway, beneath which are several sculptural bas-reliefs in the Socialist Realist style.

St Volodymyr's Cathedral
Map pp50-1

Although not one of Kyiv's most important churches, **St Volodymyr's Cathedral** (bul Tarasa Shevchenka 20) arguably has the prettiest interior. Built in the late 19th century to mark 900 years of Orthodox Christianity in the city, its yellow exterior and seven black domes conform to standard Byzantine style. However, inside it breaks new ground by displaying Art Nouveau influences.

Huge murals, flecked with golden accents, include a painting of Volodymyr the Great's baptism into Orthodox Christianity in Chersonesus (see p18 and p140) and of Kyiv's citizens soon afterwards being herded into the Dnipro River for a mass baptism into the same faith (see p18).

Golden Gate
Map pp50-1

Part of Kyiv's fortifications during the rule of Yaroslav the Wise, the famous **Golden Gate** (Zoloti Vorota; vul Volodymyrska) sounds much better than it looks. Matters haven't been improved in recent years by a closure for renovations that has dragged on and on.

Erected in 1037 and modelled on Constantinople's Golden Gate, this was the main entrance into the ancient city, with ramparts stretching out from both sides. However, the gate was largely destroyed in the 1240 Mongol sacking of Kyiv, and what you see today is a 1982 reconstruction. The statue to the side is of Yaroslav.

Chimera Building
Map pp50-1

The very Gaudí-like **Chimera Building** (vul Bankova 10), with its demonic-looking animals and gargoyles, is Kyiv's weirdest building. Built at the start of the 20th century by architect Vladislav Horodetsky, it's been more recently used as a presidential administration office.

Babyn Yar & St Cyril's   Map p48

Just outside metro Dorohozhychi, is **Babyn Yar** – a Nazi execution site during WWII. More than 100,000 *Kyivlany* (Kyivans), many of them Jewish, were murdered here between 1941 and 1943 and buried in the now covered-in ravine.

The place's dreadful history only came to light after the war, and three monuments have been erected over time. The first was a huge Soviet effort dating from 1976, which is found in the southern sector of today's park. Its monumental style divides opinion sharply; some love it, others hate it. What's certain is that it's in the wrong spot, as the massacre took place north from here. Follow the path from vul Melnikova 44, past a TV station, to the secluded spot where you'll find the 1991 Jewish memorial, a hanukiah, which better marks the spot. Another monument was erected in 2001 beside the metro station to commemorate the children who were massacred at Babyn Yar.

About 1.5km northwest across the Babyn Yar parkland, between vul Oleny Telyhy, vul Melnikova and vul Dorohozhytska, is **St Cyril's** (☎ 435 2123; ◷ 10am-5.30pm, to 4.30pm Thu, closed Fri; Ⓜ Kyrylivska Tserkva). Its striking interior bears numerous **murals** covering more than 800 sq metres. Those in the choir (1888) feature the descending of the Holy Spirit. They're accessible via a steep stone staircase.

Take trolleybus No 27 from Shulyavska or Petrivka metro to the Kyrylivska Tserkva stop on vul Oleny Telyhy, from where steps lead up to St Cyril's green domes.

Bulgakov Museum   Map pp50–1

The early home of the much-loved author of *The Master and Margarita* has become the **Bulgakov Museum** (☎ 425 5254; Andriyivsky uzviz 13; admission 3uah; English guide 20uah; ◷ 10am-5pm Thu-Tue). However, don't expect too much about that particular literary classic; Mikhail Bulgakov lived here long before writing it, between 1906 and 1919. Rather, this building was the model for the Turbin family home in *The White Guard,* his first full-length, typically controversial and largely autobiographical novel. Dealing with how the events of the 1918 Russian civil war affected those in Kyiv, parts of it originally appeared in literary magazine *Rossiya* in 1925, when the author was 34 years old.

KILLING FIELDS

On 29–31 September 1941, Nazi troops rounded up Kyiv's 34,000-strong Jewish population, marched them to the Babyn Yar ravine, and massacred them all within the next 48 hours. Victims were shot and buried in the ravine. Romany people, partisans and even footballers (see boxed text, p73) were also executed at Babyn Yar during the next two years.

Furthermore, between 1941 and 1943, the Nazis used Babyn Yar as a concentration camp, called Syrets after the Kyivan suburb it was in. During the early Soviet era, the ravine was filled and topped in parts with concrete apartment blocks. It was only in the 1970s that the massacres began to be rightfully acknowledged.

The museum's curators prefer people to enter with a guide (several languages available). Sometimes the schoolma'amish way they try to insist on this can be offputting, but they have a point. The white rooms flooded in ultraviolet light do create a memorable impression, as do the rooms hidden behind the false back of a cupboard. However, without having someone to explain who's who in the family photos and so on, the experience is a bit empty.

A restaurant just down the street has a bolder reference to *The Master and Margarita* with the figure of a smug, fat black cat – the devil's mischievous sidekick, Behemoth – adorning its façade.

Museum of One Street   Map pp50–1

The individual histories of the buildings along Andriyivsky uzviz are laid out in the award-winning **Museum of One Street** (☎ 425 0398; Andriyivsky uzviz 2B; admission 5uah; ◷ noon-6pm Tue-Sun). The exhibition consists of separate glass cases containing memorabilia found at each address. So, the history of the structure at No 9, say, will be revealed through the personal identity papers, work utensils and personal effects of successive inhabitants from the late 19th to the mid-20th century. Then you will move on to number 11. The sheer jumble-sale eclecticism of the collection – showcasing the lives of dressmakers, soldiers, a rabbi and more – exudes bags of charm.

KYIV

Pyrohovo Museum of Folk Architecture   Map p48

Ukraine is dotted with 'open-air' museums like this, full of life-size models of different rustic buildings. However, the **Museum of Folk Architecture & Everyday Life** (☎ 266 5542; vul Chervonopraporna; admission 10uah; ☼ 10am-4pm Thu-Tue), 12km south of Kyiv, is one of the most fun and best maintained.

Two things make it stand out. Firstly, the quaint 17th- to 20th-century wooden churches, cottages, farmsteads and windmills are divided into seven 'villages' representing regional areas of Ukraine. So in just one long afternoon you can journey from the architecture of eastern to western to southern Ukraine. Manicured flower and vegetable gardens line the paths to the buildings and visitors can look at the traditional furniture and textiles in the interiors.

Secondly, in summer, workers enact different village roles, carving wood, pottering, doing embroidery and driving horses and carts. There are restaurants, pubs and stalls selling barbecued *shashlyk*. The place is perfect for those with children.

Summer long, the museum is filled with people strolling, sunbathing or sprawled out around a picnic hamper. Throughout the year the museum hosts various festivals. Ukrainian musicians play at weekends.

The museum is near Pyrohovo village. To get here, take bus No 27, trolleybus No 11 or *marshrutka* No 24 from the Lybidska metro station; the entrance is hard to miss. A taxi will cost about 40uah to 50uah one way.

Other Museums

Overall, the standard of museums in Kyiv is lower than in comparable European cities, but longer-term visitors might find the following interesting.

The **Russian Art Museum** (Map pp50-1; ☎ 224 6218; vul Tereshchenkivska 9; admission 7uah; ☼ 10am-6pm Fri-Sun, from 11am Mon & Tue, closed last Mon of month) has two thousand paintings that comprise the largest collection of Russian artwork outside Moscow and St Petersburg.

Ukraine's only contemporary arts centre, the **Centre for Contemporary Art** (Map pp50-1; ☎ 238 2446; vul Skovorody 2; admission free; ☼ 1-6pm Tue-Sun), makes a change from all its history. It's in the Kyiv-Mohyla Akademy (p56).

The **National Art Museum** (Map pp50-1; ☎ 228 7454; vul Hrushevskoho 6; admission 6uah; ☼ 10am-

6pm Tue-Thu, Sat & Sun, 11am-7pm Fri) displays early Ukrainian icons, and paintings from the 14th to the 19th centuries, including some by polymath national poet Taras Shevchenko.

More than 4000 items of Shevchenko's artistic and literary works are displayed in sumptuous settings at the **Taras Shevchenko National Museum** (Map pp50-1; ☎ 234 2556; bul Tarasa Shevchenka 12; adult/child 3/1uah; ☼ 10am-5pm Tue-Sun, closed last Thu of month). There's more Shevchenko at the **Taras Shevchenko Memorial House Museum** (Map pp50-1; prov Tarasa Shevchenka 8A; ☼ 10am-6pm Wed-Sun, noon-8pm Tue), a beautifully restored, 19th-century wooden house, where the great man once lived.

Museum Hetmanstva (Map pp50-1; ☎ 462 5290; vul Spaska 16B; admission 1uah; ☼ 10am-5pm Sat-Thu) has a modest exhibition dedicated to Cossack leader Ivan Mazepa, (see p20), and other hetmans. Mazepa reputedly once lived here.

Other Churches

Vydubytsky Monastery (Map p48; vul Vydubytska 40; Ⓜ Druzhby Narodiv) is attractive and so is its location – overlooking the Dnipro from the edge of the city's 'Central' Botanical Gardens. Walk from Druzhby Narodiv metro. Alternatively, tram No 27 and 35 from Arsenalna metro, or No 21, 31, 32 and 34 from Dnipro metro head to Paton Bridge.

One rare Catholic house of worship in Orthodox Kyiv is **St Alexander Church** (Map pp50-1; vul Kostyolna 17). This 19th-century Polish church has a large central dome and twin bell towers. Sunday mass at 6pm is in English.

Originally a Byzantine cathedral, **St Illya's Cathedral** (Map pp50-1; vul Pochaynynska 2) has been rebuilt so many times that it's now a bit of a hotch-potch. However, it's popular and a good place to people-watch.

St Nicholas Naberezhny (Map pp50-1; vul Pochaynynska 4) is dedicated to Nicholas Naberezhny (Nicholas by the River), the patron saint of sailors and others journeying along the river to do business.

Florivsky Monastery (Map pp50-1; vul Prytytsko Mykilska) is a 15th-century women's convent that defiantly remained open during the communist era. Through its bell tower are several attractive churches. The nearby **Church of Mykola Prytysko** (Map pp50-1; vul Prytytsko Mykilska) survived the 1811 fire that destroyed much of Podil. This 1631 church is the oldest structure in the district.

ACTIVITIES
Beaches & Hydropark

City beaches are a hot talking point these days, thanks to Paris' *plage,* but Kyiv had them long before sand along the Seine was even a grain of an idea. The beaches on the islands in the Dnipro are packed with thousands of sunbathers in summer and even see winter bathers too. It's better to merely sunbathe than to spend much time in the river, which is polluted. This includes some radioactive silt from Chornobyl – although no-one knows the extent of the contamination. Urban myth also has it that a family of huge, mutant crocodiles lives in the river. That's extremely unlikely to be true and it doesn't stop some of the faithful taking a quick dip during Epiphany in January (see right).

The beaches are found on Trukhaniv Island or in the two-island recreation zone of **Hydropark**, which also boasts parkland, walking trails, food stalls and an amusement park. Explore and you'll find gay, straight, clothed and nude beaches.

Entertainment complex **Sun City Slavutych** (Map p48; ☎ 451 6585; Venice Beach, Hydropark) rents out jet-skis. It also has a volleyball court, two pools for actual swimming and a nightclub. To get to the islands, take the metro to Hydropark, or cross over the Dnipro footbridge directly below the rainbow arch to Trukhaniv. You could try to find a boat across, but services are increasingly limited.

River Trips

Kyiv panorama boats – great for cooling down amid the scorching heat – sail in summer. Boats (one to two hour trips cost 10uah to 30uah) don't seem to have reliable schedules. Just ask at one of the ticket windows at the pier or contact Mandrivnyk (p53) at the boat terminal for assistance.

WALKING TOUR   Map p64

Setting out on foot is a good way to orientate yourself in the Ukrainian capital before plunging on into some of its more time-consuming highlights.

Start at **maydan Nezalezhnosti** (**1**; p53), before heading eastwards up Khreshchatyk. As you come to the end of the street, a dull, metal parabola is visible to the right above the trees. This is the inappropriately

---

Distance: 6.5km
Duration: two hours

named rainbow arch, part of the **Friendship of Nations Monument** (**2**) celebrating the 1654 'unification' of Russia and Ukraine. Beneath the arch, stand two 'brothers' – Russia and Ukraine – with fists raised.

Take the laneway off Evropeyska pl (Europe Sq) to get a better vantage point not just of this monstrosity, but also of the excellent river views behind. With Ukraine now independent, the monument is as controversial as it is ugly and has been joined recently by a more politically correct statue of Cossacks and other Ukrainian patriots.

Turn right up the stairs at the back of the monument and climb the hill. From the high footbridge crossing the busy road, you'll spy **Dynamo Stadium** (**3**; p72) to the right. Continue through the park until you come to the baroque **Mariyinsky Palace** (**4**), based on a design by Italian architect Bartelomeo Rastrelli, who built much of St Petersburg and Kyiv's St Andrew's Church (p55). Pause to admire the palace and walk over to the railings on the river embankment for fantastic views of the Dnipro and the monolithic suburbs on the other bank. Then head inland to the **Verkhovna Rada** (**5**; Parliament Building). Like the palace, this is off limits to the public, but both were the scenes of votes, talks and huge demonstrations during the Orange Revolution. Return to Khreshchatyk via vul Hrushevskoho, past the huge **Government Administration Building** (**6**), smaller **National Art Museum** (**7**; opposite) and Dynamo Stadium.

Opposite the **National Philharmonic** (**8**; p72) on Volodymyrsky uzviz, climb the grassy hill and follow the trail right into Volodymyrska Hirka park. Turn left up the ramp, then right again to the edge of the embankment. From here, you can gaze down on the **statue of Volodymyr the Great** (**9**) – who brought Christianity to the eastern Slavs in 988 – and out across the Dnipro.

Continue round the elevated riverbank, past a children's playground, to the **funicular** (**10**; p56) which heads down to the river

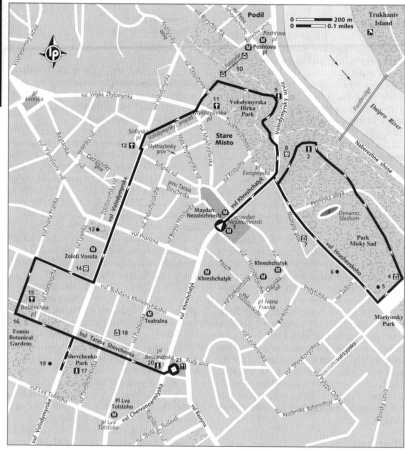

pier and the artisans' district of Podil. That deserves a separate trip, though, so for now it's better to turn left to the blue and gold **St Michael's monastery** (11; p56). From Mykhaylivska pl, you can see the tall bell tower and gold domes of **St Sophia's Cathedral** (12; p55), which you should now head towards. Turn left into vul Volodymyrska, and two long blocks along, on your right, you'll pass the **Golden Gate** (13; p60), before shortly coming to the **Shevchenko Opera & Ballet Theatre** (14; p72).

Turn right into vul Bohdana Khmelnytskoho and, two blocks later, left into vul Ivana Franka. At the end this road on the left stands **St Volodymyr's Cathedral** (15; p60). Across the road, you'll see the beginning of

the **Fomin Botanical Gardens** (16) named after 1920s botanist Alexander Fomin.

Turning left, you're on bul Tarasa Shevchenka – named after the Ukrainian national poet, Taras Shevchenko, with good reason. On the right, is his **statue** (17) in Shevchenko Park. On the left, you'll soon pass the **Taras Shevchenko National Museum** (18; p62). A quick detour will give you a look at **Kyiv University** (19). In 1901 Tsar Nicholas I ordered this building to be painted blood red in response to student protests against army conscription. When the building was reconstructed after WWII it was kept the same shade of red.

At the end of the street stands Kyiv's last remaining **Lenin statue** (20), a fairly modest affair. Take the stairs down in front of it, and cross the road via the underground shopping passage. On the other side, you'll pop up before the wonderfully atmospheric **Bessarabsky market** (**21**; p70) at the southwestern end of Khreshchatyk.

FESTIVALS & EVENTS
Some of the most important annual events in Kyiv are:

Epiphany Come January, scores of the (more hardy) faithful leap into the Dnipro River to celebrate the arrival of Christianity in Kyivan Rus. Those not so keen on swimming in the ice-cold river bring buckets of water to the islands just off Hydropark to be blessed by the Kyiv patriarch.

Kyiv Days Centred around Andriyivsky uzviz, this celebration of spring brings musicians and street performers to the capital on the last weekend of May

Kyiv International Music Festival Kicks off during the first week in October.

Kyiv International Film Festival Molodist (www .molodist.com) An annual event that takes place during the last week in October.

SLEEPING
Kyiv's budget and midrange hotels are both poor quality and rather expensive by general European standards. Even Londoners will find the city's accommodation overpriced. Yet, there are several easy ways around this problem. Particularly if you wish to spend less than $75 a night, you should bypass hotels altogether and rent an apartment instead. This cannot be overemphasised and applies even for short stays. Those with deeper pockets will also find that an apartment offers a substantial saving – up to 40% – on the same level of hotel accommodation.

If you must stay at a hotel, some have slightly discounted rooms available through travel agencies (p53) or online hotel booking sites. Try www.allrussiahotels.com, www.kiev-hotel.com, www.ukraine-travel .de or just type what you're looking for into Google. However, do check prices carefully directly with the hotels or against those in this guide.

Many hotels have different room categories, offering everything from budget to luxury accommodation under one roof. In these instances, the hotel has been placed in the category where it offers the best value. Therefore, it pays to read a few reviews outside your preferred budget range.

Budget
APARTMENTS
Always ensure the apartment has 24-hour hot water and preferably its own central heating controls (see p172).

Absolut (☎ 530 8150; www.hotelservice.kiev.ua) Although one of the city's better-known outfits, Absolut has just 20 apartments. Prices start at $25 for a one-bedroom flat (but which sleeps four) somewhat out of the centre. A central location means at least twice the price. A discount applies after three days.

Ukraine Apartments (☎ 205 9292, 8-067 742 6868; www.uaapartments.com) Run by hip young things, this friendly service is well suited to younger travellers on a budget, with a range of centrally located apartments, from $39-per-night studios to $139 for two double bedrooms. The apartments themselves are renovated – although most modestly – and have hot water, but you are sharing an ordinary block with locals. Long-term rentals are available.

Kiev Apartment Hotel Service (☎ 234 7795, 8-050 330 2236; www.kievhotelservice.com) Past guests rave about the personal care and attention you get when booking with this family-run operation, and they're particularly impressed with the apartment at vul Desyatynna. However, there is only a handful of flats ($40 to $55), so you should book ahead.

Also recommended:

Kiev Bed & Breakfast (☎ 220 4461, 8-067 960 0597; www.bedandbreakfast.kiev.ua; apt $50-90) Several apartments, pleasantly renovated.

Kiev Apartments (☎ 238 9333; www.kievapart ments.net; apt $50-160) American-owned and run, with another office in London (☎ 020-7241 7222; uko@kiev apartments.net).

HOTELS
Hotel Express (Map pp50-1; ☎ 239 8995; www .expresskiev.com; bul Tarasa Shevchenka 38/40; s/d $40/50, with private bathroom from $70/100; P ❖ 💻 ; M Universytet) The hulking concrete exterior is reminiscent of George Orwell's Ministry of Truth, but renovations have improved the inside. Down a well-trodden path from the railway station, the Express fills up quickly. Beware that cheaper rooms cunningly aren't on the website.

Hotel Bratislava (Map p48; ☎ 559 6920; vul Malyshka 1; www.bratislava.com.ua; s/d $40/60, renovated s/d $65/95; P 💻 ; M Darnystya) Like so many ex-Soviet establishments, the Bratislava is a hotel of two halves, with renovated rooms on some floors and unreconstructed accommodation, including very basic bathrooms, on others. It's definitely worth the extra to go upmarket. From here, it's a 10- to 15-minute metro ride into town.

Hotel Sport (Map pp50-1; ☎ 220 0252; vul Chervonoarmiyska 55a; s/d/tr $50/60/75; **P** ; **M** Respubliskansy Stadion) Considering its central location – and ignoring its silly metal 'crown' – this could easily be touted as excellent value. That is, were it not for the dormant building site next door, which raises questions of possible noise – ask for a room on a higher floor. The retro bedrooms are modest, but bathrooms are good.

Hotel Tourist (Map p48; ☎ 517 8832; Rayisy Okypnoyi 2; www.hotel-tourist.kiev.ua; s/d $45/50, superior s/d from $52/65; **P** ☐ ; **M** Livoberezhna) This 'complex' is not much to look at from the outside and it is some way from the centre. However, there are much worse-value rooms in town, there's a metro station right next door and the huge infrastructure means lots of services – internet, restaurants, pub, tourist bureau – are on hand. If you're looking for funny stories about Soviet attitudes, you can find those here too.

For those prepared to endure a little discomfort to save money, here are some of the cheapest hotels in town:

Hotel Holosiyivsky (Map p48; ☎ 258 2911; hotel@hotelgolos.kiev.ua; pr 40-richchya Zhovtnya 93; s/d without breakfast from $10/18)

Hotel St Petersburg 2 (Map pp50-1; ☎ 229 5943; s-peter@i.kiev.ua; vul Volodymyrska 36; s/d/tr/q from $15/22/30/35; **M** Teatralna/Zoloti Vorota) Don't confuse this cheapie with the Hotel Saint Petersburg on bul Tarasa Shevchenka, which isn't particularly nice either, but can be expensive.

RAILWAY STATION

Like most Ukrainian train stations, Kyiv's offers overnight rooms, principally for those departing early in the morning or pulling in on a late-night service. Happily, here the rooms (about $20 per night) are located in the new end of the terminal building. So while bathrooms are shared, everything is quite decent and clean. Just look for the bed signs in the southern part of the station.

HOMESTAYS

Locals renting out rooms aren't quite so obvious at Kyiv train station as in other cities. It seems the authorities don't welcome them here, and they tend to be outside the main station building or near the Vokzalna metro station. They'll generally offer *'kimnaty'* or *'komnaty'* (rooms) verbally, but will sometimes have discreet signs advertising 'кімнати' or 'комнати'. Check exactly where the room is on a map before agreeing on a price; see p171 for more.

CAMPING

Prolisok Tourist Complex (Map p48; ☎ 451 8038, 451 9037; fax 451 9039; pr Peremohy 139; per person $5) This is 12km west of the centre and a hassle to reach by public transport, so quiz yourself hard whether you really want to be camping when visiting Kyiv? From Svyatoshyn metro station, take bus No 37 westwards down pr Peremohy, or trolleybus No 7 which turns off pr Peremohy halfway.

Midrange
APARTMENTS

Kiev Apartments (☎ 413 5914; www.kievapartment.com) These are slightly more upmarket and expensive apartments than the norm, with prices ranging from $75 for a studio to $140 for a two-bedroom.

Kiev Hotel Luxe (☎ 229 2874; www.kyivhotel-luxe.com) Aimed at wealthier travellers, with pleasant, renovated apartments usually starting at €70 to €90 per day, this service also has a few bargains from €40 to €50 daily.

HOTELS

In all the following hotels, some English is usually spoken and credit cards accepted, unless otherwise noted.

Sherborne Guest House (Map pp50-1; ☎ 490 9693, 490 9699; www.sherbornehotel.com.ua; Sichneviy prov 9; s/d $85/110; **P** ☐ ; **M** Arsenalna) A rare Ukrainian apartment-hotel, this is very salubrious both on the inside and out, offering 12 apartments where you can cook for yourself and go about your business unhindered. The company also has another 13 apartments dotted throughout the centre.

Hotel Kyiv (Map pp50-1; ☎ 253 3090; www.hotelkiev.com.ua; vul Hrushevskoho 26/1; s/d $80/90; **P** ☐ ; **M** Arsenalna) Don't be fooled by the sleek new lobby; most rooms are quite quaint, with frilly glass light shades, solid wooden furniture and even some Hutsul-patterned bedspreads. However, most have bathtubs and many offer balconies with great views.

The hotel overlooks the parliament, so fellow guests will include lots of men in white shirts and black suits. Breakfast is $15 extra. No credit cards.

Hotel Gintama (Map pp50-1; ☎ 228 5092; www .gintama.com.ua; vul Tryokhsvyatytelska 9; s/d $140/170; P ✕ ⚄ ⚏ ; M maydan Nezalezhnosti) This friendly family-run hotel has understated style, with individually decorated rooms tending towards the traditional, but with cleaner lines and fewer florals than usual. Although in a quiet spot near St Alexander's Catholic church, the hotel is extremely central.

Hotel Rus (Map pp50-1; ☎ 256 4000; www.hotel rus.kiev.ua; vul Hospitalna 4; s/d $90/105, superior s/d $100/115; P ✕ ⚄ ⚏ ; M Palats Sportu) This now feels like a Western hotel throughout. True, some of the corridors still need work, but the lobby and rooms have been renovated, the latter mostly in red. They are compact, but offer the same standard as the Hotel Dnipro (following) while being slightly cheaper.

Hotel Dnipro (Map pp50-1; ☎ 254 6777; www .dniprohotel.kiev.ua; vul Khreshchatyk 1/2; s/d $110/130, Sat & Sun $90/105, superior s/d $185/205, Sat & Sun $150/165; P ✕ ⚄ ⚏ ⚏ ; M maydan Nezalezhnosti) 'Post-Soviet' and 'chic' don't really go together that often without irony, but at this conveniently located former-Intourist hotel they do. The grand scale and faint whiff of Cold War history leave you feeling at the hub of things, but the modernised rooms are small for the price. Standard class means masculine blues and blond wood; superior means dusky rose and Indian overtones. There's not much else to differentiate them.

Hotel Domus (Map pp50-1; ☎ 462 5120; www .domus-hotel.kiev.ua; vul Yaroslavska 19; s/d $150/210; ✕ ⚄ ⚏ ; M Kontraktova pl) This is in the same mode as Gintama, although neither quite as nice nor as central. Light-filled modern rooms have hypoallergenic beds, wooden floors and showers (no bathtubs).

Hotel Adria (Map p48; ☎ 516 2459; www.adria .kiev.ua; Rayisy Okypnoyi 2; s/d $100/120; P ⚄ ⚏ ; M Livoberezhna) Welcome to a hotel within a hotel – a sort of *matryoshka* (Russian stacking doll) of the accommodation world. The popular Adria occupies several floors of the lower-quality Hotel Tourist and its pleasant rooms really stand out, while online discount sites (see p65) sometimes offer more realistic prices for a hotel this far from the centre. Some taxi drivers don't know the Adria, so ask for the Hotel Tourist instead.

Boatel Dniprovsky (Map pp50-1; ☎ 490 9055; www.capitan-club.kiev.ua; Berth 2, vul Naberezhno-Khreshchatytska; d from $135; ⚄ ; M Kontraktova pl) This floating hotel on the Dnipro is novel and its cabins offer good value for couples. The decoration is thankfully restrained, unless you opt for a more expensive and opulent suite. Enjoy the summer breezes, or watch the mist rise off the icy river in winter, cosy in your heated cabin or the restaurant-breakfast room.

Hotel Ukraina (Map pp50-1; ☎ 228 2804, 229 0266; www.ukraine-hotel.kiev.ua; vul Instytutska 4; s/d from $55/70; M maydan Nezalezhnosti) Once you accept that the only service with a smile will be when *you* break into a grin at some of the reception staff's brazen rudeness, you'll be fine at the Ukraina. The rooms are all tolerable, including the older, budget categories, but those from $75/85 for a single/double are even pleasant (for Kyiv). The hotel's location just behind maydan Nezalezhnosti can't be argued with. Reception staff speak English – grudgingly.

Top End
Hotel National (Map pp50-1; ☎ 291 8888; www .natsionalny.kiev.ua; vul Lypska 5; s/d from $175/230; P ✕ ⚄ ⚏ ; M Arsenalna) This grandiose place near the parliament building makes no bones about its exclusivity, nay, snobbery.

AUTHOR'S CHOICE

If you're coming to Kyiv for a weekend break from somewhere in Europe, or on business, you might be looking for a boutique hotel with individual style.

In Kyiv, that market pretty well begins and ends with just one place – the **Hotel Vozdvyzhensky** (Map pp50-1; ☎ 531 9900; info@vozdvyzhensky.com; vul Vozdvyzhenska 60; standard s/d without breakfast $115, superior s/d with breakfast from $140/215; ✕ ⚄ ; M Kontraktova pl). Tucked away in a nook just off Andriyivsky uzviz, it has just 22 rooms, all designed in an individual style that is cool and stylish without being intimidating or cold. There's a range of business and tourist facilities. Best of all, from the new roof terrace you can dine overlooking the rooftops of Podil.

Previous guests have included Jacques Chirac and billionaire George Soros. It is not the sort of place to walk in off the street and ask if they have any rooms. You must book.

Radisson SAS (Map pp50-1; ☎ 492 2200; www .radissonsas.com; vul Yaroslaviv Val 22-24; r from $330; Ⓜ Zoloti Vorota) Regular business visitors to Kyiv are hoping the 2005 arrival of the city's first international hotel will help drive up standards of service as the city's hoteliers get a taste of how things operate in the outside world. The hotel is in the diplomatic district.

Premier Palace (Map pp50-1; ☎ 244 1200; www .premier-palace.com; bul Tarasa Shevchenka 5-7; s/d $405/445; ☒ ☒ ☒ ; Ⓜ Teatralna) You're paying for location and prestige at this, Kyiv's first five-star hotel. However pleasant, the rooms are small and overpriced.

EATING

Kyiv's dining prospects match those of most European cities – in choice and price. For further options, see the *Kyiv Post, What's On Kiev*, or the oddly spelled www.chiken .kiev.ua.

Ukrainian

Za Dvoma Zaytsamy (Map pp50-1; ☎ 229 7972; Andriyivsky uzviz 34; mains 50-130uah; Ⓜ Kontraktova pl) 'Sweet' and 'delightful' are two adjectives commonly used to describe this restaurant. The name, 'Chasing Two Hares,' comes from a Soviet film (see the boxed text, right) and the décor – from the doorman in period dress to the old theatre posters and the cutlery – evokes its backdrop of 19th-century Kyiv. The food, which is tasty and good value, naturally includes some rabbit.

Kozak Mamay (Map pp50-1; ☎ 228 4273; vul Prorizna 4; mains 20-80uah; Ⓜ 9am-11pm; Ⓜ maydan Nezalezhnosti/Teatralna) Patronised by numerous English and German speakers, with waiters in Cossack costumes and a folksy interior, Kozak Mamay could have been a tourist trap. Fact is, it carries this all off with such aplomb and has such tasty food that it emerges as one of Kyiv's best restaurants. It's also easy to reach.

Khutorok (Map pp50-1; ☎ 460 7019; Berth 1, vul Naberezhno-Khreshchatytska; mains 20-100uah; Ⓜ Kontraktova pl) This wooden paddle-steamer moored on the Dnipro has a cosy Carpathian-style interior. Sit on the deck in summer, or huddle up to the fire in winter, while partaking of delicious *shashlyk*, green *borshch*, *khrushch-*

enky (beef roulades) or vegetarian options. Watch out for the wandering musicians, though. Credit cards accepted.

Puzata Khata (Map pp50-1; ☎ 246 7245; vul Baseyna 1/2; mains 10-15uah; Ⓜ 8am-11pm; Ⓜ Teatralna) Cafeteria-style 'Hut of the Pot Belly' is an excellent place for budget travellers to sample traditional Ukrainian cuisine. There are cheap veggie options, delicious pastries and beer, while those into the harder stuff can enjoy a tipple of rum.

Varenichnaya #1 (Map pp50-1; ☎ 227 1539; vul Esplanadnaya 28; mains 25-35uah; Ⓜ 24hr; Ⓜ Palats Sportu) Specialising in – and offering the city's widest assortment of – *varenyky* (Ukrainian dumplings), this mimics the homy interior of an early-20th-century private apartment. Nearly 30 different *varenyky* fillings are offered, from liver to mushrooms, accompanied by salads laid out in two 'wells'. Surely, though, the live piglet in the basket near the door (so cute!) must deter anyone from ordering pork?

Tsarske Selo (Map p48; ☎ 290 3066, 573 9775; vul Sichnevoho Povstannya 42/1; mains 35-130uah; Ⓜ 11am-1am; Ⓜ Arsenalna) This is Kyiv's quintessential Ukrainian theme restaurant, decorated in

---

CULT MOVIES, CULT RESTAURANTS

Two listed restaurants take their names from cult Soviet movies.

- **Za Dvoma Zaytsamy** (1961) The title, *Chasing Two Hares*, comes from a Ukrainian proverb that if you chase two hares, you'll catch neither. In this comic movie, itself based on a play, a poor Ukrainian barber in late-19th-century Kyiv puts on Russified airs and graces to woo two wealthy women but is exposed for his duplicity; see left.

- **Mimino** (1977) Georgian pilot 'Mimino' (Falcon) is sick of delivering cows by helicopter and goes to Moscow to retrain as an Aeroflot captain. He befriends an Armenian truck driver, and the comedy revolves around the country bumpkins' adventures in the big city. Despite many mishaps, Mimino achieves his dream, but decides he prefers Georgia after all. (Available on Russian DVD, with English subtitles.) See opposite.

rustic 18th-century style and popular for corporate entertaining or large celebratory groups (credit cards accepted). Ukrainian staples are done superbly, but the most famous dish is the dessert of *salo* (pig fat) in chocolate – only for the most adventurous. In summer, Tsarske Selo has an adjoining open-air restaurant, **USSR** (☎ 290 3066), where you can sample the culinary delights of each former Soviet republic.

Mlyn (Map p48; ☎ 516 5728; M Hydropark) Panoramic views of the Dnipro and its beach activities can be enjoyed from the balcony terrace of waterfront Mlyn, housed in an old wooden mill. An old Hydropark fave.

Most pubs and clubs also serve food. Viola's Bierstube (p70) and Art Club 44 (p71) dish up the city's best-presented (but not necessarily best-tasting) *borshch* – in a hollowed-out circular bread loaf.

International

Mimino (Map pp50-1; ☎ 417 3545; vul Spaska 10A; mains 50-100uah; M Kontraktova pl) Outstanding Georgian cuisine – at least for carnivores – served by staff dressed as air stewards, in reference to another popular Soviet film (see the boxed text, opposite). Lamb features prominently – grilled, baked, ground or *shashlyk* – and there's *suluguni* cheese, *khinkali* (dumplings) and fiery spices. Vegetarian options don't pack the same oomph, but still this is one of the best restaurants in the city.

Limoncello Grill's Pizza Terrace (Map pp50-1; ☎ 254 2024; vul Moskovska 22; mains 30-100uah, pizzas 40-60uah; ☺ 10am-1pm; M Arsenalna) The main restaurant is quite formal and foists live music on customers in the evenings. However, in summer you can escape to the terrace for Kyiv's best pizza – wood-fired in an oven imported from Italy.

Osteria Pantagruel (Map pp50-1; ☎ 229 7301; vul Lysenka 1; mains 45-150uah; M Zoloti Vorota) Homemade pasta, risotto and bruschetta is turned out at this whitewashed cellar restaurant by the Golden Gate. Summer sees tables and chairs spill onto the square outside.

Peschera (Map pp50-1; ☎ 244 3372; vul Tarasivska 10A; mains 25-75uah; M pl Lva Tolstoho/Universytet) It's back to the scientifically well-documented Flintstone era at gimmicky but popular 'Cave', where imitation Easter Island statues, primitive cave drawings and waiters in leopard skin greet you. Stone-grilled meat is the speciality.

Himalaya (Map pp50-1; ☎ 462 0437; vul Khreshchatyk 23; mains 25-55uah; M Teatralna) The Indian cuisine here is better than you might expect, given Eastern European unfamiliarity. But in the greater scheme of things, it's mild and mediocre. Weekday set lunches are only 40uah, and there are many veggie options.

Marrakesh (Map pp50-1; ☎ 494 0494; vul Petra Sahaydachnoho 24; couscous dishes 50-100uah; M Poshtova/Kontraktova pl) This showcases three things Kyiv has been having a love affair with lately – '1001 Nights' Arabian design, couscous and hookah pipes. However, the food is usually too bland for connoisseurs of spicy cuisine.

Marocana (Map p48; ☎ 254 4999; vul Lesi Ukrainky 24; mains 15-140uah; ☺ 8am-2am; M Percheska) This trendy joint offers a better North African experience, but is a bit further out, and quite showy.

Nobu (Map pp50-1; ☎ 246 7734; vul Shota Rustaveli 12; sushi per portion 10-45uah M pl Lva Tolstoho) Within this minimalist interior, you'll find Kyiv's best – and priciest – sushi. Miso soup, salads and desserts like green-tea ice cream are also served.

Fellini (Map pp50-1; ☎ 229 5462; vul Horodetskoho 5; mains 50-150uah; ☺ 24hr; M maydan Nezalezhnosti) Despite being themed around the great Italian film director, this upscale outlet does a mixture of Italian and French food. There are some classics like onion soup and frog's legs, but mostly the restaurant gives things a modern twist, turning out very appealing modern international cuisine. The terraces are great for people-watching in summer.

Concord (Map pp50-1; ☎ 229 5512; 8th fl, vul Pushkinska 42/4; mains 45-140uah; M pl Lva Tolstoho) Atop the Donbas centre, this elegant restaurant offers great views. The 'ethnic' décor is vaguely North African while the food is described as 'French fusion'. That means anything from rabbit leg in Calvados or New Zealand shrimp to veal médaillons served with soy and spicy rib of lamb on couscous.

Empire (Map pp50-1; ☎ 244 1235; 18th fl, bul Tarasa Shevchenka 5-7; breakfast 135uah, mains 60-140uah; ☺ 7am-11pm; M Teatralna) For an even more jaw-dropping view over Kyiv's golden church domes – all the way to the Caves Monastery – pop up to the 18th-floor restaurant of the Premier Palace hotel. Be prepared, before the bill arrives, for that panorama to come at a price.

Sam's Steakhouse (Map pp50-1; ☎ 227 2000; vul Zhylyanska 37; steaks 50-70uah; 🕓 11.30am-1am; Ⓜ pl Lva Tolstoho) This American bistro bar serves everything from brownies, waffles and hot-fudge sundaes to burgers and all-day breakfasts. Steaks come in separate men's and women's sizes.

Steakhouses are big business in Kyiv and other popular options include the long-standing American-style **Arizona** (Map pp50-1; ☎ 425 2438; vul Naberezhno-Khreshchatytska 25; steaks 110-150uah; 🕓 8am-last customer; Ⓜ Kontraktova pl) and the newer, Argentinean-run **El Asador** (Map pp50-1; ☎ 425 4402; vul Nyzhniy Val 29; steaks 35-70uah; Ⓜ Kontraktova pl).

Cheap Eats

Gourmet (Map pp50-1; vul Chervonoarmiyska 12; dishes 5-10uah; Ⓜ pl Lva Tolstoho) Colourful, regional foods are eye-catchingly displayed in the stainless-steel trays in the window of this cheap cafeteria.

Makabi Kosher (Map pp50-1; vul Shota Rustaveli 15; dishes 5-20uah; Ⓜ pl Lva Tolstoho/Palats Sportu) This long, narrow space feels a bit like a deli, with Jewish stews, salads and soups made to order or under the glass counter.

Perepichka (Map pp50-1; vul Bohdana Khmelnytskoho 3; sausages 2uah; Ⓜ Teatralna) Want to grab one of those fairground-style sausages deep-fried in batter, which everyone seems to be munching on at the corner of Khreshchatyk and vul Bohdana Khmelnytskoho? This hole in the wall is where they emanate from. Greasy.

Pita Inn (Map pp50-1; vul Bohdana Khmelnytskoho 12B; pitas 3-6uah; Ⓜ Teatralna) Falafel comes to Kyiv! And that's such a delight that it's easy to forgive the strip-lighting and Formica tables. Chicken and meat kebabs are also served.

Non-Stop (Map pp50-1; ☎ 216 4073; pr Peremohy 6; 🕓 24hr; Ⓜ Vokzalna/Universytet) Spitting distance from the airport bus stop on pr Peremohy, this café has a delightful terrace and serves a good selection of salads, mains and crepes.

Self-Catering

Central Gastronom (Map pp50-1; ☎ 229 2288; vul Khreshchatyk 40-42 4A; 🕓 8am-10pm; Ⓜ Teatralna) With its high-profile location, this late-night supermarket is full of locals and bemused tourists stocking up on alcohol and basic essentials – which is all that's on offer. Don't overlook the basement floor. Bags must be put in lockers before entering.

Gourmet Furshet (Map pp50-1; ☎ 230 9522; Basement, Mandarin Plaza, vul Baseyna 4; 🕓 24hr; Ⓜ pl Lva Tolstoho) Less apparent than Central Gastronom, this round-the-clock outlet is part of a leading supermarket chain. Many expats would be lost without it.

Megamarket (Map pp50-1; ☎ 248 7387; vul Horhoko 50; 🕓 9am-11pm; Ⓜ Respublikansy Stadion) Another leading chain outlet, a little further out.

Bessarabsky Market (Map pp50-1; ☎ 224 2317; pl Bessarabska; 🕓 8am-8pm Tue-Sun, to 5pm Mon; Ⓜ Teatralna) The arrangements of colourful fruit, vegetables, meat and even flowers in this light-filled hall are works of art and it almost seems a shame to disturb them by buying – almost, but not quite. The market was built in 1910–12 for traders coming to Kyiv from Bessarabia. Some imported produce is on sale (at a high price).

Volodymyrsky Market (off Map pp50-1; ☎ 260 0101; vul Horkoho 115; 8am-8pm Tue-Sun; Ⓜ Palats Ukraina) One block west of Palats Ukraina metro station, this is a very crowded, local market with cheaper prices.

DRINKING
Pubs & Bars

Eric's Bierstube (Map pp50-1; ☎ 235 9472; vul Chervonoarmiyska 20; 🕓 10am-2am; Ⓜ pl Lva Tolstoho) Eric is the East German mastermind behind many of Kyiv's clubs. This, his first bar, is a relaxed cellar establishment where an assortment of expats and wealthier locals retire for a well-priced beer every evening of the week. There's a bar menu, including a hangover breakfast, and some DJ nights. Through the archway, head for the right-hand corner.

Viola's Bierstube (Map pp50-1; ☎ 235 3751; bul Tarasa Shevchenka 1a; 🕓 8am-2am; Ⓜ Teatralna/ploshcha Lva Tolstoho) Matching pubs, ain't that sweet? Viola's is the *femme* version of Eric's – with the same underground brick arches, but adding the peculiarly Ukrainian phenomenon of Fashion TV continually on screen. It's good to pop into during the day, too, for a serving of *borshch* in a bread basket. The dark wooden door is on the left, at the end, but still under, the archway leading to the courtyard.

O'Brien's Irish Pub (Map pp50-1; ☎ 229 1584, vul Mykhaylivska 17A; 🕓 8am-2am; Ⓜ maydan Nezalezhnosti) Kyiv's original Irish pub is only concerned with having a rollicking good expat time, so the complete lack of class isn't an issue. A huge screen showing big football matches hangs behind the stage where crappy cover bands play – and, bizarrely, the two even kick off in tandem sometimes. It's a good place to come to on your own, though, as you can easily blend in with the crowd and get chatting.

Château (Map pp50-1; ☎ 228 7800; vul Khreshchatyk 24; ⏰ 24hr; Ⓜ maydan Nezalezhnosti) Mainstream by location and comfortably mainstream by nature, this popular brewery pub has large picture windows overlooking Kyiv's main drag. Order a Slavutych beer; it's brewed on the premises.

Blindazh (Bunker; Map pp50-1; ☎ 228 1511; vul Mala Zhytomirska 15; ⏰ 8am-2am; Ⓜ maydan Nezalezhnosti) Those looking for something a little more alternative will enjoy the Bunker. It's a basement 'dive' bar decorated with Red Army camouflage and other paraphernalia.

Also recommended:

Baraban (Drum; Map pp50-1; ☎ 229 2355; vul Prorizna 4a; ⏰ 11am-11pm; Ⓜ maydan Nezalezhnosti) Difficult to find, hole-in-the-wall favourite expat hang-out, in the back of the courtyard.

Golden Gate Irish Pub (Map pp50-1; ☎ 229 1584; vul Volodymyrska 40/2A; ⏰ 8am-1am; Ⓜ Zoloti Vorota) Renowned for its pub cuisine, particularly its breakfasts.

Sunduk (The Chest; Map pp50-1; ☎ 228 78 00; vul Mykhaylivska 16; ⏰ 11am-11pm; Ⓜ maydan Nezalezhnosti) The Chest (as in pirate's chest) is a fairly traditional-looking pub with a youngish clientele and one allegedly nonsmoking room.

Wall (Map pp50-1; ☎ 235 8045; pl Bessarabska 2; ⏰ 9am-midnight; Ⓜ Teatralna) Small studenty pub-cum-café at the back of Bessarabsky Market. Look for a small red sign over a doorway.

Cafés

Kaffa (Map pp50-1; ☎ 464 0505; prov Tarasa Shevchenka 3; ✕ ; Ⓜ maydan Nezalezhnosti) Hallelujah! Real heart-pumping, rich-tasting brew. You might have forgotten what this tastes like after a time in Kyiv, which is lousy with instant coffee. Admittedly, you do have to wade through a long menu and wait some time to be served. While you do, peer around the hushed, whitewashed African-inspired interior – all ethnic masks, beads and leather – and at your fellow customers, most in middle youth.

Marquise de Chocolate (Map pp50-1; ☎ 464 0505; vul Prorizna 4; Ⓜ maydan Nezalezhnosti/Teatralna) This cosy, red-velvet-lined café serves delicious

pastries and, unsurprisingly, hot chocolate. It's above restaurant Kozak Mamay.

Kofiym (Map pp50-1; ⏰ 8am-midnight) maydan Nezalezhnosti (☎ 228 0490; vul Kostyolna) Arsenalna (☎ 290 5796; vul Sichnevoho Povstannya 3) The Arsenalna branch of Kofiym is populated by hip students and other arty types, while the 'cigar, cognac and coffee' downtown outlet feels more like a smoking club. Still, however you cut it, these are two of the city's better coffeehouses.

A busy assortment of cafés, bars and clubs are also found along Khreshchatyk pasazh, a hip street accessed through an ornate archway of the main street. The upmarket **Passazh** (Map pp50-1; ☎ 229 1209; ⏰ 8.30am-11pm Mon-Fri, 11am-11pm Sat & Sun; Ⓜ Khreshchatyk) is like an Austrian coffeehouse. Great for people-watching as you tuck into some of its delicious cakes.

For something funky and laidback, try the Baboon Book Coffee Shop (p49).

ENTERTAINMENT
Clubs

The following are just the unmissable heavy-hitters, which avoid the worst excesses of Kyiv nightlife (ie strip shows and prostitutes). The printed editions of *What's On Kyiv* and the *Kyiv Post* include full listings, the latter including gay and lesbian venues.

Art Club 44 (Map pp50-1; ☎ 229 4137; vul Khreshchatyk 44; admission varies; ⏰ 10am-2am; Ⓜ Teatralna) This basement club is the best venue in the city for those who prefer an unpretentious, uncomplicated vibe, albeit sometimes cramped and a little sweaty. Officially, it's a jazz club, but lots of local and international rock groups and DJs pass through, too. Once in the courtyard at 44, turn through the door under the red sign in the middle of the left wall and keep bearing left through another door.

Cocktail Bar 111 (Map pp50-1; ☎ 238 0286; pr Peremohy 1; admission varies; ⏰ 10pm-4am; Ⓜ Vokzalna) In short – Kyiv's foremost pick-up joint. This bar in the Hotel Lybid is renowned for its signature 111 cocktails and a revolving bar, along which the bar staff like to strut. The DJs are infamously below par, tending towards mainstream cheese. However, nothing puts this up-for-it crowd off its stride.

ModaBar (Map pp50-1; ☎ 428 7388; www.2k.com.ua; Berth 6, vul Naberezhno-Khreshchatytska; admission free; ⏰ 8pm-6am; Ⓜ Kontraktova pl) Aboard a moored ship, below the 'Mandarin' Chinese restaurant, the ModaBar likes to boast it has the longest bar in Europe. What it certainly has is regular fashion shows on its Perspex catwalk, pop music, pricey drinks and a flirty atmosphere.

Opium Dance Club (Map pp50-1; ☎ 205 5393; vul Saksahanskoho 1G; admission varies; ☼ 10pm-6am Fri & Sat; Ⓜ Palats Sportu) A German-designed dance/rave club, Opium has room for 1500 punters, spread between a huge dance floor, VIP areas and a chill-out zone with hookah pipes.

Tchaikovsky (Map pp50-1; ☎ 234 7406; pl Bessarabska 1; admission for men about 50uah, women free; ☼ 10pm-6am; Ⓜ Teatralna) With a 2nd-floor balcony great for people-watching, this glam club mostly offers the house and disco music that is par for the course in Kyiv. However, on Thursday nights, it's caught the imagination of many with its hip-hop and R & B night. The entrance is near Metrograd.

Decadence House (Map pp50-1; ☎ 206 4920; vul Shota Rustaveli 16; admission varies; ☼ nightclub 10pm-6am Fri & Sat; Ⓜ pl Lva Tolstoho) You might hear a lot about this VIP place, but you will have to pass the strictest 'face control' (door policy) to get in. Otherwise, if you want to see what the fuss is about, pop in during the week when it functions as a swanky Italian restaurant.

During summer, Kyiv hosts many open-air club events. One of the most popular venues is **Sun City Slavutych** (Map p48; ☎ 451 6585; Venice Beach, Hydropark; Ⓜ Hydropark).

Rock

Palace of Sport (Map pp50-1; ☎ 246 7253, 246 7406; pl Sportyvna 1; Ⓜ Palats Sportu) This multifunctional venue plays host to sporting fixtures and major rock and pop concerts, including the Eurovision Song Contest.

Ukraina Palace (Map p48; ☎ 247 2376, 247 244; vul Chervonoarmiyska 103; Ⓜ Respublikansky Stadion/Palats Ukraina) The other major venue for international rock and pop concerts.

Classical Music

Tickets to classical music and opera performances are significantly cheaper than in the West, ranging on average from 10uah to 100uah in Kyiv. To get a decent seat will usually only set you back about 20uah.

National Philharmonic (Map pp50-1; ☎ tickets 228 1697, information 228 6291; www.filarmonia.com.ua; Volodymyrsky uzviz 2; ☼ ticket kasa noon-3pm & 4-7pm Mon-Sat; Ⓜ maydan Nezalezhnosti) Originally the Kyiv Merchants' Assembly headquarters, this beautiful building is now home to the national orchestra.

St Nicholas' Church (Map p48; ☎ 268 3186; vul Chervonoarmiyska 75; Ⓜ Respublikansky Stadion/Palats Ukraina) Organ and chamber music recitals are hosted here, the only truly Gothic building in the city.

Cinema

Kyiv (Map pp50-1; ☎ 221 0881, 234 7381; www.kiev kino.com.ua in Russian; vul Chervonoarmiyska 19; Ⓜ pl Lva Tolstoho) is the only cinema in Kyiv showing films in English. It takes a break during the summer months.

Theatre

Kyiv has more than 20 theatres, including the semi-avantgarde **Koleso Kafe-Theatre** (Map pp50-1; ☎ 425 0527; Andriyivsky uzviz 8A; Ⓜ Kontraktova pl). They all perform in Ukrainian or Russian, so check listings magazines for more details.

Advance tickets and schedules are available at the **Teatralna Kasa** (vul Khreshchatyk 21; Ⓜ Khreshchatyk). Tickets are available at the theatres about an hour before the curtain rises.

Opera & Ballet

The **Shevchenko Opera & Ballet Theatre** (Map pp50-1; ☎ 224 7165, box office 229 1169; vul Volodymyrska 50; Ⓜ Teatralna) is a lavish theatre (1899-1901); a performance here is a grandiose affair.

Sport

Dynamo Kyiv is one of the most recognisable names in European football (soccer) and **Dynamo Stadium** (off Map pp50-1; ☎ 229 0209; vul Hrushevskoho 3; Ⓜ maydan Nezalezhnosti) is the team's modestly sized home. It's worth a visit if you're a fan, or perhaps to see the memorial to WWII team Start (see the boxed text, opposite).

However, most of Dynamo's European matches kick off at the larger **Olympic/Respublikansky Stadium** (Map pp50-1; ☎ 246 7007; vul Chervonoarmiyska 55; Ⓜ Respublikansky Stadion/Palats Ukraina). Tickets for this Olympic Stadium's 100,000 seats are sold at kiosks in front of the entrance gates.

Cobbled Andriyivsky uzviz (p52) winds up to St Andrew's Church, Kyiv

CAROL ANN WILEY

PETER WILLIAM THORNTON

'Radioactive' sign at the Chornobyl Museum (p56), Kyiv

CHRISTINA DAMEYER

Rodina Mat (p60), Kyiv

'Walrus' swimming (p173), Kyiv

AFP/GETTY IMAGES

JEFF GREENBERG

Ivan Franko Opera & Ballet
Theatre (p91), Lviv

JONATHAN SMITH

The old market square (p85) and
Armenian Cathedral, Lviv

Locals prepare to symbolically burn a straw figure to
celebrate the end of winter

PHOTOBANK.KIEV.UA/VLADIMIR

Kamyanets-Podilsky (p105), Western Ukraine

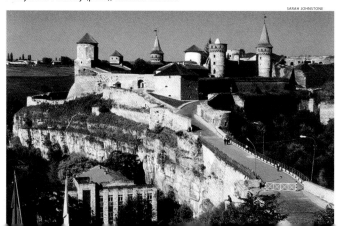
SARAH JOHNSTONE

LOSE OR DIE

During WWII, when Kyiv was occupied by Nazi Germany, the members of the talented Dynamo football team were challenged to a public match with a team of German soldiers. The Ukrainians formed a team called Start, and despite physical weakness brought on by the occupation, they were soon ahead in their first match. At half-time, German officers came into the dressing room and commanded them to let up. Nevertheless, Start continued to play hard, and before the game finished the referee blew the whistle and called it off (with a score of 4–1).

The Germans reshuffled their players, and Start was offered another chance to lose. Instead they won. Next, Start was pitted against a Hungarian team – and won again. Finally, the enraged Germans challenged Start to a match against their finest, undefeated team, Flakelf. When the 'Übermensch' of Flakelf lost, the Nazis gave up – and proceeded to arrest most of the Start players, several of whom were executed at Babyn Yar (p61). A monument to them still stands in Dynamo Stadium in Kyiv. Their story inspired the movie *Victory*, starring Sylvester Stallone and soccer-legend Pele. Andy Dougan's *Defending the Honour of Kyiv* (2001) is a readable, well-researched account of the incident.

Other sporting events take place at the Palace of Sport (opposite).

SHOPPING

Long-term residents – some of them not even over the age of 40 – complain Kyiv has become one big shopping mall. But, although you can buy most things here, it's not a particularly inspiring retail destination. Clothes outlets line Khreshchatyk and fill the enormous underground Metrograd shopping mall and the Globus mall at maydan Nezalezhnosti. However, prices aren't always cheap and some of the fashions (including fur) might not appeal to Western tastes.

Apart from vodka, which is available everywhere including the airport, something to look out for is Kyivsky Tort, a nutty, layered sponge sold in circular cardboard cartons. Stalls around the train stations have huge stockpiles.

TsUM (Map pp50-1; ☎ 224 9505; vul Bohdana Khmelnytskoho 2; 🕐 9am-8pm Mon-Sat; Ⓜ Teatralna) With a little nod to Harrods, and a huge bowing of the head to the musty 1970s department store in *Are You Being Served?*, this monolithic building is where you should head to when replacing any lost or damaged essentials.

Ukrayina Department Store (Map pp50-1; ☎ 496 1601; pl Peremohy 3; 🕐 10am-9pm, to 10pm Fri & Sat; Ⓜ Vokzalna) Completely revamped in 2003, this now offers five floors of shopping, a cinema and a round-the-clock supermarket, bookshop and pharmacy on the ground floor.

Bessarabsky Market (Map pp50-1; ☎ 224 2317; pl Bessarabska; 🕐 8am-8pm Tue-Sun, to 5pm Mon; Ⓜ Teatralna) Grocery shopping is rarely such an aesthetically pleasing experience, so this market full of colourful fruit and veg should definitely not be missed.

Dynamo Kyiv club shop (Map pp50-1; ☎ 227 0576; vul Chervonoarmiyska 86; Ⓜ Respublikansky Stadion) Snaffle up the club strip of the Ukrainian capital's football team and various other branded goods.

Popular Andriyivsky uzviz (p53) is lined with stalls selling cheap – and often tatty – souvenirs. For more expensive artworks, head for the galleries behind the stalls about halfway down the street.

GETTING THERE & AWAY
Air

Most international flights (except a handful to/from Moscow and Eastern Europe) use **Kyiv Boryspil airport** (☎ 296 7609, 296 7243; www.airport-borispol.kiev.ua), about 40km east of the city. Domestic flights use **Zhulyany airport** (Map p48; ☎ 242 2308; www.airport.kiev.ua, in Ukrainian), 12km west of the centre. For more details, see p185.

Ukraine International Airlines (Map pp50-1; ☎ 461 5656; www.ukraine-international.com; vul Bohdana Khmelnystkoho 63A; Ⓜ Universytet) and **Aerosviot** (Map pp50-1; ☎ 490 3490; www.aerosvit.com; bul Tarasa Shevchenka 58A; Ⓜ Universytet) are the two main national airlines. Most major European airlines have an airport and city centre office, listed in the *Kyiv Business Directory, Kyiv In Your Pocket, Kyiv Post,* and *What's On Kyiv.* For carriers' phone numbers see p185.

Plane tickets are also sold at **Kiyavia** (Map pp50-1; ☎ 056, 490 4956; www.kiyavia.com; pr Peremohy 2). It also has offices at Boryspil and Zhulyany airports and at vul Horodetskoho 4.

Boat

Kyiv is the most northerly passenger port on the Dnipro and the usual starting or finishing point of river cruises. Boats sail between May and mid-October. Contact Chervona Ruta or other travel agencies for details (see p53).

Shorter-distance boats to Cherkasy, Kaniv and Pereyaslav-Khmelnytsky had all been cancelled at the time of research, but ask at the **boat passenger terminal** (Map pp50-1; richny vokzal; Poshtova pl 3; Ⓜ Poshtova pl) to see whether they've resumed.

Bus

There are seven bus terminals, but most buses run from the **Central Bus Station** (Map p48; Tsentralny avtovokzal; ☎ 265 0430; pl Moskovska 3), one stop from Lybidska metro station on trolley-bus No 4, 11 or 12, or tram No 9 or 10.

Autolux (☎ 451 8628; www.autolux.com.ua; ⏱ 7am-11pm) operates buses from Boryspil airport via Kyiv's central bus station to various destinations, including Odesa (55uah, eight hours, four per day), Kharkiv (60uah, 7½ hours, six daily) and Lviv (72uah, 10 hours, twice daily). Buses coming into Kyiv arrive at the central bus station first, before terminating at Boryspil. Tickets are sold at both the central bus station and the airport.

Car

The major car rental companies are:
Avis (Map pp50-1; ☎ 490 7333; www.avis.com; Hotel Rus, vul Hospitalna 4) Also at the airport, with the same contact details.
Europcar town (Map pp50-1; ☎ 238 2691; fax 238 2692; vul Horkoho 48A); airport (☎ /fax 296 7737)
Hertz town (Map pp50-1; ☎ 494 4935; rent@hertz.ua; vul Pymonenka 13); airport (☎ 296 7614; hertzua@i.kiev.ua)

Train

You can get everywhere in the country from **Kyiv train station** (Map pp50-1; ☎ 005, 223 1111; pl Vokzalna 2). It just might take time. For international train information, see p186. The train station, newly remodelled in recent years, is in front of Vokzalna metro station.

Heading west, there are at least three daily trains to/from Lviv (40uah to 60uah, nine to

---

USING THE TRAIN STATION LOCKERS

There is a left-luggage room at Kyiv's main station, but the self-service lockers are more convenient. They're in the new southern terminal, in the basement near the telephone/internet centre. Pay 2uah at the counter for a token *(zheton)*, then select an empty locker. Dial your chosen code using the four knobs on the *inside*, before holding the door shut and inserting the token. When you come to reopen the locker, pay another 2uah for another token. Dial your code on the outside this time, then insert your token to open the door.

---

11 hours), while twice-daily trains to/from Uzhhorod (50uah to 55uah, 18 to 20 hours) and the daily train to Ivano-Frankivsk (45uah, 12 hours) also pass through. There's an overnight train to Kamyanets-Podilsky (30uah, 12 hours) and one to Chernivtsi (50uah, 14 hours).

Heading south, there are three daily services to Odesa (40uah to 60uah, 12 hours). The two daily services to Sevastopol (50uah to 55uah, 17 hours), go through Simferopol (one at an ungodly hour). The other two daily trains terminating in Simferopol (55uah to 75uah, 15 to 17 hours) are at least as expensive as the train to Sevastopol and take as long, although covering a shorter distance.

Heading east, there are at least four daily trains to Kharkiv (35uah to 65uah, six to eight hours), which all go through Poltava. There is one direct train to Poltava (30uah, seven hours). Daily there are also some eight trains to Dnipropetrovsk (35uah to 65uah, six to eight hours), three to Donetsk (50uah to 70uah, 10 to 12 hours) and one to Zaporizhzhya (45uah to 55uah, 10 hours).

Impending departures and arrivals are notified on the board in Ukrainian and English. If you can read Cyrillic, there are automatic machines dotted throughout the concourse – looking like ATMs – that will give you detailed schedules, prices and seat availability on every service.

Windows Nos 40 and 41 in the southern section of the station are reserved for foreign customers and international bookings, should you choose to use them. Staff don't speak English, but there are rarely queues.

The advance **train ticket office** (Map pp50-1; bul Tarasa Shevchenka 38/40; ⏰ 8am-7pm Mon-Fri, 9am-6pm Sat & Sun; Ⓜ Universytet), a five-minute walk from the station, is next to Hotel Express.

You can also buy train tickets from desk No 6 or 7 inside the **Kiyavia** (vul Horodetskoho 4) office, or at their office on pl Peremohy. Reservations can be made by telephone on ☎ 050.

GETTING AROUND
To/From the Airport
Catching a **Atass bus** (☎ 296 7367) is the usual way to Boryspil airport (10uah, 45 minutes to one hour). Buses (marked either Атасс/політ or simply Атасс) depart from behind the new southern terminal of the train station every 15 to 30 minutes between 4.40am and 1.20am. Five minutes later they pick up at another airport bus stop on pr Peremohy, near a LukOil petrol station. At Boryspil, buses arrive/depart from in front of the international terminal and terminate at the central train station.

Autolux (☎ 230 0071; ⏰ 7am-10pm) buses also travel between Boryspil and Kyiv's main bus station (35 minutes).

To get to Zhulyany airport, take trolley-bus No 9 from pl Peremohy (40 minutes).

Public Transport
Kyiv's metro is clean, efficient, reliable and easy to use if you read Cyrillic (see the Metro Map p54). Trains run frequently between around 6am and midnight on all three lines. Blue-green plastic tokens (*zhetony*) costing 50 kopecks (good for one ride) are sold at kiosks at metro station entrances. During the first week of the month you can buy a monthly pass, good for all forms of transportation.

Buses, trolleybuses, trams and many quicker *marshrutky* serve most routes. Tickets for buses, trams and trolleybuses cost $0.10 (50 to 60 kopecks) and are sold at street kiosks or directly from the driver/conductor. *Marshrutky* tickets are 1uah to 2uah.

A funicular links the main river terminal on vul Naberezhno-Khreshchatytska with Mykhaylivska pl (see p56).

Taxi
Catching a taxi from the train station, on pl Peremohy and outside hotels inevitably incurs a higher price, so try to find one elsewhere on the street. Try to look for newer, official-looking cars, which are more likely to have a meter and hence won't rip you off. Metered cabs are rare, however. By phone, try **Kyiv-Taxi** (☎ 459 0101).

AROUND KYIV

Outside the capital, you'll find yourself plunged into the heart of rural Ukraine, where small villages and simple farming towns neighbour endless stretches of prairie-like land and steppe.

But as well as the provincial towns of Chernihiv, Pereyaslav-Khmelnytsky and Uman, or the rural idyll of Kaniv, more adventurous tourists can now see the Chornobyl (Chernobyl in Russian) nuclear reactor for themselves. Most day trips from the capital tend to involve a long day, with four to six hours' travelling. However, Chornobyl is slightly closer in.

CHORNOBYL ЧОРНОБИЛЬ
It's the world's weirdest day trip, one for extreme tourists and a once-in-a-lifetime experience that you probably *won't* want to repeat. A package tour to the Chornobyl exclusion zone will take you to the heart of an apocalypse and sear itself into your memory.

In truth, such tours are nothing new. They follow the same years-old arrangements for ferrying scientists into this prohibited zone, which has been closed to the general public ever since the 1986 Chornobyl nuclear accident (see p34). In 2004, however, the website of one Elena Filatova, aka kiddofspeed at www.kiddofspeed.com, brought them to international prominence and they don't seem to have gone away since. Despite claims that Filatova drove her motorcycle through the zone, all she did was ride it to the gates. From this point she, her husband and their camera continued on an official tour – that comes from the travel agent who booked it.

So what's the deal? Well, first you have to decide whether to risk it. According to travel agents, you receive no more radiation on your three hours or so in the zone that you would on a New York–London flight. But they would say that wouldn't they? And it's difficult to check unless you wear your

KYIV

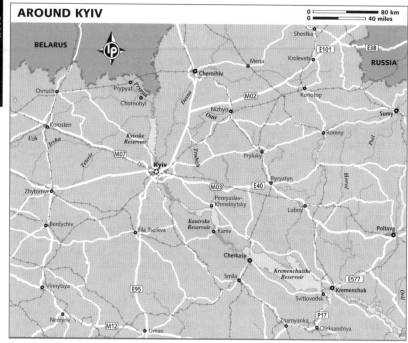

AROUND KYIV

own radiation exposure strip (used by X-ray technicians and easily purchased from medical suppliers back home).

Usually, no overalls or special shoes are supplied and you really don't need them anyway. Just keep off the particularly radioactive moss and watch where you put your hands. You will be closely accompanied by a guide, who takes a Geiger counter. At brief moments – including near the reactor or near moss – this will beep its way up to 600 or 800 micro-roentgens, when normal background radiation is 14. There are a few heart-stopping moments when you're checked for radiation when entering working buildings and leaving the zone. Reportedly, no-one's received an accidental overdose since 1992, but guides venturing out alone admit to sometimes having to throw away their shoes.

Another risk factor to consider is the instability of the sarcophagus covering the exploded reactor (see p34).

Next, arrange your tour. It's not a matter of attaching yourself to an existing group; that's not allowed. You have to bring your own companions. If you're travelling to Ukraine alone or in a small number this can mean huge expense and a lack of people to share observations with. A tour costs from $220 for one person and $290 for two.

Finally, you have to cope with the experience. Not that you see anything remotely gruesome, it's just unbalancing and discomforting. You might find it incredibly moving and upsetting. Then again, there's nothing very emotional left to see, and you might come away feeling like a voyeur and morally ambivalent. Between the right-on stilted conversation and outbreaks of gallows humour, don't be utterly surprised to catch yourself thinking, 'What am I doing here?'.

Since the kiddofspeed publicity raised some interesting issues about sightseeing around the scene of a major disaster, organising authority Chornobyl Interform has taken greater control of tours. You'll be driven about two and half hours from Kyiv to its office in the outer 30km exclusion zone, where a guide will accompany you in the car to the inner 10km exclusion zone. Tours usually visit the reactor information centre and the giant catfish in the river (reportedly this big because of a lack of predators and competitors, rather than through mutation). They also pass by the graveyard of helicopters, fire trucks and other rescue vehicles used in the clean-up operation and can drop in on one of the 358 zone residents. Lunch at Chornobyl Interform is also included.

The most sobering sight is the ghost town of Prypyat, where workers at Chornobyl and their families once lived. Today, deserted buildings and overgrown streets present a genuinely postapocalyptic scenario, and the 'devil's playground' aura is only underscored by the herds of wild boar crashing through the trees.

The travel agents arranging Chornobyl tours include New Logic, Sam and Solo-East Travel (see p53). Some supply a bottle of red wine as 'the best protection against radiation'. Bizarrely, this *was* tried at Chornobyl in the accident's aftermath. Theoretically, alcohol speeds up the metabolism, and hence your body's excretion of radionuclides, especially iodine. However, iodine

CHORNOBYL AFFECTED AREA

0 ▭▭ 20 km
0 ▬▬ 12 miles

BELARUS
▦ Outer Exclusion Zone
▨ Inner Exclusion Zone

Mazyr ○
Prypyat River
○ Hojniki
River
Dnipro River
Slavutych
Prypyat
Chornobyl Nuclear Power Plant (now decommissioned) ○
Poliske ○
Chornobyl
Opachichi ○
Dytyatky ○
To Moscow
UKRAINE
Kyivske Reservoir
Ivankiv ○
Desna River
To Lviv
KYIV

has a half-life of eight years, so you won't be absorbing any of that nearly 30 years after the accident. Caesium 137 in the soil is the biggest issue now. To avoid dehydration, a bottle of water is a better drink to bring.

UMAN УМАНЬ
☎ 04744 / pop 95,000
Sofia Pototsky was a legendary beauty, and Uman's stunning **Sofiyivka Park** (☎ 322 10; adult/child 4/2uah, tours per person from 10uah, minimum of 4; ☼ 9am-6pm May–mid-Nov) is her husband Felix' monument to her physical perfection. Having bought Sofia for two million zloty from her former husband (she had been sold into slavery at an early age by her Greek or Turkish parents), the Polish count set to landscaping this 150-hectare site with grottoes, lakes, waterfalls, fountains, pavilions and 500 species of tree. The result was Ukraine's answer to Versailles.

Today, sights are strung along the Kamenka River, particularly around the upper and lower ponds, the former having the **Island of Love** with a Renaissance-style rose pavilion (1850–52) on it. Tradition demands that when stepping foot on the island you shout the name of your loved one. Other highlights include the **Grotto of Fear and Doubts**, the **Fountain of Three Tears**, the **Grotto of Venus** (1760–1800) and the fabulous **Dead Lake** and **Underground River Styx**. In summer, you can hire boats here. While visiting the park, take time to learn about the Pototskys themselves. Sofia broke Felix' heart before he died, having an affair with his son.

HASSIDIC PILGRIMS
Ever since the death of Rabbi Nakhman (1772–1810), Jewish pilgrims have flocked to his graveside in Uman to pay homage to this 18th-century sage who founded the Breslov trend of Hassidism. The rabbi was born in Medzhybizh, 120km east of Ternopil in western Ukraine, but later moved to Uman where he died of tuberculosis.

The pilgrimage – strictly male only – takes place each year in September or October during Jewish New Year (Rosh Hashanah). In 1994 a 2000-seat synagogue and Jewish centre was built to accommodate the estimated 5000 pilgrims that journey to Uman each year.

KYIV

Uman is midway between Kyiv (210km) and Odesa (280km), easily reached by **Autolux bus** (www.autolux.com.ua). The park headquarters is near the bus station. From here follow the 'Sofiyivka' signs – Софіївка – to the entrance at vul Sadova 53.

Should you wish to stay overnight, there's the modern **Hotel Muzey** (☎ 335 27; d from $30) next to the park entrance.

Uman is also an important Jewish pilgrimage site (see the boxed text, p77).

CHERNIHIV ЧЕРНІГІВ
☎ 04622 / pop 313,000

Chernihiv (Chernigov in Russian) is revered in Slavic culture as an important town dating from Kyivan Rus. Inside the Boryso-Hlibsky Cathedral, looking at a plan of the old 10- to 12th-century town on the wall, you'll see it must have really been something once. As a raised bluff of land, it formed its own natural fortress and commanded trade routes south to Kyiv. Today, the main reasons to visit are the Antoniy caves, kayaking on the Desna River and a tight cluster of churches, which rise up from the plain as you approach town. Otherwise, Chernihiv makes a relaxing, rather than exciting, retreat.

Sights
Find pl Chervona (see Getting There & Around, right), a wide square with a huge neoclassical theatre. Two blocks southeast along vul Myra is the historic core. Stand in front of the theatre, with your back to it and facing the square, and head up the street to your left. This historic core is known as Dytynets (Ramparts), because it was the site of the raised natural strategic fortress. Today, you're looking for a leafy park.

In the park, you'll discover a complex of several buildings, including the **Spaso-Preobrazhensky Cathedral** (1017) with its two distinctive, missile-like corner bell towers. Within its dark interior are the tombs of several Kyivan Rus royalty, including both the younger brother and son of Yaroslav the Wise. The smaller 12th-century **Boryso-Hlibsky Cathedral** next door is worth visiting for the stunning silver **Royal Doors**, commissioned by the famous Cossack leader Ivan Mazepa.

Lining the southern edge of the Dytynets park is a row of 18th-century **cannons** overlooking the embankments and once pro-

tecting the fortified southern entrance to the city.

ANTONIY CAVES, ILLINSKY CHURCH & TROYITSKY MONASTERY
From Dytynets, it's about a 3km walk to **Troyitsky Monastery**, which you can see in the distance. However, it's easier to take trolleybus No 8. To know when to get off, look out for the 58m-high **bell tower** beside the road. If you get off at the stop after the bell tower, which you probably will, walk back past the monastery to the dirt path heading downhill beside its far monastery wall. Where the path divides, head left down the hill and you'll reach the 1069 **Illinsky Church** (admission church & caves 2uah; ☺9am-5pm Fri-Wed). Alternatively, you can walk back a bit further still to the bus stop and dilapidated park, and head straight down the hill.

Underneath the Illinsky Church are the **Antoniy Caves**, 315m of passageways, galleries and chapels constructed from the 11th to 13th centuries. These are very different from those at Kyiv's Caves Monastery (p56). Mostly wider, taller and quite deserted, they are lit with electric lamps and even have English signs. Look out for the **Chapel of the Tomb** – the bones of several monks killed during the Tatar-Mongol sacking of the church in 1239 are encased behind glass here. There are a few, short dark tunnels to explore, too.

Activities
The **Centre for Green Tourism** (www.explorecherni gov.narod.ru) offers day and multi-day kayak trips for about $20 a day. It also runs city tours in English.

Sleeping
The **Centre for Green Tourism** (www.explorecherni gov.narod.ru) can arrange overnight stays in local villages. Otherwise, there's the typically half-renovated Intourist-style **Hotel Hradetsky** (☎ 450 25; vul Myra 68; s/d from $15/20), 2km northwest of pl Chervona.

Getting There & Around
The train and bus stations are 2km west of pl Chervona, on pl Vokzalna. Trolleybus No 1 runs between the stations and the centre, stopping a block north of pl Chervona. Ask for directions to the square from here.

The electric *Chernihiv Express* (6uah each way) leaves Kyiv's local (*prymisky;* приміський) train station (next to Vokzalna metro station) around 8am daily. It takes three hours to arrive and departs Chernihiv for Kyiv around 4pm (check the departures board in the station for exact current times). Mainline trains, including the morning Kyiv–St Petersburg service, pass through, but are slower and more expensive.

Marshrutky and buses leave from Kyiv's central bus station at least every hour or two (12uah, two to 2½ hours). Check for services coming back, as they stop fairly early in the evening.

KANIV КАНІВ
☎ 04736

When Taras Shevchenko died in 1861, his famous poem *Zapovit* (Testament) requested his countrymen bury him on a hill overlooking the great Dnipro River where, after rising up and liberating the land, they could 'freely, and with good intent, speak quietly of him'.

Kaniv, 162km down the Dnipro from Kyiv, is the spot. In 1925 the steep and scenic bluff overlooking the river called Taras' Hill (Tarasova Hora) was designated a State Cultural Preserve. On a hill above the (mainly disused) river pier you'll find the poet's tomb, which is crowned with a statue of the man himself. There is an observation point in front offering great views of the river. Beside the grave is the **Shevchenko Monument & Literary Memorial Museum** (☎ 223 65; admission 5uah; 9am-6pm). Behind

this, a path leads to the tomb of Yadlovsky, the man who guarded Shevchenko's body from 1883 to 1933.

About 15km south of the city is the **Kaniv Nature Reserve**, some 2000 hectares of pristine forest and hills with over 5000 species of plants indigenous to the area.

The nearest train station is in Lipylava, 7km away. Some Cherkasy buses from Kyiv also stop in Kaniv (two hours). There used to be a Kaniv hydrofoil making a relaxing day trip from Kyiv on Saturdays and Sundays, which might be restarted. Or check with travel agencies to see if they offer special chartered tours (see p53).

PEREYASLAV-KHMELNYTSKY ПЕРЕЯСЛАВ-ХМЕЛЬНИЦЬКИЙ
☎ 04467 / pop 24,000

Pereyaslav-Khmelnytsky was the hometown and stronghold of Cossack leader Bohdan Khmelnytsky, and also where he signed the infamous agreement accepting Russia's overlordship of Ukraine on 18 January 1654.

Today the whole town, with its numerous museums, has been declared a historical preserve. The highlight is probably the **Folk Architecture Museum** (admission 3uah; ⊙ 10am-5pm, from noon Fri, closed Wed). Many sights in the town centre are clustered on central pl Vozyednannya, which lies off the main street, vul Khmelnytsky. The square's southwestern side is dominated by the **Ascension Monastery**.

Most buses between Kyiv's main bus station and Cherkasy (about six daily) stop at Pereyaslav-Khmelnytsky.

Western Ukraine
Західна Україна

CONTENTS

The west is a special case in Ukraine. It likes to think itself more quintessentially Ukrainian than the rest of the country; at the same time it considers itself more European. Thanks to its different history, it manages to be both. Having kept the nationalist home fires burning during centuries of Polish, Lithuanian and Austrian rule, it still shows greater pride in Ukrainian traditions and language than elsewhere. Yet overseas visitors will find this one of the most familiar feeling and friendly regions of Ukraine – poorer than, but not so different from, neighbouring Hungary, Poland or Slovakia. Here, where Moscow ruled for only 50 years, there's less of that surly 'no-can-do' Soviet bureaucracy than still permeates eastern regions. Attitudes are more relaxed and there's even a greater willingness to speak English, in the cities at least.

One of those cities, the Galician capital Lviv, is a true gem that's only now starting to get the attention it deserves. Its historic core mixes classic Central European flair with surprising Italian detail. Dramatic Kamyanets-Podilsky also stays in the mind, with its medieval old town perched on a tall rock 'island' in the middle of a wide river canyon.

No discussion of western Ukraine would be complete, however, without mention of the eastern arc of the Carpathian Mountains – sometimes called 'the Hutsul Alps' after the folk who live here. These scenic peaks constitute Ukraine's premier skiing spot and one of its hiking highlights, too. Relatively remote and wild, they're still largely a secret to the outside world. But pioneering foreigners are already arriving to climb the country's highest peak, Hoverla, or to catch a glimpse of the rich culture that underpinned Ukraine's win in the Eurovision song contest 2004.

WESTERN UKRAINE

HIGHLIGHTS

- Call off the search for the new Prague! **Lviv** is it (p83)
- Bungee jumping – or even just looking – into the spectacular **Kamyanets-Podilsky gorge** (p108)
- Climb Ukraine's highest peak, **Hoverla** (p96), and walk along the Carpathians' Chornohora ridge
- Count your eggs at the oval-shaped **Pysanky Museum** (p100) in pretty Kolomyya
- Have a lazy Sunday picnic at **Khotyn fortress** (p109) on the Dnister River
- Visit the Orthodox monastery at **Pochayiv** (p110)
- Expand your mind at the striking **Chernivsti university** p102)

★ Pochayiv
★ Lviv

Kolomyya ★ Kamyanets-
★ Podilsky
Mt Hoverla ★ ★ Khotyn
Chernivtsi

- POPULATION: 14.5 MILLION
- HIGHEST POINT: MT HOVERLA (2061M)

WESTERN UKRAINE

History

Mongols overrunning the rest of Kyivan Rus in 1240 never made it as far west as the powerful province of Galicia-Volynia. They did occasionally knock on its door, but the region was largely left to enjoy self-rule under Prince Roman Mstyslavych, his son Danylo Halytsky and their descendants.

This idyllic state was shattered in the 1340s when Polish troops invaded, but western Ukraine never lost its taste for independence. Several centuries of Polish domination saw the rise of a unique 'Ruthenian' identity, which is the basis for much contemporary Ukrainian nationalism. Many Galician nobles or 'boyars' – often sent over from Poland, Germany or Hungary – adopted the Polish language and Roman Catholicism. However, the peasants or 'Ruthenians' remained Orthodox. They were only persuaded to join the new Ukrainian Catholic or Uniate Church in 1596 (thereby acknowledging the pope's spiritual supremacy) because it agreed to retain Orthodox forms of worship. Other Ruthenians fled southeast to set up Cossack communities.

In 1772 Galicia became part of the Habsburg Austro-Hungarian Empire, and to this day Ukrainians touchingly remember the Austrians as liberal, tolerant rulers. Serbian separatists so chaffed under the Austrian yoke that they even started WW1 in 1914 to rid themselves of it, but the Habsburgs allowed Ukrainian nationalism to reemerge

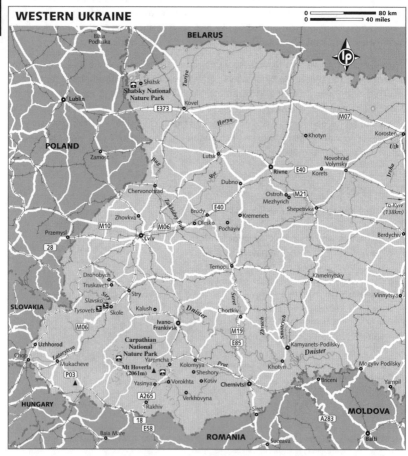

WESTERN UKRAINE

0 ――――― 80 km
0 ――――― 40 miles

and that made them good guys here. Western Ukraine even enjoyed a few days' independence as the Habsburg Empire collapsed at the end of WWI, but it soon found itself under the dreaded Polish thumb again.

Then, at the outbreak of WWII in September 1939, things went from bad to worse in local eyes. The Red Army marched in and asserted Moscow's control over the region for the first time in history. Finally dispatching the Nazis after bloody battles during WWII, the Soviets hung around until 1991, when the USSR imploded.

LVIV REGION

LVIV ЛЬВІВ
☎ 032 (7-digit Nos), 0322 (6-digit Nos)
pop 685,600

From its popular Castle Hill, it's obvious where Lviv derived the nickname 'the Florence of the east'. As evening sunlight is refracted through a mild haze, green church domes and red roofs make it seem as if that Italian city has been picked up and transported. And the fact that it appears to have been transported to the Moscow suburbs only adds to the surreal quality of the vision.

But you needn't go near those Soviet-like suburbs; Lviv's superb historic centre is where it's at. It was built like a rich layer-cake, as a succession of foreign rulers poured neoclassical architecture upon rococo, baroque, Renaissance and Gothic. Remarkably, it escaped damage during WWII. Now this quaint Central European city looks rather nibbled around the edges, but it's no less charming still.

With faded, ornate buildings and friendly, unjaded locals, it's reminiscent of Prague before it was refurbished and inundated with tourists. As you wander Lviv's uneven cobblestone streets, sticking your head into hidden courtyards, admiring ornate churches and eating cake in Austrian-style coffee houses, it does seem too good to be true – just like a mirage from a hilltop. Luckily, instead, it proves to be very, very real.

History
Lviv has had as many names as rulers. It took its first from Lev, the son of Prince

Danylo Halytsky who founded a hilltop fort here on Castle Hill in the 13th century. When the Poles took over 100 years later, the place became known as Lwow, as it still is in Poland. Austrians called it Lemberg between the 18th and 20th centuries, and can't stop doing so today. The Russians, who later christened it Lvov, continue to use their historical name. All are variations on a theme. Since each is rooted in the meaning 'lion', the city has always taken the big cat as its symbol.

Lviv (luh-*veev*) had another set of unwelcome occupiers, also calling the place Lemberg – the Nazis, who invaded in 1941 and weren't driven back by the Soviets until 1944. During these three years, 136,000 people are reported to have died in Lviv's Jewish ghetto and nearly 350,000 in nearby concentration camps. For more about this era, read Robert Marshall's *In the Sewers of Lvov: A Heroic Story of Survival from the Holocaust.*

The Galician capital was a major mover within the movement that led to Ukrainian independence in 1991. Ukrainian nationalism and the Ukrainian Catholic Church reemerged here in the late 1980s, and in the early 1990s its people unanimously elected nationalist politicians and staged mass demonstrations. Today, it still has its eyes focused more on Europe than Russia and has been a stronghold for Western-orientated politicians like Viktor Yushchenko.

Orientation
Lviv's main street is the 600m-long pr Svobody (Freedom), which runs north from pl Mitskevycha to the Ivan Franko Opera & Ballet Theatre. Directly east are the narrow, old-quarter streets around the central pl Rynok. Westwards, 19th-century streets lead to Ivan Franko Park. Most sights are within this roughly 1.25 sq km area, overlooked from the northeast by Zamkova Hora (Castle Hill).

From the central train station, take tram No 1 or 9 to the southern end of pr Svobody. *Marshrutka* No 95 goes from the airport to the centre.

Information
BOOKSHOPS
Books (Map p86; ☎ 722 550; pl Mitskevycha; ⏰ 10am-6pm Mon-Fri, 10am-3pm Sat) This large, central bookshop has local maps and guides.

WESTERN UKRAINE

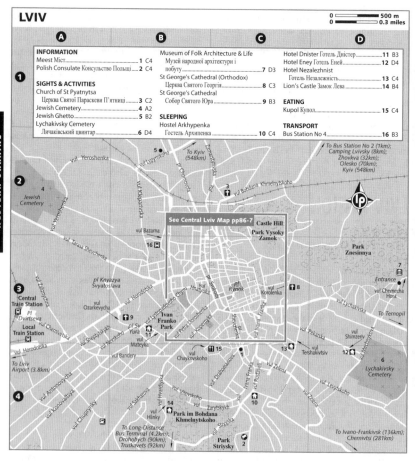

LVIV

INFORMATION
Meest Міст..**1** C4
Polish Consulate Консульство Польщі.....**2** C4

SIGHTS & ACTIVITIES
Church of St Pyatnytsa
　Церква Святої Параскеви П'ятниці.........**3** C2
Jewish Cemetery....................................**4** A2
Jewish Ghetto.......................................**5** B2
Lychakivsky Cemetery
　Личаківський цвинтар..........................**6** D4

Museum of Folk Architecture & Life
　Музей народної архітектури і
　побуту...**7** D3
St George's Cathedral (Orthodox)
　Церква Святого Георгія........................**8** C3
St George's Cathedral
　Собор Святого Юра.............................**9** B3

SLEEPING
Hostel Arkhypenka
　Гостель Архипенка.............................**10** C4

Hotel Dnister Готель Дністер....................**11** B3
Hotel Eney Готель Еней..........................**12** D4
Hotel Nezalezhnist
　Готель Незалежність............................**13** C3
Lion's Castle Замок Лева........................**14** B4

EATING
Kupol Купол..**15** C4

TRANSPORT
Bus Station No 4...................................**16** B3

INTERNET ACCESS

Komp'yuterny Klub (Map p86; pr Shevchenka 14; per hr 3.30uah; ☼ 10am-10pm) This gaming centre is full of adolescent boys, but does offer cheap internet access.

Pavuk (Map p86; ☎ 725 084; pr Svobody 7; per hr 4uah; ☼ 10am-10pm) 'Spider' has a long bank of terminals in a relatively sedate environment.

MONEY

In addition to at the banks listed below, credit-card cash advances are also available at Western Union/X-Change Points inside the central train ticket office or in the main post office.

Oschadny Bank (Map p86; ☎ 272 793; vul Sichovykh Striltsiv 9) Full banking services, including cashing of traveller cheques.

Privatbank (Map p86; pr Svobody & pr Shevchenka) Well-placed ATMs, accepting all cards; the second is behind McDonald's, next to Baskin & Robbins.

POST

Central post office (Map p86; ☎ 065; vul Slovatskoho 1; ☼ 9am-5pm Mon-Fri, 8am-2pm Sat)

TELEPHONE

Central telephone office (Map p86; vul Petra Doroshenka 39; ☼ 24hr)

TOURIST INFORMATION

Tourist Information Centre (Map p86; ☎ 975 767; www.tourism.lviv.ua; vul Pidvalna 3; ☼ 10am-1pm & 2-6pm Mon-Fri) Free maps and brochures; staff speak some English and can organise guided tours.

TRAVEL AGENCIES

Lviv Ecotour (☎ 276 5121; www.lvivecotour.com)
Owner Vladyslav 'Slav' Tsarynnk knows the region very
well, has plenty of experience in guiding foreigners and
speaks English like a native. Highly recommended. Can also
arrange accommodation.

Meest (Map p84; ☎ 297 0852; www.meest-tour.com; pr
Shevchenka 34) This larger agency also gets good reports.
English-speaking staff offer a range of travel services,
including the booking of air tickets.

Sights

PLOSHCHA RYNOK   Map p86

Lviv's splendid array of buildings meant it
was declared a Unesco World Heritage Site
in 1998, and this old market square lies at
its heart. The square was progressively rebuilt after a major fire in the early 16th century destroyed the original. A 19th-century
town hall *(ratusha)* stands in the middle of
the plaza, with fountains featuring Greek
gods on each of its corners. You can climb
the neo-Renaissance **tower** (adult/child 2uah/50
kopecks; ☺ 10am-5pm Mon-Fri, 11am-7pm Sat & Sun).
However, the 40-odd buildings around the
square's perimeter are more interesting.

Most of these have uniform dimensions,
with only three windows overlooking the
square. This was the maximum allowed tax-
free, and those buildings with four or more
windows belonged to the extremely wealthy.

House No 4, the Black Mansion, has one
of the most striking façades. Built for an
Italian merchant in 1588–89, it features a
relief of St Martin on a horse. The Kornyakt
House at No 6 is named after its original
owner, a Greek merchant. An interesting
sculptural row of knights along the rooftop
cornice makes it a local favourite. Together,
Nos 4 and 6 house the largest portion of the
Lviv History Museum (p88).

House No 10 has a mural of cannon and
cannonballs on its lower corner and a face-
less Roman legionnaire looming high above
the parapet. It owes its grandiose, 18th-
century appearance to the Polish Lyubo-
myrsky family, its former owners, and is
now a branch of the Museum of Ethnography, Arts & Crafts (p88). The Venetian
consul lived at No 14 in the 17th century.

A highlight is the **Boyim Chapel**, just off the
square's southwestern corner. The burial
chapel (1617) of a Hungarian merchant
family, its blackened façade is covered in
magnificent carvings, including portraits of

PHONE WARNING

Lviv's change from analogue to digital
phone lines has caused some confusion,
and sometimes when calling within Lviv,
you might have to put a 2 in front of a
six-digit number. If a listed number fails to
work, that's the first thing to try.

---

the Boyim family patriarchs above the door.
Atop the cupola is an unusual sculpture of
Christ sitting with his head in one hand,
pondering his sorrows. At the time of research, the chapel seemed to be permanently
closed, with a 'back in 10 minutes sign' continuing to hang on its door.

Opposite the chapel, on pl Katedralna
(Cathedral Sq) is the working **Roman Catholic
Cathedral** (1370–1480). From this vantage
point, you can see a cannonball hanging off
its corner, which miraculously failed to pene-
trate its walls during a historic battle. If you
walk around the cathedral, on the other side
you'll see a relief of Pope Jean Paul II, erected
to commemorate his visit to Lviv in 2001.

VULYTSYA VIRMENSKA
& AROUND   Map p86

By some accounts, Lviv has more than 80
churches and it's all too easy to overdose
on ornate interiors and golden iconostases.
However, two of the most beautiful examples are within easy reach of pl Rynok: the
1363 **Armenian Cathedral** (vul Virmenska 7), which
has another entrance on vul Krakivska, and
the late-17th-century **Transfiguration Church**
(cnr vuls Krakivska & Lesi Ukrainky; ☺ evening prayers 7pm
Wed-Sun). The latter was the first church in
the city to revert to Ukrainian Catholicism
(aka the Uniate Church or Greek Catholicism) after independence in 1991. Watching a sung evening prayer service here is
quite a moving and mystical experience.

PROSPEKT SVOBODY   Map p86

Just in case it should ever slip your mind
that Lviv is Ukraine's most patriotic large
city, it boasts an enormous **statue of Taras
Shevchenko** in the middle of its central avenue. A gift from the Ukrainian diaspora in
Argentina, the statue of the revered national
poet stands beside a wave-shaped relief of
religious folk art. In summer, the broad
pavement in the middle of the prospekt

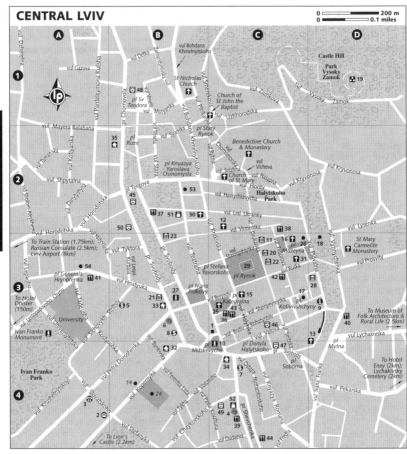

CENTRAL LVIV

WESTERN UKRAINE

is the town's main hang-out and the hub of Lviv life, and lovers pose for photos at Shevchenko's feet. People promenade along the 'Planta', as older locals call the boulevard, while ponies and tricycles are rented out for children and older locals sometimes gather in singing groups. At the northern end is the **Ivan Franko Opera & Ballet Theatre** (1897–1900), at the southern end a statue of the Polish poet Adam Michiewicz stands in pl Mitskvycha. The street is closed to traffic on weekends.

VULYTSYA PIDVALNA
& AROUND   Map p86
Take a quick stroll around the area east of pl Rynok. Down vul Stavropihiyska, is the

large dome of the **Dominican Church & Monastery** (1745–64). Don't bother going inside however, as Lviv's finest bit of rococo looks better from the exterior. Instead, skirt right (east) around the side of the church, where you'll come to the former **royal arsenal** and a square with a statue of a monk with a book. This is Federov, who brought printing to Ukraine in the 16th century. Fittingly, there's a used-book market here on weekends. In the park across the street is the **Gunpowder Tower** (1554–56), part of the old system of walls and bastions.

Turning right and heading south along vul Pidvalna you'll come to the **Uspensky Church & Three Saints Chapel** (vul Pidvalna 9). The church is easily distinguished by the 65m,

INFORMATION		
Books Книги	**1**	C3
Central post office Поштамт	**2**	A4
Central telephone office Укртелеком	**3**	A4
Grand Hotel Tour Agency		
Гранд-Готель туристичне агенство	(see 33)	
Komp'yuterny Klub		
Комп'ютерний клуб	**4**	C4
Oschadny Bank Ощадний банк	**5**	B3
Pavuk Павук	**6**	B3
Privatbank ATM Приватбанк	**7**	C4
Privatbank ATM Приватбанк	**8**	B3
Tourist Information Centre		
Туристичне бюро	**9**	D3
SIGHTS & ACTIVITIES		
Adam Michiewicz statue		
Статуя Адаму Міцкевичу	**10**	C4
Apteka Museum Аптека-музей	**11**	C3
Armenian Cathedral		
Вірменський собор	**12**	C2
Arsenal Museum		
Музей старовинної зброї	(see 28)	
Bernardine Church & Monastery		
Бернардинців костьол і монастир	**13**	D3
Birthplace of Leopold von Sacher-Masoch		
Будинок Леопольда ван Сачер-Масоч	**14**	B4
Boyim Chapel Боїм Каплиця	**15**	C3
Dominican Church & Monastery		
Костьол та монастир домініканців	**16**	C3
Former synagogue Колишня синагога	**17**	C3
Gunpowder Tower Порохова вежа	**18**	D3

High Castle Високий замок	**19**	D1
Lviv History Museum		
Історичний музей	**20**	C3
Museum of Ethnography		
Gift Shop	(see 20)	
Museum of Ethnography, Arts & Crafts		
Музей етнографії та художнього		
промислу	**21**	B3
Museum of Ethnography, Arts & Crafts		
Музей етнографії та художнього		
промислу	**22**	C3
National Museum		
Національний Музей	**23**	B3
Pototsky Palace Палац Потоцького	**24**	B4
Roman Catholic Cathedral		
Романо-Католицький собор	**25**	C3
Royal Arsenal Королівський арсенал	**26**	C3
Statue of Taras Shevchenko		
Пам'ятник Тарасові Шевченку	**27**	C3
Three Saints Chapel		
Каплиця трьох святителів	(see 31)	
Town Arsenal Міський Арсенал	**28**	D3
Town Hall Ратуша	**29**	C3
Transfiguration Church		
Храм Преображення Господнього	**30**	B2
Uspenska Church Успенська церква	**31**	C3
SLEEPING		
Banking Academy Hostel	**32**	B4
Grand Hotel Гранд-Готель	**33**	B3
Hotel George Готель Жорж	**34**	C4
Hotel Lviv Готель Львів	**35**	B2

EATING		
Amadeus Амадеус	**36**	C3
Chelentano Челентано	**37**	A4
Dzyga Дзиґа	**38**	C2
Europa Європа	**39**	C4
Italian Courtyard	(see 20)	
Kulchetskoho Pizza Піцца Кульчицького	**40**	D3
Olesya Олеся	**41**	A3
Pid Synioyu Pliashkoyu	**42**	C3
Tsukarnia Цукарня	**43**	C3
Veronika Вероніка	**44**	C4
ENTERTAINMENT		
Ivan Franko Opera & Ballet Theatre		
Театр Опери та балету ім Івана Франка	**45**	B2
Korzo Pub Корзо паб	**46**	C3
Lyalka Лялька	**47**	C4
Millennium Міленіум	**48**	B1
Philharmonia Філармонія	**49**	C4
Teatralna Kasa Театральна каса	**50**	B2
SHOPPING		
Outdoor Arts & Crafts Market		
Відкритий ринок по продажу виробів		
мистецтва та художнього промислу	**51**	B3
Svitoch Світоч	**52**	C3
TRANSPORT		
Bus Ticket Office Центральні каси по		
продажу автобусних квитків	**53**	B2
Train Ticket Office		
Центральні залізничні каси	**54**	A3

triple-tiered **Kornyakt Bell Tower** rising beside it, named after its Greek benefactor (a merchant who was also the original owner of No 6 on pl Rynok, Kornyakt House). The church, reached through the gate to the right of the tower, is only open for services (usually at 5pm). However, it's worth seeing inside, because this is another beautiful interior and, being Orthodox (albeit Ukrainian Orthodox), is slightly unusual for Lviv.

Further along is the 1554–56 **Town Arsenal & Arsenal Museum** (vul Pidvalna 5). This was also part of the city's original fortification system, albeit rebuilt; see p88 for details. Crossing vul Valova and following Pidvalna as it curves right, you'll come across the last standing section of the old town fortifications. Beyond this is the 17th-century **Bernardine Church & Monastery** complex, now the Ukrainian Catholic Church of St Andrew. Walking from here back to pr Svoboda, you'll pass pl Danyla Halytskoho and the statue of Prince Danylo, Lviv's founder.

HIGH CASTLE HILL

Visiting the **High Castle** (Map p86; Vysoky Zamok) on Castle Hill (Zamkova Hora) is a quintessential Lviv experience. Whoever first called the city 'the Florence of the east' was surely standing here when they did so.

The 14th-century ruined stone fort at the summit was Lviv's birthplace and offers the best vantage point of the modern city. Sunset is a good time to visit. Newlyweds like to pop the cork on a bottle of champagne here, while enterprising locals rent binoculars and sell souvenirs.

To reach the peak, cross vul Pidvalna and climb the stairs into the park behind. Head left to the corner of vuls Vynnychenka and Kryvonosa. Bear left, following the curving road uphill. You'll reach the first crest near a restaurant. Continue past this, and up the steel stairs behind. Turn left at the tree-lined road, walking until you reach a set of stone stairs around the summit. Bear right and follow the trail to its end.

LYCHAKIVSKY CEMETERY

Don't even think of leaving town until you've seen the **Lychakivsky Cemetery** (Map p84; Lychakivsky Tsvyntar or Kladovyshche; admission 3uah; ☾ 9am-6pm Apr-Sep, to 5pm Oct-Mar), even though it is a short journey from the centre. This is the Père Lachaise of Eastern Europe. With the same sort of overgrown grounds and Gothic aura as the famous Parisian necropolis, Lychakivsky is the final resting place for more than 400,000 people.

Unlike in Paris, no-one's holding a vigil beside the grave of Doors singer Jim Morrison, of course. However, the revered nationalist poet Ivan Franko is buried here (in sector four, diagonally right from the entrance), alongside dozens of other famous Ukrainians and Poles. Thousands of soldiers are also remembered at the rear of the 42-hectare site. Ultimately, you needn't recognise a single soul to be moved by the mournful photos of loved ones, ornate tombstones and floral tributes.

The cemetery is five stops on tram No 7 from vul Pidvalna; when you see the flowersellers you're there.

MUSEUMS

Its buildings are Lviv's strong point, rather than its museums, but it's also worth popping your head into one or two of them. At the time of research, a post office museum was being constructed on the corner of pl Rynok.

Lviv History Museum (Map p86; ☎ 720 671; ⏰ 10am-6pm Thu-Tue) is split between three collections dotted around pl Rynok. The best part of this museum is at **No 6** (admission 3.50uah, temporary exhibitions extra 1uah). Here you get to enjoy the Italian-Renaissance inner courtyard and slide around in cloth slippers on a woodcut parquet floor upstairs. It was also here on 22 December 1686 that Poland and Russia signed the treaty that partitioned Ukraine. **No 4** (admission 1uah) covers 19th- and 20th-century history, while **No 24** (admission 1uah) expounds on the city's earlier history, including some Cossack displays.

Small but fun, the **Apteka Museum** (Map p86; ☎ 722 041; vul Drukarska 2; admission 1.50uah; ⏰ 10am-6pm Mon-Fri, 10am-4pm Sat & Sun) is located inside the city's oldest working pharmacy (1735), which is colourfully named the Black Eagle. Pay the pharmacists to open the museum, and you enter a world of containers, drawers, herbs and tinctures and salves. You can buy a bottle of iron-rich medicinal wine, if you can bear the temporary tooth discolouration. Ask for 'vino'.

The **National Museum** (Map p86; ☎ 742 280; pr Svobody 20; admission 11uah; ⏰ 10am-6pm Sat-Thu) is most notable for its 15th- to 19th-century religious icons and medieval books, which are quite impressive if you're a fan. The temporary exhibitions by local artists are of a more variable quality.

The **Museum of Ethnography, Arts & Crafts** (Map p86; ☎ 727 808; pr Svobody 15 & pl Rynok 10; admission 2uah; ⏰ 11am-5.30pm Wed-Sun) has displays of furniture, dress, woodcarvings, ceramics and farming implements that give a basic introduction to Carpathian life. However, much is faded and little is noteworthy. The Hutsul museum (p100) is Kolomyya is superior.

If you're into cannons and armour, the **Arsenal Museum** (Map p86; ☎ 721 901; vul Pidvalna 5; admission 1uah; ⏰ 10am-5pm Thu-Tue) contains a variety of weaponry from more than 30 countries, .

Museum of Folk Architecture & Life (Map p84; Muzey Narodnoyi Arkhitektury i Pobutu; ☎ 718 017; vul Chernecha Hora 1; adult/child 1.50uah/75 kopecks; ⏰ 11am-7pm Tue-Sun Apr-Oct, 11am-6pm Tue-Sun Nov-Mar) is not the best place in Ukraine to appreciate the different regional styles of farmsteads, windmills, churches and schools, as many of the wooden buildings are in a state of disrepair. Still, if you're keen and not heading to Kyiv (see p62), take tram No 2 or No 7 and get off on vul Lychakiska, following Map p84 to the museum.

CHURCHES

On a hilltop beyond Ivan Franko Park stands **St George's Cathedral** (Map p84; Sobor Yura; pl St Yura 5). This is the historic and sacred centre of the Ukrainian Catholic Church, which was handed back after 44 years of compulsory Orthodox control. Constructed in 1774–90 in baroque style, this yellow building is pleasant enough, especially since a refurbishment for the pope's 2001 visit. However, perhaps it's not as striking as some of Lviv's less important churches. For nonbelievers, the most memorable element is the 3-D icon of Christ near the far right corner from the door. It presents Christ's living face from one angle, and the image from the shroud of Turin from another.

The other **St George's Cathedral** (Map p84; vul Korolenka 3) is the city's only Russian Orthodox church. It has an eye-catching white and red-brick exterior.

One of the best iconostases is found in the **Church of St Pyatnytsa** (Map p84; vul Bohdana Khmelnytskoho 77). However, it's a fair walk to the church and, unfortunately, it isn't always open.

OTHER SIGHTS

South off pl Mitskevycha runs Lviv's lesser grand boulevard, **prospekt Shevchenka**, adorned with rows of attractive early-20th-century buildings. At its far southern end is a statue of a seated Mykhailo Hrushevsky, Ukraine's most famous historian and the country's first president during its brief independence in 1918.

Opposite the charming **Pototsky Palace** (Map p86; vul Kopernyka 15), the home of Polish nobles, is the **birthplace of Leopold von Sacher-Masoch** (vul Kopernyka 22), the world's original 'masochist'. The author of the novel *Venus in Furs* came into the world here in 1835, although he spent most of his subsequent 60 years begging to be whipped in Austria, Germany and Italy.

Despite some Jewish history, there aren't really many Jewish sites in Lviv. The **former synagogue and baths** (Map p86) behind the Town Arsenal & Arsenal Museum are overgrown and covered in graffiti. The **Jewish Cemetery** (Map p84) lies northeast of the centre, along vul Tarasa Shevchenka, while the **former Jewish Ghetto** (Map p84) is northeast of the intersection of pr Chornovola and vul Lypynskoho.

Sleeping
BUDGET

Lviv has a range of budget accommodation, to suit most tastes.

Hostels

Shockingly for a Ukrainian city, Lviv has some. They're run through a central booking organisation, which will pick you up from the airport or train station.

Banking Academy Hostel (Map p86; ☎ 296 5734; info@hihostels.com.ua, lviv@hihostels.com.ua; vul Kopernyka 14; dm $20; ☺ Jun-Sep) A small wing of this financial school's student quarters becomes a hostel between June and September. The building is new, well built and very central. It's most memorable for its fantastic, light-filled inner courtyard, but there's also a kitchen, a games room/lounge downstairs and a sauna.

Hostel Arkhypenka (Map p84; ☎ 296 5734; info@hihostels.com.ua, lviv@hihostels.com.ua; vul Arkhypenka 2; dm/d $20/40; ℗ ▯) Neither as flash nor as central as its sister establishment, this is, however, open all year. It's in a wooden house, with bunk beds crowded into most of the

rooms, but there's also what staff laughingly dub a 'honeymoon suite' – a kitsch, 1970s retro double bedroom. You can shoot basketball hoops in the grounds.

Apartments

Trident (☎ 297 1332; travel@utel.net.ua) has an apartment a little from the centre for $35 a night.

Lviv Ecotour (p85) has a two double-bedroom apartment (sleeping one to four people) for $60 a night. It's very central and well equipped.

Hotels

Hotel George (Map p86; ☎ 725 952; www.georgehotel.ukrbiz.net; pl Mitskevycha 1; r without private bathroom $20-25, s/d with private bathroom from $55/60) Behind its renovated Art Nouveau façade, the central Hotel George is the epitome of faded grandeur, with creaky wooden floors and scuffed carpets alongside high ceilings, an elegant staircase and stained-glass windows. The bathrooms are clean however, while staff speak some English and are very accommodating. (If you're actor Ewan McGregor they might even let you park your motorbike in the lobby.) Breakfast is 20uah extra, but not really worth it. A word of warning: be prepared to pay more, as you might not get the class of room you've booked.

Also available:

Hotel Nezalezhnist (Map p84; ☎ 757 224; vul Tershakivtsiv 6; s/d from $20/25) Probably the best Soviet-era cheapie in town.

Hotel Lviv (Map p86; ☎ 728 651; pr Chornovola 7; s/d without private bathroom $9/15, with private bathroom $20/27) Not the best, but cheap.

Camping

Camping Lvivsky (☎ 721 373, 721 473; ☺ closed winter) Some 10km northeast of the centre on the Kyiv road near the village of Dublyany, this place has tent and caravan sites.

MIDRANGE

Lion's Castle (Map p84; ☎ 238 6115; www.lionscastle.com; vul Hlinky 7; r $70-130; ℗) This hotel is spread across two neighbouring buildings in a leafy upmarket neighbourhood. The main building is a castle-shaped stone mansion, where there are five, creaky, characterful and enormous doubles, with striking baths. The nine rooms in the newer building are a slight step down in standard and size. The one cheap room (single/double $40/45) is in a basement, but it has a window and is more than bearable. Credit cards accepted.

Hotel Eney (Map p84; ☎ 768 799; www.eney.lviv.ua; vul Shimzeriv 2; d €70-80, ste €90-120, apt €190; **P ⚒ ☒**) Towards Lychakivsky Cemetery, this new hotel feels like a small private villa, with green lawn behind iron gates. The rooms are small, but comfy and modern. In summer you can take breakfast on the garden terrace; all year-round there's a Finnish sauna. Credit cards accepted.

Hotel Dnister (Map p84; ☎ 297 4305; www.dnister.lviv.ua; vul Mateyko 6; standard s/d $55-80, superior s/d $100-115; **P ⚒ ☐**) The monolithic Dnister's primary audience is business travellers, and while superior rooms now meet modern corporate standards, the hulking great façade isn't too pretty. Still, you don't have to look at that from the inside, and the hotel is near a leafy park. Facilities and service are good, with some staff speaking English. Credit cards accepted.

TOP END

Grand Hotel (Map p86; ☎ 724 042; www.ghgroup.com.ua; pr Svobody 13; s/d from $100/145; **P ✗ ⚒ ☐ ☒**) Lviv's only honest-to-goodness Western-standard four-star hotel has tastefully restrained décor and a prime location on pr Svobody. Behind the restored, plum-coloured neoclassical exterior, there's lots of iron-lace stair railing, black-and-white tiled lobbies, a bar and (overpriced) restaurant. Use of a nearby fitness centre is included. Credit cards accepted.

Eating
RESTAURANTS

Chelentano (Map p86; ☎ 741 135; pr Svobody 24, entrance on Lesi Ukrayinky; mains 5-8uah) Proof that fast-food pizza, Western-style, just ropes in young Ukrainians, the Lviv branch of this popular chain is always full. You have to order individual toppings at the counter; if you don't speak Ukrainian, use p44 to point, or try to pick up an English menu. Salads and pastas are available, too.

Kulchetskoho Pizza (Map p86; vul Vynnychenka 12; mains 5-12uah; ⌚ 10am-7pm Mon-Sat) Proving just how unpopular Eastern European–style slow food and pizza can be, this quiet nationalist bookshop and canteen is nonetheless more interesting than Chelentano for foreigners. Despite the portraits of Ukrainian heroes, including Stepan Bandera and

AUTHOR'S CHOICE

Tucked away up a small hill is the restaurant **Kupol** (☎ 274 4254; vul Chaykovskoho 37; mains 16-35uah; ⌚ 9am-11pm). It's designed to feel like stepping back in time – to 1938 in particular, 'the year before civilisation ended' (ie before the Soviets rolled in). How well this former mansion and arts salon recreates that specific year is moot, but, goodness, is the overall effect winning. The olde-worlde chintzy interior is lined with framed letters, ocean-liner ads, antique cutlery, hampers and other memorabilia. There's also a hillside terrace that's perfect in the summertime. The Polish/Austrian/Ukrainian food is delicious and beautifully garnished; try the green *borshch*, stuffed aubergine or pork chop with cranberry sauce. Credit cards accepted.

Taras Shevchenko, there's still a brown wrapping-paper, Soviet atmosphere.

Olesya (Map p86; ☎ 272 1601; vul Hnatyuka 11; mains 5-50uah) A little musty and sometimes so deserted you have to wonder whether this touristy restaurant is open. It usually is, delivering honest Ukrainian and Central European cuisine. Choose from things like *borshch*, *varenyky* or carp in beer.

Europa (Map p86; ☎ 272 5862; pr Shevchenka 14; mains 12-25uah; ⌚ 8am-11pm Mon-Fri, 10am-11pm Sat & Sun) This rustic café/bar is a locals' hangout, where people seem to be on friendly terms with the staff or owner, or pop in to watch the football on TV. The Ukrainian/Russian food won't blow a hole in your wallet and it's good for a quick meal.

Amadeus (Map p86; ☎ 297 8022; pl Katedralna 7; mains 30-75uah) Everything from fondue and risotto to meat and potatoes are available at this small, upscale bistro. The ambience is quite refined, with the music turned right down.

CAFÉS

The following all serve snacks and/or cakes.

Dyzga (Map p86; vul Virmenska 35) This café-cum–arts centre has a relaxed vibe. It's particularly popular with bohemian, alternative types, but seems to attract pretty well everyone, really.

Pid Synioyu Pliashkoyu (Map p86; vul Ruska 14) With its nostalgia for the Polish/Austrian past and its dark interior, this tiny café/bar at the back of a courtyard has a cosy, secretive atmosphere. Look for the sign with the blue bottle. It serves sandwiches and fondues, as well as coffee with pepper.

Tsukarnia (Map p86; vul Staroyevreyska; ☺ 9am-10pm) A little gem of a sweet shop, whose good coffee and pastries mean it's always crowded. It's tucked away behind the restaurant Amadeus and the Roman Catholic Cathedral.

Veronika (Map p86; pr Shevchenka 21; ☺ 10am-midnight) This upmarket Cafe-Konditorei is so convincing, you could almost be in Vienna once you step inside; only the average coffee lets the side down. Besides Veronika's small ground-floor salon, there's also a smoky basement floor and, in summer, a pavement terrace.

Italian Courtyard (Map p86; pl Rynok 6) Even if you decide to skip the Lviv History Museum, it's worth popping in for a coffee in its lovely inner courtyard. You usually have to pay a cover charge, which in principle is an outrage, but it is only 50 kopecks (10¢).

Entertainment
BARS & CLUBS
Dyzga and Pid Synioyu Pliashkoyu (both opposite) are also good places for a drink.

Korzo Pub (Map p86; vul Brativ Rohatyntsiv 10) Bars are thin on the ground in Lviv and this is the closest the city has to an Irish pub. There's food and sometimes an English-speaking happy hour from 6pm Thursdays.

Lyalka (Map p86; Doll; pl Danyla Halytskoho 1; admission Sat & Sun 10uah) This favourite disco/club among Lviv's university students has a good vibe. It's beneath the marionette theatre.

Millennium (Map p86; ☎ 240 3591; pr Chornovola 2; ☺ from 9pm Tue-Sun) Attached to a restaurant, this mainstream club, with cocktails and 'show programs' (everything from fashion shows to go-go dancers) is the most popular among a wider audience. Admission varies.

OPERA, THEATRE & CLASSICAL MUSIC
For an evening of high culture, and to enjoy the ornate building, take in a performance at the **Ivan Franko Opera & Ballet Theatre** (Map p86; ☎ 728 562; pr Svobody 28). Alternatively, be wooed by the sweet strains of the **Philharmonia** (Map p86; ☎ 741 086; vul Chaykovskoho 7). Advance tickets are sold at the **Teatralna Kasa** (Map p86; pr Svobody 37; ☺ 11am-2pm & 5-7pm).

Prices range from 5uah to 100uah, with a decent seat usually 20uah to 25uah.

Shopping
Outdoor arts & crafts market (Map p86; cnr vuls Lesi Ukrainky & Teatralna; ☺ 10.30am-6pm) This large market sells rugs, embroidered blouses, wooden *pysanky* (patterned eggs), woodcrafts and lots of everyday knick-knacks.

Museum of Ethnography gift shop (Map p86; ☎ 727 808; pr Svobody 15; ☺ 10am-6pm) The souvenirs are better quality here than at the market, particularly the *pysanky*, which use real eggshells and are arguably better than those in the museum itself.

Svitoch (Світоч) is one of Ukraine's most popular brands of chocolate, and the company has many 'own-brand' shops. These include the well-stocked confectionery outlet **Svitoch** (Map p86; pr Shevchenka 10).

Getting There & Away
AIR
The **airport** (☎ 692 112; www.avia.lviv.ua in Ukrainian) is about 9km west of the centre. It's small and basic, with no ATM or currency exchange (so arrange for a transfer to your hotel beforehand). The main international flights are via Vienna on Austrian Airlines. However, you should insist on longer than 30-minute's transfer in Vienna, whatever the airline says. People regularly mention their luggage not making their onward flight to Lviv with that margin. It happened to this guide's author, too.

BUS
There are eight bus stations, but mostly you'll only need the **long-distance bus station** (☎ 632 473; vul Stryska 271), 8km south of the centre. It's reached by *marshrutka* No 71 from pr Svobody or trolleybus No 5 from pl Petrushevycha – about a 45-minute journey. From here buses go to Ivano-Frankivsk (10uah to 11uah, three hours, hourly), Chernivtsi (25uah, 7½ hours, at least one daily), Kyiv (52uah, nine hours, three daily) and some international destinations (see p186). Buses to Belarus leave from **Bus Station No 2** (☎ 520 489), which is about 3km north of the centre at the end of tram line 6.

Advance tickets are sold at the **bus ticket office** (Map p86; vul Teatralna 26; ☺ 9am-2pm & 3-6pm). Alternatively, for bus information, call ☎ 004 (until 8pm).

WESTERN UKRAINE

TRAIN

Lviv's refurbished train station is 2km west of the centre, connected to town by tram Nos 1 and 9.

Services go northeast to Kyiv (40uah to 55uah, nine to 11 hours, at least four daily), Lutsk (four hours) and Rivne (4½ hours, at least twice daily). Most services to Kyiv pass through Ternopil (10uah, three hours). There are three daily Lviv–Ternopil *elektrychky* (5uah, three hours).

Heading south into the Carpathians, there are twice daily mainline trains to Ivano-Frankivsk (three hours) and to Kolomyya (30uah, five hours). Daily trains to Rakhiv (45uah, nine hours) arrive at midnight. Further south, there are services to Odesa (55uah, 12 hours, daily) and Simferopol (75uah, 24½ hours, daily). Heading east, you reach Uzhhorod (25uah, seven hours, at least three daily).

The most painless way to acquire a train ticket is to buy it in advance at the **train ticket office** (Map p86; ☎ 748 2068; vul Hnatyuka 20; ⊙ 8am-8pm Mon-Fri, 8am-6pm Sat & Sun, closed 2-3pm). For train information call ☎ 005.

Those wanting to travel to/from Kyiv in style can opt for a cabin aboard the Grand Tour, a luxury carriage on the express night trains. Tickets (190uah one-way) can be reserved through the **Grand Hotel Tour Agency** (☎ 769 170; grand@ghgroup.com.ua), situated in the same building as the Grand Hotel (p90), or in Kyiv (☎ 044-223 5106).

DON'T LET THIS HAPPEN TO YOU

When travelling by train between western Ukraine and southern Ukraine, be very warned: Some of those trains travel through Moldova, for which you need a visa if you don't want to be tossed off the train at the border (probably at night).

The person selling you your ticket won't just offer up a warning. If you don't speak Ukrainian, ask '*tsey poh-*yizd ee-*di che-*ryes mal-*dah-*vu?' (Does this train go through Moldova?) or point to this: Цей поїзд їде через Молдову?

Although the train between Kyiv and Chernivtsi briefly crosses into Moldova, Moldovan immigration officials don't seem perturbed if you can prove that you're going back into Ukraine.

Getting Around

From the central train station, take tram No 1 or 9 to the southern end of pr Svobody; tram No 6 will take you to the northern end. A taxi is the easiest way in from the airport and should cost 25uah to 35uah. Otherwise, take trolleybus No 9 to the university or *marshrutka* No 95 to the centre. Tram and trolleybus fares are usually 50 to 60 kopecks, *marshrutky* 1uah.

AROUND LVIV

An enjoyable day trip from Lviv is to the historical town of **Zhovkva** (Жовква), 32km north. Although much more unkempt than it was during its 17th-century heyday as an artists' colony, it has a **Renaissance palace** and some nice parkland. Cossack hero Bohdan Khmelnytsky and his men reportedly marched through the 17th-century **Zvirynetska Gate** when liberating the town from the Poles in 1648. There are about eight buses daily to Zhovkva (45 minutes) from Lviv's bus station No 4. This is next to Krakivsky market at vul Bazarna 11 (a 10-minute walk northwest from the opera theatre).

Also worth seeing is the French chateau-style hilltop castle at **Olesko** (Олесько), about 70km east of Lviv. This 18th-century castle was restored in 1960–75. It's built on the site of a medieval fortress, destroyed by Tatar attacks in the 15th century. To get to Olesko, take a bus (1½ hours, eight daily) from bus station No 2 in Lviv, about 3km north of the centre at the end of tram line No 6.

See the travel agencies listed in Lviv (p85) for organised day-trips.

Some 90km southwest of Lviv lies the extremely scenic town of **Drohobych** with an historic old town centre and a brace of wooden churches. Just 20 minutes further by train is the famous spa town **Truskavets**. Four *elektrychka* leave daily to Truskavets (5uah, 2½ hours), stopping at Drohobych en route. Two mainline trains also pass through.

THE CARPATHIANS

Those who know Ukraine regard the Carpathian Mountains as a byword for hiking and skiing; they also call them a land that time forgot. Here horse-drawn carts clip-clop along potholed roads as weather-beaten folk till the neighbouring fields, and babushkas herd their geese home or take their solitary cow to be milked. Apart from the clusters of tourist development, existence is overwhelming rural. Destined to simply watch the *marshrutky*, army surplus trucks and the odd black Mercedes from Kyiv speed past, many people live off the land in the same way their ancestors did.

The mountains are divided into three sections: the low hills south of Lviv, the remote Horhanys and the southern Chornohora Range, which includes Hoverla (2061m), Ukraine's highest peak. This is modest by world standards, but what the Carpathians lack in size, they make up for in wilderness and scenery. Driving through the foothills, a gently rolling landscape dotted with peculiarly embossed tin roofs meets the eye. Once you've reached the peak of one Chornohora mountain, you can see and hike along the rest of the spectacular ridge.

Ivano-Frankivsk is the major gateway, and heading deeper into the Carpathians alone will not be for everyone. Fewer train connections mean tourists generally must rely on local buses or taxis and many hiking trails are overgrown. Furthermore, hotels, while improving fast, still tend to be either very basic or relatively expensive. So those partial to middle-class comfort, or prone to getting lost, might be better off on a guided tour. However, for adventurous travellers with plenty of time and a willingness to splash out occasionally, these mountains offer an insight into a fascinating world that few Westerners have seen.

IVANO-FRANKIVSK
ІВАНО-ФРАНКІВСЬК

☎ 0342 (6-digit Nos), 03422 (5-digit Nos)
pop 204,200

What would revered poet-patriot Ivan Franko have made of his namesake? The moniker was just a Soviet sop in 1962 to try to appease Ukrainian nationalist guerrillas in the surrounding hills, who'd been taking pot shots at them since WWII. The town once known as Stanyslaviv still has a Polish feel.

Today, with the city centre smartened up, the effect is also like being in an unfinished colouring-in book. From pl Rynok (Market Sq) to the cobbled pedestrian precinct of Vichevy maydan and vul Nezalezhnosti, the baroque churches, onion-domed cathedrals, neoclassical shopfronts and even

vulgar modern additions are all in pretty pastel tones. But move outside this central core and you still feel like you're stepping off the page into a monochrome past.

Information

Bukinist (☎ 238 28; vul Nezalezhnosti 19; ☼ 10am-6pm Mon-Fri, 10am-2pm Sat) Local maps are sold here. Bukinist is the smaller of the two bookshops here, with the far-right corner entrance.

Central post office (☎ 231 041; vul Sichovykh Striltsiv 13A)

Exim Bank (vul Nezalezhnosti 10) Has a 24-hour ATM.

Internet Point (☎ 552 580; vul Nezalezhnosti 6; per hr 4uah; ☼ 9am-9pm Mon-Fri, 9am-7pm Sat & Sun)

Nadiya Tours (☎ 537 042; tour@nadia.if.ua; vul Nezalezhnosti 40) In Hotel Nadiya; can arrange hotels in the region and conducts Carpathian tours.

Tourist Information Centre (☎ 502 474; www .tourism-carpathian.com.ua; pl Rynok 4; ☼ 11am-4pm Mon-Fri) Still finding its feet, this privately run centre is a start at least, with some English-language pamphlets about regional cities.

Ukrtelekom (vul Nezalezhnosti 9; ☼ 7am-11pm) Long-distance phone calls and internet access.

Sights

Most travellers will simply stop over in Ivano-Frankivsk en route to the surrounding mountains, but its charming centre is worth an hour or two's exploration. This charm won't be immediately obvious when you alight at the train or bus station, but it's only 10-minutes' walk into more salubrious surrounds, including the main pedestrian drag of **vulytsya Nezalezhnosti**, with all its refurbished neoclassical buildings.

If vul Nezalezhnosti is the city's modern soul, its traditional heart is **ploshcha Rynok**, where a mix of colourful buildings circle the angular star-shaped town hall. This building, built in 1929, houses a rather run-down and depressing **Regional Museum** (☎ 223 26; pl Rynok 4A; adult/child 60/40 kopecks; ☼ 10am-5pm Tue-Sun). The best things tend to be the temporary exhibitions on the 1st floor. Otherwise, you're looking at things like moth-eaten, taxidermied animals and a worryingly threadbare Cosmonaut's suit.

Much more interesting is the **Art Museum** (☎ 300 39; maydan Sheptytskoho 8; adult/child 2uah/50 kopecks; ☼ 10am-6pm Wed-Sun), with its range of icons and other religious art, in the 1703 Parish Church (Church of the Blessed Virgin Mary).

WESTERN UKRAINE

WESTERN UKRAINE

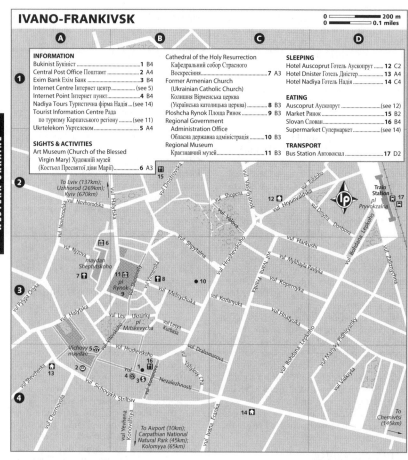

IVANO-FRANKIVSK

0 — 200 m
0 — 0.1 miles

INFORMATION
Bukinist Букініст **1** B4
Central Post Office Поштамт **2** A4
Exim Bank Ексім Банк **3** B4
Internet Centre Інтернет центр ....(see 5)
Internet Point Інтернет пункт...................**4** B4
Nadiya Tours Туристична фірма Надія ...(see 14)
Tourist Information Centre Рада
    по туризму Карпатського регіону ....(see 11)
Ukrtelecom Укртелеком **5** A4

SIGHTS & ACTIVITIES
Art Museum (Church of the Blessed
    Virgin Mary) Художній музей
    (Костьол Пресвятої діви Марії)................**6** A3

Cathedral of the Holy Resurrection
    Кафедральний собор Страсного
    Воскресіння **7** A3
Former Armenian Church
    (Ukrainian Catholic Church)
    Колишня Вірменська церква
    (Українська католицька церква).............**8** B3
Ploshcha Rynok Площа Ринок **9** B3
Regional Government
    Administration Office
    Обласна державна адміністрація **10** B3
Regional Museum
    Краєзнавчий музей...........................**11** B3

SLEEPING
Hotel Auscoprut Готель Аускопрут **12** C2
Hotel Dnister Готель Дністер **13** A4
Hotel Nadiya Готель Надія **14** C4

EATING
Auscoprut Аускопрут ....(see 12)
Market Ринок **15** B2
Slovan Слован **16** B4
Supermarket Супермаркет....................(see 14)

TRANSPORT
Bus Station Автовокзал **17** D2

Across from the Art Museum/Parish Church is the baroque **Cathedral of the Holy Resurrection** (maydan Sheptytskoho 22), a Ukrainian Catholic church. East of pl Rynok is the 1762 **former Armenian church** (vul Virmenska 6) with an attractive, undulating baroque façade and twin, rounded bell towers.

The hulking Soviet-realist edifice of the **regional government administration office** (vul Hrushevkoho 21) is unfortunately hard to miss.

Sleeping

Hotel Nadiya (☎ 537 077; www.nadia.if.ua; vul Nezalezhnosti 40; basic s/d $20/35, renovated r from $45; P) The grey-white lobby with its world clocks is very nouveau riche, but the rooms are still catching up. Cheaper accommodation features slightly itchy blankets and medical-looking shower attachments, but the more expensive modern rooms are cheerful and decent value, especially if you're travelling as a couple.

Hotel Auscoprut (☎ 234 01; www.auscoprut.if.ua; vul Gryunvaldska 7/9; s $30-60, d $40-80, ste from $85; P ✷) This quaint hotel in a 1912 private residence constitutes luxury in these parts. With only 25 rooms, there's a real personal charm and staff speak some English. The bedroom furniture is a little creaky, but the bathrooms are good, and the occasional whiff of hospital-strength disinfectant is testament to the place's spotlessness.

If you're really on a tight budget, there's the Soviet-style **Hotel Dnister** (☎ 235 33; vul Sichovykh Striltsiv 12; s/d with shared bathroom $8/12, d with private bathroom $22, ste $30-35).

Eating

There are cheap pizza and jacket-potato restaurants dotted along vul Nezalezhnosti, a reasonable supermarket next to Hotel Nadiya and a market north of vul Shpytalna that sells fresh produce.

Slovan (☎ 225 94; vul Komarova 4; mains 9-25uah) Located in the pedestrian zone, this is a local favourite for its pizza, ice-cream sundaes and specialities of the day (usually things like veal Marengo, cayenne pork and chicken fillet Hawaiian). However, it also serves Ukrainian cuisine. The low-lit interior, with its black-and-white floor tiles and black-and-white attired waiters, has Italian overtones. In warm weather, there's also outdoor seating.

Auscoprut (☎ 234 01; vul Gryunvaldska 7/9; mains 6-14uah; ☒ 8am-11pm) This hotel restaurant seems criminally underused – at least when we visited – so head up for its delicious mix of Ukrainian, Georgian, Serbian and other Central European cuisine. There's a range of wines (80uah to 110uah a bottle) to match.

Getting There & Away

AIR

Ivano-Frankivsk's tiny **airport** (☎ 598 348; vul Evhena Konovaltsya 264A) is 10km south of the city, served every 15 minutes by bus Nos 21, 24 and 65 (60 kopecks, 30 minutes) from the train station.

BUS

The bus station is right next to the train station on pl Pryvozksalna, and buses are the usual choice for heading into the Carpathians. Dozens of buses and *marshrutky* go to Yaremcha (7uah, one to 1½ hours), Vorokhta (8uah, two hours), Chernivtsi (12uah, 3½ hours, thrice daily) and Rakhiv (five hours). At least 12 buses daily go to Lviv (10uah to 12uah, 3½ hours).

Longer-distance buses also go to Kyiv (38uah to 44uah, 12 hours, twice daily) and Uzhhorod (24uah, nine hours, twice daily).

TRAIN

There are daily trains to Kyiv (42uah, 14 hours) and twice-daily trains to Lviv (20uah, 3½ to seven hours). On odd dates, there is one train to Odesa (43uah, 21 hours) and Uzhhorod (24uah, 11 hours).

Local train services serve Kolomyya (5uah, four to five daily), and Rakhiv (4uah, 5½ hours, twice daily). Three trains daily pass through to Chernivtsi (18uah, 3½ hours), but only one at a sensible time. There's another service, very early in the morning, on even dates.

CARPATHIAN NATIONAL NATURE PARK

This is the heart of the Carpathians and Ukraine's largest national park. However, it's a very different sort of national park from that which is generally understood – one in which industrial logging occurs, for example. It turns out that only about a quarter of the area is completely protected, but that hasn't detracted too much from the natural beauty of the place…yet.

Founded in 1980, the park covers 503 sq km of wooded mountains and hills, in parts sheltering wolves, brown bears, lynx, bison, deer and a host of other fauna and flora. A maze of hiking trails crisscrosses the region, which becomes a playground for skiers come winter snow. Hoverla (2061m), Ukraine's highest peak, lies within the park.

There are several villages in which to stay, discussed under individual headings later. Getting between them using public transport does require tenacity, however. If you're going to do this, leave yourself plenty of time and also budget to catch a few taxis. Otherwise, agencies in Lviv (p85), Ivano-Frankivsk (p93) and Kolomyya (p101) can organise guided tours and transportation.

Orientation

The Carpathian National Nature Park (CNNP) straddles the Ivano-Frankivska and Zakarpatska regions (*oblasti*). From the city of Ivano-Frankivsk, the A265 cuts southwards into the heart of the park. Yaremcha, 60km south of Ivano-Frankivsk, sits across the park's northern boundary. Yasinya, 37km further south along the A265, marks the park's westernmost point. Rakhiv, 62km south of Yaremcha on the A265, is just outside the southwestern boundary, but serves as a good back door into the park.

MAPS

Maps No 165 and 184 in the Topograficheskaya Karta map series (see p178) cover the park and surrounding area (1:100,000 scale), but feature few hiking trails. Mandrivnyk produces a map of Yaremcha (available in Kyiv and probably elsewhere) that marks the start of the Dovbush trail.

Activities

Although you will see plenty of churches and Hutsul buildings alongside the roads, hiking and skiing are the major reasons to be here. The following is a very brief sample of the dozens of walks in the area. Other popular destinations include Lake Nesamovyte and Mt Khomyak; detailed information on how to reach these can be found at www.members.aol.com/chornohora under 'travel info/hiking trails'.

HIKING HOVERLA

It's not the most remote trail in the Carpathians, but the popular ascent to Ukraine's highest peak (2061m) is pretty straightforward and easy to boast about to the folks back home. On a clear day, the expansive views from Mt Hoverla are also breathtaking. Initially, the trail follows the road, so how much of the way you want to hike and how much you want to cover by *marshrutka* (as far as Vorokhta) or taxi is up to you.

About 6km south of Vorokhta, you need to take the right fork in the road, west to Zaroslyak, where there's a **hotel** (☎ 03434-415 92; r from $6). En route, you will cross the boundary into the **Carpathian National Nature**

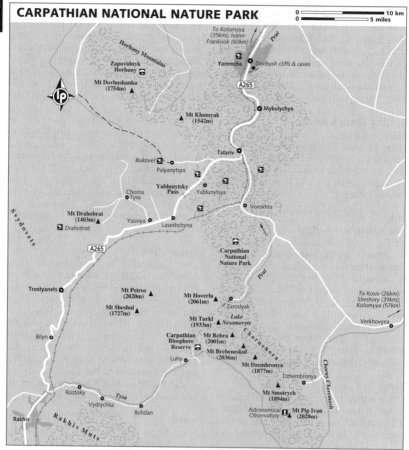

CARPATHIAN NATIONAL NATURE PARK

0 — 10 km
0 — 5 miles

To Kolomyya (35km); Ivano-Frankivsk (60km)

Horhany Mountains

Zapovidnyk Horhany

Yaremcha   Dovbush cliffs & caves

Mt Dovbushanka (1754m)

A265

Mt Khomyak (1542m)   Mykulychyn

Tatariv

Bukovel
Palyanytsya

Chorna Tysa

Yablunytsky Pass   Yablunytsya

Mt Drahobrat (1403m)   Yasinya   Laseshchyna   Vorokhta

Drahobrat

A265

Svydovets

Carpathian National Nature Park

Prut

Trostyanets   Mt Petros (2020m)   Mt Hoverla (2061m)

Zaroslyak

To Kosiv (26km); Sheshory (39km); Kolomyya (57km)

Mt Sheshul (1727m)   Mt Turkl (1933m)   Lake Nesamovyte

Bilyn   Carpathian Biosphere Reserve   Mt Rebra (2001m)   Verkhovyna

Luhy   Mt Brebeneskul (2036m)

Chornohora

Mt Dzembronya (1877m)   Dzhembronya

Roztoky   Tysa   Vydrychka   Bohdan   Mt Smotrych (1894m)

Chorny Cheremosh

Rakhiv   Rakhiv Mnts   Astronomical Observatory   Mt Pip Ivan (2028m)

Park (adult/child 5.50/1.50uah), where you must pay an entrance fee. From Zaroslyak (20km from Vorokhta) it's about 3.5km to the summit, which is marked with a big iron cross and Ukrainian national flag.

The route can get reasonably crowded in summer and litter has been a problem. At the start of the landmark 2004 presidential election campaign, Viktor Yushchenko led a large group of supporters to the peak of Hoverla on a symbolic clean-up mission.

IN ROBIN HOOD'S FOOTSTEPS

The hike to the Dovbush cliffs and caves is a relaxed three- to four-hour return walk through pleasant forest just outside Yaremcha. This area is reputed to be one of the many hideouts of Oleska Dovbush, the Ukrainian Robin Hood, and, according to legend, the site of buried treasure. During the upheavals of the early 18th century,

just after the Cossacks lost their crucial battle against Poland, Dovbush and his band of *opryshki* (highway robbers) would raid foreign landowners, killing the cruellest of them and taking their wealth to redistribute among the local Ruthenians. A series of boulders that were pushed off a cliff form 'caves' outside Yaremcha sometimes provided these folk heroes with shelter.

To get to the start of the trail, head south out of the village, cross the road over the Prut River and start on the incline past the restaurant Hutsulshchyna, continuing about 1km (passing the hotel u Galiny and restaurant Kolyba) to where a trail turns left off the road rising over the rocky drop to the river.

TO THE OBSERVATORY

The southern Chornohora peak of Pip Ivan (2028m) is well known for the abandoned

WESTERN UKRAINE

HUTSUL-MANIA

When Ukrainian pop star Ruslana stormed the stage during 2004's Eurovision song contest – and decisively snatched the crown – it was the first most dumbfounded foreigners ever heard of the country's Hutsul people. With her hair flying and feet stamping, Ruslana's anthemic *Wild Dances* strictly had more to do with skimpy outfits and leather cuffs than with authentic folkloric tradition. But if her dress and music lacked the necessary degree of flowery embroidery, the shouty singer's attitude perfectly encapsulated this hardy mountain people.

Fiercely independent and individualistic, the Carpathian-dwelling Hutsuls are a mainstay of Ukrainian national identity. They were first identified as a separate group at the end of the 18th century. But, according to some accounts, they encompass several tribes – including Boiki, Lemi and Pokuttian – so who and what they are is open to some interpretation.

Ethnographers talk of a life dominated by herding sheep from high mountain pastures *(polonyny)* to lowland fields, with a little agriculture and forestry thrown in. They point to a dialect incomprehensible to other Ukrainians, a canon of pre-Christian, pagan legends and a diet based on mountain ingredients, including mushrooms, berries, *brynza* (a crumbly cow's or goat's cheese tasting like feta) and corn-based *mammalyha* (like polenta).

Wooden architecture, particularly churches, and a host of handicrafts are also totems of Hutsul culture, from decorated ceramics and embroidered shirts to woollen rugs and embossed leather.

But whereas a traditional Hutsul would dress colourfully, carry an ornate *toporet* (hatchet) and play the *trembita* (a long alpine horn), most modern Hutsuls obviously don't bother much with any of these. The few occasions on which they are likely to drag out their folk costumes include dances and weddings. The dances, in which men in baggy trousers and women with floral hair arrangements jump up and down, are much sweeter-natured than Lviv-born Ruslana's interpretation would lead you to believe. The truly wild dances are at the weddings, where guests deck trees with paper flowers and ribbons, eat special flat breads and imbibe lots of vodka.

Hutsul souvenirs are touted throughout the region, particularly in Yaremcha. If you want more, keep an eye out for the Hutsul festivals that take place around the Carpathians each summer. There's usually one in Rakhiv in the first week of September. For more on the Hutsuls, see the boxed text, p100.

astronomical observatory atop it. The Poles completed this observatory just before WWII and anything of value has naturally been looted, but the place stills retains atmosphere. (Singer Ruslana and her crew even turned it into their studio when recording parts of the best-selling album *Wild Dances*.)

One of the routes to Pip Ivan is over Mt Smotrych from the village of Dzembronya, although even this 24km return journey usually requires a night's camping out. Afterwards, you could also continue on to Rakhiv, via Luhy.

Another option is to reach Pip Ivan by following the crest of the Chornohora ridge from Mt Hoverla via Lake Nesamovyte. This route follows the interwar border between Poland and Czechoslovakia and passes old boundary markers. At more than 40km return, the hike will take at least three days.

CARPATHIAN BIOSPHERE RESERVE
In contrast to much of the CNNP, the flora and fauna in the Carpathian Biosphere Reserve are fully protected and shelters Europe's only remaining virgin beech forest.

Ecotourism is still in its infancy here, but tours can be organised in Rakhiv, at the **Carpathian Biosphere Reserve headquarters** (☎ /fax 221 93; http://cbr.nature.org.ua; Krasny Pleso 77), 3km from the town centre. Information and a map of the reserve are available on the website.

Sleeping
For more accommodation options throughout the region, look under the individual town and village sections that follow and check out the **Bukovel** (http://bukovel.com) website.

HOMESTAYS
Many locals throughout the Carpathian region rent out rooms in their houses to travellers and those who speak a little Ukrainian or Russian – or are comfortable just gesturing – might want to look into this as a way of being part of a Ukrainian home, however temporarily. The main organisation is the **Ivano-Frankivsk Regional Association for Green Rural Tourism** (☎ 03422-730 07; www.members.aol.com/chornohora, www.greentour.com.ua). The first website is very old, but does print the addresses and contact details of

participating homeowners so you could take a chance and just turn up, or try ordering a bed through the second website. The CNNP recreation department (opposite) and CARD (p100) can also help.

CAMPING
Camping in the wild is allowed in the park, although technically you have to pay the CNNP entrance fee (adult/child 5.50/1.50uah). Lighting fires is also prohibited, although everyone does.

Getting There & Around
BUS
Buses and *marshrutky* heading south from Ivano-Frankivsk pass through the main axis of the park, including Yaremcha, Tatariv, Vorokhta and Verkhovyna. Buses heading north from Chernivtsi also go to Yaremcha. See Getting There & Around under each city for details.

TRAIN
Two trains chug their way daily across the park from Rakhiv in the southwest to Kolomyya (5uah, 4½ hours) in the northeast and back. Stops along the tunnel-clad rail route include Yaremcha (2uah, two hours).

For trains into the park from Ivano-Frankivsk and Lviv, see Getting There & Around under each city.

Yaremcha Яремча
☎ 03434 / pop 7600
Yaremcha is a pretty resort strung out along the highway. Ukrainians will warn you that it's touristy, meaning it has a large souvenir market and gets very busy in both the summer hiking and winter skiing seasons. Indeed, they're right that some of Yaremcha's 'Hutsul' restaurants and gifts seem a little too folksy. However, from a Westerner's perspective, the village is comparatively easy to reach, has some good places to stay and makes a reasonable hiking base. The trail to the Dovbush cliffs (and 'caves') lies just outside town, if you want a not-too-taxing half-day's trek. Yaremcha is also a good staging point for an ascent of Hoverla. Catching a *marshrutka* or taxi to Vorokhta or beyond, you can get to Ukraine's highest peak and back in a day or two, depending on your preferred pace. The wilder Eastern Horhany Mountains can also be reached from here.

There is usually someone in the recreation department at the **CNNP office** (☎ 211 57; cnnp@jar.if.ua; Room 20, 1st fl, vul Stussa 6; ☺ 8am-5pm Mon-Fri) who speaks English. From the main street in the village (A265), cross the railway tracks; the park office is recognisable by the stained-glass window that adorns its façade.

While it's kind of a blot on the landscape when you're looking at it from below, the **Karpaty** (☎ /fax 221 34; karpaty@itc.if.ua; vul Dachna 30; s/d full board from $32/46; ℗ ⌘ ⌂) resort complex on the hillside above the Prut River offers reasonable comfort. It has tennis courts, a sauna and solarium and is open year-round.

The three cottages on offer at **U Galiny** (☎ /fax 222 41, 227 91; www.ugaliny.com.ua; vul Svobody 333; per person from $30, 4-6 person cottage $150; ℗ ⌨ ⌂) are best for those travelling in a family or small group, as each has several bedrooms. They offer every modern comfort, but are built in a traditional style.

The red-brick gingerbread-style **Krasna Sadyba** (☎ /fax 222 53, 212 75; vul Ivasyuka 6; s/d $50-100; ℗) really does look like something out of a fairytale. Its prices are high for the region, though, so it's for those who really

want to pamper themselves after a hike, including in the *banya* (sauna).

The souvenir market is behind the theme restaurant **Hutsulshchyna** (☎ 223 78; vul Svobody), on the southern edge of town just after you cross the Prut River and start uphill.

Tatariv Татарів

A popular Central European resort at the turn of the 20th century, Tatariv is somewhat overlooked today. However, it is conveniently located for both hikes north into the Eastern Horhany Mountains, particularly Mts Khomyak and Synyak, as well as south to Hoverla. **Hotel Pigy** (☎ /fax 03434-354 04) offers simple B&B accommodation and has a restaurant.

Vorokhta Ворохта

This quiet village is the closest to Hoverla, and offers comfortable but very reasonably priced accommodation at **Kermanych** (☎ /fax 03434-410 82; vul Danyla Halytskoho 153; s/d/tr full board $40/50/90), where pleasant new log cabins have been built around a restaurant, a Russian *banya* and a Finnish sauna – great for relaxing after a hike.

OFF PISTE

The Carpathians are one of Eastern Europe's premier skiing regions and if you're already coming this way – flights are too expensive for a special trip – these slopes provide an unusual alternative to the continent's west. Prices for ski passes are 20uah to 75uah ($4 to $14) a day, and equipment rental costs around the same. Hotels can go up to $90 a double in high season, but homestays can be as cheap as $20.

- **Piligrim** (☎ 032-297 0551; www.piligrim.lviv.ua) and **Lviv Ecotour** (☎ 032-276 5121; www.lvivecotour .com) both have information on their websites and can book accommodation and/or help with transfers.

- **Slavsko** (www.slavsko.com.ua in Ukrainian) The most popular resort has blue, red and black runs, but slopes tend to get bumpy and icy by the season's end. Slavsko is 130km south of Lviv, on the railway line to Uzhhorod.

- **Bukovel** (http://bukovel.com) With a flash modern hotel, this is the place 'new Ukrainians' come to ski and be seen. The most expensive option, it also has an informative website. It's possible to visit Bukovel for the day from Yaremcha.

- **Drahobrat** (www.ski.lviv.ua/drahobrat in Ukrainian) Want to go skiing in May? At Drahobrat, 1400m above sea level, you often can. Sometimes described as offering the wildest skiing in Ukraine – the place is remote and conditions suitable only for the experienced – it's also popular with snowboarders. The resort is 18km from Yasinya.

- **Tysovets** (www.ski.lviv.ua/tysovets in Ukrainian) Once the winter sports base for the Soviet army, this has well-maintained slopes, even if some facilities are a little old. Tysovets is relatively uncrowded, as it can only be reached by road. Skole is the nearest train station, 32km away.

Dzembronya Дземброня

Past the logging trucks and the eyesore of the concrete electricity poles along the rough road in, this tiny village is in a remote, idyllic valley. You're really out in the sticks here. Dzembronya's location at the foot of Mt Smotrych makes it an ideal starting point for hikes to Pip Ivan. One villager offers homestays. If you speak Ukrainian or Russian, call her daughter Mariya on her mobile for directions: ☎ 8-067-661 7377.

Rakhiv Рахів

☎ 03132 / pop 16,000

Charming Rakhiv serves as a southern gateway to the park. Although it is more difficult to reach than Yaremcha, 65km north, it's a good jumping-off point to Romania and for hikes to Pip Ivan.

The **Carpathian Agency for Regional Development** (☎ /fax 214 06; card@rakhiv.ukrtel.net, rda@rakhiv .net; vul Myru 1) can find accommodation in *turbazy* (tourbases) and private homes, as well as ecotours. English-speakers should contact the agency via email.

One of the best places to stay is the cosy guesthouse **Smerekova Hata** (☎ 212 92; www .rakhiv-tour.narod.ru/info.html; vul Shevchenko 8; per person $5-8; [P]). There's also the ageing but larger **Turbaza Tisa** (☎ 226 90; fax 211 62; vul Ivana Franko 1; d $15).

Rakhiv hosts an annual **Hutsul cheese-making festival** early in September.

AROUND THE CNNP

Kolomyya Коломия

☎ 03433 / pop 58,700

Pretty as a picture, Kolomyya is one of the best introductions to the Carpathians for foreigners, despite being more than 50km east of the main Chornohora Range. Spruced up in 1999–2000 to host a Hutsul folk festival, it has the feel of an Austrian spa town, with a couple of good accommodation options and two interesting museums. In another country, Kolomyya might be too twee and touristy, but in Ukraine it's a breath of fresh air.

The most eye-catching attraction is the **Pysanky Museum** (☎ 278 91; vul Chornovola 39; admission 1uah; ☎ 10am-6pm Tue-Sun), which showcases the colourful, hand-painted Easter eggs *(pysanky)* that are a Ukrainian tradition (see p31). Any visiting Australians will immediately rename this the 'Big Egg' as the two-storey museum is itself that shape – reminding one of the many 'big things' that infamously dot the landscape Down Under. Inside, there are hundreds of *pysanky*, decorated in various regional designs.

Behind the Pysanky Museum, cut diagonally left towards the next street, to the **Museum of Hutsul Folk Art** (☎ 239 12; vul Teatralna 25; adult/child 2/1uah; ☎ 10am-6pm Tue-Sun). This well-curated exhibition is probably the best of its kind in Ukraine, with decorated stove tiles and other ceramics, musical instruments, carved wooden tools, boxes, furniture,

---

SHADOWS OF FORGOTTEN ANCESTORS

'A god-forsaken Carpathian region; a land of Ukrainian Hutsuls'. So declares an opening screen of one of the most celebrated Soviet films, Sergei Paradzhanov's *Shadows of Forgotten Ancestors* (1964). Paradzhanov's judgment of the Carpathians is a bit harsh, but it's no doubt made to set the scene for the tragic tale that follows. Part *Romeo and Juliet,* part *Wuthering Heights,* it's the story of how Hutsul shepherd Ivan is haunted by the untimely death of his childhood sweetheart Marika, the daughter of a rival family.

However, it's not the simple plot – based on an 1894 novel by Ukrainian writer Mykhailo Kotysyubinsky but originally emanating from folklore – that makes this a spellbinding movie. It's the flamboyant cinematography. Paradzhanov intersperses saturated colour with a black-and-white interlude and uses Hutsul customs and the primeval howl of *trembity* (long alpine horns) to great effect.

Stylised camerawork makes the movie resemble a medieval fairground one moment, and avant-garde French New Wave the next. Underpinning it all is a gut-wrenching melancholy as a heartbroken Ivan rejects all around him, resulting in tragedy. This vintage movie is still available on video occasionally, if you hunt around. The winner of 16 international film awards, it makes great viewing before visiting the Carpathians. For more on Hutsul culture, see the boxed text, p97).

AUTHOR'S CHOICE

We don't mean to spoil it by raving too much. However, past visitors have already written 'the best place I stayed in Ukraine' into the guest book of humble B&B **On the Corner** (☎ 274 37; Hetmanska 47A, Kolomyya; per person $12; **P** 🖵). And if you think travel is more about meeting people than swanning around in five-star accommodation, you might find it hard to disagree.

Whirlwind Vitaliy and his family take you into their bosom, making you feel at home. You're (over)fed delicious, Ukrainian cuisine by mother Ira – who also speaks Italian. And you're offered some of the percolated coffee that keeps twentysomething Vitaliy talking fast in Ukrainian, German and English. Help is provided in abundance, from transfers from the train station (included in the price), hiking guides (from as little as $10 a day), and rafting trips down the Dnister River, to nightclub recommendations and billiards 'lessons' from fellow guests.

On the Corner can also organise other accommodation, including homestays with a local family or a wonderful, newly-built romantic hideaway in the nearby village of Sheshory. The latter is actually extremely well priced, from about $25 per room, and easy to imagine as another best place to stay in Ukraine.

traditional and embroidered folk dress and woven wall-hangings.

In the heart of town, facing the Pysanky Museum across a pedestrian square, the relatively new **Hotel Pysanky** (☎ 203 56; hotel@yes .ko.if.ua; vul Chornovola 41; s/d/tr from $23/30/38; 🔀) has 23 cosy rooms. These already show a few minor signs of wear and tear, but they're still good value. Breakfast is served downstairs.

The train station is northeast of town. Head right down vul I Krypyakevycha and left into vul Sichovykh Striltsiv, continuing into Chornovola to the centre. There are a few trains a day from Lviv to Kolomyya, including the Moscow train via Lviv's main train station (30uah, 5½ hours,). At least four trains a day leave to/from Ivano-Frankivsk (5uah, two hours) and three or four from Chernivtsi (4uah, 2½ hours).

The bus station is southwest of the centre along vul Hrushevskovo. Buses go every half hour to Chernivtsi (7uah, 1½ hours) and every 15 minutes to Ivano-Frankivsk (7uah to 10uah, one hour). There are also regular buses to Kosiv, Verkhovyna, Vorokhta, Yaremcha and other towns in the Carpathian National Nature Park.

Bus No 12 runs between the Kolomyya train and bus stations, stopping in the centre en route.

Kosiv Косів
☎ 03433 / pop 9000

Further south, Kosiv is famed for its Saturday-morning **craft market** (🕐 6am-2pm Sat), which is a good place to pick up Hutsul crafts. Artisans from the hills roll down in their carts in

the early morning to set up shop. The best buys are snatched up by 8am. At least three daily buses go to/from Kolomyya.

Verkhovyna Верховина
☎ 03432 / pop 5300

Just as you can base yourself in Yaremcha to reach Hoverla, but actually have to go through Vorokhta, so you can base yourself in Verkhovyna for a longer trek through Dzembronya towards Mt Smotrych and Pip Ivan. Try **Hotel Verkhovyna** (☎ 215 71; vul Popov-ycha 9; s/d from $18/32; **P**).

CHERNIVTSI & KHMELNYTSKY REGIONS

CHERNIVTSI ЧЕРНІВЦІ
☎ 03721 (6-digit Nos), 03722 (5-digit Nos)
pop 260,000

Leafy Chernivtsi has lopsided charm. While in some neighbourhoods, the city is an obvious nomination for the worst-pavements-in-Ukraine award, overall it's lively and energetic. That's partly due to its student population, and a photo of its phantasmagoric university building – all red-brick Hanseatic façades, green domes and a few Moorish touches – is instantly intriguing. This, and prevailing transport routes, make the city an excellent quick stopover between the Carpathians and Kamyanets-Podilsky.

WESTERN UKRAINE

Chernivtsi was once the chief city of Bukovyna (Beech Tree Land), the northernmost part of old Moldavia (now Moldova), and it remains the 'capital' of the unofficial Bukovynian region today. In the 19th century, it was part of the Habsburg Empire and after WWI it was temporarily drawn into Romania. All this mixed history and past Jewish, Armenian and German communities have bestowed varying architectural styles and a cosmopolitan atmosphere.

Orientation

Chernivtsi is on the Prut River but the centre is a good 3km south of it. The old core surrounds pl Tsentralna. Trolleybus Nos 3 and 5 run between the bus station and the train station, stopping en route in the centre and along vul Holovna.

Information

InfoCom (☎ 552 739; vul Universytetska 1; per hr 6uah; ◷ 8am-7pm Mon-Fri, 10am-4pm Sat) A small internet centre set back off the street, with four terminals.
Kretm (vul Holovna 41; per hr 4uah; ◷ 10am-10pm) Gaming centre with an occasionally temperamental internet connection.
Post office (vul Khudyakova 6) A block north of pl Tsentralna; there's also a telephone office next door.
Privatbank (pl Rynok; ◷ 8am-7.30pm Mon-Fri, 10am-4pm Sat)
Ukrtelekom (pl Rynok 9; per hr 3.50uah; ◷ 8am-6.30pm Mon-Fri, 9am-4pm Sat, closed 1-1.30pm) Another small centre with just four computers. Ask if they're free – the 'customers' are sometimes just bored staff.

Sights

CHERNIVTSI UNIVERSITY

University buildings are often called 'dreaming spires', but Chernivtsi's is more like a trip on LSD. This fantastic red-brick ensemble, with coloured tiles decorating its pseudo-Byzantine, pseudo-Moorish and pseudo-Hanseatic wings, is the last thing you'd expect to see here. The architect responsible was Czech Josef Hlavka, who was also behind the Armenian Cathedral on the other side of the city, as well as large chunks of Vienna. He completed this building in 1882 for the metropolitans – Orthodox Church leaders – of Bukovyna as their official residence. The Soviets later moved the university here.

The wings all surround a landscaped court. Immediately to your left as you pass the gatehouse is the **Seminarska Church**

and the former theological seminary. The church, with its elongated central cupola, is now used for concerts and ceremonies. Walk through the arch into the arcaded garden off the courtyard, and around the back of the church to the door. The interior is strikingly Byzantine.

On the opposite side of the complex is the main **University Building**, its central clock tower composed of a unique, staggering cluster of forms rising up to a central cupola.

The building straight ahead as you first enter is the former main **palace residence of the metropolitans**. Two remarkable staircases are located in the far back corners, above which there's the fantastic **Marmurovy Zal** (Marble Hall). Unfortunately one of the staircases is permanently locked and you'll usually be told off if you attempt to ascend the other. However, it's always worth trying!

The university is about 1.5km northwest of the centre. Any trolleybus heading down vul Universytetska will take you there, particularly trolleybus No 2.

THE CENTRE

The **City Hall** (1847) on the southern side is the nicest thing about pl Tsentralna. The Art Nouveau building housing the **Regional Museum** (☎ 226 071; pl Tsentralna 10; adult/child 3/1uah; ◷ 9am-5pm Tue-Sun) is also appealing. Otherwise, the 'historic' town centre has been rather defiled by dirty concrete constructions.

The best thing to do is to head off for a stroll down the main pedestrian venue of vul Olgy Kobylyanskoyi. Named after a 19th- to 20th-century writer and civil activist, its vine-covered Habsburg façades give the street an attractive and aged look.

The **Music & Drama Theatre** on pl Teatralna is an attractive building, designed in the De Stijl style by the same Viennese architects who designed the opera house in Odesa (see p122).

CHURCHES

One of Ukraine's most unusual churches is **St Nicholas Cathedral** (vul Ruska 35). It's called the 'drunken church' because of the four twisted turrets surrounding its cupola. Painted dark blue with golden stars, these create an optical illusion, much like an Escher painting. The church is a 1930s copy of a 14th-century royal church in Curtea de Argeş (Romania) and was repainted in 2004.

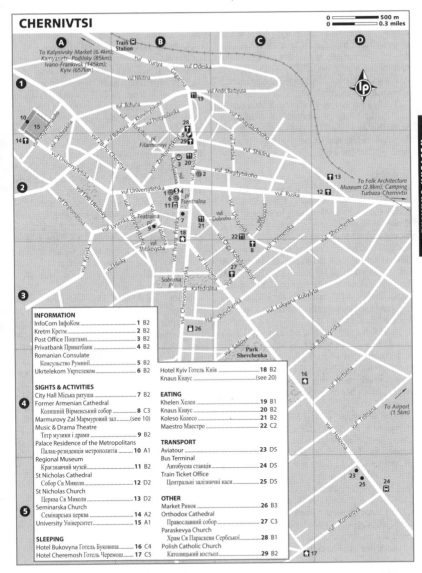

CHERNIVTSI

WESTERN UKRAINE

The other **St Nicholas** (vul Sahaydachnoho 29) is a wooden church and Chernivtsi's oldest (1607).

Not far from vul Olgy Kobylyanskoyi is the former **Armenian Cathedral** (vul Ukrayinska 30). Based on ancient Armenian architecture, it features beautiful masonry detailing. Excellent acoustics saw it turned into an organ and concert hall by the Soviets, which it still is today.

OTHER SIGHTS
Even more than the university, the reason for Chernivtsi's sense of energy is the huge **Kalynivsky Market** on its outskirts. As a conduit into Ukraine for goods from neighbouring

countries, it attracts some 50,000 shoppers a day and is frenetic. You might not want to buy anything, but all human life is here. Take any of the numerous *marshrutky* (1uah) to калинівський ринок; many leave from in front of the train station. Mornings are best; things are winding down by 3pm.

Trolleybus No 4, which runs east down vul Ruska from pl Tsentralna, goes past St Nicholas Cathedral to the open-air **Folk Architecture Museum** (Muzey Arkhitektury; admission 1uah; ☑ 10am-6pm Tue-Sat).

Sleeping

Hotel Bukovyna (☎ 585 625; www.hotel.cv.ua; vul Holovna 141; s/d $18/35, renovated s/d from $32/60; (P)) Ladas park beside Mercedes in front of this flower-festooned, cheery yellow concrete block, a clear giveaway that this is another hotel of two halves. Several floors offer flash new accommodation, while others proffer unrenovated rooms. Even the latter are bearable, despite their cracked bathroom tiles. There's a hilariously folksy Bukovynian farmhouse restaurant and the cheerful Pink Rhinoceros bar.

Hotel Kyiv (☎ 222 483; vul Holovna 46; s/d $10/22) 'Mod cons' here mean that bathrooms now have their own water boiler, guaranteeing the hot stuff on tap. Otherwise, the best you can say about this budget hotel is that it's central…but then that also means noise from the street.

Hotel Cheremosh (☎ 247 500; fax 413 14; http://cheremosh.chv.ukrpack.net/e_home.html; vul Komarova 13A; r without private bathroom $12, s/d/ste with private bathroom from $25/30/70; (P)(🏊)) This 326-room monolith would be the best value in town, if you could be sure that it was in town, that is. The 3.5km distance from the centre is a pain. Still, once you get through the giant-sized reception area resembling a train station hall, there are good rooms and lots of facilities, including a sauna. Trolleybus No 6 runs from here to central pl Soborna, but a taxi is easier.

Knaus (☎ 510 255; www.knaus.cv.ua not in English; vul Holovna 26A; s/d $45/65; (P)) This German restaurant rents a nearby apartment in the same courtyard. It's a charmingly renovated early-20th-century interior, with a modern bathroom added, in a very central location. Unfortunately, the apartment doesn't have a kitchen. In the warmer months, if the courtyard ever gets into full swing with

drinkers, you might not get to sleep very early, either.

Camping Turbaza-Chernivtsi (☎ 250 37; 2-3-person bungalows per person $5; ☑ May-Oct) This site has bungalows plus room to pitch your tent. Reception is open from 9am to 5pm. Trolleybus No 4 from pl Tsentralna ends at the camping ground, across the street from the Folk Architecture Museum.

Eating

Khelen (☎ 237 00; vul Sahaydachnovo 2; mains 1-5.50uah; ☎ 9am-10pm Mon-Sat) This is a very laidback local café with humble food that's excellent value. Choose a Formica table near the counter, or head for one of the private booths.

Koleso (☎ 237 00; vul Olgy Kobylyanskoyi 6; mains 4-30uah) Swing doors lead to the cellar bar of this rustic Bukovynian inn, where staff are dressed in folk costumes. Dishes include *varenyky*, crispy *mammalyha* and Hutsul salads. There's an English menu and a terrace decked out with beer barrels.

Knaus (☎ 510 255; vul Holovna 26A; mains 5-25uah) It's only really the beer that's German at this upmarket beer garden, and perhaps the decision to offer fresh juices and herbal teas. Otherwise the food is predominantly Slavic, from *borshch* and *banush* (wet polenta) to crepes with red caviar and *pelmeni* (Siberian-style dim sum).

Maestro (☎ 281 47; vul Ukrayinska 30; mains 15-25uah) Interesting Ukrainian cuisine and a wonderful, sun-flooded terrace overlooking the former Armenian Cathedral help make this banquet restaurant Chernivtsi's top choice. Weddings or other large parties do sometimes rent out the whole place.

Getting There & Away

AIR

Chernivtsi has a very basic airport, 5km from the centre. See **Kiyavia** (www.kiyavia.com) for schedules and prices.

BUS

The **bus station** (☎ 416 35; vul Holovna 219) is 3.5km southeast of the centre. It's best to take a bus or *marshrutka* to Kamyanets-Podilsky (8uah to 10uah, 2½ hours, at least 11 daily). Services go regularly to Kolomyya (7uah, 1½ hours), and also to Ivano-Frankivsk (12uah, four hours, at least three daily) and Khmelnytsky (20uah, six hours, three daily). Longer-distance services to Kyiv (40uah, 12

Catacombs (p123) below Odesa

JONATHAN SMITH

Potemkin Steps (p119), Odesa

JONATHAN SMITH

Odesa nightlife on vulytsya Derybasivska (p125)

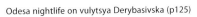

ALLOVER PHOTOGRAPHY / ALAMY

Mt Ay-Petri looms over Alupka Palace (p152), Crimea

SARAH JOHNSTONE

PETER WILLIAM THORNTON

Uspensky Monastary (p137), Bakhchysaray, Crimea

Beach at Hurzuf (p153) backed by the Genoese Cliff, Crimea

JONATHAN

hours, daily), Odesa (56uah, 10 hours, twice daily) and Simferopol (84uah, 11 hours, daily) are also available.

TRAIN
The **train station** (☎ 005, 592 432; vul Yuriya Gagarina 38) is 1.5km north of the centre. Advance train tickets are sold at the **train ticket office** (☎ 429 24, 055; vul Holovna 128; ☺ 9am-7pm).

Chernivtsi is close to the rail border at Vadul-Siret (Romania). All trains heading to Ukrainian destinations to the east, northeast or southeast pass briefly through Moldova (see the boxed text, p92).

There are local trains to Kolomyya (3uah, 2½ hours) or Ivano-Frankivsk (4uah, four hours) at least three times a day.

Mainline services include to Lviv (25uah, eight hours, one direct service daily) and Odesa (52uah, 14 hours, three daily). Services to Kyiv (44uah, 11 to 16 hours, four daily) stop at Khmelnytsky en route.

Getting Around
While trolleybus Nos 3 and 5 run between the bus station and the train station, in practice they are so jam-packed, you might decide to walk or negotiate with a taxi. Taxis are easy to find, but do quote high prices. Try not to pay more than 5uah from either the bus or train station to the centre.

Trolleybuses cost 40 kopecks, buses cost 50 kopecks and *marshrutky* 1uah (pay on board).

KAMYANETS-PODILSKY
КАМ'ЯНЕЦЬ-ПОДІЛЬСЬКИЙ
☎ 03849 / pop 108,000
Kamyanets-Podilsky is the sort of place to have writers lunging for their thesauruses in search of superlatives. Even 'dramatic, stunning, breathtaking' just will not do. Like the Swiss capital Bern, or Český Krumlov in the Czech Republic, it's located where a sharp loop in a river has formed a natural moat. However, Kamyanets-Podilsky is much wilder and more arresting. The tree-lined Smotrych River canyon is wide and 40m to 50m deep, leaving the 11th-century old town standing clearly apart on a tall, sheer-walled rock 'island'. Access is mainly via two bridges. To the southwest, there's a medieval construction, which is structurally sound enough to take only pedestrians but leads to the town's famous castle. To the

east lies a rickety Soviet bridge that shakes as cars zoom across, high above riverside houses and allotments on the lush canyon floor. Some nutters actually bungee jump here – and have lived to tell the tale.

History
Named after the stone on which it sits, Kamyanets-Podilsky existed as early as the 11th century as a settlement of Kyivan Rus. Like much of western Ukraine, the town spent periods under Lithuanian and Polish rule, with the latter dominating from the 15th to 17th centuries. Unlike much of western Ukraine, however, it fell briefly to the Ottoman Turks. They conquered it in 1672 and ruled for 27 years. Returned to Poland, Kamyanets-Podilsky was then – also atypically for a western city – conquered in 1793 by the Russians. They used its castle as a prison for Ukrainian nationalists.

In the 20th century the town's singular natural setting saw it both crowned and desecrated. In 1919 it became the temporary capital of the brief Ukrainian National Republic. However, during WWII the Germans misused the old town as a ghetto, where an estimated 85,000 people died. Intensive fighting and air raids destroyed some 70% of the old town.

Orientation
Central vul Knyaziv Koriatovychiv runs for some 1km east–west through the Soviet-style new town, from the bus station in the far east to the old town in the far west. The train station is 1km north of the bus station on vul Pryvokzalna.

Information
Aval Bank (☎ 233 44; vul Starobulvarna 10) Changes money, cashes travellers cheques and gives credit-card cash advances.
Filvarky Centre (☎ 360 24; www.filvarki.km.ua; vul Lesi Ukrainky 99) Can arrange bungee jumping, plus hiking or biking tours.
Post & telephone office (vul Soborna 9)
Post office (vul Troytska 2)

Sights
It's important not to judge Kamyanets-Podilsky too early. You'll arrive in the new town and it's impossible to appreciate the beauty of the place until you reach the bridge to the old town. Even then, many

buildings are quite run-down and feel a bit bare. It some ways, however, this just adds to the stark melodrama of the landscape.

Although Mother Nature calls most of the shots in Kamyanets, the town does have one famous man-made attraction, namely its **fortress**. You must walk across the 'island', passing many other sights, to reach this.

The old town was settled mainly by Ukrainians, Poles, Armenians and Jews. Under the medieval Magdeburg Laws, each occupied a different quarter.

EN ROUTE TO THE FORTRESS

Cross the New Bridge, stopping to admire the amazing views of the canyon floor below. Over your right shoulder on the new-town side of the canyon, you will see a **waterfall** trickling down the cliff and steps leading down to a **footbridge**. You can follow this route to the canyon floor at another time. However, all the baying dogs in poorly fenced gardens, plus nervous goats and sheep, mean a walk alongside the river is not as idyllic as possibly imagined. For now, keep on walking across the bridge overhead, observing to your left the **Black Tower** (1583) on the Old-Town side. Follow the road off the bridge, continuing as it curves to the left. After another 100m or so and you will arrive in the **Polish market square**. On your right, through a small triumphal gate lies the **Cathedral of SS Peter & Paul** (see the boxed text, p108).

WESTERN UKRAINE

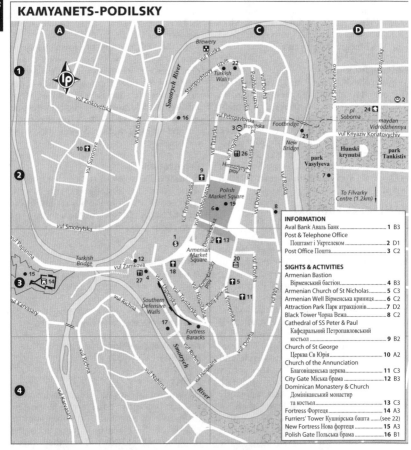

KAMYANETS-PODILSKY

In the centre of the market square you'll see the 14th-century **former town hall**, which now houses an **art gallery** (admission 2uah; 10am-5pm Tue-Sun). Nearby is an enclosed **Armenian well** (1638), and as you continue straight ahead you come to the **Armenian market square**.

Turn right here, past the red-roofed 18th-century **St Trinity's** Ukrainian-Catholic church and a clutch of cheap souvenir stalls. Beyond, the road dips past further fortifications on the northern side of vul Zamkova, the 16th-century **Armenian Bastion** and main **City Gate**. Great views of the castle are had by climbing the grassy knoll to the left of vul Zamkova, behind the restaurant Kafe Pid Bramoyu (p109).

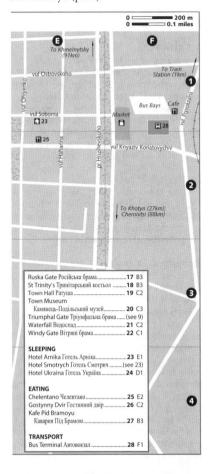

Ruska Gate Руська брама................................**17** B3	
St Trinity's Трінітарський костьол **18** B3	
Town Hall Ратуша **19** C2	
Town Museum	
Кам'янець-Подільський музей...............**20** C3	
Triumphal Gate Тріумфальна брама .....(see 9)	
Waterfall Водоспад....................................**21** C2	
Windy Gate Вітряні брама........................**22** C1	

SLEEPING
Hotel Arnika Готель Арніка......................**23** E1	
Hotel Smotrych Готель Смотрич.........(see 23)	
Hotel Ukraina Готель Україна.................**24** D1	

EATING
Chelentano Челентано...............................**25** E2	
Gostynny Dvir Гостинний двір **26** C2	
Kafe Pid Bramoyu	
Каварня Під Брамою..................................**27** B3	

TRANSPORT
Bus Terminal Автовокзал.........................**28** F1	

Anyone wishing to enter the fortified city had to initially pass the massive castle guarding the western side of the 11th-century **Turkish Bridge**; these days you walk from the east across this bridge. The name is slightly misleading, as this is essentially a medieval construction whose arches were filled in and fortified by Turks in the 17th century. Today, it's only strong enough to take pedestrians.

THE FORTRESS

Built of wood in the 10th to 13th centuries, then redesigned and rebuilt in stone by Italian military engineers in the 16th century, the **fortress** (admission 3.50uah; 9am-6pm) is a complete mishmash of styles. It's certainly not one of those attractions where you have to keep off the grass, or watch what you touch. You're given free rein to clamber all over it, which can be slightly worrying at times, especially when you feel the walkways creak below your feet and see the odd sign warning of life-threatening danger! It's best to tread carefully.

The castle is in the shape of a polygon, with nine towers of all shapes and sizes, as well as dungeons, turrets and galleries. There's a plan, with some English explanations, on a billboard just to the left after the gate. Over your right shoulder, the **New East Tower** (1544) contains a **well** and a huge winch stretching 40m deep through the cliff to bring up water. In the courtyard, stairs lead downwards to the **debtors' hole**, where locals behind in loan repayments were kept until their debt was covered; in bad years, many people smothered in the overcrowded hole.

To the far left lies the tall **Papska** or **Karmalyuk Tower** (1503–17), which was used as a prison. A plaque commemorates the folk hero Ustym Karmalyuk, imprisoned here three times between 1817 and 1823.

On the northern side of the courtyard (ahead, to your right) is an extremely musty **Ethnographic Museum** (admission 3uah), which can easily be skipped. Behind the castle to the west is the **New Fortress**, a series of earth ramparts and 17th-century stone walls.

OTHER SIGHTS

Once you've seen the fortress, you can head back to the Armenian market square. The main attraction here is the small **town**

WESTERN UKRAINE

TOP THAT!

The Cathedral of SS Peter & Paul perfectly illustrates how the Polish and Turkish empires collided in Kamyanets-Podilsky. Built in 1580 by the Catholic Poles, the cathedral was made a mosque when the Turks took over in the late 17th century; they even built an adjacent 42m-high minaret. Legend has it that when the town was handed back to the Poles by treaty in 1699, the Turks specifically stipulated that the minaret could not be dismantled. So the Poles topped it with its current 3.5m-tall golden statue of the Virgin Mary instead.

The triumphal gate leading to the cathedral has its own tale. Erected in 1781 in honour of a visit by Polish King Stanislas II Augustus, it was visited by former president Leonid Kuchma during both the 1994 and 1999 election campaigns. Each time he walked through the gate, Kuchma made a wish to be the president, and each time he won. Afterwards, reform-minded locals swore that Kuchma and his ilk should never be let near the gate again.

museum (admission 1uah; ☼ 9am-5pm Tue-Sun), which contains religious icons and scenes from folkloric tales interestingly cut from paper in an Oriental-style technique known as *vytynanka*. A Soviet-era statue of a monk carrying a naked girl in the basket on his back is also quite amusing. Ask an attendant if you can flick the switch to get him to spin around.

Besides the museum there is a brace of churches in the vicinity of the square, including the striking ruins of the 15th-century **Armenian Church of St Nicholas**, beside a reconstructed defensive bell tower, to the south. Beyond this is the refurbished **Church of the Annunciation**. To the north of the square lies the **Dominican Monastery & Church**.

If you're keen, you can check out the very north of the old town, behind the Cathedral of SS Peter & Paul, although parts of these backstreets are particularly run-down. At the northern edge of the old town is the 16th-century **Windy (Vitryani) Gate**, where Peter the Great's hat blew off in 1711. Connected to it is the seven-storey stone **Furriers' (Kushnir) Tower**, a defensive structure funded by artisans who lived nearby. From the

tower, Staroposhtovy uzviz turns southwest and descends steeply into the ravine down to the **Polish Gate**. This gate was named after the historic Polish section of the city, which was on the other side of the river around the hill dominated by the attractive 19th-century Orthodox **Church of St George**, with its five cupolas painted in brilliant turquoise. (You see this church from the fortress.)

Both the Polish Gate and the **Ruska Gate**, on the south side of the isthmus, where the Ruthenian (Ukrainian) quarter was centred, were built in the 16th to 17th centuries to guard the two most vulnerable entrances into the old town. Both gates were ingeniously fashioned with dyke mechanisms that could alter the flow of the Smotrych River and flood the entrances – an engineering feat for the time.

Activities

If you're one of the foolhardy ones who wants to **bungee jump** from the New Bridge, contact the Filvarky Centre (p105). Do have a proper look at the bridge first, though.

For something just a little less extreme, head for the very creaky **Ferris wheel** (2uah) in the local **Attraction Park** (vul Lesi Ukrainky; ☼ 10am-10pm). You have a great panorama of the old town as the wheel goes over the top.

Festivals & Events

In May **Kamyanets-Podilsky Day** is celebrated with a hot-air balloon festival. In September there are displays of jousting, horsemanship and swordsmanship in the fortress, during the **International Tournament of Knights**.

Sleeping & Eating

There are no hotels in the old town, but the first three listed here are within a 10-minute walk of it.

Hotel Arnika (☎ 318 17; arnika@kp.rel.com.ua; 8th fl, vul Soborna 4; s/d/ste $11/17/37; P) Off the dark-pink stucco hallway – better looking than it sounds – lie Kamyanets' most comfortable, clean and modern rooms. Each fitted bathroom has its own hot-water heater and singles even come with a French bed, while the young, friendly staff speak some English. Check in at the ground floor Arnika desk, to the left. Breakfast costs 30uah extra.

Hotel Smotrych (☎ 303 92; 6th & 7th fl, vul Soborna 4; s/d/tr $11/14/17; P) If Arnika is full, taking a room at Smotrych seems the easiest option. The two hotels are in the same ugly tower block, so you can just move to the reception desk to your right. Be aware, however, that the tiny drop in price brings a clunking great drop in standard. Stained carpets, older bathrooms and some dodgy electrical sockets make this only passable. No breakfast.

Hotel Ukraina (☎ 323 00; vul Lesi Ukrainky 32; s/d without private bathroom from $5/8, s/d/tr with private bathroom from $15/27/37) You'll probably find yourself rattling around this large but strangely empty hotel, although it's arguably the second-best choice in town. The rooms are typically Soviet – cosy but a throwback to a 1970s style of faux Persian rugs and polyester-fibre sofas. No breakfast.

Filvarky Centre (☎ 360 24; www.filvarki.km.ua; vul Lesi Ukrainky 99; s/d from $15/20; P) This is a popular place for locals to drink, but it's probably a bit too far out to make it anything but a last choice for accommodation. The reception area is dark and the furniture is older than you'd expect from the modern façade, but the bathrooms sparkle at least.

Gostynny Dvir (vul Trotiyska 1; mains 4-9uah) If you can forgive the spreadeagled bearskin pinned to the far wall, this refined restaurant is by far the best in the old town for food, service and even price. Despite the carnivorous, mainly Russian menu, they'll rustle up meat-free options if you tell them you're vegetarian.

Chelentano (vul Knyaziv Koriatorychiv; pizzas from 5uah) The Kamyanets branch of this pizza/pancake/salad chain is typically mobbed with young locals. There's no obvious street number, but a tacky plastic palm tree marks the spot.

Kafe Pid Bramoyu (Turkish Bridge; mains 2-17uah) It's a shame the service here is so outrageously bad and the long-awaited food so ordinary, for this *shashlyk* restaurant-café overlooks the castle and canyon, and the view is astounding. It's better to just come for a beer.

Getting There & Away

The limited long-distance transport to Kamyanets-Podilsky is one reason it hasn't lived up to its enormous tourist potential. The only direct train services are overnight to Kyiv (30uah, 12 hours), and a service to Odesa (35uah, 10 hours), which is daily May to October and every second day during the rest of the year. Otherwise, you need to make

a fairly inconvenient change in Khmelnytsky (15uah, three hours, three daily).

In fact, from Chernivtsi or Khmelnytsky, you're better coming by bus. At least eight daily buses run to/from Khmelnytsky (10uah to 12uah, three hours,) and Chernivtsi (8uah to 10uah, 2½ hours). All the buses making the 88km journey to Chernivtsi stop in Khotyn en route.

There are several bus services a day to Kyiv (30uah to 35uah, 12 hours), and one or two daily to Ivano-Frankivsk (16uah, five hours) and Odesa (50uah, 13 hours). Buses to Odesa usually don't cross the border into Moldova, but it's best to check (see p92).

Getting Around

The **train station** (vul Pryvokzalna) is 1km north of the bus terminal. You can take bus No 1 into the new or old town, or catch a taxi, which should cost 5uah to 7uah.

The **bus terminal** (vul Knyaziv Koriatovychiv) is 500m east of the new town, and about 1km from the bridge that leads into the old town. To orientate yourself when you arrive, look for the huge buzzing market to the west of the terminal.

Having checked in to your hotel, it's easiest to proceed on foot, although *marshrutka* No 19 does run from the new town into the old town.

KHOTYN ХОТИН

Although you might first pass it on the way from Chernivtsi, Khotyn is closest to Kamyanets-Podilsky and best visited as a day trip from there. There is no hotel in town.

While Kamyanets-Podilsky is awesome taken as a whole, its castle building is upstaged by **Khotyn fortress** (admission 3uah; ☾ 10am-6pm). Eastern European film makers love to use this massive fort overlooking the Dnister River as a location and it's been undergoing renovation in recent years.

With walls up to 40m high and 6m thick, today's stone fortress was built in the 15th-century, replacing an earlier wooden building. Its location safeguarded trade routes along the river and made it a sought-after prize. The defining moment in its long, interesting history came in 1621, with a threatened Turkish invasion. The incumbent Poles enlisted the help of 40,000 Cossacks and managed to rout a 250,000-strong Turkish army. This improbable victory made a hero of Cossack leader Petro Sahaydachny, whose huge statue greets you soon after you enter the fortress grounds. However, any notion that the fortress was impregnable was dispelled in 1711 when the Turks finally conquered it. The Russians took over in the 19th century.

The fortress walls have red Turkish markings and a mystery damp spot, but it's the large riverfront grounds that really make the place. Some of the outer fortification walls remain and you can clamber precariously over these. In one far corner, locals even pose for pictures where it appears they're jumping over the fortress. See if you can find the spot (facing the back of the fortress, looking at the left-hand corner). Oh, and bring a picnic.

Getting There & Around

There are regular *marshrutky* making the 27km trip between Kamyanets-Podilsky and Khotyn (3uah, 30 to 45 minutes) and every Kamyanets-Podilsky–Chernivtsi bus stops en route. The fortress is about 4km north of the bus station. It's simplest to get a taxi from across the street (about 7uah), but if you want to walk, turn right at the bus stop and head back the way you've come from Kamyanets-Podilsky. It's a 45-minute walk north along vul Shevchenko, across the market square and beyond, following the occasional sign that says 'Fortetsya' (фортеця). Turn right after the road curves and head towards a statue in the distance. Walk past the statue, through the first set of walls and through to the other side for a spectacular view down a grassy hillside towards the fortress, perched above the river.

TERNOPIL REGION

POCHAYIV ПОЧАЇВ

Its ornate golden domes rising up from the surrounding plain, **Pochayiv Monastery** (Pochayivska Lavra; ☎ 612 44; admission free; ☺ grounds 24hr, excursion bureau 11am-4pm) is a beacon of Ukrainian Orthodoxy on the edge of a largely Ukrainian Catholic region. Indeed, it's the country's second largest Orthodox complex after the Caves Monastery (p56) in the capital, and was founded by monks fleeing that mother ship when the Mongols sacked Kyiv in 1240.

The atmosphere is much more devout than at the Caves Monastery. The place is still frequently packed, but tourists are outnumbered by pilgrims visiting the Mother of God icon (1597) or the 'footprint of the Virgin Mary'. The busiest religious festivals are the Feast of the Assumption on 28 August and the Feast of St Iov on 10 September.

There are beds for Orthodox believers to stay overnight. However, the monks are cautious of curious foreigners, so tourists will almost always visit Pochayiv as a day trip, most probably from Ternopil, 75km south, but possibly even Lviv.

Even the casual visitor will find the monastery's ornate golden dome and church interiors beautiful and its mystical aura intriguing.

Both of the famous religious relics are found in the baroque **Uspensky Cathedral** (1771–83), whose entrance is straight ahead to your left, on the crest of the hill after you enter the main gate. The famed footprint of Mary, reportedly left after the Virgin appeared to a local monk and shepherd, has a holy spring with purportedly healing waters. The Mother of God is imbued with the power to work any miracle. Both are to the right of the central aisle.

The 65m-tall baroque **bell tower** (1861–71) is worth climbing for the view, if you can sneak in with a tour group or monk. Its central knocker weighs over 315kg.

On the far side of the Uspensky Cathedral is a building with a door leading down the **Cave Church**. Pilgrims come here to pay their respects to the relics (ie remains) of Saint Iov.

Because this is an Orthodox place of worship, men are not allowed to wear hats or shorts, and women must cover their head, knees and hands (no trousers, shorts or skirts above the knee). Trouser-clad women can borrow a wraparound skirt from the excursion bureau. The souvenir stalls on the way up to the monastery do a roaring trade in headscarves.

Getting There & Away

The bus station is just west of the monastery grounds. There are three daily buses to/from Ternopil (two hours), six daily to Brody (from where you can transfer to Rivne or Lutsk), and one to Lviv. There are at least seven daily buses to/from Kremenets (40 minutes).

TERNOPIL ТЕРНОПІЛЬ
☎ 0352 / pop 206,000
Ternopil's leafy, lakeside city centre is much more inviting than its wide sprawl of concrete suburbs on the way in would suggest. It has a few nice buildings and pleasant streets. As the only city in the area with halfway decent hotels, it's also the logical base for visiting Pochayiv and Kremenets. Dating from 1549, today's city was founded on the site of an earlier 14th-century fortress.

Orientation
The town centre sits between the artificial lake (to the west) and the train station (to the east). Exit into the square in front of the train station and, crossing vul Bohdana Khmelnystkoho, continue straight ahead down vul Zaliznychna for two blocks until you get to bul Tarasa Shevchenka, with the central maydan Tealtralni at its northern end. Just southwest, the main pedestrian artery, vul Hetmana Sahaydachnoho, runs west through maydan Voli to the eastern shore of the lake and Hotel Ternopil.

There's a separate cluster of development on the lake's southwestern shore, where you'll find the Hotel Halychyna.

The bus station is about 1km south of the centre; trolleybus No 9 or bus No 20 go to the centre.

Sights & Activities
The **Dominican Church & Monastery**, at the western end of vul Hetmana Sahaydachnoho where it opens up into maydan Voli, is the city's finest silhouette. Built in the mid-18th century, its twin towers rise from a baroque façade. Halfway down vul Hetmana Sahaydachnoho, opposite a fountain, vul Valova leads south (right) through a vaulted gateway onto vul Ruska and the 17th-century **Rizdva Khrystovoho Church**. The small interior is an explosion of gilded colour. From here, walk 100m south along vul Zatserkovna to Ternopil's **Regional Museum** (☎ 251 459; maydan Mystetstv; admission 3uah; guided tour 5uah; ☺ 10am-5pm Thu-Sun & Tue). Skip the stuffed animals on the ground floor and ascend to the upper two floors, which are full of impressive historic and ethnographic displays.

Bulvar Taras Shevchenko, the town's leafy showpiece and popular hang-out, is a nice venue for a stroll, with landscaping and fountains. Its northern end is maydan Teatralni, with the neoclassical **Shevchenko Theatre**.

Behind Hotel Ternopil is a bit of parkland on the lakeside with views across the water to bland postwar development. Southwest, near the water's edge, is the small 450-year-old **Zavyzhenska Church**. It is referred to as the 'Church on the Pond', as it's supposedly where Cossack leader Bohdan Khmelnytsky and his men prayed before their infamous 1649 battle against the Polish King Casimir II near Zboriv, 35km northwest.

The Ternopil region is home to dozens of karst caves, including the 212km-long **Optimistic Cave**, one of Europe's largest. These are all 100km south of Ternopil, near Borschiv. It's not really safe to visit without a tour, but unfortunately, as with so many Ukrainian sightseeing gems, tours are sometimes tricky to arrange. Try well beforehand with Lviv's **Fund of Support for Scientific and Creative Initiatives** (☎ 0332-240 4624; www.cave-ua.narod.ru) or ask at your hotel.

Sleeping
Hotel Ternopil (☎ 224 397; www.hotel.te.ua; vul Zamkova 14; s/d from $22/25) The more conveniently located of the city's two main hotels, Hotel Ternopil also has the better restaurant. On the downside, it's older, poorer quality and there have been reports of strange goings-on. The more expensive rooms offer relatively better value. Breakfast is 20uah extra.

Hotel Halychyna (☎ 533 595; vul Chumatska 1A; s/d/ste $40/55/110) On the opposite side of the lake, 1km west of the centre, this renovated, Soviet-style monolith is more modern and nicer than Hotel Ternopil, but also more inconveniently located. Take *marshrutka* No 15 or 16 from the train station.

Getting There & Away
Daily domestic services include several trains to/from Lviv (10uah, 3½ hours) and Kyiv (45uah, nine hours), plus one daily to/from Odesa (45uah, 13 hours), Simferopol (70uah, 17 hours), Kharkiv (55uah, 11 hours) and Chernivtsi (25uah, four to five hours).

A bus shuttles back and forth continually to Pochayiv (1½ hours) and there are at

WESTERN UKRAINE

least five buses a day to Kremenets (6uah, two hours) and eight to Lviv (10uah, three hours). Other destinations reached by bus from Ternopil include Chernivtsi (20uah, 4½ hours, four daily) and Kamyanets-Podilsky (20uah, four hours, two daily).

KREMENETS КРЕМЕНЕЦЬ
☎ 03546 / pop 22,000

Kremenets is a striking ruined fortress with an extremely picturesque town attached. The paisley swirl–shaped 12th-century fortress atop the Zamkova Hora (Castle Hill) was much fought over throughout history. The Mongols made it this far in the 1240s, but could never capture it from Prince Danylo. All that remains is a ring of walls and a gate tower, but it's still extremely memorable. At the foot of the hill is the **Mykolayivsky cathedral**.

The town is famous for several other things. During the Khmelnytsky uprising against Poland in 1648 (see the boxed text, p20), it was liberated by a group of Cossacks, and it was the birthplace of renowned violinist Isaac Stern in 1920. Jewish communities lived here, on and off, from the 15th century until 1942, when the Nazis massacred 15,000 people, herded into the ghetto here.

The old town centre is 2.5km south of the bus station along the main artery, vul Shevchenka, and then one block west (right) uphill. The centrepiece is the **former Jesuit Cathedral** (1731–43), built by the Poles when they regained control of the town from the Cossacks, and converted into a lyceum in 1805.

Once you've looked around the town and been to the top of the castle hill, you can stop at the **Pyatnytske Kladovyshche** (cemetery) where 100 or so of the Cossacks who died during the 1648 battle are buried. Weathered stone crosses scattered about, some bearing faint Slavonic inscriptions, mark the graves. To get there, walking north, back towards the bus station, take the first right off vul Shevchenko past the town market. Bear left when the road forks and walk for some 10 minutes uphill (northeast).

From Kremenets there are some 10 daily buses to/from Ternopil (two hours), and seven daily to/from Pochayiv (30 minutes). In addition six buses a day go to/from Rivne (2½ hours) and one bus daily goes to Lviv.

VOLYN & RIVNE REGIONS

LUTSK ЛУЦЬК
☎ 0332 (6-digit Nos), 03322 (5 digit Nos)
pop 216,000

Lutsk is well off the beaten path. The chief city of the Volyn region, it mixes Soviet architecture with a few historic gems, and the only foreigners in town are usually visiting friends or those looking for family roots, like the hero in Jonathan Safran Foer's cult novel *Everything is Illuminated*, who comes here. True, the Shatsky (or Shatsk) National Nature Park lies 160km northwest in the corner between Belarus and Poland, with some 200 lakes, rivers and streams. However, while fascinating to scientists, Ukraine's wild 'Lakes District' and its deep lake Svytyaz is a long way from appealing to all but the most adventurous of Western tourists.

Orientation & Information
The most interesting parts of town are south of pl Teatralna, at the western end of the main street, pr Voli. The traffic-free section of vul Lesi Ukrainky is the city's main pedestrian artery. It leads southwest from pl Teatralna across busy vul Kovelska, a former moat, down into the old town in a bend of the Styr River.

Sights
Known as Lubart's Castle after the Lithuanian prince who had it built in the 14th century, **Lutsk Castle** (◷ 10am-6pm) is the centrepiece of the old town. Its 13m-high brick walls are topped with three tall towers.

The real gem, however, is just west of the castle in the Jesuits' complex on vul Kafedralna. The stately white and blue façade of its Roman Catholic **Saint Peter's & Paul's Cathedral** was originally built in 1610. Its renovated interior – painted in pink and yellow tones – resembles the inside of a massive Easter egg. To one side is an entrance to the town's huge network of underground **tunnels**. Since the 16th century, locals have used these to move about freely without being seen by the authorities, whether they be Poles, Nazis or Soviets.

Between the church and the castle is the wide-open cobbled pl Zamkova. Down vul Kafedralna to the south is the plain, 17th-century **Birgittine monastery**, converted into a prison in 1846; it's now Lutsk's music academy. Across the street is a tiny park and **memorial** to Pasha Saveleva, a WWII partisan burnt alive in the prison yard by the Nazis.

If you are interested in heading to the **Shatsky National Nature Park**, catch one of the frequent buses heading to Kovel and change to the village of Shatsk. Daily buses also go direct to Shatsk. Don't consider heading this way without lashings of mosquito repellent! Start by asking at the Hotel Ukraina (following) about guides into the park.

Sleeping

Hotel Ukraina (☎ 788 118; www.hotelukraine.lutsk.ua; vul Slovatskoho 2; s/d €21/30, superior s/d €30/42; [P] [X]) Recently renovated, this 96-room, three-star hotel is central and the best in town. Even the cheapest rooms have simple modern furniture, although the curtains and bedspreads are old-fashioned. The travel bureau can help with information and excursions. Credit cards accepted.

Hotel Svityaz (☎ 434 81; fax 490 00; vul Naberezhna 4; s/d/tr $18/28/35; [P] [💺]) Overlooking the old town and on the bank of the Styr River, this larger hotel is of a slightly lower quality, but isn't an awful second choice. It does have lots of services.

Getting There & Away

The train station is 2km northeast of the centre; bus No 8 and trolleybus Nos 4 and 7 go from the station to pl Teatralna. Trains go daily to/from Rivne and Kyiv (30uah, 11 to 12 hours). Kyiv–Minsk trains (see p187) pass through. The only sensibly timed train from Lviv is the evening *elektrychka* (6uah, six hours), arriving at midnight.

The bus ticket and information office is at vul Striletska 23. There are at least three buses a day to/from Lviv (12uah, 4½ to five hours), six a day to/from Rivne (4uah, 1½ hours) and frequent services to all surrounding destinations.

RIVNE РІВНЕ

☎ 0362 / pop 250,000

Rivne is pretty dreary, and if you're staying here the best thing is to make a day trip south to **Ostroh**, where there's an attractive fortress, and **Mezhyrich**, where there's a monastery. As the Nazi's administrative capital in Ukraine, the city itself was des-

troyed during WWII and has been unattractively rebuilt since. The main street, vul Soborna, does have one nice building, the pretty **Resurrection Cathedral** (1895) at No 36, while pleasant parkland lines the Ustie River snaking through the city. In summer locals flock to **Gilcha Lake**, about 20km south of Rivne on the road to Ostroh.

Off the northeastern end of maydan Nezalezhnosti, the former Intourist **Hotel Mir** (☎ 290 470; vul Mitskevycha 32; s/d/ste from $25/45/80; [P]) is a large, concrete block, but the rooms are OK. **Hotel Tourist** (☎ 267 413; vul Kyivska 36; s/d/ste $25/55/90; [P]) tells the usual Ukrainian story: some rooms have been remodelled, others have not. This hotel is 4km from the town centre but near the bus station (and highway).

Rivne is on some major north–south train lines, with daily trains to/from Kyiv (7½ hours) and Minsk (10 hours). There is a daily *elektrychka* from Lviv (7uah, 4½ hours).

There are frequent bus services to most outlying towns and larger cities, including six daily buses to Lutsk (1½ hours), Ostroh (1½ hours) and Ternopil (four hours via Kremenets).

TRANSCARPATHIA

UZHHOROD УЖГОРОД

☎ 0132 (6-digit Nos), 01322 (5-digit Nos)

pop 110,000

Uzhhorod (formerly Ungvar) is a typical border town – buzzing, full of energy, and often quite brusque. You'll probably only pass this way if entering or leaving the country via Hungary (25km away) or Slovakia (4km distance). However, it is quite pretty, particularly the old town centre and tree-lined river embankments.

The main town of the Transcarpathian (Zakarpatska) region, it has large Hungarian and Romanian minorities, giving it a Balkan feel. The long autumn is the best season to visit, with the beeches turning and the grape harvest coming in. Troyanda Zakarpatya (a red dessert wine) and Beregivske (a Riesling) are among the best-known Transcarpathian wines.

Orientation

The old town centre lies on the northern bank of the Uzh River, which wends its way roughly east–west through town. The train and bus stations are 1km directly south, but most traffic heads northwest up pr Svobody, before crossing the main bridge (near the Hotel Uzhhorod) and turning back east to the pedestrian area and pedestrian bridge. The castle and museum of folk architecture lie about 400m northeast of this. See opposite for details on getting into town.

Information

Banks and ATMs dot the centre and aren't hard to find. There are Hungarian and Slovakian consulates in Uzhhorod (see p176).

Planeta I-Net (nab Nezalezhnosti 1; per hr 4uah; ☼ 24hr) Low-lit gaming centre–cum-office for the self-employed, offering internet access.

Post and telephone office (vul Mynayska 4) Opposite Hotel Zakarpattya, this also has internet terminals.

Sights

On the hill overlooking town is the 15th-century **Uzhhorod Castle** (vul Kapitalna; adult/child 3uah/50 kopecks, grounds only 1uah; ☼ 9am-5pm Tue-Sun), with massive walls and big bastions built to stand against the Turks. The **Transcarpathian Museum of Local Lore** inside the castle isn't completely fabulous, but it does have its moments, and the grounds are peaceful. Wander behind the building to the far corner where you can peer over the thick wall and look down on the town below.

Doing this, you'll also spy the open-air **Folk Architecture & Life Museum** (adult/child 3/1uah; ☼ 10am-6pm Wed-Mon) next door. It's one of the tidiest and nicest of its kind in the country, albeit small. The highlight, **St Michael's Church**, is shut and but can be admired from the exterior.

Between the pedestrian bridge and the castle are the Moorish red-brick **Philharmonia building** (☎ 332 38; pl Teatralna) and the tiny **Transcarpathian railway**, which putts 1km east along the river in summer.

Sleeping

Hotel Atlant (☎ 614 095; www.hotel-atlant.com; pl Koryatovycha 27; s/d from $18/34; P ⚅) This cosy, friendly place is the most central and pleasant in town, with homy rooms and its own heating. The only downside is that it only has 21 rooms and so you usually need to book. Credit cards accepted.

Hotel Uzhhorod (☎ 235 060; hotel@email.uz.ua; pl Bohdana Khmelnytskoho 2; standard s/d $16/32, 'luxury'

s/d $34/50; P) Renovations are slowly transforming this 200-bed monolith, but work might still be needed on the slightly temperamental hot water and the heating. At least the service is friendly. Chocolates on your pillow might be naff elsewhere, but in Ukraine it strangely feels like luxury.

Hotel Zakarpattya (☎ 975 10; fax 973 04; pl Kyryla i Mefodya 5; s/d $37/50; P ⌨) Much the same as the Uzhhorod – huge, concrete, Soviet-style and chilly in autumn. However, this is the most convenient for the train and bus stations. You might get a kick out of the rooms if you're into 1970s retro kitsch, but the poor lighting – no ceiling lights just standing lamps – is a tad impractical.

Hotel Svitanok (☎ 343 17; svitanok@svitanok.uzhgorod.ua; vul Koshytska 30; s/d $8/16) Uzhhorod's cheapest accommodation is ironically on a street 1km north of the centre called 'millionaires' row'. This is really a budget hotel selling itself as a hostel, but is quite decent – and probably more so seen without a citywide power outage (as when we visited). Three buildings here are called Svitanok; you want the white one with blue edging.

Eating & Drinking

Delfin (☎ 350 93; nab Kyivska 2; mains 15-60uah) Uzhhorod isn't exactly a culinary capital, but this is highly rated by locals. It serves a mix of European and Ukrainian dishes, and is on the southern bank of the river.

Pid Zamkom (Under the Castle; ☎ 369 83; vul Ivana Olbrakhta 3; ☼ 7.30am-11pm) Full of Transcarpathian knick-knacks from bottles to antique motorbikes, this smoky pub is a magnet for Uzhhorod's alternative types. Very basic snacks are served.

Getting There & Away

AIR

There's at least one flight an evening (and sometimes two) from Kyiv to Uzhhorod's **airport** (☎ 975 04, 428 71; vul Sobranteska 145), 2km northwest of the centre. Check the website of **Kiyavia** (www.kiyavia.com) for flight details.

BUS

Uzhhorod's **bus station** (vul Zaliznychna 2) is opposite the train station at the southern end of pr Svobody. Daily cross-border buses link Uzhhorod with Michalovce (27uah, three hours) and Košice (13uah, two hours) in Slovakia and with Nyíregyháza (26uah, three hours) in Hungary.

Marshrutky go to Chop (2uah, 45 minutes) roughly every 15 minutes, and to Mukacheve (3uah, 50 to 60 minutes), nominally every half hour, but more likely when they're full. There are twice-daily buses to Lviv (20uah, four hours) and to Chernivtsi (32uah to 35uah, 10 to 12 hours), the latter stopping en route at Rakhiv (20uah, 6½ hours). An overnight service run by **Autolux** (www.autolux .com.ua) goes to Kyiv (65uah, 14 hours).

TRAIN
Daily trains to Kyiv pass through nearby Chop from Slovakia and Hungary, so Uzhhorod makes a good stopover, particularly when travelling eastwards. In this direction, it's easier to get off at the border and take a bus or taxi to Uzhhorod, to avoid the long wait while the train's wheel-gauge is changed (see p187).

Onwards, there are trains thrice-daily to Lviv (25uah, seven hours) and two services daily to Kyiv (50uah to 55uah, 20 to 21 hours), one of which leaves from Chop. There are also a couple of services every other day to Carpathian towns, such as to Ivano-Frankivsk (25uah, 11 hours).

Heading westwards from here, take a bus to Chop, and hop on the train there.

Getting Around
On leaving the train station, you'll see the bus station diagonally to the left (west). Directly ahead, across the roundabout, a street to the station's right heads northwest. This is pr Svobody. Go to the bus shelter on pr Svobody that's opposite the bus station, where *marshrutka* No 5 or 16 will take you into town, past the hotels Zarkarpattya and Uzhhorod, landing you near the market, which is right by Hotel Atlant.

Alternatively, it's about a 1.5km walk. After 1km, you should turn right along the embankment after you cross the main bridge. A taxi from the train station to the centre should cost no more than 5uah to 6uah.

MUKACHEVE МУКАЧЕВО
☎ 03131 / pop 90,000
Arriving by road from Uzhhorod, Mukacheve's Zamkova Hora (Castle Hill) seems to pop up like a fairy-tale fantasy from the surrounding flat plain; the city's refurbished pedestrian centre reinforces the picturebook impression, with cobblestones and pastel-coloured neoclassical façades. Things are more chaotic around the edges, but the rustic horses and carts competing for road space with weaving *marshrutky* and speeding taxis keep up the romantic image.

Mukacheve's 14th-century **Palanok Castle**, atop Zamkova Hora, is as charming up close as it seems from a distance. Although a lot of it's bare, there are a couple of good exhibits – with a few English explanations – and very pleasant views (including from the ladies' toilet in the upper courtyard!). The castle is particularly famous among Hungarians, as the base for princess Ilona Zrini, whose army fought off invaders for years.

To get here, catch bus No 3-4, No 3-9, No 14-1 or any bus or *marshrutka* heading to тімірязева. These leave from the busy bus stop at the opposite end of the pedestrian zone to the hard-to-miss **Hotel Star** (☎ 548 80; www.star-ar.mk.uz.ua in Ukrainian; vul Myru 10-12; s $35, d from $45, semideluxe r from $70, ste $125; P ⚙). This yellow neoclassical building on the edge of the pedestrian zone houses a 60-room, truly Western-standard hotel that's astoundingly good for a town this size and exceeds anything in downtown Uzhhorod. Rugs run down stone-floored halls and dark wooden doors lead to spotless new rooms with minibar, international satellite TV and safe. Marks deducted for the jolting lift.

Getting There & Away
The train station is 1.5km southwest of central vul Myru. To get to the centre from the train station, head straight up vul Yaroslava Mudroho (вул Ярослава Мудрого), which brings you to the pedestrian zone on vul Myru, with the Hotel Star one block to your left. Services between Kyiv and Budapest stop on the way through. If you break your train journey in Mukacheve on the way out of Ukraine, be prepared for the long border wait an hour down the line at Chop (see p187) when you recommence your journey.

Heading eastwards, daily trains go to Lviv (30uah, six hours) and Kyiv (50uah to 60uah, 19 hours).

To get to Uzhhorod (3uah, 50 to 60 minutes, every half hour) it's much faster to take the bus. The bus station is 1.5km east of the centre off vul Myru, the street extending southeast from pl Myru.

Southern Ukraine
Південна Україна

This southerly region once helped make Russian empress Catherine great. As part of her territorial acquisitions in the late 18th century, it vastly expanded her dominion and brought Russia huge wealth by opening it on to the Black Sea. Novorossiya, or new Russia, as it was ambitiously christened, had been a wild-west no-man's-land between the domain of the Cossacks and that of the Crimean Tatars. Under Catherine, it became a melting pot, as Bulgarians, Germans, Greeks, Italians, Moldavians, Russians, Swedes and many others were invited to populate the area and set up business along this trading coast.

That history, coupled with a temperate climate, has shaped the character of today's region, especially the largest city, Odesa (Odessa in Russian). Entrepreneurial and cosmopolitan, with Russian, French, Greek, Italian and Jewish cultural touchstones, Odesa is also Ukraine's capital of hedonism. Closer than Crimea to Kyiv, with sandy beaches and a wicked nightlife, it's a favourite weekend break from the capital and is in many ways cooler.

However, southern Ukraine has more to offer than Odesa's *joie de vivre* and attitude. It's also home to three major river estuaries. The Dnipro empties into the Black Sea 60km east of Odesa and the mouth of Dnister estuary is 40km southwest. But the most spectacular – and, sadly, the most threatened – is the Danube estuary in the country's far southwest corner. Here, in the small Ukrainian nook of Europe's largest wetlands, you'll find more than 300 different bird species, 90 types of fish, and animals such as mink, freshwater otter and monk seal.

Even nature seems to emphasise the multicultural theme. Elsewhere around southern Ukraine you'll find an African-style safari park created by a German settler, the 'Ukrainian Venice' and an isolated city of Swedes.

SOUTHERN UKRAINE

HIGHLIGHTS

- Enjoy a movie moment on Odesa's massive **Potemkin Steps** (p119)
- Hit the restaurants in and around central **vul Derybasivska** (p125)
- Enter the **catacombs** (p123) that WWII partisans made their base when fighting pro-Nazi Romanian troops
- Do a club-crawl around **Arkadia beach** (p122 and p126) during summer
- Spend a winter's evening with Odesa's much-lauded **orchestra** (p126)
- Punt down the canals of the Ukrainian Venice, **Vylkovo** (p128)
- Spot zebras, bison and flamingos at the **Askaniya Nova Reserve** (p128)

Odesa Catacombs ★
★ Odesa
Askaniya Nova ★ Reserve
★ Vylkovo

- POPULATION: 4.8 MILLION
- HIGHEST POINT: NOTHING OVER 200M

SOUTHERN UKRAINE

ODESA ОДЕСА

☎ 048 (7-digit Nos), 0482 (6-digit Nos)
pop 1 million

Odesa is a city straight from literature – an energetic, decadent boomtown. Its famous Potemkin Steps sweep down to the Black Sea and Ukraine's biggest commercial port. Behind them, a cosmopolitan cast of characters makes merry among pastel neoclassical buildings lining a geometrical grid of leafy streets.

Immigrants from all over Europe were invited to make their fortune here when Odesa was founded in the late 18th century by Russia's Catherine the Great. And these new inhabitants gave Russia's southern window on the world a singular, subversive nature.

As well as becoming a duty-free port and a major mafia stronghold – it still is the latter – Odesa also attracted ordinary holidaymakers with its sunny climate, self-confidence and sandy beaches. True, the city's appearance grows tattier as you head south past half-empty sanatoriums towards its beachside nightclubs. However this East–West crossroads makes up for that with sheer panache.

Local writer Isaac Babel claimed Odesa had 'more charm than any city in the Russian Empire' and that's probably still true in modern-day Ukraine. The credit must go to Odesans themselves. A breed apart, they're stylish, cultured, funny, savvy and not that easily impressed.

History

Catherine the Great imagined Odesa as the St Petersburg of the South. Her lover, general Grygory Potemkin, laid the groundwork for her dream in 1789, by capturing the Turkish fortress of Hadjibey, which previously stood here. But Potemkin died before work began on the city in 1794 and his senior commanders oversaw its construction instead. The Spanish-Neapolitan general Jose de Ribas, after whom the main street, Derybasivska, is named, built the harbour. The Duc de Richelieu, an aristocrat fleeing the French Revolution, became the first governor from 1803 to 1814. The city's name harks back to early Greek civilisations along this coast.

In 1815 things really began to boom, when the city became a duty-free port. Its huge appetite for more labour meant the city became a refuge – 'Odesa Mama' – for runaway serfs, criminals, renegades and dissidents. By the 1880s it was the second-biggest Russian port, with grain the main export, and an important industrial base.

This was the crucible of the early 1905 workers' revolution, with a local uprising and the mutiny on the battleship *Potemkin Tavrichesky*. And between 1941 and 1944, Odesa sealed its reputation as one of Stalin's 'hero' cities, when partisans sheltering in the city's catacombs (see p123) during WWII put up a legendary fight against the occupying Romanian troops (allies of the Nazis).

Odesa was once a very Jewish city, too, from which its famous sense of humour derives. Jews initially came to escape persecution, but tragically suffered the same fate here. In the early 20th century, they accounted for one third of the city's population, but after horrific pogroms in 1905 and 1941 hundreds of thousands emigrated. Many moved to New York's Brighton Beach, now nicknamed 'Little Odesa'.

Orientation

Central Odesa is laid out in a grid, stretching south from Prymorsky bul, which overlooks the passenger port. The port is in the middle of a 35km S-bend in the coast, with the city stretching several kilometres back from the seafront to the north and south. Most activity occurs on and around vul Derybasivska, part of which is pedestrianised.

Odesa is a mainly Russian-speaking town, rather than Ukrainian-speaking. Street signs are in both languages, but often twisted in the wrong direction.

Information
BOOKSHOPS
Knizhnaya Perlina (☎ 358 404; vul Derybasivska 14; 🕑 10am-10pm) A few maps and some English-language books.

INTERNET ACCESS
Internet Planet (☎ 724 2177; vul Rishelevska 58; per hr 6uah; 🕑 24hr)

INTERNET RESOURCES
www.odessaglobe.com News and some basic city information.
www.theodessaguide.com Comprehensive listings, although a bit out-of-date.

POST
Central post office (☎ 266 467; vul Sadova 10)

TRAVEL AGENCIES
Eugenia Travel (☎ 220 554; janna@eugen.intes.odessa .ua; vul Rishelevska 23) Manager Janna is one of those rare gems of a Ukrainian travel agent who speaks excellent English, knows her stuff and offers good service and some of the best prices. Eugenia also has a branch at the port.
Katamaran Tour (☎ 358 508; office@katamarantour .com; vul L Schmidta 16/2) Relatively new travel agency, which offers tours and apartments to rent.
London Sky Travel (☎ 729 3196; lstravel@lst.com.ua; Boat Passenger Terminal, vul Prymorska 6) Arranges boat and other journeys.

Dangers & Annoyances

Even lovable rogues are sometimes just rogues and Odesa has a marginally higher rate of petty street crime than many Ukrainian cities, including bag snatching. Be careful on less-well-lit streets. There is also the occasional drunken scuffle along the Arkadia Beach strip at night.

Odesa is unfortunately a huge mecca for 'dating/marriage agency' clients from the West. Along with nearby Mykolayiv, it's also the epicentre of Ukraine's runaway HIV epidemic (see p195).

All in all, though, the city's seedy underbelly is easy to avoid if you stick to the mainstream.

Sights & Activities
POTEMKIN STEPS & PRYMORSKY BULVAR
If you've ever been to the movies, you'll want to head to the **Potemkin Steps**; they're the site of one of cinema's most famous scenes (see the boxed text, p122).

The stairs are in the renovated, most beautiful part of town and reached along the tree-lined **Prymorsky bulvar**, a pedestrian zone with replica 19th-century gas lamps, to which the whole city gravitates. At the boulevard's eastern end, you'll pass the pink and white colonnaded **Odesa City Hall**, originally the stock exchange and later housing the Regional Soviet Headquarters. The cannon here is a war trophy captured from the British during the Crimean War.

Continuing along the boulevard, you'll reach a **statue** of Odesa's first governor, the Duc de Richelieu, looking like a Roman in a toga at the top of the stairs. The view from here is of the passenger port, the towering

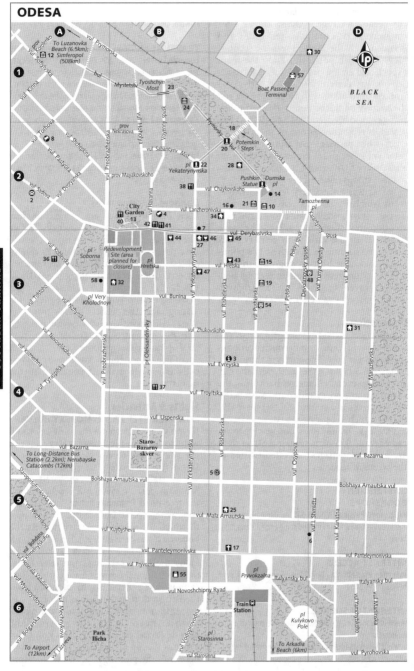

ODESA

BLACK
SEA

SOUTHERN UKRAINE

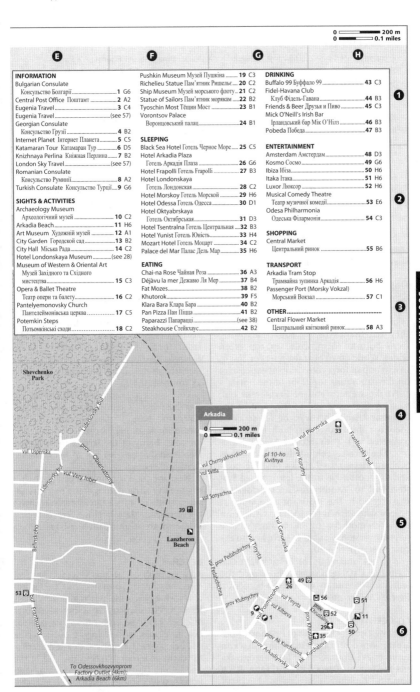

INFORMATION
Bulgarian Consulate
　Консульство Болгарії..........................1 G6
Central Post Office Поштамт 2 A2
Eugenia Travel 3 C4
Eugenia Travel ....(see 57)
Georgian Consulate
　Консульство Грузії 4 B2
Internet Planet Інтернет Планета....5 C5
Katamaran Tour Катамаран Тур 6 D5
Knizhnaya Perlina Книжная Перлина.......7 B2
London Sky Travel............................(see 57)
Romanian Consulate
　Консульство Румынії 8 A2
Turkish Consulate Консульство Турції ..9 G6

SIGHTS & ACTIVITIES
Archaeology Museum
　Археологічний музей 10 C2
Arkadia Beach 11 H6
Art Museum Художній музей 12 A1
City Garden Городской сад 13 B2
City Hall Міська Рада 14 C2
Hotel Londonskaya Museum ....(see 28)
Museum of Western & Oriental Art
　Музей Західного та Східного
　мистецтва 15 C3
Opera & Ballet Theatre
　Театр опери та балету....................16 C2
Pantelyemonovsky Church
　Пантелеймонівська церква 17 C5
Potemkin Steps
　Потьомкінські сходи.......................18 C2

Pushkin Museum Музей Пушкіна 19 C3
Richelieu Statue Пам'ятник Рішельє....20 C2
Ship Museum Музей морського флоту.21 C2
Statue of Sailors Пам'ятник морякам 22 B2
Tyoschin Most Тёщин Мост...............23 B1
Vorontsov Palace
　Воронцовський палац......................24 B1

SLEEPING
Black Sea Hotel Готель Черное Море.....25 C5
Hotel Arkadia Plaza
　Готель Аркадія Плаза 26 G6
Hotel Frapolli Готель Frapolli 27 B3
Hotel Londonskaya
　Готель Лондонская 28 C2
Hotel Morskoy Готель Морской 29 H6
Hotel Odessa Готель Одесса 30 D1
Hotel Oktyabrskaya
　Готель Октябрьская.........................31 D3
Hotel Tsentralna Готель Центральная 32 B3
Hotel Yunist Готель Юність 33 H4
Mozart Hotel Готель Моцарт 34 C2
Palace del Mar Палас Дель Мар.........35 B2

EATING
Chai-na Rose Чайная Роза 36 A3
Déjàvu la mer Дежавю Ля Мер...........37 B4
Fat Mozes...38 B2
Khutorok..39 F5
Klara Bara Клара Бара 40 B2
Pan Pizza Пан Пицца 41 B2
Paparazzi Папараци ....(see 38)
Steakhouse Стейкхаус.......................42 B2

DRINKING
Buffalo 99 Буффало 99 ....43 C3
Fidel-Havana Club
　Клуб Фідель-Гавана......................44 B3
Friends & Beer Друзья и Пиво 45 C3
Mick O'Neill's Irish Bar
　Ірландський бар Мік О'Нілл.........46 B3
Pobeda Победа..................................47 B3

ENTERTAINMENT
Amsterdam Амстердам......................48 D3
Kosmo Космо.....................................49 G6
Ibiza Ібіза..50 H6
Itaka Ітака..51 H6
Luxor Люксор....................................52 H6
Musical Comedy Theatre
　Театр музичної комедії.................53 E6
Odesa Philharmonia
　Одеська Філармонія.......................54 C3

SHOPPING
Central Market
　Центральний ринок........................55 B6

TRANSPORT
Arkadia Tram Stop
　Трамвайна зупинка Аркадія 56 H6
Passenger Port (Morsky Vokzal)
　Морський Вокзал 57 C1

OTHER
Central Flower Market
　Центральний квітковий ринок.............58 A3

SOUTHERN UKRAINE

AS SEEN ON SCREEN

Regularly voted one of the most influential films of all times, Sergei Eisenstein's *Battleship Potemkin* (1925) has guaranteed Odesa cinematic immortality. The B&W classic's most renowned sequence is a massacre of innocent civilians on the Potemkin Steps, during which a baby in a pram is accidentally pushed off the top and bounces in agonising slow motion down the 192 stairs.

But as with all great art, the scene is partly fiction. Sailors aboard the battleship *Potemkin Tavrichesky* did mutiny over maggot-ridden food rations while in Odesa harbour, and that mutiny did spark a revolution in 1905. However, locals running to the shore to support the sailors were never shot by tsarist troops on the steps – although they were killed elsewhere in the city.

None of this, however, detracts from the drama of the great Russian director's brilliant edit, which still moves audiences today. Made as Soviet propaganda, his film was banned in some Western countries for years, but since reemerging it's been frequently copied. Babies in prams have bounced down stairs in many films, most notably Brian de Palma's *The Untouchables* (1987).

In 2004 the Pet Shop Boys composed a new *Potemkin* soundtrack. It wasn't very well-received, but it did reawaken interest in the original film. *Battleship Potemkin* and its pivotal staircase sequence went on to appear at the 2005 Berlin Film Festival... Oh yeah, the baby survives.

Hotel Odessa and the Black Sea. The scene is probably better from the bottom of the steps, where the designer's optical illusion takes effect. The stairs seem higher than they are, thanks to a gradual narrowing from bottom (21m wide) to top (13m wide). While down near the port you might like to pop in for a coffee (albeit expensive) on the panoramic top floor of the hotel.

At the western end of Prymorsky bul, back up the stairs and to the right, is the **Vorontsov Palace**. This was the residence of the city's third governor, built in 1826 in a classical style with interior Arabic detailing. The terrace behind the palace offers brilliant views over Odesa's bustling port, and the footbridge to the left is called **Tyoschin Most** or 'Mother-in-Law's Bridge'. It was erected in the 1950s for a communist official who wished to facilitate visits from his wife's mother – or, in the story's more popular version, wanted to leave her no excuse to stay overnight.

A block inland is pl Yekaterynynska, featuring a **statue of sailors** who staged the famous 1905 mutiny aboard the battleship *Potemkin Tavrichesky*.

CITY CENTRE

The low-rise blocks south of Prymorsky bul are tree-lined, and at their liveliest on warm summer evenings. On vul Lanzheronivska sits the famous **Opera & Ballet Theatre**. It's a beautiful building, designed in the 1880s by Viennese architects in Habsburg baroque style. However, it's become a running city joke. Covered in scaffolding since 1996 for renovation, it was still shut some eight years later when, despite a personal order from then–Ukrainian president Leonid Kuchma to hurry up, the money for the facelift ran out. It possibly remains closed as you read this.

Odesa's main commercial street, vul Derybasivska, is jam-packed with restaurants and bars. It also contains the **city garden** where all manner of tacky souvenirs are sold. Many of the streets radiating off Derybasivska are also full of bars, restaurants and shops.

Near the train station you can't help but spy the five silver domes of the newly renovated, 19th-century **Panteleymonivsky Church** (vul Panteleymonivska 66). However, churches in Odesa are – unusually for Ukraine – a minor attraction.

BEACHES

Lots of people do swim at Odesa's crowded, dirty beaches in summer, but that's not really what beach-life here is about. With its English, Victorian-style sideshows and lines of cafés, bars and clubs, the most popular beach, **Arkadia**, is for hanging out – seeing and being seen. It's one of the easiest beaches to reach; take tram No 5 to the end of the line, along the lovely tree-lined **bul Frantsuzsky**. As you travel down the boulevard, enjoy the views of the old sanatoriums. Number 10, with an elaborate, iron-lace gate designed in the shape of grapes is the **Odessovkhozvynprom factory outlet** (☎ 221 774; wineprom@farlep.net; ☼ 8am-3pm Mon-Fri).

Lanzheron Beach, near Shevchenko Park, has a more family-orientated atmosphere, with a cable car and a dilapidated fun fair.

The further south you go, the cleaner and less crowded the sand becomes. Good options are **Kurortny** and **Zoloty Plyazh** (Zolotoy Bereg in Russian, or Golden Beach). Both are in the area known as Bolshoy Fontan. To get here by public transport requires a few changes, so it's better to catch the tram to Arkadia and catch a taxi onwards.

There's also a popular beach about 6km north of the centre, called **Luzanovka**.

With a recent clean up of the beaches, the local government has declared the water around Odesa is no longer a health risk to swim in, although you still might want to exert some caution.

CATACOMBS

The sandstone on which Odesa stands is riddled with some 1000km of tunnels, and these have always played an important part in the city's history. Quarried out for building in the 19th century, they were first used to hide smuggled goods. But during WWII they sheltered a group of local partisans, who waged a war of attrition against the occupying Romanians and forced the Nazis to keep more men in the area.

With some visitors having become lost in the catacombs never to return, it's foolhardy not to take a guided tour. Ask your hotel or a travel agency – Eugenia Travel (p119) offers this tour for $25. Cheaper, Russian-language tours leave from outside the train station in summer. Keep an eye out for guides with megaphones.

Today, the tunnels contain rusty bedsteads, school desks, pictures of Soviet leaders and old ammunition. They exit into the musty **Museum of Partisan Glory**.

MUSEUMS

Odesa's museums are of a high standard for Ukraine, but in such an outdoorsy city they seem a bit out of place.

The **Museum of Western & Oriental Art** (☎ 224 815; admission 2uah; vul Pushkinska 9; ☼ 10.30am-6pm Thu-Tue) covers Chinese and Japanese porce-

lain, European masters (such as Caravaggio and Canaletto) and Russian art.

Gold jewellery and coins from early Black Sea civilisations (and a few Egyptian mummies) are showcased at the **Archaeology Museum** (☎ 226 302; vul Lanzheronivska 4; admission 2uah; ☼ 10am-6pm Tue-Sun).

Pushkin Museum (☎ 251 034; vul Pushkinska 13; admission 3.50uah; ☼ 10am-5pm Tue-Sun) is where Alexander Pushkin spent his first days in Odesa, after being exiled from Moscow by the tsar in 1823 for radical ideas. But governor Vorontsov humiliated the writer with petty administrative jobs, and it took only 13 months, an affair with Vorontsov's wife, a simultaneous affair with someone else's wife and more radical ideas for Pushkin to be thrown out of Odesa too. Somehow, he still found time while in town to finish the poem 'The Bakhchysaray Fountain' (see p137), write the first chapter of *Eugene Onegin* and scribble the

---

MUSEUM ETIQUETTE

Most museums in Ukraine are state-owned and desperately short of funds. So much so, they keep the lights off when rooms are empty. This, combined with a generalised notion that there's a right way of seeing things, means that when you enter many provincial Ukrainian museums you'll be expected to follow a predefined trail. Don't think that, as a paying customer, you can skip the bits that bore you; you'll be told which room to enter first and the attendant will follow you to turn on the lights. Thereafter, you'll be shadowed and directed where to go.

Meanwhile, many attendants are amateur artists and will try to sell you examples of their own handiwork to supplement their meagre income. If you like the works, buy them. If you don't want to be approached, keep moving quickly.

…But not too quickly, as whizzing through even the mustiest exhibits is seen as ignorant and insulting. In Odesa's Pushkin Museum (above), this guide's author glanced too quickly over portraits of the poet's relatives, and – hilariously – was hauled back like a naughty schoolchild and given an on-the-spot quiz/lecture on Pushkin's rather fraught love and family life!

TALES OF ODESA

Odesa could have come from the imagination of German playwright Bertolt Brecht, but in reality it had its own chronicler, Isaac Babel. Indeed, the city's colourful image is often rooted more in his fiction than in strict fact.

Babel was born in 1894 in Odesa to a middle-class Jewish family. His most famous creation was Benya Krik, a Jewish gangster boss whose exploits dominate the *Odesa Tales* (1922–27). Based on a real mobster who used the improbable nom de guerre Mischa Yaponchik (Micky Japanese), Benya has an idiosyncratic code of honour. In 'How it was Done in Odesa', our 'hero' stages a lavish funeral for the accidental victim of his henchman Savely Butzis, before insisting the huge crowd of mourners move over to the graveside of 'Savely Butzis, unknown to you, but already deceased…'. In 'The King', he falls in love at first sight with his soon-to-be wife while slaughtering her father's cows and forestalls a police raid of his sister's gangster-filled wedding by arranging a fire in the police station.

Told in Babel's wonderfully terse, ironic style and set against a backdrop of Odesa's imported riches, swaggering mafioso and 'bawdyhouses' (brothels), such lightweight anecdotes gained immense popularity. But like so many writers unfortunate enough to be contemporaries of Stalin, Babel himself fared less well. The authorities objected to his portrayal of Soviet officers in his semiautobiographical account of the 1917 Civil War, *Red Cavalry* (1926), as well as to other works. He was arrested in 1939 and died in a Siberian gulag, his exact fate unknown.

Babel's goodfellas and their real-life prototypes reigned over Odesa's Moldavanka quarter. Some hotel tourist bureaus now offer short tours of this 'Criminal Odesa'. Alternatively, contact Katamaran Tour (p119).

---

notes and moaning letters found in this humble museum.

Olde-worlde **Hotel Londonskaya Museum** (☎ 738 0102; Prymorsky bul 11; admission free) pays tribute to past guests, including Anton Chekhov, Isadora Duncan, Robert Louis Stevenson, Marcello Mastroianni and Vladimir *(A Conversation with the Tax Inspector About Poetry)* Mayakovsky.

The **Ship Museum** (☎ 240 509; vul Lanzheronivska 6; admission 3uah; 10am-5pm Fri-Wed) displays models of sailing ships and other boats, compasses, sextants and so on in a baroque palace, while the **Art Museum** (☎ 237 287, 238 272; vul Sofiyivska 5A; 10am-5pm Fri-Mon) has a collection of Russian and Ukrainian art including a few seascapes by master talent Ayvazovksy.

Festivals & Events

Odesa's annual **Carnival Humorina** (☎ /fax 252 273; org@humor.odessa.ua), celebrated on 1 April, is no joke. The festival fills the streets with carnival floats and processions and is the biggest party of the year for most Odesans.

Sleeping

BUDGET

There are always babushkas (old women) offering *komnaty* or *kimnaty* (rooms) for about 40uah to 70uah a night. As always, check about the location and arrangements.

A scheduled redevelopment of the huge Passazh building on the corner of vuls Derybasivska and Preobrazhenska is about to deprive Odesa of all its central budget accommodation. However, remembering the delays affecting the Opera House renovation, you could check if the best option, **Hotel Tsentralna** (☎ 268 406; fax 268 689; vul Preobrazhenska 40; s/d/tr $22/44/66), is still open.

Hotel Yunist (☎ 738 0405; www.yunost.com.ua; vul Pionerska 34; r $12-85; P) , a decent but fairly old building towards Arkadia, runs the gamut from dirt-cheap to midrange, but the cheapest rooms are the best value and budget travellers are less likely to object to the unrenovated public areas. Take tram No 5 to 'база моряків'.

MIDRANGE

Black Sea Hotel (☎ 242 025; www.bs-hotel.com.ua; vul Rishelevska 59; s $90, d $110-160, unrenovated s/d $40/80; P) A short walk from the train station, this ugly 1970s concrete tower is an easy option rather than a positive choice. The refurbished rooms are pleasant and the unrenovated ones are bearable, although they have older bathrooms and thin curtains. There are lots of services, such as laundry, restaurants and a tour bureau. Credit cards accepted. Staff speak some English.

Hotel Oktyabrskaya (☎ 280 666; vul Kanatna 35; d $60-70) Towards Shevchenko Park, this isn't bad for a Soviet-era establishment. There are no hot-water problems and it even has a bed-and-breakfast feel.

Hotel Morskoy (☎ 357 357; www.morskoy.com; prov Khrustalny 1/1; standard s/d $70/80, superior s/d from $80/90; **P** ⊠ 🖳 ⚊) Right near Arkadia beach, this is a good place for well-heeled party animals in summer, and an anomaly at other times of year. The modern designer interior uses blue and yellow tones to create a crisp Mediterranean atmosphere. Triple-glazed windows reportedly dampen the noise from nearby clubs. Credit cards accepted. Staff speak some English.

Hotel Frapolli (☎ 356 801; www.odessapassage .com; vul Derybasivska 13; s/d from $100/130; 🖳) Identikit pale-green and white rooms look clean and businesslike, but noise wafts in from the busy street in summer. Winter is a better time to power up the internet-enabled computer that's provided in every room; online access costs 10uah per hour. Credit cards accepted. Some staff speak English.

TOP END

Odesa's hotel market is top-heavy with luxury establishments. Credit cards are accepted in all and staff speak good English.

Mozart Hotel (☎ 378 900, 379 00; www.mozart -hotel.com; vul Lanzheronivska 13; s $120-140, d $170-185, ste $305-335; **P** ⊠ ⚊ ⚊) As the name suggests, this top choice offers classic European luxury, with elegant furnishings and a calm, light-filled interior. Behind its refurbished neoclassical façade, Mozart has 40 rooms.

Hotel Londonskaya (☎ reservation 738 0110, reception 738 0102; www.londred.com; Prymorsky bul 11; s $100-130, d $130-160; **P** ⊠ ⚊) Last refurbished in the early 1990s, the rooms of Odesa's oldest luxury hotel are becoming dated, but with iron-lace balustrades, stained-glass windows, parquet flooring and an inner courtyard, the place still oozes Regency charm. It boasts a primo position, an excellent restaurant and even a museum (opposite).

Hotel Odessa (☎ 729 4808; www.hotel-odessa.com.ua; vul Prymorska 6; s/d from $195/230; **P** ⊠ ⚊ ⚊ ⚊) Towering above the passenger port, this conference-sized hotel is a swish but soulless business-travellers' haunt. However, its

19th-floor Panorama restaurant is worth a quick visit by all for the view.

Also recommended are two recently built luxury hotels at Arkadia beach:

Hotel Arkadia Plaza (☎ 307 100; www.besteastern.com; vul Posmitnoho 1; s/d from $145/165; **P** ⊠ ⚊ ⚊)

Palace del Mar (☎ 301 900; www.besteastern.com; prov Khrustalny 1; s/d from $145/165; **P** ⊠ ⚊ ⚊)

Eating

Dress at least smart casual for a night out in Odesa; the place can be pretty posey. Restaurants tend to open earlier than elsewhere in Ukraine, serving good breakfasts.

Klara Bara (☎ 200 331; Gorsad; mains 30-65uah; ⏲ 9am-midnight) Tucked away in a quiet corner of the city garden, this modern ivy-covered café and restaurant has a cosy atmosphere. It serves European fare with Thai touches, plus brilliant Turkish coffee.

Steakhouse (☎ 287 775; vul Derybasivska 20; mains 30-135uah; ⏲ 9am-midnight) A local institution that produces souvenir T-shirts, Steakhouse is more upmarket than the name suggests. The brightly lit interior is a cross between Nordic and Japanese minimalism, while the clientele includes a lot of expats and trendy couples. The meat and fish cooked on the open grill is given creative flavourings, but the salads are a bit oily.

Fat Mozes (☎ 714 4774; vul Yekaterynynska 8/10; mains 15-45uah; ⏲ 8am-midnight) Sounds like a New York deli, doesn't it? But, apart from the roast-beef sandwiches, it isn't quite. The atmosphere is more of a cosy, unpretentious bistro, serving an eclectic mix, that includes souvlaki, goulash and Jamaican chicken.

Paparazzi (☎ 348 070; vul Yekaterynynska 8; mains 40-55uah; ⏲ 10am-midnight) Next door to Fat Mozes, this more fashionable outlet is renowned for its stone-grilled meats – if you can get past the 'arty' pictures of women on the menu, that is.

Khutorok (☎ 735 3873; Shevchenko Park, Lanzheron Beach; mains 45-135uah) Particularly brilliant for a slap-up Sunday lunch, this excellent Ukrainian restaurant is housed in a series of thatched-roof cottages overlooking the water near Lanzheron Beach. It's worth the half-hour walk, or short taxi ride, from the centre, although its hugeness makes it more conducive to kicking back in a group (or family) than for an intimate tête à tête.

Déjà vu la mer (☎ 377 574; vul Troytska; mains 35-55uah; ⏲ 10am-midnight) *Déjà vu* was a cult Soviet gangster film shot in Odesa, but this name-sake is more like an American diner, with half a helicopter and similar accoutrements hogging the space. Still, it's very popular.

Chai-na Rose (☎ 731 5127; vul Koblevska 46; snacks 5-14uah) With green plastic chairs, black-and-white photos and a single flower in a vase on each table, this looks like an art-gallery teahouse – as pretty as the iced biscuits on its snack menu (ranging from tostadas to cake). The name, actually meaning 'Tea Rose' in Russian, is a play on words.

Pedestrianised vul Derybasivska is lined with cafés for a quick, cheap bite to eat, including the ubiquitous **Pan Pizza** (vul Derybasivska 22; pizzas 25-45uah, pasta 10-20uah).

Drinking

Mick O'Neill's Irish Bar (☎ 268 437; vul Derybasivska 13; ☷ 24hr) At one time the sole meeting point for Odesa's expat community, this long-standing Irish pub is still one of the best places to start a long evening. There's ale and Guinness, food and even a very expensive internet terminal.

Friends & Beer (☎ 769 1998; vul Derybasivska 9; ☷ 10am-midnight) Proof that 'Retro Soviet' doesn't have to mean political posters and Constructivist art is this charming re-created USSR-era living room. However the food is average and seemingly aimed at Brits – with jacket potatoes, Yorkshire puddings and even bhajis – so it's best to come just for a beer. The huge TV screen showing football is possibly not authentic for the period…

Two enduringly popular, American-style sports bars are **Fidel-Havana Club** (☎ 227 116; vul Derybasivska 23; ☷ 24hr) and **Buffalo 99** (☎ 731 4187; vul Rishelevska 5; ☷ 9am-midnight). Both sell food, but be warned the former has strip shows on Saturday evenings.

For something a little more local, try the basement **Pobeda** (☎ 728 7838; vul Hretska 25).

Entertainment

CLUBS
Odesa has dozens of clubs, ranging from the flirty to the seriously sleazy. As always in Ukraine, fashion shows and go-go dancers are common, even at the more respectable end of the spectrum, such as these. Door prices generally range from 10uah to 40uah.

Ibiza (☎ 777 0205; Arkadia Beach; ☷ summer) Mixing 'troglodyte' desert architecture with a Spanish name, this white, free-form open cave structure is a good-natured pick-up joint, with DJs and go-go dancers.

Itaka (☎ 349 188; Arkadia Beach; ☷ summer) This seaside amphitheatre tips a nod to Odesa's Greek name with columns and statues right out of ancient Athens. The music policy tends more towards Russian pop, however, as artists sometimes blow into town from Moscow to play live.

Luxor (Arkadia Beach; ☷ summer) It might be ancient Greece over at Itaka, but at this ever-growing superclub it's ancient Egypt. Confused? Best to just grab a beer or cocktail.

Kosmo (☎ 688 203; Gagarinske plato 5; ☷ from 10pm Fri & Sat winter) Twentysomethings and teens come to this spaceship-shaped club to hear DJs play the latest drum 'n' bass, or nu skool anything.

Amsterdam (☎ 741 1116; Devolanovsky spusk 11; ☷ year-round) This more grown-up variety theatre/club is easier to reach from the centre. It has live cabaret floorshows and big-band entertainment.

CLASSICAL MUSIC
The best regional orchestra within the former Soviet Union, the **Odesa Philharmonic** (☎ 256 903; vul Bunina 15) has been granted 'national' status within Ukraine, but doesn't play during summer. Plus: charismatic and energetic American conductor Hobart Earle, a former student of Leonard Bernstein's. Minus: the improved but still not brilliant acoustics of its hall, the former stock exchange.

Conversely, opera performances in Odesa rarely matched the quality of the world-class opera building, even when it was open. Today, they take place in the **Musical Comedy Theatre** (☎ 250 924; vul Panteleymonivska 3).

Shopping
Odesa's weekend *tovkuchka* or *tovchok* (both meaning 'crush' or 'push') is one of the country's biggest flea markets – full of junk and of life. It's on the city's western edge. Take southwest bound tram No 4 from vul Uspenska to the end of the line, then bus No 160.

The central market is on vul Privozna at the southeastern end of pr Oleksandrivsky.

Getting There & Away

AIR
Odesa is better linked to Europe than any other Ukrainian city besides Kyiv. There are international connections to Vienna

---

WHAT THEY SAID ABOUT ODESA

'I have not felt so much at home for a long time as I did when I "raised the hill" and stood in Odesa for the first time,'

Mark Twain, Innocents Abroad, 1869

'Odesa has more colour, more spunk, more irreverence than any other Soviet city,'

Maurice Friedberg, How Things Were Done In Odesa, 1972

'Odesans, from the city's raffish gangsters to its lissom girls, are convinced that they are superior in culture and style to anyone in Moscow or London, let alone the hicks from Kyiv… And they are absolutely right.'

Simon Sebag-Montefiore, the Independent, 2000

---

and Istanbul (see p185), while LOT and Malév offer flights five or six times a week to Warsaw and Budapest. There are four to five flights a day to Kyiv.

BOAT

From the passenger port there are regular ferry services to Istanbul, plus some to Haifa and Varna in summer (see p188). Odesa is also a terminus for the Dnipro River hydrofoils and passenger boats (see p189) and summertime catamarans from Yalta and Sevastopol. Eugenia Travel (p119) can help in all instances.

BUS

Odesa's **long-distance bus station** (☎ 004; vul Kolontaevska 58) is 3km west of the train station. Take tram no 5 heading away from Arkadia to the other end of the line. Alight in this dingy neighbourhood, walk towards the front of the tram and take the first street right, then look for the coaches down this street.

There are at least eight buses daily to Kyiv (45uah to 60uah), stopping en route at Uman (28uah). **Autolux** (www.autolux.com.ua) runs four services daily. The exact journey time will depend on whether the new highway to Kyiv has finally been completed (see p190). With Autolux, count on roughly four or five hours to Uman and seven or eight to Kyiv.

Other buses head for Simferopol (45uah, 12 hours, one daily), Zaporizhzhya (45uah, 12 hours, two daily) and Dnipropetrovsk (60uah, 10 to 11 hours, three daily).

There are at least nine daily buses to Chişinău (15uah to 25uah, five to seven hours). Call **Arman Tours** (☎ 728 9518, 245 161) for bus journeys to Istanbul or Prague. It has an office upstairs at the train station.

TRAIN

From **Odesa train station** (pl Pryvokzalna) there are three overnight trains to Kyiv (42uah, nine to 11 hours), plus daily trains to Dnipropetrovsk (50uah, 10 hours), Kharkiv (52uah, 14 hours), Izmayil (25uah, eight hours) and Simferopol (30uah, 13 hours). Longer-distance services go to Minsk, Rostov and (summer only) St Petersburg.

There are also trains to Chernivtsi and Lviv, but most pass through Moldova, for which a visa is required (see p92). If you have a visa and want to reach Chişinău, there are three trains a day (44uah, four to five hours).

Getting Around

Odesa airport (☎ 658 186, 213 576, 006) is about 12km southwest of the city centre, off Ovidiopilska doroha. Bus No 129 goes to/from the train station; bus No 101 runs to/from pl Hretska in the city centre.

To get to the centre from the train station (which is about a 20-minute walk), there are several options: bus Nos 137 and 146 pass the train station en route to pl Hretska. Bus Nos 155 and 109, and trolleybus Nos 4 and 10, go up vul Pushkinska before curving around to vul Prymorska past the passenger port and the foot of the Potemkin Steps.

Tram No 5 travels between the bus station and Arkadia beach. It passes by the train station en route, but misses the city centre.

Taxis in Odesa charge incredibly high prices (because the rough streets destroy their cars, one driver told us). Hotel staff say a taxi from the airport should cost 25uah, but you're more likely to pay three times more. Never catch a cab in front of a hotel if you can help it. Try **Elit-Taxi** (☎ 371 030) for a reliable service.

SOUTHERN UKRAINE

AROUND ODESA
Bilhorod-Dnistrovsky
Білгород-дністровський
☎ 04849 / pop 48,500

The 'White City on the Dnister', is an ordinary industrial port, but with an impressive **fortress** (admission 5uah; ☼ 10am-6pm). First settled by Greeks, the river estuary was controlled by many different peoples before Stefan II of Moldavia built this fortress here in the 13th century. Slightly unkempt today, the castle is still one of Ukraine's largest. You can walk along most of the walls, which stretch nearly 2km.

Bilhorod-Dnistrovsky is 55km from Odesa, and there are eight *elektrychka* (electric trains) daily between the two cities, taking 2½ hours. Trains between Odesa and Izmayil also stop en route. To reach the fortress from the train station, walk along vul Vokzalna and, after the park, turn right onto vul Dzerzhinskoho. From here, the fortress is a 1.5km walk.

Vylkovo Вилково
☎ 04843 / pop 9000

Not many Westerners venture this way, but those who do rave about the place. It really is the Venice of Ukraine, a quaint fishing village with onion-domed churches set on a series of canals. Cossack descendants founded the village after fleeing persecution in Zaporizhzhya. They built their houses on the river flood plain, digging out soil to create high platforms and leaving ditches that later filled with water to become canals.

Vylkovo is also the headquarters for the **Dunaysky Biosphere Reserve**, the Ukrainian section of the Danube Biosphere Reserve. The entire region, which stretches well into Romania, constitutes Europe's largest wetlands and is home to many species of birds, including pelicans and cormorants.

It was a cause of international consternation when the government of Leonid Kuchma started deepening a canal in this environmentally sensitive region in 2004, to allow greater shipping. Recent political events might or might not have halted construction.

As you journey by boat down Vylkovo's streets, the most feasible option for visiting here is on an excursion from Odesa. Eugenia Travel (p119) charges $85 to $90 per person for a one-day tour, although a two-day trip is really preferable. Odesa's Black Sea Hotel (p124) also organises tours.

Alternatively, if you speak Russian and trust your ability to negotiate with local boatmen, you could try heading to Izmayil and proceeding from here. There's a daily train from Odesa to Izmayil, taking eight hours. From the train station, bus No 10 goes to the centre.

KHERSON & ASKANIYA NOVA
ХЕРСОН ТА АСКАНІЯ НОВА
☎ 0552 / pop 307,000 (plus some wild animals)

Kherson is attractively situated at the mouth of the Dnipro River, but the main reason to visit is for the unusual experience of going on safari in Europe. The area that's now the 2300-hectare **Askaniya Nova Reserve**, some 100km east of Kherson, was populated by animals from several continents by a slightly mad German settler in the late 19th century. There's antelope, bison, deer, emus, gnus, wild Przhevalski horses, zebras, and many types of bird, ranging from pink flamingos to the rare steppe eagle.

Poorly timed bus services and a lack of operational hotels or restaurants near the park mean an organised tour from Kherson or negotiating with a taxi driver are the only sensible options.

Kherson's former Intourist hotel **Fregat** (☎ 280 139, 280 003, 240 522; www.hotelfregat.com; vul Ushakova 2; s/d $22/36, tr $48-34; 🅿 🖳 🛗) organises day trips to the reserve, from about $80 for one person or $100 for three, including a translator at the reserve. It also does tours to the Swedish village of **Zmiyivka** – whose first citizens begged Catherine the Great to move them here to escape serfdom in Russian-governed Sweden in the late 18th century. Zmiyivka remains a quirky enclave of Swedishness in today's Ukraine. You reach the Fregat from the train station by trolleybus No 13 or from the bus station by bus No 6.

The **Brigantina Hotel** (☎ 273 551, 273 731; www.brigantinaua.com/e/; vul Patona 4; s/d from $25/45; 🅿 🖳) offers better-value rooms, but is inconveniently located (you'll need to take a taxi) and doesn't offer Askaniya Nova tours.

Kherson lies on the train line between Kyiv (12 hours) and Simferopol. From Odesa, you can arrive by train (six hours) or bus (five hours).

Crimea Крим

The landscape is the star in Crimea; even those initially lured by the peninsula's fascinating past usually come to agree. Not that 'landscape' means the pebbly Black Sea beaches, crumbling concrete high-rises and post-Soviet kitsch of the main resort, Yalta, which isn't going to steal the market from Benidorm any time soon. Rather, it's the sheer mountain cliffs rising behind a coastline covered with cypress, juniper and grape vines that make the Tatar homeland so breathtakingly exotic and unique. High limestone plateaus, expansive vistas, bizarre rock formations and a series of Byzantine 'cave cities' all lie inland from such historical landmarks as Balaklava, Sevastopol or Livadia, where Churchill, Roosevelt and Stalin shaped the face of postwar Europe. So, all in all, it's just as important to remember walking shoes as it is to pack your swimming costume.

A stop on the Silk Road from China, and occupied throughout history by ancient Greeks, Genoese, Mongols and Tatars, Crimea came under Russian rule in the late 18th century. Inevitably, these northerners seized upon the Mediterranean-style climate as perfect for a holiday retreat. The Russian monarchy began spending summers outside Yalta during the 1860s. Millions of ordinary workers united in their desire to vacation here – year in, year out – during the Soviet era.

That heyday as a workers' paradise is now past, but a decade and a half after Ukrainian independence this semi-independent republic is still the 'Russian Riviera'. More than 60% of locals are of ethnic Russian descent, Moscow's tricolour frequently flies alongside the Ukrainian flag, people speak Russian and regularly quote prices in roubles. While those prices demonstrate a firm grasp of latter-day capitalism, standards of service can be an amusing communist throwback, too.

CRIMEA

HIGHLIGHTS

- Visit the **Livadia** (p150) or **Alupka** (p152) palaces outside Yalta
- Clamber over the Byzantine 'cave cities' of **Chufut-Kale** (p137) and **Manhup-Kale** (p139)
- See how the medieval Tatars lived at the **Khans' Palace** (p136), Bakhchysaray
- Quaff champagne on the beaches of **Novy Svit** (p154)
- Take the cable car to the desert-like peak of **Mt Ay-Petri** (p151)
- Take a stop along the Silk Road – drop in on the impressive fortress at **Sudak** (p154)
- Hike among the dramatic volcanic rock formations of the **Kara-Dah Nature Reserve** (p155), the original Jurassic Park
- Scurry and crawl through **Sevastopol's** catacombs (p142) or dive into **Balaklava's** hidden submarine factory (p144)

- POPULATION: 1.9 MILLION
- HIGHEST POINT: MT ROMAN KOSH (1543M)

History

The central theme of Crimean history revolves around the struggle between the Turkic and Slavic peoples for control of the peninsula. However, the stage is also littered with cameo appearances, from 6th-century Greeks who built Chersonesus (p142) to the 15th-century Genoese merchants behind the impressive Sudak fortress (p154), as well as Cimmerians, Scythians, Samartians and Jews. As a constant reminder of the region's essential multiculturalism, these bit players have taken some heat out of the central rivalry.

This rivalry began in 1240, when Mongols conquered parts of Kyivan Rus, including Crimea. They ruled for two centuries, when control of the peninsula passed to their descendants, the Tatars, for more than 300 years (see the boxed text, p138).

In 1783 Russia invaded. Tatars began emigrating to the lands of their close ally, the Ottoman Empire, while Russians, Ukrainians, Bulgarians and even some Germans were invited to resettle Crimea.

Such Russian expansionism soon began to worry great powers Britain and France.

As Russia tried to encroach into the lands of the decaying Ottoman Empire, the Crimean War erupted in 1854 (see the boxed text, p143).

With close ties to the monarchy, Crimea was one of the last White bastions during the Russian civil war, holding out till November 1920. It was occupied by German troops for three years during WWII and lost nearly half its population. In its aftermath, Stalin deported all remaining Crimean Tatars (see the boxed text, p138).

In 1954 Ukrainian-born Soviet leader Nikita Khrushchev created the Autonomous Crimean Soviet Socialist Republic and transferred legislative control to the Ukrainian SSR. Hence, despite the name, the peninsula is really only semi-independent.

When the USSR disintegrated, Russia and Ukraine wrestled over control of the region and the Black Sea Fleet. The disputes were resolved remarkably peacefully, but underlying tensions remain. The Crimean parliament has many times attempted to make Russian the official language or gain economic independence from Kyiv, and in

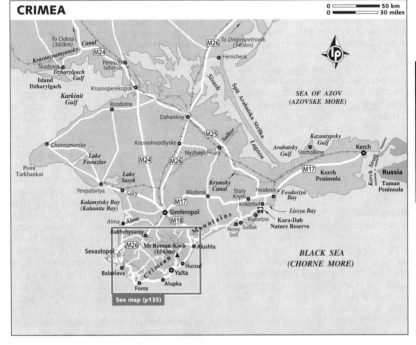

CRIMEA

THE LANGUAGE IN THIS CHAPTER

As noted in the introduction, Crimea remains largely Russian speaking. As it is a region of Ukraine, however, we have chosen to use the – usually very similar – Ukrainian renditions of places names as often as possible. Only where Russian names have passed into English usage (eg Livadia, Sapun Gor), where a change to Ukrainian could confuse readers (eg bus-stop names) and in a few other necessary instances have we stuck with the Russian.

---

the aftermath of 2004's disputed election it made noises about secession. For now, the main rivalry for control of the peninsula is between two Slavic peoples – Russian and Ukrainian – while the fate of the returned Crimean Tatars (who overwhelmingly backed Viktor Yushchenko) is being overshadowed.

SIMFEROPOL СІМФЕРОПОЛЬ
☎ 06521 / pop 345,000

For many people, the Crimean capital is nothing but a night-time blur outside the taxi window as they race from the airport to the coast. Others only glimpse the city as they transfer from the train station to the trolleybus.

Neither group is missing much, aesthetically speaking. However, in contrast to the superficial, seasonal, merry-go-round of Yalta, Simferopol is a working city that marches on throughout the year. With more reasonable prices than at the seaside, it's a handy base for cost-conscious travellers wishing to explore the Tatar capital of Bakhchysaray (p136), the Valley of the Ghosts (p154), or the caves of Chatyr-Dah (p153).

Orientation

The town centre is south of the airport, lying approximately midway between the train station (to the northwest) and the central bus station (to the east). From the airport, trolleybus No 9 goes to the train station. *Marshrutky* travelling west from the central bus station (from across the road) also go to the train station. To get downtown, you should look out for 'т украина' on the destination sign. See p135 for more details.

Information

Central post office (vul Rozy Lyuxemburg 1) Contains a telephone centre, 24-hour internet café charging 4uah an hour, and 24-hour ATM.

Internet Café (☎ 273 377; vul Pavlenko 20; per hr 4uah; ☒ 24hr) Has a dozen computers.

Sights

A young city, founded in the 18th century under Russia's Catherine the Great, Simferopol contains no must-sees. Remnants do survive, however, of earlier civilisations on the same site. The most interesting is the restored 16th-century **Kebi-Djami mosque** (vul Kurchatova 4), which dates back to the Crimean Tatar town of Ak-Mechet (White Mosque). It's in a neighbourhood repopulated by returning Crimean Tatars.

There's little sense of history about the much-touted **Neopolis** (btwn vuls Vorovskoho & Chervonoarmiyska), 2km east of the centre. However, it offers a good view of Simferopol in all its Soviet-constructivist glory, should you be tempted by such things. Archaeological excavations of a late Scythian city (300 BC–AD 300) have been abandoned. Nowadays, the 20-hectare hilltop site is where locals take their goats or cattle to graze, or teenagers meet for illicit drinking.

The memorable thing about the modest **Crimean Ethnographic Museum** (☎ 255 223; vul Pushkina 18; admission 2uah; ☒ 9am-5pm, closed Tue) is its first room. It boasts a 3-D relief map of Crimea, populated with nearly 50 colourful small statues representing the peninsula's different peoples throughout history. The five-domed **Three Saints Church** (vul Hoholya 16) is nearby.

Sleeping

Hotel Ukraina (☎ 510 165; jscukrcomp@crimea.ua; vul Rozy Lyuxemburg 7; s/d from $35/50; Ⓟ) Recent renovations, a central location and a smattering of English information make this Simferopol's best option. With modern bathrooms, TV, phone and minibar, even the lowest-priced rooms will satisfy most travellers. Others rise to $80. The construction is a little cheap, though, so the new look might not wear well. The entrance is through the car park and courtyard behind the pinkish building to right of the hotel sign.

Turbaza Tavriya (☎ 232 024; vul Bespalova 21; refurbished s/d from $15/20) The inconvenient location

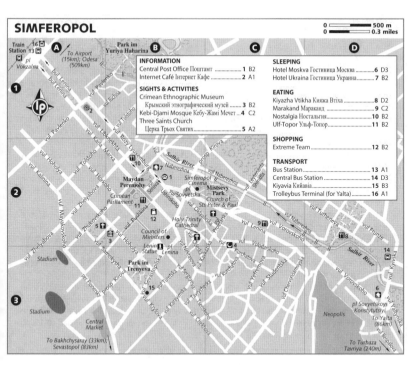

SIMFEROPOL

0 ——— 500 m
0 ——— 0.3 miles

INFORMATION
Central Post Office Пошгамт **1** B2
Internet Café Інтернет Кафе **2** A1

SIGHTS & ACTIVITIES
Crimean Ethnographic Museum
    Крымский этнографический музей **3** B2
Kebi-Djami Mosque Кебу-Жамі Мечет ... **4** C2
Three Saints Church
    Церква Трьох Святих **5** A2

SLEEPING
Hotel Moskva Гостиница Москва **6** D3
Hotel Ukraina Гостиница Украина **7** B2

EATING
Kiyazha Vtikha Княжа Втіха **8** D2
Marakand Мараканд **9** C2
Nostalgia Ностальгия **10** B2
Ulf-Topor Ульф-Топор **11** B2

SHOPPING
Extreme Team **12** B2

TRANSPORT
Bus Station **13** A1
Central Bus Station **14** D3
Kiyavia Киявіа **15** B3
Trolleybus Terminal (for Yalta) **16** A1

spoils an otherwise gem. Refurbished rooms (going up to $55) are relatively cheap, although many bathrooms – ahem, in the Japanese 'wet' tradition – have no shower cubicle; there's just a modern showerhead and drain. At about only $6 less than the cheapest new rooms, the older wing is possibly not worth it.

Hotel Moskva (☎ 237 520; fax 239 795; vul Kiyivska 2; s/d/tr from $18/35/46; **P**) This former Intourist hotel does boast larger luxe rooms ($80 to $115), but its dark halls, truculent staff and not particularly tasteful furniture mean it's a fall-back option. Within walking distance of the central bus station, it's reached from the train station on trolleybus No 1, 2 or 6.

Eating

Ulf-Topor (☎ 254 270; vul Karla Marxa 14; pizzas 3-8uah, other mains 8-17uah) This bar/café takes its theme from a Russian fairy tale, with murals, various knick-knacks and even a fake tree in the middle of its basement. Students and other locals descend for tasty pan pizzas, salads and other dishes.

Nostalgia (vul Rozy Lyuxemburg 12; mains 6-18uah; 🕙 9am-11pm) Hard to tell exactly what they're nostalgic for here – ancient Egypt, Africa, the Crimean War or something else – but the eclectic decoration gives a homy atmosphere. The local clientele enjoying the modest range of omelettes, *blyny* (pancakes) with jam, cutlets and *borshch* add to that feel.

Marakand (☎ 524 698; vul Vorovskoho 17; mains 1-6uah; 🕙 closed Sun) *Plov* (meat and rice) and *shashlyk* grilled over an open fire are served at this Uzbek restaurant, popular with local Tatars.

Kiyazha Vtikha (☎ 291 489; vul Turheneva 35; mains 18-38uah) The obligatory Ukrainian theme restaurant sometimes goes a bit over the top with the cheesy band and cheek-to-cheek dancing, but the food is tasty. In summer, you can escape the music in an outdoor hut.

Shopping

Extreme Team (☎ 546 781; Office 5, vul Karla Marxa 6) A small selection of last-minute camping and hiking supplies.

CRIMEA

HEADING DOWN TO YALTA

With no direct trains from Simferopol to Yalta, you need to make the trip by road. It's an infamous journey for two reasons – the taxi prices and the traffic.

Taking a taxi might not be as easy to avoid as you first expect, because, quite simply, the alternative forms of transport are cramped or hellishly slow – and frequently both. Historically, this gave taxi drivers carte blanche to rip people off. They still try, of course, but if you're leaving from the airport, scheduled fares to different destinations have finally been posted on an official billboard. According to this **central cab firm** (☎ 545 676), Simferopol to Yalta should cost 120uah ($25) in a normal taxi, 190uah ($35) in a bigger vehicle or 280uah ($55) for a VIP, air-conditioned transfer. Use this knowledge to negotiate at the train station, too.

The traffic is difficult to avoid, but it's renowned as the craziest in Ukraine, thanks to poorly marked overtaking lanes. In fact, there's only one overtaking lane, in the middle of the road, which is 'shared' by traffic in both directions. For several hundred metres, priority is given to southbound traffic to overtake, before northbound traffic is given right of way. To the uninitiated it's a little unnerving at first, but local drivers know the rules well.

The slowest moving vehicles along this route are the Simferopol–Yalta trolleybuses. Trolleybus No 52 serves Yalta (2½ hours, every 20 minutes between 5.30am and 8pm). Covering 85km, it's the world's longest – and slowest! – trolleybus route. Trolleybus No 51 only goes to/from Alushta. Trolleybuses depart from the terminal next to the train station clock tower (to your left when exiting the train station). A single ticket for Yalta costs 6uah. Large bags theoretically need a separate ticket.

Much speedier are the *marshrutky* that plough to/from Yalta (1½ to two hours), departing from the bus stop between the train and trolleybus stations. Buses depart when full. Alternatively, take a regular Yalta-bound public bus (2½ hours, hourly departures) from the small bus station opposite the trolleybus terminal. On average, prices for buses and *marshrutky* are 9uah to 15uah to Yalta (or 6uah to 7uah to Alushta).

Getting There & Away

AIR
Simferopol airport (☎ 295 516; www.airport.crimea .ua) is 15km northwest of the town centre and is accessible by trolleybus No 9 (50 kopecks, 30 minutes) as well as myriad *marshrutky,* including Nos 49, 50, 98, 113 and 115.

Aeroflot, El Al and Turkish Airlines all operate direct flights in season and there are charter flights from Germany and the UK (see p185). Domestic flights in summer include services to Kyiv (two to three a day) and Kharkiv (one a day).

Kiyavia (☎ 272 116; info@ticket.crimea.ua; vul Sevastopilska 22; 8am-5.45pm Mon-Fri) sells both international and domestic air tickets.

BUS
Most Crimean cities apart from Sevastopol (train) are better reached from Simferopol by road. From the small bus station opposite the train and trolleybus stations, there are daily services to Sudak (18uah, 2½ hours, up to 22 daily) and Yevpatoriya (10uah, 1¾ hours, 11 daily).

Some Sudak and Yevpatoriya buses also pick up passengers at the **central bus station** (☎ 275 211; vul Kyivska 4). There are regular services to/from Odesa from here (40uah to 60uah, 12 hours, two daily), Feodosiya (16uah to 26uah, three hours, 16 daily), Kerch (30uah, 4½ hours, at least eight daily) and Rostov (80uah, 14 hours, twice daily).

Buses to Bakhchysaray (4uah, one hour) go from the central bus station, too. Only four services a day are timetabled, but more actually leave.

TRAIN
Simferopol is Crimea's main railway junction, with two trains daily to/from Kyiv (75uah, 14 to 15 hours) and Moscow (235uah, 21 to 26 hours); and a daily service at least to/from Donetsk (45uah, 12 hours), Dnipropetrovsk (40uah, 11 hours), Lviv (75uah, 21 hours), Kharkiv (45uah, 10 hours) and Odesa (40uah, 13 hours). Other destinations include Minsk (190uah, 29 hours, every other day) and St Petersburg (275uah, 35 hours, every other day). There are seasonal services to/from Rostov-on-Don (14 to 15 hours).

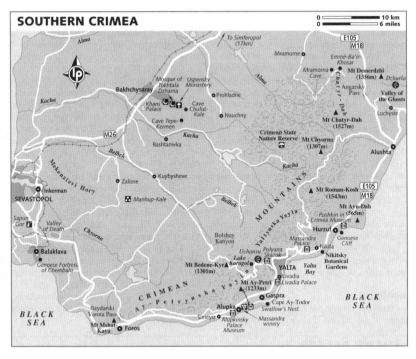

SOUTHERN CRIMEA

Local *elektrychka* run regularly along the Crimean peninsula to/from Yevpatoriya (two hours, 11 a day in each direction) and Sevastopol (two hours, seven daily in each direction). The latter service stops en route in Bakhchysaray (40 minutes). Prices are all 5uah or less.

Getting Around

Trolleybus No 9 goes from the airport to the train station and to get to the centre from here you need to take trolleybus No 5 or 2 eastwards, or a *marshrutka* or bus from near McDonald's with 'г украина' on its side. Alternatively, some *marshrutky* and buses – eg Nos 49, 98 and 113 – go straight from the airport to the town centre. Alight at the central Hotel Ukraina stop on vul Rozy Lyuxemburg.

Although *marshrutky* travelling west from opposite the central bus station go to the train station, they usually skirt the city centre. To be sure to get downtown, look out for the 'г украина' sign. Taking a trolleybus, you will have to take a No 2, 4 or 6.

YEVPATORIYA ЄВПАТОРІЯ
☎ 06569 / pop 106,000

One of Crimea's few sandy coastlines, this area is lined with health resorts and sanatoriums. The waters of Kalamita Bay are relatively calm and inviting, while refurbishment in 2001 has injected a bit of cheer along the promenade.

Yevpatoriya was a slave-trading market in the 15th century and the Turkish buyers and sellers left their mark. The **Dzhuma-Dzhami Mosque** (1552), in a park near pl Prymorska on the seafront, is Crimea's largest and frequented by returned Crimean Tatars.

Most sanatoriums demand a week's stay. For shorter visits, try the renovated **Yevpatoriya** (☎ 303 39; vul Kirova 50; d $50). The cheaper **Hotel Krym** (☎ 234 12; vul Revolyutsy 46; per person $12) is near the waterfront.

There are about 11 buses daily from Simferopol to Yevpatoriya bus station (10uah, two hours). The bus and train stations are near one another, 1.5km northwest of the old town. Take tram No 3 to pl Teatralna, then tram No 1 along the waterfront to the old town.

CRIMEA

BAKHCHYSARAY БАХЧИСАРАЙ

☎ 06554 / pop 27,500

Bakhchysaray is emblematic of the Crimean Tatar condition. It *sounds* so lush and exotic – just let the syllables back-*chee*-sa-rye roll off your tongue – but the reality is a little dusty and down-at-heel. The name means 'garden palace' in Turkish, and was conferred when the town was the capital of the powerful Crimean Khanate between the 15th and 18th centuries. Today, after significant destruction by both the Russian crown and the Soviets, Bakhchysaray and its newly returned Tatar inhabitants are still getting back on their feet (see the boxed text, p138).

Luckily, the place has managed to keep a few serious aces up its elaborately embroidered sleeves. The khans' original palace survives, as does a thoroughly entrancing 'cave city' dating back to the 6th century. In between them, an Orthodox monastery has been built into the side of a hill.

Sights

To truly appreciate Bakhchysaray, don't just come to the Khans' Palace. Make a proper day trip of it and visit all three following sights. They lie along the same road, several kilometres apart. See p139 for details on how to proceed.

KHANS' PALACE

When she was busy ordering the mass destruction of Bakhchysaray's mosques in the 18th century, Catherine the Great spared the **Khans' Palace** (Khansky Palats; www.hansaray.iatp .org.ua; vul Lenina 129; admission 14uah; 9am-5.30pm daily Jul & Aug; 9am-4.30pm Wed-Mon May, Jun, Sep & Oct; 9am-4.30pm Thu-Mon Nov-Apr). Her decision was reportedly based on the building's being 'romantic', and it is sweet. While it lacks the imposing grandeur of Islamic structures in, say, Istanbul, the stories behind it and the sheer incongruity of finding such architecture in Crimea add to its appeal.

The palace's intricate designs and minarets were erected by Russian and Ukrainian slaves in the 16th century under the direction of Persian, Ottoman and Italian architects. Fire and other damage necessitated rebuilding, but the structure still resembles its original state.

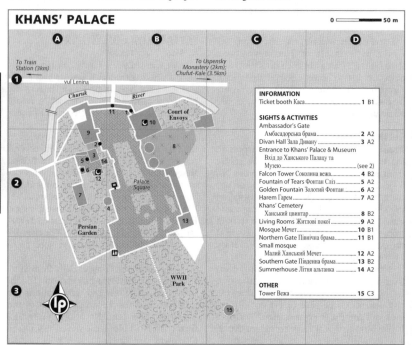

Today's circuit begins through the main gate on the courtyard's right-hand side (although the ticket booth is to the left). Passing through the back of the finely carved **Ambassador's Gate** (also called Portal Aleviza after its Italian designer Alevisio Novi), you enter the west wing and the dimly lit **Divan Hall**. This was the seat of government where the khan and his nobles discussed laws and wars.

Through the hall lies the inner courtyard, containing two fountains. With its white marble ornately inscribed in gold leaf, the **Golden Fountain** (1733) is probably the more beautiful. However, the neighbouring **Fountain of Tears** (1764) is more famous, thanks to Alexander Pushkin (see the boxed text, right). It's tradition that two roses – one red for love and one yellow for chagrin – are placed atop the fountain; Pushkin was the first to do this.

Off the courtyard are two other rooms: a **small mosque**, restored to its original 16th-century appearance, and the 18th-century **summerhouse**, with stained-glass windows and divans arranged around a central fountain.

Behind the palace is the only surviving **harem** of the four that were traditionally attached to the palace and belonged to the khan's wives. Across the yard, you can see the **Falcon Tower**.

The palace's north wing houses the **main exhibition hall**, 12 rooms featuring various historical exhibits on Tatar culture (nothing on the deportations) and the life of the khans. There are some interesting books and pieces of jewellery, although the displays are a bit moth-eaten.

The main palace **mosque** (1740), in the east wing, is closed to the public. The **Khans' Cemetery** behind it is also closed, but in this case it's just for restoration. Plans are to open the cemetery and several new parts of the palace in coming years.

Souvenir and fast-food stalls line the street in front of the palace and dot the main courtyard, selling *chebureky* (a meat-filled pastry), baklava, and hiking maps to Chufut-Kale.

USPENSKY MONASTERY

Stop for a moment and say 'aah!'. Possibly the cutest little church in a country absolutely jam-packed with them is attached to the small monastery at Uspensky. It's been built into the limestone rock of the

---

THE BAKHCHYSARAY FOUNTAIN

The Fountain of Tears in the Khans' Palace is a real case of life imitating art imitating life. It was commissioned for the last Crimean khan, Giri, whose hard heart was revealed to have a chink when he fell in unrequited love. His 'paramour' was a Polish beauty, captured and enslaved in his harem. But she resisted his advances and wasted away, unable to endure harem life.

When she died, the khan began weeping day and night uncontrollably. Worried important state matters were being neglected, the court ordered the Persian master craftsman Omer to build the fountain to give an outlet to the Khan's grief. Originally placed by the girl's tomb, it was moved to the courtyard by Catherine the Great.

On visiting the fountain, Russian writer Alexander Pushkin was so moved by the tragedy he wrote the poem 'The Bakhchysaray Fountain' (1823). The verse became so famous in Russia, it continued to ensure the survival of the palace itself.

---

surrounding hill, most probably by Byzantine monks in the 8th or 9th century. If that theory is correct it's the oldest, as well as the cutest, church in Ukraine. Besides the **gold-domed church**, whitewashed monks' cells, a 'healing' fountain and tiled mosaics all cling to the hillside.

Of course, the Soviets closed the place down, but it's been operating again since 1993. Despite – or possibly because of – all the tourists, today's eight monks work hard to maintain a devout atmosphere. The usual dress code for Orthodox churches applies and you're not even supposed to smoke within a 100m range. The interior is also tiny, so you might want to make do with climbing the stairs to the church door and enjoying the excellent views from there.

CHUFUT-KALE ЧУФУТ-КАЛЕ

For many visitors, Chufut-Kale (chew-*fewt* kar-*lay*) will prove to be Bakhchysaray's highlight. Rising 200m, this long and bluff plateau houses a honeycomb of caves and structures where for hundreds of years people took refuge. It's wonderful to explore, especially (but gingerly) the burial chambers and casemates with large open

CRIMEA

CRIMEA

THE TATAR BURDEN

Just who are the Tatars? Thanks to an unfortunate linguistic tic, English-speakers often know the word as an insult and are unaware that it also refers to a group of living people. The definition properly applies to a descendant of Turkic peoples who moved into Europe from Central Asia. The Crimean Tatars are descended from soldiers of Mongol leader Batu Khan, who expanded the Golden Horde into Ukraine in the 13th century.

In 1428, with the horde disintegrating, the Crimean Khanate became an independent political entity under Haci Giray. In 1475 it was invaded by the Ottoman Empire. However, despite spending 300 years as a Turkish vassal state it enjoyed a good deal of political freedom. But it was a different story when the Russians arrived in 1783 and began their persecutions. Most of the peninsula's four to five million Tatars emigrated to the Ottoman Empire.

Although advanced in culture and the arts, the Khanate's main economic activity had been trading in slaves, captured during regular raids into Russian, Ukrainian or Polish territory. In his 1999 book *Ethnic Cleansing in the USSR, 1937–1949*, J Otto Pohl notes: 'The image of the Crimean Tatar as a raider and slave trader has remained strong in the minds of many Slavs.'

This attitude ignores the fact that for the last 250 years, the Tatars have been the oppressed rather than the oppressors. Returning to Crimea with high hopes of independence during the Russian revolution, they soon found themselves the victims of a Stalinist genocide. Accusing them of Nazi collaboration, Stalin deported all 250,000 Tatar inhabitants to Uzbekistan, Kazakhstan and Siberia over the course of a few days, beginning on 18 May 1944.

Thousands died in transit, and an estimated half did not survive the first year. Their Turkic language was banned and all traces of Tatar culture were obliterated. Mosques were destroyed, while the area was repopulated with Ukrainians, Russians, Bulgarians and Germans.

Given an official apology by Khrushchev in 1967, the Tatars were finally granted permission to return home in 1989. Since then, some quarter of a million have, accounting for 12% of the Crimean population today. Life still hasn't been easy, as they struggle against racist attitudes to build a new life. It is only just now that many from Uzbekistan are being issued Ukrainian passports and new homes are being built for the dispossessed. In their native land, their homeland, thousands of Tatars remain in makeshift camps.

'windows' in the vertiginous northern cliff. These are truly breathtaking, as is the view into the valley below. Although the joint entrance to the Uspensky Monastery and Chufut-Kale looks a bit touristy, the 1.5km walk to the cave city ensures it's not too overrun with people.

First appearing in historical records as Kyrk-Or (Forty Fortifications), the city was settled sometime between the 6th and 12th centuries by Christianised descendants of Samartian tribes. Around 1400 the last powerful ruler of the Golden Horde, Tokhtamysh, sheltered here after defeat in the 1390s, and the first Crimean Khanate was established here in the 15th century, before moving to nearby Bakhchysaray. After the Tatars left, a dissident Jewish sect, the Karaites, occupied the city until the mid-19th century. This won the mountain its current name of 'Jewish Fortress'.

Following the track from Uspensky, the best idea is to keep bearing right. The main

entrance is not under the flat tin roof to the left of the Chufut-Kale sign, but further up the hill to the right. At this, the 14th-century main **South Gate**, you might, or might not, be hit for an 8uah entrance fee – rather a cheek given it's a mountain you're visiting!

Soon after the gate, you enter a Swiss-cheese composition of carved-out rooms and steps. Behind this, a stone path heads along the top of the plateau, past two locked *kenassas* (Karaite prayer houses) in a walled courtyard to the right. To the left of the first intersection stands the red-tile roofed **Muslim mausoleum** (1437) of Dzhanike-Khanym, daughter of Tokhtamysh; to the right is an archway. Head left behind the mausoleum towards the cliff edge and enjoy the view into the valley below. To the right (east), a grassy track leads to two **burial chambers** in the northern side of the cliff.

Wading through long grass and ducking tree branches, you can continue along this edge, where there are other caves with gaping holes in the cliff face. Or you can return to the stone path. Either way, eventually, you will reach the locked **East Gate**. Here, the road loops back on itself towards the main gate. It passes several homesteads and the archway you previously saw to the right; this is a remnant of the **Middle Defensive wall** built in the 6th century and reinforced in the 15th century.

Camping in the wild is allowed near (although sadly not on) Chufut-Kale; water is available from a fountain at the chapel next to the Uspensky Monastery. Bring your own food and supplies.

Getting There & Away

There's no difficulty finding transport to Bakhchisaray. At least 11 buses a day travel from Sevastopol (6uah, one hour) and up to 26 a day are scheduled in summer. At Simferopol's central bus station (4uah, one hour), only four services daily to Bakhchisaray are on the timetable, but more leave. Buses between Simferopol and Sevastopol also go through Bakhchisaray.

Meanwhile, local *elektrychka* between Sevastopol and Simferopol shuffle back and forth seven times a day in each direction. For these, you will need to buy your ticket at the *prymisky kasa* (local ticket office) of either train station. Trains from Simferopol (2uah) take 45 minutes, those from Sevastopol (3uah) 1½ hours. Some mainline train services heading north out of Sevastopol (eg to Kyiv or Donetsk) stop at Bakhchisaray, but it's cumbersome catching these over a short distance and usually much more expensive.

Getting Around

All buses to Bakhchisaray stop at the train station, 3km west of the Khans' Palace. On the way into town, they make a loop further into the city, so you want to alight when the driver, or another passenger, shouts '*vokzal*' (often at the entrance to the station plaza, away from the main building). When leaving town, buses leave from outside the station.

From here, bus No 2 (50 kopecks, 11 a day) stops in front of the palace. However, many of the frequent *marshrutka* services (1.50uah) leaving from the plaza follow the same route. Simply ask the driver '*doh*

khansky palats?'. Alternatively, you can take a taxi for 6uah to 7uah.

To get to the palace on foot (a 45-minute hike), walk 300m east of the train station, to the large intersection, then continue straight ahead (third road from left).

Having visited the palace, you can stick out your hand for a *marshrutka* or bus to take you further up the road to Uspensky Monastery and Chufut-Kale – they are all going that way now. Or you can continue to walk. After about 500m, you'll pass the small Mosque of Tokhtala-Dzhama. Another 1.5km on, you'll arrive in the hamlet of Starosele. You'll know you're in the right place, because enterprising restaurateurs have opened a small cluster of Tatar establishments to serve the growing tourist trade.

Past the bus stop and small car park, there's a paved path heading up the hill on the right to Uspensky Monastery (a five- to 10-minute walk) and Chufut-Kale beyond. In season, touts will try to sell you a ticket to Chufut-Kale. You can easily ignore them here, but might have more trouble refusing at the city gates.

MANHUP-KALE МАНГУП-КАЛЕ

If you like Chufut-Kale, or you would prefer to devote an entire day to a cave city, head to Manhup-Kale. Located 22km south of Bakhchisaray, it's larger than Chufut-Kale, more remote and even more spectacular.

This plateau is in the shape of a hand with four fingers. Formerly the ancient capital of Feodor, the principality of the 6th-century 'Crimean Greeks' (actually Greeks, Goths and Samartian descendants), its sheer cliffs made it an excellent fortress. It was finally abandoned in the 15th century.

The closest village to Manhup-Kale, Zalisne, is reached from Bakhchisaray bus station by two daily buses. The easiest way to reach the village is to hitch or take a taxi (about 50uah).

From the southern end of Zalisne walk about 1km until you see, on your left, four rock peaks rising in a row out of wooded ravines. Turn off the road towards the small hamlet at the base of the ridge. On the furthest fingertip east you'll see small holes and some cave openings – that's where the biggest concentration of caves is. The other three fingers have only a few scattered walls.

CAVE CITIES

Many readers will have heard of Göreme in Turkey's Cappadocia region. Crimea's cave cities, while smaller, are roughly a similar deal. Manhup-Kale and Chufut-Kale (p137) are just two of about 20, with the most obvious third choice to visit being Tepe-Kermen, about 2km east of Chufut-Kale. If you really get the bug, you'll find hiking maps to all the cave cities are sold at the souvenir stalls in Starosele at the foot of the path to Chufut-Kale. Most maps are in Russian, but keep an eye out for the English-language booklet *Cave Cities of the Crimea*.

The best way up is between the first two fingers; a trail leads up to your right just as you approach the small group of cottages.

At the top of the ridge follow the trail to the furthest finger of land until you see a large stone gateway and long wall. Beyond are the carved-out chambers and caves. Explore along the far eastern edge of the cliff; many chambers have windows looking out over the vast vista. The most impressive is the final cave room carved out of the very tip of the cliff with stairs leading down the west side to a burial chamber with tiny cells.

SEVASTOPOL СЕВАСТОПОЛЬ

☎ 0692 / pop 330,000

If only all former Soviet cities were as clean as Sevastopol! Spick and span, it always seems ready for military inspection. Whitewashed neoclassical buildings and stone forts stand to attention before a cerulean bay, and there's a palpable sense of civic pride as cleaners sweep the waterfront promenades in the early morning light.

Those military analogies aren't pure fancy. Until 1996 this naval base was closed to outsiders and both the Russian and Ukrainian Black Sea fleets remain anchored here. Russia has a lease on the port until 2019 and its continued presence isn't by any means unwelcome. It's a fond reminder of a communist era that was unusually good to Sevastopol and gave it a head start. A prominent statue of Lenin still watches from a hill as black-uniformed Russian sailors and their green-clad Ukrainian counterparts go about their business.

History

Modern Sevastopol (pronounced see-vas-*to*-pple locally) has an attractive appearance, but it was a different story when the city was making international headlines during the Crimean War. After 349 days of bombardment by the British, French and Turks in 1854–55, it lay devastated by the time of its defeat. Arriving 10 years later, Mark Twain still felt moved to remark: 'In whatsoever direction you please, your eye encounters scarcely anything but ruin, ruin, ruin!'

History repeated itself in 1942, when the city fell to the Germans after a brutal 250-day siege. Stalin promptly proclaimed it a 'hero city' for holding out so long. Only 10 buildings in town today date from before 1945.

Orientation

The train station is south of the town centre and main seafront. To get into town, cross the metal pedestrian bridge over the tracks and wait at the bus shelter for any trolleybus or *marshrutka* marked 'центр' or '5км'. The main street, pr Nakhimova, begins soon after you pass the roundabout with the unmistakable Admiral Nakhimov monument. It heads west (left) along the waterfront. Some 600m on, you turn left (south) into vul Bolshaya Morskaya for the famous panorama.

Information

There are 24-hour ATMs along pr Nakhimova and vul Bolshaya Morskaya.

Central post office (☎ 544 881; vul Bolshaya Morskaya 21; ☽ counters 9am-7pm Mon-Fri, to 2pm Sat, internet centre 8am-7pm Mon-Fri, to 6pm Sat & Sun) Internet costs 5uah per hour.

Exim Bank (pr Nakhimova 15; ☽ 9am-4.30pm Mon-Fri) Offers ATM access and credit-card advances, and even cashes travellers cheques.

Sevram (☎ 555 878, 550 829; office@sevram.com; Office 63, Palace of Childhood, pr Nakhimova 4) This Crimean War specialist offers English-speaking guides for about $12 to $15 an hour. Other languages and tours available. The office is tucked away, so ring or email first; staff speak English.

Telephone office (☽ 9am-10pm) In the side street next to the post office.

Sights & Activities

Climate and environment make Sevastopol a pleasant sojourn for anyone. Most overseas visitors, however, will be in town because of an interest in the Crimean War.

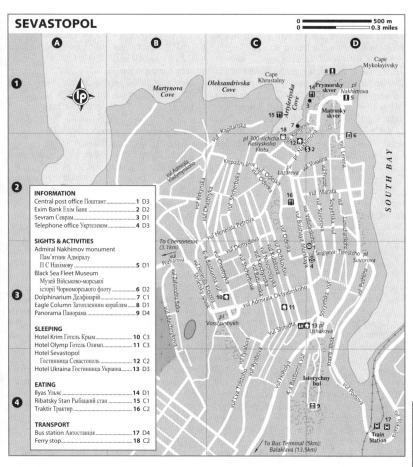

SEVASTOPOL

0 ——— 500 m
0 ——— 0.3 miles

Some of that history is celebrated in city monuments. The **Eagle Column** (1904), atop a rock in the sea, commemorates Russian ships deliberately scuppered at the mouth of the harbour in 1854 to make it impossible for enemy ships to pass. The **Admiral Nakhimov monument** (1959) literally puts on a pedestal the man who led the city's sea and land defence.

But for military buffs, the centrepiece of Sevastopol's war-time memories is the **painted panorama** (bul Istorychny; adult/child/concession 12/6/8uah, English/German guide 14uah extra; 9.30am-5pm, closed Mon), on a hill near the centre of town. A painting around the inner wall of a circular building is supplemented with 3-D props designed to bring the 349-day siege of

Sevastopol to life. Entry is only as part of a group tour, leaving at allotted times (usually every hour in summer). The commentary is in Russian, although you can buy English-language assistance and some of the signage below the platform is in English.

Behind the panorama are several original gun emplacements and redoubts employed in the Crimean War. From here, you can also see today's Black Sea Fleet nestling in South Bay (Pivdenny Bay). Some 460 vessels belong to Russia, 162 to Ukraine. To learn more about the controversial fleet's earlier history, head to the **Black Sea Fleet Museum** (542 280; vul Lenina 11; admission 10uah; 10am-5pm Wed-Sun). The many ship models include the famous battleship *Potemkin Tavrichesky*, whose sailors helped fuel the move to anti-Tsarist revolution in the early part of the 20th century (see the boxed text p122).

The Crimean War and naval history aside, the ruins of the **ancient Greek city of Chersonesus** (admission 10uah; ☺ 9am-7pm) are a delight. Founded in 422 BC, Chersonesus (Khersones locally) is the spot where Volodymyr the Great was famously baptised as a Christian in 989 AD, thus launching what would become the Russian Orthodox Church. Tatars destroyed the city in the 14th century, but much has been excavated. The highlight is a row of marble columns from an early Christian church, a few metres from the shore. The **Prince Volodymyr Cathedral** was also magnificently restored in 2004, but the accompanying museums can easily be skipped.

Except at the height of summer, when some *marshrutky* reportedly run, a taxi is the only option. On the street, drivers will quote up to 20uah. If you get your hotel to call, it should be around 7uah to 10uah.

Urban adventurers will relish the chance to get under Sevastopol's skin with a tour of its **catacombs** (☎ 8-050 244 3962; www.sevdig.sevastopol .ws; admission for 2 $50-75) which are much more extensive than those in Odesa. The 350,000 sq metres of chambers and tunnels include the former emergency headquarters of the Black Sea Fleet – once top-secret – plus subterranean command posts, artillery batteries, fortifications and casemates, some dating back to the days of Catherine the Great.

If you've still got time on your hands, you can catch a **ferry** across the bay to the north shore – just for the views. The **dolphinarium** (☎ 559 955; nab Kornylova 2; admission 18uah; ☺ 10am-4.30pm Tue-Sun) sounds better than it looks, based on rumours that these dolphins were once engaged in military missions. Frankly, their current quarters are cramped and you'll just feel pity for the poor creatures.

Sleeping

Hotel Ukraina (☎ 542 127; www.ukraine-hotel.com.ua; vul Hoholya 2; s/d/ste from $50/65/90, 'king' r $85; **P** 🔀) This friendly hotel evinces a vague sense of style. The black wood panelling in the lobby is a Viennese Secessionist/Bauhaus touch, and some of the 'king' rooms feel remotely Japanese, with a voile curtain separating the bedroom from the living room and kitchenette. If you can, nab one of these.

Hotel Sevastopol (☎ 466 400; fax 466 409; pr Nakhimova 8; s/d from $8/11, with private bathroom $15/25, ste from $55) This creaky old pile seems to have a brilliant location, until you realise you can't sleep for the noisy seaside revelry. Balconies slope and the large, digital clocks make one feel like a nervous athlete, but the white, neoclassical façade, decent bathrooms and seafront views strangely make up for these. Cheaper rooms go very early and foreigners are frequently offered a suite.

Hotel Olymp (☎ 455 758; www.olymphotel.com; vul Kulakova 86; s $100, d & tw $110, ste $130; **P** 🔀 🔀) The faux-Greek motifs are a trifle nouveau riche, but it's hard to complain about the level of comfort offered here. Staff speak some English and are helpful.

Hotel Krim (☎ 469 000; vul Sheshtaya Bastionna 46; s from $20, d & tr from $30; **P** 🖥) The Krim is slightly better than expected for a Soviet-era establishment. Rooms are old and modest, but offer OK value for prices that don't go above $40, including breakfast. Once you get past the bizarre mix of car showroom, casino, marriage agency and photocopy shop that is the entrance, some of the higher floors have expansive sea views.

Eating & Drinking

Possibly because the city was closed for so long, the notion of good service seems a foreign concept. For cheap eats, head to the waterfront, particularly behind the Hotel Sevastopol, where there are some pizza places and kebab outlets. Bars and clubs are found down here, too.

Rybatsky Stan (☎ 557 278; Harbour; mains 25-85uah; ☺ 11am-3am) This is possibly the best seafood restaurant in Crimea, although it also serves delicious poultry, meat, lip-smacking salads and even frog's legs and snails. Its success is down to fresh and 'ecologically clean' ingredients, combined with chefs who seem comfortable catering to Western palates and standards. Its wooden deck on the waterfront is a lovely spot for a drink at dusk, although when cruise ships are in they obscure some of the view.

Ilyas (☎ 544 766; pr Nakhimova 2; mains 10-25uah; ☺ 9am-11pm) You want a table by the window here, especially at midday when the harbour shimmers all the way out to the fort. The seafood isn't as spectacular, so you might prefer the Tatar menu of *shashlyk*, pilaf, *manti* (minced-lamb in home-made pasta), *bureks* (deep-fried parcels of pastry filled with meat or cheese) and samosas. The place is popular with tour groups.

Traktir (☎ 52 21 27; vul Bolshaya Morskaya 8; mains 18-30uah) Right down to the waiters and waitresses deck out in jaunty white and blue sailors suits, this place is a bit too gimmicky. Lots of dishes allude to the Crimean War in name – pies called 'Malakhov Hill', for example – and the service is especially awful. Admittedly, something smelled delicious when we here, but it wasn't our *kurnyk* (chicken, kasha and pancake pie).

Getting There & Away

There are two mainline trains a day from Kyiv direct to Sevastopol (50uah to 60uah, 17 hours). Local *elektrychka* run regularly to/from Simferopol (5uah, two hours, seven daily in each direction). The latter service stops en route in Bakhchysaray (2uah, 1½ hours).

There are buses every half-hour or hour to/from Bakhchysaray (6uah, one hour), Yalta (9uah to 12uah, two hours) and Simferopol (8uah to 12uah, two hours).

AROUND SEVASTOPOL
Balaklava Балаклава
☎ 0692

Put aside ideas of the balaclava that covers the head and neck, leaving only a slit for the eyes. Balaklava, the village, might have given that woolly cap its name, but it's a far more picturesque sight. Strung along a narrow, curving Black Sea inlet, with scrubby hills on either side, its charming buildings and blue waters are overshadowed by the ruins of a Genoese fort. An irresistible, 20-minute climb gives you a bird's-eye view of both the coast and the cove. Alternatively, you can live out Cold War spy fantasies by exploring the remains of a secret Soviet submarine factory.

HISTORY

The British navy made Balaklava its base during the Crimean War, but during the stormy winter of 1854 many ships sank and sailors began dying of cold. Reading about this in the *Times,* concerned English women began knitting full-cover woolly caps and sending them to 'Balaclava'. They became known as Balaclava helmets and eventually just balaclavas.

> ### THE CAUSES OF THE CRIMEAN WAR
>
> The Crimean War of 1854–56 resulted from imperial Russia's attempts to gain unfettered access to the Mediterranean. It lost the war, but within 20 years was breathing down the back of the Balkans again.
>
> Russia initially wanted control over parts of the decaying Ottoman Empire (particularly Moldavia and Walachia) to secure a route from the Black Sea to the Mediterranean. Britain and France opposed the move as it was a threat to their routes to India and their North African colonies. The first skirmishes were in Turkey in 1853, from which the Russians quickly withdrew. However, the allies were now fired up and joined the Turks in sending a punitive invasion force to Crimea the following year.
>
> The fighting centred on Sevastopol, Russia's main Black Sea port, which the allies surrounded for 349 days.
>
> Each side lost an estimated 250,000 during the war. Many allied soldiers died from disease, bad hospitals and poor supplies, all conditions to which British nurse Florence Nightingale drew attention.

During the war, Florence Nightingale ran a field hospital on one of the plateaus above the village, and the infamous charge of the ill-fated Light Brigade took place in a valley north of the city (see the boxed text, p144).

SIGHTS & ACTIVITIES

Unsurprisingly, others discovered this wonderful cove before the British navy; the settlement is about 2500 years old and even mentioned in Homer's *Odyssey* as a pirate's den. Today, however, the oldest surviving reminders of earlier habitation only date back to the 15th century. These are three towers from the **Genoese Fortress of Chembalo**, which you immediately see on the hills above town. Chembalo was the village's name before 1475, when conquering Turks rechristened it Balaklava, or 'Fish's Nest'.

The surrounding hills are perfect for scrabbling over, and the most obvious thing to do is to walk up to the lowest fortress tower (passing the town's public toilets; many cafés don't have any). However, keep

CRIMEA

heading south along the base of this hill and you'll arrive at the eastern point above the mouth of the cove, where you will be rewarded with even better views of coastline and the bay.

Back in town, opposite the main stretch of restaurants and cafés, there's a concrete opening in the harbour wall. This is the mouth of the 'fish's nest', a natural underwater cave and harbour inside the hills, which the Soviets turned into a **secret nuclear submarine factory**. Plans are to create a naval museum inside, but meanwhile you can still visit the factory tunnels by hiring a small boat from in front of the cafés, or by taking a scuba-diving trip. **Akvarmarin** (☎ 530 352; www .voliga.ru; vul Nazukina 5; qualified dives from 160uah, equipment hire daily from 140uah) offers this and other dives, while an English-speaking, PADI-qualified instructor works with the company during summer. Tour operators along the harbour tout regular, short **cruises**.

Just back up the road from the bus terminus, look for the **Exhibition on the**

Crimean War (☎ 595 007, 531 072; Balaklava Centre of Culture & Rest, vul Seventh of November 6; admission 5uah; ☺ 9am-6pm). Memorabilia from each army camp – Russian, English, French and Turkish – includes small chess pieces made from bullets. The helpful, English-speaking curator, Nadejda, can offer advice on finding various battlefields. The exhibition is due to stay open at least until the end of 2006.

SLEEPING

Most travellers will view Balaklava as a day trip from Sevastopol, but there are a few rooms available.

Golden Symbol (☎ 535 557, 535 624; www.golden symbol.com not in English; vul Nazukina 2; r $50) Right on the waterfront, this new hotel could easily be mistaken for the local port or yacht club, but just head right in. With pine floors and furniture, rooms are basic, clean and modern. There's a restaurant and bar on site.

Balaklava Hostel (☎ 538 580, in Russian; www .hostels.org.ua; vul Drapushko 18; dm $7) Recommended

---

INTO THE VALLEY OF DEATH

Unquestioning loyalty, bravery and inexplicable blunders leading to tragedy – these ingredients turned an engagement lasting just minutes into one of the most renowned battles in military history. The action in question is the ill-fated charge of the Light Brigade, which occurred during a Russian attempt to cut British supply lines from Balaklava to Sevastopol during the Crimean War.

The battle began northeast of Balaklava early on 25 October 1854. Russian forces based on the east–west Feduikine Hills also wrested control of allied gun positions (Turkish-held) lining the parallel southern ridge of Causeway Heights. Then they moved towards Balaklava itself.

Initially, the Russians were blocked by the 'thin red line' of the British 93rd Highlanders, and repulsed by Lord Lucan's Heavy Cavalry Brigade. But four hours later, they appeared to be regrouping at the eastern end of the valley between the Feduikine Hills and Causeway Heights. British army commander Lord Raglan sent an order for the cavalry 'to try and prevent the enemy carrying away the guns'.

The order was vague – which guns exactly? – and misinterpreted. The Earl of Cardigan headed off down the wrong valley, leading his Light Cavalry Brigade into a cul-de-sac controlled on three sides by the enemy. The numbers are disputed, but nearly 200 of 673 were killed.

'C'est magnifique, mais ce n'est pas la guerre,' exclaimed a watching French general. ('It's magnificent, but it's not war.') Later, romantic poet Lord Alfred Tennyson would lionise the 'noble six hundred' who rode into 'the valley of death'. His poem 'The Charge of the Light Brigade' did more than anything to mythologise the event for posterity. On its 150th anniversary, the charge was even recreated in front of British dignitaries, including Prince Phillip.

Online encyclopedia Wikipedia is altogether less reverent about the whole affair, stating simply: 'Initially the Russian commanders believed the British soldiers must have been drunk and it improved the reputation of British cavalry.'

The 'Valley of Death' is now a vineyard, just north of the M18 road from Sevastopol to Yalta. You can look down on it from the WWII Diorama and Memorial at Sapun Gor (Сапун гор). Catch a taxi, or contact travel agency Sevram (p140) to take you to the memorial for British soldiers.

only for determined backpackers wanting a slice of the 'real' Ukraine. Rooms are basic, although a distinct improvement on the almost-derelict exterior. The out-of-the-way location, halfway between Sevastopol and Balaklava, is the biggest drawback; see the website for directions. Lone women will feel uncomfortable in this remote, run-down neighbourhood at night.

GETTING THERE & AWAY

In Sevastopol, take any trolleybus (0.50uah) or *marshrutka* (1uah) heading away from the train station or south down vul Bolshaya Morskaya to '5km'. (The sign looks the same in Cyrillic). This transport terminus 5km south of town is huge, chaotic and hectic. The bus drops passengers off at one entrance and the *marshrutky* to Balaklava (2uah to 3uah) leave from the back of the far left-hand corner here. Continue along the food-stall lined footpath until you see a white cabin set back from the street on your left. Cut through the forecourt here to the street behind, and *marshrutka* No 9 to Balaklava departs to your left.

Sevastopol to Yalta

The drive between Sevastopol and Yalta is one of the two most scenic in Crimea. The road twists and turns along a coastal escarpment, with the Black Sea far below and the sheer cliffs of the Crimean Mountains rising behind. Vineyards and cypress trees line the route.

Thirty kilometres from Sevastopol lies the small village of **Foros**, notable for three things. Firstly this is where Gorbachev was held under house arrest during the 1991 counter-Soviet coup attempt in Moscow. Locals will happily point out his dacha, which has a terracotta roof.

The second attraction is the small, gold-domed Resurrection Church dramatically overlooking the sea from the top of a precipitous crag. The 19th-century tea tycoon Alexander Kuznetsov built the church in thanks for the survival of his daughter, whose runaway horse stopped at the edge of the cliff.

Thirdly, Foros is popular with rock climbers, because of the left-hand face of Mt Mshat-Kaya, the Forosskiy Kant, which rises up above the village. The face lies above today's Sevastopol–Yalta road, near the Baydarsky Vorota pass. For a detailed description of climbing routes, see www.risk.ru/eng /regions/crimea/long/foros/index.html.

YALTA ЯЛТА

☎ 0654 / pop 82,000

It's just too easy to make fun of Yalta – an exclusive 19th-century resort founded on the Russian aristocracy's struggle with tuberculosis, then a 20th-century workers' paradise where model Soviet citizens frolicked between concrete sanatoriums and pebbly beaches. Twinned with the English seaside town of Margate, it's an easy satirical target, what with all the speak-your-weight machines lining its waterfront promenade. That's not to mention the opportunity of having a souvenir photo taken in a crinoline, on a Harley Davidson or with a possum (fortunately not all at once).

However, Crimea's leading tourist trap has much more to offer than a celebration of kitsch. It bursts with so much good-time energy that people remain unruffled by the high-season downsides of crowding, high prices and poor service.

The setting is convenient and extremely beautiful, too, with waving palm trees in the background and the chalky mountain faces rising up to bluey-green tips. Gazing up at yet another statue of Lenin to survive in Crimea, you're forced to reflect that the socialist leader could rarely have been in such luxuriant surrounds.

Orientation

Yalta lies on the gently curving shore of Yalta Bay (Yaltinsky Zaliv), with two rivers flowing at opposite 45% angles flowing into the sea here. The waterfront promenade, nab Lenina, stretches from the mouth of the Bystra (Bystraya) River west to the Vodopadna (Vodapadnaya) River.

The Yalta main bus station is 1.5km north of the centre. Take trolleybus No 1, 2 or 3 down (not up) the hill to the town centre.

Information

In town, currency exchange kiosks dot the waterfront. Dozens of tourist booths line the waterfront and around. Some sell maps, others sell very cheap Russian-language day tours. Remember, some attractions don't need much commentary. Many hotels can also help with information. If calling

CRIMEA

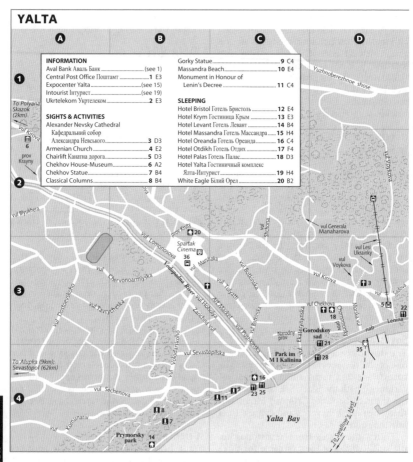

YALTA

INFORMATION
Aval Bank Аваль Банк ....(see 1)
Central Post Office Поштамт **1** E3
Expocenter Yalta.....................................(see 15)
Intourist Інтурист....................................(see 19)
Ukrtelecom Укртелеком.............................**2** E3

SIGHTS & ACTIVITIES
Alexander Nevsky Cathedral
  Кафедральний собор
  Александра Невського...........................**3** D3
Armenian Church.....................................**4** E2
Chairlift Канатна дорога............................**5** D3
Chekhov House-Museum............................**6** A2
Chekhov Statue.......................................**7** B4
Classical Columns....................................**8** B4

Gorky Statue...**9** C4
Massandra Beach...................................**10** E4
Monument in Honour of
  Lenin's Decree **11** C4

SLEEPING
Hotel Bristol Готель Бристоль **12** E4
Hotel Krym Гостиница Крым **13** E3
Hotel Levant Готель Левант **14** B4
Hotel Massandra Готель Массандра **15** H4
Hotel Oreanda Готель Ореанда...........**16** C4
Hotel Otdikh Готель Отдих **17** F4
Hotel Palas Готель Палас.........................**18** D3
Hotel Yalta Гостиничный комплекс
  Ялта-Интурист **19** H4
White Eagle Білий Орел............................**20** B2

from abroad – mobile numbers especially – please note the time difference.

Aval Bank (pl Lenina 1) Booth No 14 of the post office; handles Western Union and cash advances.

Central post office (☎ 312 073; pl Lenina 1; 🕐 8am-8pm)

Expocenter Yalta (☎ 272 546, 8-050 324 2350; www .travel2crimea.com; Hotel Massandra, vul Drazhynskoho 48; 🕐 9am-5pm Mon-Fri, plus 9am-5pm Sat May-Sep) With years of experience, excellent English and a helpful manner, owner Ihor Brudny runs a superior travel service. Website is in conjunction with guide Sergey Sorokin.

Intourist (☎ 327 604; Hotel Yalta, vul Drazhynskoho 50; 🕐 8am-8pm summer, 9am-5pm other times) If you're happy to tag along on one of Intourist's many crowded day tours, great. If you want something different, tough. Customisation isn't a speciality here.

Ukrtelecom (vul Moskovska 9) Telephone and internet centre.

Sights & Activities
THE WATERFRONT

Step right up! Take a stroll along **naberezhna Lenina**, the good-time seaside promenade. The sea view is not at its best here – rusting ships along the jetty, anyone? – but it's the town's main artery, pulsing with life. The pedestrian zone passes palm trees, restaurants, clubs, shops, stalls and photographers before reaching Prymorsky Park.

En route, you'll pass the way to the **chairlift** (return trip 10uah; 🕐 10am-5pm Apr-Sep) that swings above the rooftops to Darsan, a temple-like lookout on the hill. The

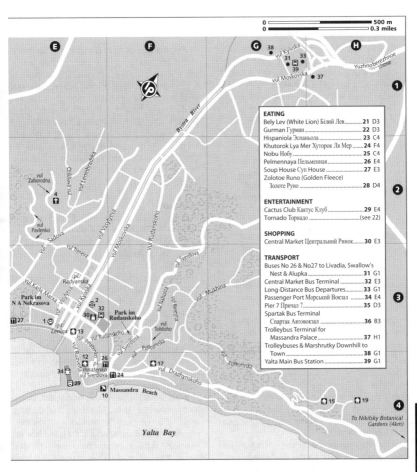

EATING
Bely Lev (White Lion) Білий Лев............**21** D3
Gurman Гурман **22** D3
Hispaniola Эспаньола **23** C4
Khutorok Lya Mer Хуторок Ля Мер **24** F4
Nobu Нобу **25** C4
Pelmennaya Пельменная **26** E4
Soup House Суп House **27** E3
Zolotoe Runo (Golden Fleece)
Золоте Руно **28** D4

ENTERTAINMENT
Cactus Club Кактус Клуб **29** E4
Tornado Торнадо ....(see 22)

SHOPPING
Central Market Центральний Ринок.......**30** E3

TRANSPORT
Buses No 26 & No27 to Livadia, Swallow's
Nest & Alupka **31** G1
Central Market Bus Terminal **32** E3
Long-Distance Bus Departures............**33** G1
Passenger Port Морський Вокзал **34** E4
Pier 7 Причал 7.......................................**35** D3
Spartak Bus Terminal
Спартак Автовокзал **36** B3
Trolleybus Terminal for
Massandra Palace **37** H1
Trolleybuses & Marshrutky Downhill to
Town **38** G1
Yalta Main Bus Station **39** G1

CRIMEA

boarding point is behind nab Lenina 17, along vul Kirova.

Just before Hotel Oreanda, there's an **art and souvenir market** stretching along vul Pushkinska, next to the small Vodopadna River. Heading inland here will take you to the Spartak cinema and bus stop.

Prymorsky Park itself has several statues of great Russians, from Anton Chekhov to Maxim Gorky, plus a monument inscribed with part of Lenin's 1920 decree 'On the Use of the Crimea for the Medical Treatment of the Working People'.

CHEKHOV HOUSE-MUSEUM
With many of Yalta's attractions a short distance away, the **Chekhov House-Museum**

(☎ 394 947; vul Kirova 112; foreign adult/student 10/5uah; ☉ 10am-5.15pm, last entry 4.45pm Wed-Sun, closed last day of the month) is the only must-see in town. It's sort of *The Cherry Orchard* incarnate. Not only did Anton Chekhov (1860–1904) pen that classic play here, the lush garden would appeal to the most horticulturally challenged audience.

A long-term tuberculosis sufferer, the great Russian dramatist spent much of his last five years in Yalta. He designed the white dacha and its garden himself and when he wasn't at his desk, producing plays like *Three Sisters* and *The Cherry Orchard,* he was a legendary host and *bon vivant*. The great Russian singer Fydor Chaliapin and composer Rachmaninov played the piano

---

HIKING GUIDES IN CRIMEA

Crimea has some fantastic hiking opportunities, but a scarcity of really good topographical maps and marked routes and a total lack of English signs mean that many hikers will find the going more challenging than usual. If you enjoy that, fine. If not, consider hiring a guide. Those to contact include:

- **Sergey Sorokin** (www.mt.crimea.com) Experienced 20-something mountain guide who speaks English and French and charges around €50 a day. Tours include to Crimea's 'Grand Canyon' and mountain-biking trips to the Valley of the Ghosts.
- **Han-Tengry** (☎ 0512-362 936; www.han-tengry.mk.ua) Based in Mykolayiv (also called Nykolayiv), this agency offers Crimean treks. Prices range from €10 per person per day for 10-day-long tours for big groups to €100 to individual luxury day trips. Guides speak English.

Some areas, including Crimea's highest mountain, Roman Kosh, near Alushta, are legally off limits without a mountaineering guide.

---

that's still on view in the 1st-floor sitting room. Writer Maxim Gorky had a favourite garden bench and author Leo Tolstoy was another guest.

After the exhibition at the entrance, you head down the path to the dacha, where all nine rooms are pretty much as Chekhov left them upon his departure from Yalta for Germany in May 1904. Explanation sheets are available in several languages.

Take *marshrutka* No 8 from the Spartak bus terminus to the Dom-Muzey A P Chekhova stop, or catch trolleybus No 1 from pl Radyanska (Sovietskaya), alight at the sixth stop, walk up the concrete stairs shortly afterwards to the right at Krajnij pereulok and turn left into vul Kirova at the top. However, to walk the whole distance only takes 15 to 20 minutes from nab Lenina.

OTHER SIGHTS

Alexander Nevsky Cathedral off vul Sadova is a beautiful piece of neo-Byzantine architecture with fantastic detailing. Way up the

hill off vul Zahorodna is the **Armenian church** (1909–17).

Polyana Skazok (Fairy-Tale Glade; ☺ 8am-8pm 15 May-15 Sep, 9am-5pm & closed Wed rest of the year) is an open-air museum featuring statues of Ukrainian, Russian and Western fairy-tale characters. Be warned, though, that the park might be a bit humble for contemporary Western children's tastes. To get here, take bus No 8 from the Spartak bus terminus to the end of the line, or bus No 26, 27, 28 or 11 from Yalta main bus station to the Polyana Skazok bus stop and walk 1km. (Follow the locals.)

Sleeping

The English tour operator **Black Sea Crimea** (☎ +44-20-8200 6834; www.blacksea-crimea.com) offers a whole range of apartments, from €40 a night for a single-bedroom apartment to €120 a night for two double bedrooms. All are bookable online. In summer, locals at Yalta main bus station offer homestays – *komnati* (Russian) or *kimnaty* (Ukrainian). Expect to pay no more than $15 a night.

Prices for the hotels listed here are for the high season in July to August, when it's recommended you book ahead. Out of season, rates reduce progressively. In many hotels, fellow guests include large package-tour groups.

Hotel Otdikh (☎ 353 067; otdyh@yalita.com; vul Drazhynskoho 14; d $15-65; ⊠) Hotel 'Relaxation' was a 19th-century brothel for visiting government dignitaries; now it's a good budget *pension*. The rooms are pleasant, staff speak English and it has a private stretch of beach.

Hotel Bristol (☎ 325 860; vul Ruzvelta 10; s/d from $70/75; ⊠) A rare three-star Ukrainian hotel that lives up to its rating – and possibly even exceeds it – the anglophile Bristol is central and comfortable. Sunny rooms in yellows and blues are thoroughly Western-standard and there's a huge breakfast buffet. For young families, cots can be arranged. It's good value particularly in the off season.

White Eagle (☎ 327 702, 8-050 324 21 61; prov Kruty 13; d $80-100; ☺ summer P) A boutique hotel in Ukraine? Blimey, they do exist. Built like a 19th-century private villa with just half a dozen rooms, this is away from the waterfront. However, its small hillside terrace – where you can eat – has views over the neighbouring rooftops. The lobby is just a touch fanciful, but room décor is tasteful and restrained.

Hotel Massandra (☎ 327 800; vul Drazhynskoho 48; s/d $18/28, superior s/d from $30/40; **P**) This is reasonably pleasant, even considering the older bathrooms, the tiny, scratchy towels, and the fact you have to pay separately for breakfast in the neighbouring café. The big drawback is the location, about 1.5km east of the centre. It's a half-hour walk or short, hairy drive down narrow, winding, poorly lit streets. *Marshrutka* No 34 from the central market stops nearby.

Hotel Yalta (☎ 350 150; www.hotel-yalta.com.ua; vul Drazhynskoho 50; s/d from $24/30; **P** 🖳 🏊) No-one chooses the famous Yalta for comfort or convenience. They stay for the novelty of checking-in to a 2230-bed ex-Soviet behemoth and because it's relatively cheap. Rooms are ordinary and the hotel is as poorly located as the neighbouring Massandra. However, given 10 bars, seven restaurants, numerous shops, a dolphinarium, a sauna, a lift to a private beach and myriad sporting activities, some guests probably never step foot off the premises.

Hotel Oreanda (☎ 274 227; www.hotel-oreanda.com; nab Lenina 35/2; s/d $155/225; superior s/d $185/275; **P** 🍴 ⚙ 🖳 🏊) The crème de la Krim. Revamped just a few years back, the Oreanda offers every luxury you would expect in a top Western European city hotel, although it does seem a little overpriced. Superior rooms are worth splashing out for, as they're the ones with sea views.

Also available:

Hotel Krym (☎ 271 701; director@hotelkrim.yalta.crimea .ua; vul Moskovska 1/6; s/d/tr from $5/10/10) Cheap, relatively unappetising Soviet-style establishment, but central at least.

Hotel Palats (☎ 324 380; fax 220 492; vul Chekhova 8; s/d from $45/50; ⚙) OK midrange choice.

Hotel Levant (☎ 231 13; www.levant.ru; Prymorsky Park; s/d from $125/140; ⚙ **P**) Award-winning new hotel facing the beach at the far end of nab Lenina.

Eating

Yalta's eating options are quite polarised. Cheap *stolovy* (canteens) are here in abundance to cater for the ordinary CIS tourist, while glitzy upmarket restaurants cater to big-spending 'new Russians'.

Pelmennaya (☎ 323 932; vul Sverdlova 8; mains 5-8uah) This is the best workers' caff in town because it makes your order fresh, rather

than doing the usual of placing dishes in a glass display cabinet for hours. *Varenyky, blyny, borshch* and good, crisp salads all join the namesake dish of *pelmeni* (ravioli-like dumplings).

Soup House (nab Lenina 7; mains 3-15uah) While its food is better earlier in the day, this nouveau *stolova* gets bonus points for its stylish, cheerful décor and wide range of Ukrainian staples, from green *borshch* and berry-filled *varenyky* to cranberry juice.

Khutorok Lya Mer (☎ 271 815; vul Sverdlova 8; mains 25-130uah; 🕙 11am-2am) Overlooking the sea at Massandra Beach, this restaurant is designed to look like the interior of a ship, but the theme isn't overdone. Delicious food and an interesting wine selection make this the place for a nice meal out. The low bar, where staff stand as if in an orchestra pit, is eye-catching, as is the menu listing of bull's testicles in horseradish sauce.

The waterfront is lined with many other restaurants, including a huge Viking ship on stilts with wobbly stairs called **Zolote Ruho** (Golden Fleece; nab Lenina; mains 25-60uah), the imperial **Bely Lev** (White Lion; ☎ 327 736; nab Lenina 31; mains 30-75uah) with chandeliers and classical music. Another two restaurants open in summer only are the galleon-shaped **Hispaniola** (☎ 390 631; nab Lenina 35/2) and ritzy sushi bar **Nobu** (☎ 274 246; nab Lenina 35/2) on a bamboo-clad open-air terrace next door. However along the promenade you'll pay more, and the food is nothing spectacular.

The exception to this is seafood restaurant **Gurman** (☎ 320 306; nab Lenina 11; mains 25-40uah), which is a local favourite.

Drinking & Entertainment

In many ways, Yalta in summer is one big nightclub. There are many more choices than the options listed here, including at several hotels. However, these are the most central.

At Massandra Beach head past the seaport building and on to the waterfront, clubs and bars around Khutorok lya Mer and you'll find one of the town's biggest hangouts.

Cactus Club (☎ 321 614; vul Ruzvelta 5) Across from the Hotel Bristol in the seaport building, this is a Tex-Mex restaurant on the ground floor, and a club with a summer terrace on the 1st floor. DJs spin everything from garage to disco.

CRIMEA

Tornado (☎ 322 036; 1st fl, nab Lenina 11) Favoured by new Russians and foreigners, this is one of Yalta's most expensive clubs and a shameless pick-up joint.

Getting There & Away

BOAT

Few boats sail in and out of the **passenger port** (morskoy vokzal; ☎ 320 094; vul Ruzvelta 5), at the end of vul Ruzvelta. From June to September there is a catamaran service between Yalta and Odesa, via Sevastopol (see p189).

BUS & TROLLEYBUS

Trolleybuses to Simferopol leave from beside **Yalta main bus station** (☎ 325 777, 342 092; vul Moskovska 8); see p134 for details.

Buses depart from Yalta main bus station to/from Sevastopol (9uah to 12uah, 2½ hours, half-hourly to hourly), Bakhchysaray (12uah, three hours, three daily) and Odesa (48uah, 12½ hours, once daily). Buses to Feodosiya (26uah, five hours, two daily) and Kerch (42uah, eight hours, once a day) go via Simferopol. Many seemingly unscheduled *marshrutky* also leave from the bus station.

If taxi drivers in Simferopol aggressively tout for custom, they're worse at Yalta bus station, where they're looking for passengers on the homebound journey. They'll even try to convince you that there's no bus going where or when you want. Check before believing them.

Getting Around

There are several bus/*marshrutka* stations in town. You'll arrive at the main bus station (see preceding section), which is about 1.5km from the waterfront. From here, trolleybus No 1, 2, or 3 goes down the hill along vul Kyivska to the town centre.

You can use this bus station again to go west to Alupka. Alternatively, you can find a *marshrutka* leaving from the bus terminus next to the central market. Buses to the Nikitsky Botanical Gardens also go from here.

Other services, including those terminating at Livadia depart from the Spartak terminus, west of Hotel Oreanda, where vuls Marshaka and Pushkinska join.

Unmetered taxis in Yalta charge high fares (up to 15uah from the bus station to Hotel Yalta). **Avka-Trans Taxis** (☎ 231 085, 8-067 563 0444) are metered and cost half as much around town (but not to Simferopol). They're often

found at the intersection of vul Ruzvelta and nab Lenina.

WEST OF YALTA
☎ 0654

Yalta's most popular attractions lie several kilometres west of the city, downhill from the Yalta–Sevastopol road, closer to the shore. As they all lie in a row, it's fairly easy to pop from one to the next. However, undoubtedly the best way to arrive at the Swallow's Nest castle is by boat – which can upset the sequence!

Orientation

Bus No 27 runs hourly from Yalta main bus station to the Alupka stop, from where you can walk across the park to the palace. The wine tasting complex is 50m back up the hill from the bus stop.

Bus No 26 goes to Simeyiz (every 45 minutes), No 39 to Foros (three times a day); both serve Yalta.

Livadia Palace Лівадія Дворец

Everyone has a favourite among Yalta's palaces. Those into history will plump for **Livadia Palace** (Livadia Dvorets; ☎ 315 579, 315 581; adult/child 15uah/7uah 🕙 10am-5.45pm Tue-Thu). It's the site of the 1945 Yalta Conference between British prime minister Winston Churchill, US president Franklin Roosevelt and Soviet leader Josef Stalin, which shaped the face of postwar Europe. The palace doesn't have the most sumptuously furnished interior in Crimea but its scale is impressive. And even as huge tour groups nearly trample you in a race to the overflowing souvenir shops in the furthest rooms, it's also hard not to be moved by the thought of Livadia's ghosts.

The Italian Renaissance-style building was designed as a summer residence for Russian Tsar Nicholas II in 1911. He and his family spent just four seasons here before their arrest by Bolshevik troops in 1917 and their execution the following year. Photos and some poignant mementos of the doomed Romanovs are still in their private apartments upstairs.

Before you get to that, however, you pass through the imposing spaces on the ground floor. Here in the enormous White Hall, the 'Big Three' and their staff met to tacitly agree that the USSR would wield the biggest influence in Eastern Europe, in exchange for its promises to keep out of the Mediterranean. Churchill, Roosevelt and Stalin sat around the small round table in the adjoining room. The crucial documents, dividing Germany and ceding parts of Poland to the USSR, were signed on 11 February in the English billiard room.

The most famous Yalta photograph of Churchill, Roosevelt and Stalin is hung on a wall, along with the awkward outtakes, which really bring history to life. (At the time of writing there was a major dispute over plans to erect a statue of the three men in the grounds, with local Tatars rejecting any memorial to Stalin.)

Other highlights inside the white granite palace include the charming Florentine and Arabic courtyards, the bedroom of the already terminally ill Roosevelt, and the Churchill room, which the curators tend only to open for British visitors and usually only if they ring ahead. The temporary exhibitions in the palace's smaller rooms can usually be skipped. Some signs in the Yalta conference section are in English.

Livadia's coastal **gardens** (admission free; dawn-dusk) are reason alone to visit. Behind the palace you'll find the start of the **Sunny Path** (Solnechnaya Tropa), built on the recommendation of the Tsar Nicholas II's doctor, who believed that regular outdoor exercise would improve the royal family's tuberculosis. The path stretches nearly 7km to Swallow's Nest, but while the first kilometre is well kept and beautifully landscaped, it becomes progressively littered, unpleasant and isolated after that. If you turn right instead of entering the Sunny Path, you'll also find the Romanovs' chapel. The family have been beatified as martyrs by the Russian Orthodox Church.

If you take bus No 26, 27, 32 or 47 to the palace, cross the road after the Livadia Dvorets stop and follow the little path off it down the hill. There are concrete stairs beside the pinky-orange building, where someone has drawn an arrow on the footpath pointing to the castle. Head down these stairs, take the stone stairs behind the big tree at their foot, and where the road forks near a sanatorium, turn left, taking the lower, larger road towards all the tour buses.

Swallow's Nest Ласточкино Гнiздо

Like many movie stars, Swallow's Nest (Lastochkyno Gnizdo) is shorter in real life than it appears in pictures. This toy-town castle is a favourite subject for Crimean postcards, but it's only big enough to house an expensive but exceedingly disappointing Italian **restaurant** (247 571).

Instead, it's the castle's precarious perch on the sheer cliff of Cape Ay-Todor, 10km west of Yalta, that gives it pulling power. Strolling along the surrounding walkway, you realise that the castle actually overhangs the cliff. From here, you have much better views than from most of the restaurant's tables.

Although the castle looks medieval in style, it was built in 1912 for German oil magnate Baron Steingel, as a present to his mistress. Destroyed by an earthquake in 1927, it was heavily reconstructed in 1970.

The most spectacular approach to the castle is over the water, via the **ferry** (adult/child 16/12uah; 4 daily) that heads from Yalta pier 7 to the beach and jetty just below Swallow's Nest.

Bus Nos 26 and 27 also pass this way, both stopping directly in front of a row of restaurants, shops and multicoloured plastic palm trees above the castle. From the road, head past Kafe Yachta to the far left-hand corner of this row, from where steps lead down. In summer, there might be a small entrance fee of 3uah to 5uah at this point of entry, although this was expected to be abolished.

Cable Car Канатна Дорога

About 1km east of Alupka, behind a little cluster of market stalls, is the **cable car** (kanata dorohy; each way 15uah; ticket office 10am-5pm, services until 6pm) up the cliff of Mt Ay-Petri. It's a truly dizzying ride across the foothills and up the mountain's sheer face, during which you overlook the coast and the sea. At the summit, there are expansive views inland, too. Best among the touristy establishments here are the very cheap, but delicious, Tatar food stalls (mains 10uah to 15uah).

There's no guarantee – as there is in Switzerland – that the cable cars are given an overhaul each year, but they seem in much better condition than most Ukrainian transport.

Alupka Алупка

Crimea's most exotic palace-park complex is 16km west of Yalta at Alupka. Wedged between the coast and Mt Ay-Petri, its setting is stunning. The palace was designed and built in 1828–46 by English architects for the English-educated Count Mikhail Vorontsov, the immensely rich regional governor. It's a bizarre combination of Scottish castle on its landward side with Arabic-Asian fantasy facing the sea. Vorontsov brought serfs from his estates all over Russia to create the palace and park. Churchill stayed here during the 1945 Yalta Conference.

Entry into the **Alupkinsky Palace Museum** (☎ 722 81; adult/child 15/7uah; 🕙 9am-6pm Jun; 8am-7.30pm Tue-Sun Jul & Aug; 9am-5pm Tue-Sun Apr, May, Sep & Oct; 9am-4pm Tue-Sun Nov-Mar) takes you firstly into the palace's luxuriant interior, which includes an imitation Wedgwood 'blue room', an English-style dining hall and an indoor conservatory. However, the best views are from the lush gardens behind the palace, where six marble lions flank the staircase up to the ornate façade, which is framed against the backdrop of Mt Ay-Petri. Unfortunately, the gardens nearest the coast have been cordoned off, giving credence to reports that the palace foundations are very slowly slipping into the sea.

To get to the palace from the Alupka bus stop, keep going straight ahead, following the path on the left-hand side of the park as it curves above the seafront for about 900m.

Fifty metres in the opposite direction from the bus stop, back up the road from which you came, is the **Massandra winery** (☎ 721 198; admission 17uah; 🕙 shop 10am-6pm Tue-Sat). Here you can participate in a tasting tour of Crimean wines, although you need to appreciate madeiras, sweet dessert wines or sherries to really enjoy the experience. Between May and November, tours kick off at 11.30am, and 12.30pm, 3pm, 4pm and 5pm Tuesday to Saturday. The rest of the year there are tours at 11.30am and 3pm Tuesday and Thursday, plus 11.30am on Saturday.

Uchansu Waterfall & Mt Ay-Petri
Водопад Учансу та Ай-Петрі

Heading northwest from Yalta, bus No 30 (four times daily) from Yalta main bus station takes you within walking distance of two beauty spots in the mountains off the Bakhchysaray road. From the Vodopad (Waterfall) stop about 11km out, you can walk to a platform beside the 100m-high **Uchansu Waterfall**. From the Karagol stop, 3km further up the road, a track leads to forest-ringed **Lake Karagol**. Both spots have a restaurant.

Continuing past the Karagol stop, the road winds spectacularly up to the top of the range 13km on; the summit of **Mt Ay-Petri** (St Peter, 1233m) sits to the left. This route, and several others up Mt Ay-Petri, are ideal for **mountain biking**. For more details, see www .mountainbiking.velocrimea.com.

The Ay-Petri cable car whisks passengers down to Alupka (see p151).

EAST OF YALTA
☎ 0654

Nikitsky Botanical Gardens
Нікітський Ботанічний Сад

Even if you're no gardener or botanist, the **Nikitsky Botanical Gardens** (adult/child 6/3uah; 🕙 8am-6pm) are worth a visit for their beauty and views. Tumbling down 3 sq km of hillside to the sea, they are home to 28,000 species, including 2000 rose types, a 500-year-old yew tree and a 1000-year-old pistachio tree.

Founded in 1812, the gardens are split into four sections: the Upper Park (Verkhny Park) and Lower Park (Nyzhny Park), together called the Arboretum; Prymorsky Park; and Cape Montedor Park (Mys-Montedor Park). The Upper Park has the rose garden and a fine observation area. Prymorsky Park has delicate subtropical plants.

From the central market bus terminus, take bus No 34 to the Upper Gate bus stop. Stroll through the gardens down to the sea, then walk a short distance back up the hill to get the return bus to Yalta from the Lower Gate bus stop. The more frequent bus No 31 to Hurzuf passes the NBS bus stop on the Yalta–Alushta highway, which is a 2km signposted walk from the gardens.

Massandra Palace Массандра Дворец

A hunting lodge built to resemble a French chateau, **Massandra Palace** (☎ 321 728; adult/child 15/7uah; 🕙 10am-6pm Wed-Mon, to 4pm Nov-Apr) was completed by Tsar Alexander III in 1889. It's better known, however, for what it became: Stalin's summer dacha.

Recently restored, the palace contains paintings and antique furniture. However, the parkland surrounding the palace is probably more beautiful. Take trolleybus No 2, heading uphill opposite the Yalta main bus station.

HURZUF ГУРЗУФ

Hurzuf's steep, winding streets and old wooden houses, backed by Mt Roman-Kosh (1543m), are a magnet for artists and writers. The village, 18km northeast of Yalta, is built around a picturesque bay with the rocky Genoese Cliff (Skala Dzhenevez) at its eastern end. Bear Mountain (Hora Medvid or Ayu-dah, 565m) looms along the coast to the east, protruding into the sea.

Overhanging wooden balconies, a few cafés and the odd shop adorn vul Leningradska, the curving, picturesque main street. The beach just west of the town centre is backed by **Hurzufsky Park**, home to some elegant wooden, 19th-century sanatoriums and lots of red squirrels. The dacha of the Duc de Richelieu, governor of Odesa (1803–14), today houses the **Pushkin in Crimea Museum** (☺ 10am-5pm Wed-Sun, closed winter), a history museum.

Chekhov's dacha (vul Chekhova 22; ☺ Tue-Sun, closed winter), also a museum, sits close to the foot of Genoese Cliff. At the eastern end of vul Leningradska are the remains of a 6th- to 15th-century **clifftop fortress**, founded by the Byzantines and rebuilt by the Genoese. A path round to the left leads through a rock tunnel to the sea-cliff edge. Beyond is a handsome swathe of beach.

Bus No 31 (every 30 to 45 minutes) links Hurzuf with Yalta main bus station.

ALUSHTA АЛУШТА

Yalta's poor sibling, 40km northeast, is a sea of high-rise concrete towers and offers little of interest to see or do. From the bus station roundabout, where the Simferopol–Yalta road touches northwest Alushta, vul Horkoho runs down to the harbour 1km away. Bus Nos 2 and 4 follow this sea-bound route.

East of the harbour is the promenade, with a few small subdivided beaches and a larger free-access, half-sand, half-rock beach at the far end. Westwards are some parks and paths leading towards the Rabochy Uholok (Workers' Corner) where most sanatoriums are concentrated.

The tall unsightly **Hotel Alushta** (☎ 550 62, 552 78; vul Oktyabrska 50; s/d $15/35; ☺ summer)

building next to Alushta bus station has grotty rooms.

Trolleybus No 52 (Yalta–Simferopol train station) trundles from Yalta through Alushta (one hour, every 20 minutes), while No 51 runs between Alushta and Simferopol train station (1½ hours, every 20 minutes).

AROUND ALUSHTA

Although the following natural attractions are closest to Alushta, that city's lack of both decent budget hotels and good looks mean that most travellers would be better served using another base, either Simferopol or Yalta.

Chatyr-Dah Чатир-Даг

Mt Chatyr-Dah (1527m) lies west of the Alushta–Simferopol road and is most famous for the numerous caves that lie beneath it. Two in particular stand out: the **Mramorna Pechera** (Marble Cave; admission from 16uah) Cave and the **Eminé-Ba'ir-Khosar** (Well of Maiden Eminé; admission from 16uah). Admission prices depend on the length of the tour.

The first is a long, shallow cave (68m deep and nearly 2km long) formed by the collapse of underground riverbeds. It's full of strangely shaped stalactites and stalagmites, which the on-site guides (Russian-speaking only) have named after various animals, objects, fairy-tale characters and international buildings, such as the leaning tower of Pisa. There's even a mini-Manhattan on the roof and the vast space at the end has been nicknamed 'Perestroika Hall'.

The second cave, Eminé-Ba'ir-Khosar, spirals down to 120m, with jade-like stalagmites, crystal flowers and a lake. According to legend, Eminé threw herself to the bottom of the cave after her lover was killed by her father's family.

The caves are tricky to reach on your own, as they lie at the end of a rough, 10km dirt road and few local taxi drivers can be convinced to drive out here. If you're coming from Simferopol, which is closer than Yalta, you can get off the trolleybus at the stop for Mramornoye and, armed with a good topographical map, hike the direct route across the mountain. By the time you visit the caves, getting there and back on foot is probably a two-day trip, so take a tent, just in case the mountain huts on site are booked.

Alternatively, settle for a day tour from Yalta. Those sold by the stalls along the promenade are always in Russian, but in high season some travel agents and hotels such as the Oreanda can arrange English-language tours. Russian-language 'extreme' tours of the lower level of the Mramorna cave (three hours) are organised by **Onyx Tour** (☎ 0652-245 822, Russian only).

Mt Demerdzhi Гора Демерджі

If you don't have time to visit the amazing Kara-Dah Nature Reserve, the **Valley of the Ghosts** under Mt Demerdzhi also contains some stunning rock formations. These have been created by wind erosion of sandstone, rather than volcanic eruptions, but the freaky pillars with vaguely human features are certainly memorable.

If you get off the trolleybus at the Angarskii Pass (coming from Simferopol is quicker than from Yalta) you can hike towards Mt Demerdzhi and the Dzhurla waterfall, before turning south to the valley. Two other options include taking a taxi towards the village of Luchistoye (Лучистое) in Russian, or Luchyste (Лучисте) in Ukrainian, and hiking north, or taking an organised mountain-bike tour (www.mt.crimea.com). If you go by yourself, take a good topographical map. Starting from either direction, the return hike is at least a full day's trip.

YALTA TO SUDAK

Visitors to eastern Crimea are much fewer than in the west, but the region has some of the peninsula's most outstanding natural attractions. For starters, the journey between Yalta and Sudak is arguably even more scenic than that between Sevastopol and Yalta. About halfway along, the lush palm trees and cypresses of warm western Crimea are replaced by stark steppe as the climate cools.

Some 7km before Sudak is the sleepy seaside resort of **Novy Svit** (Новий Світ; New World). The bay here is generally agreed to have some of the best beaches in Crimea, and is framed by the 474m Mt Sokil (or Kush-Kaja in Tatar, meaning Falcon Mountain) to the east and the much lower Mt Orel (or Koba-Kaja, Eagle Mountain) on the western cape. Mt Sokil can be climbed without a guide, taking about three hours in total.

You're not allowed on Mt Orel without a guide, but there is a path (4uah) at its base that will take you on a picturesque route along the coast to Sudak and back to Novy Svit in three hours. En route, you'll encounter a huge seaside grotto, in which a local 19th-century tycoon used to hold high society parties.

Novy Svit is also famous for its champagne, should you want to celebrate a climb or hike. There are *marshrutky* and taxis from Sudak.

SUDAK СУДАК

☎ 06566 / pop 14,500

As an important stop on the Silk Road from China, Sudak was a major, and well-defended, trading centre. Its giant **Genoese Fortress** (Sudakska Krepost; admission 4uah, still/video photography 5/15uah; ☯ 9am-8pm, to 5pm Oct-May) still stands today, wonderfully perched on a massive cliff overlooking the town and the sea. This is Ukraine's most impressive surviving fortress, resembling a mini Great Wall of China. Built by a predominantly Tatar workforce during the 14th and 15th centuries, its crenulated walls are 2m thick and 6m high. Ten of its 18 original defensive towers remain and the ramparts extend for 2km, cutting a magnificent silhouette. To the west rises Mt Perchem (576m), its face dramatically dropping into a sheer cliff; and to the far east is Mt Urmani-Ustu (352m), its two peninsular points protruding into the sea.

Most of the towers still bear their original Italian names. The main fortress entrance is via a forecourt which leads through the Holovna (Main) Gate between the **Tower of Torcello** (right) and the **Tower of Di Franco Di Pagano** (left). Inside, the walls encircle over 30 hectares of desolate sloping terrain with a few overgrown ruins and foundations lying about. The largest tower on the dramatically sloping south side along the coastline is the 14th-century, twin-towered **Consul's Tower**. The next tower up, the 14th- to 15th-century **Tower of St George** leads out to a viewpoint and a stepped path on the seaward side of the long crenulated wall that eventually leads to the apex, the remains of the 14th-century **Dozorna Tower**. It's officially forbidden to climb this last 'Virgin's Tower', but few seem to obey the rules.

There is a sporadic bus between the bus station, north of town, and the fortress.

Sleeping

Hotel Forum (☎ 338 60; vul Lenina 88; standard s/d from 40/45, superior d from $60; P ⌨ 🖵) One of the new generation of glass-and-concrete private hotels in Ukraine, the Forum doesn't exude masses of atmosphere, but it's the only truly Western-standard hotel in town and is tastefully decorated, mainly in blues and earth tones.

Hotel Horyzont (☎ 221 79; fax 211 83; vul Turist-ikoyu 8; s/d incl compulsory full board $20/40) The large Hotel Horyzont near the foot of the fortress has passable rooms, some of which have fortress views.

Getting There & Away

From Sudak there are buses to/from Simferopol (18uah, 2½ hours, seven daily), Yalta (four hours, once daily) and Feodosiya (10uah, two hours, one daily). Buses from Kerch (24uah, four hours, two daily) also pass through Feodosiya.

KARA-DAH NATURE RESERVE
КАРА-ДАГ ЗАПОВІДНИК
☎ 06562

The Kara-Dah Nature Reserve, between Sudak and Feodosiya, is a true Jurassic park. Its dramatic landscape is the work of an extinct volcano (Kara-Dah, or Black Mountain in Tatar) that spewed lava and debris over land and sea during the Jurassic period. Over millennia, the elements have moulded the volcanic rocks into striking shapes, with names like 'The Devil's Finger', 'The King and the Earth', or the 'Golden Gate', a freestanding arch in the sea. These all circle the 575m Kara Dah, or Mt Svyataya in Russian.

To top it off, the area is full of many rare minerals and crystals, as well as lots of flora and fauna. You could see cormorants, eagles and storks, and walk past pistachio, pine and juniper trees.

For environmental reasons, you cannot visit this nature reserve alone. Furthermore, some of the volcanic mountains contain so much iron that they render a compass useless. Therefore, you must go to the **visitor centre** (☎ 383 31; karadag@crimea.com) at the library of the seaside hamlet of **Kurortne**, where you can buy a ticket (15uah) for a four-hour guided hike with a group and knowledgeable Russian-speaking guide. If you want explanations in English, you will have to arrange for your own interpreter beforehand.

Several buses and *marshrutky* daily go from Feodosiya to Kurortnoe (3uah, one hour). A taxi costs about 30uah. From Koktebel, you can catch a bus to the village of Shchebetovka and then hike 3.5km south. Alternatively, catch a boat (10uah) around the coast to the pier at Kurortnoe.

If you're visiting the reserve, you might want to overnight in the artists' colony of **Koktebel**, rather than Feodosiya. Accommodation options in Koktebel include the huge, 853-bed **Turbaza Prymore** (☎ 362 75; vul Lenina 124; d incl full board $12-20; ⊙ May-Sep) at the east end of the village. Rooms have their own basic facilities and balconies, while the hotel has its own pebble beach.

Weather permitting, you could also pitch a tent at the naturist beach of **Lissya Bukhta** (Fox Bay). It's about a 2.5km walk east around the headland from Kurortnoe, or a short boat-ride west from Koktebel.

FEODOSIYA ФЕДОСІЯ
☎ 06562 / pop 74,500

There's no compelling reason to head to Feodosiya unless you're a massive fan of the renowned seascape artist Ivan Ayvazosky. However, eastern Crimea's largest city is a pleasant enough place, which mixes a busy cargo port with elegant old mansions, health resorts and some sandy beaches. It makes a reasonable base for exploring the Kara-Dah Nature Reserve.

Between 1475 and 1616, Feodosiya was the largest slave-trading centre on the Black Sea coast and was known as 'the vampire that drinks the blood of Rus' by the Slavs. Today, a brace of churches and a Genoese citadel complement the Ayvazosky museum.

Sights

The modern city centre lies northwest of the waterfront train station on tree-lined pr Lenina, while the remains of the **Genoese citadel** are even further north along the bay; exit the train station and turn right (north) to head in the direction of either of these.

The old town, on the other hand, is southeast along the curve of the bay. The 14th-century Armenian **Serhiya Church**, left (south) from the train station along pr Lenina and vul Horkoho, has exquisitely carved marble tablets embedded in its façade. Adjoining it is the **Tomb of Ayvazovsky** (1817–1900), who, although of Armenian descent, was born, lived and worked in Feodosiya.

Ayvazosky was one of the world's best painters of breaking waves, ships and moody seas, and the hometown collection contained in the **Ayvazovsky Museum** (☎ 302 79; cnr pr Lenina & vul Halereyna; admission 10uah; ☻ 10am-6pm Thu-Tue) is so large it's spread over two neighbouring buildings. There's a separate entrance and entry charge (5uah) for each.

On the main road to Simferopol, 23km west of Feodosiya, is the farming town **Stary Krym** (Старий Крим), 3km south of which is the 14th-century Armenian **Surp-Khach Monastery** (Сурп-Хач Монастирь). The complex, surrounded by dense woods, includes original monks' cells, a refectory and a beautiful church with a series of vaulted chambers.

Sleeping & Eating

Hotel Lidia (☎ 315 49; vul Libknekhta 13; s/d from $40/60; ℗ ✗ ☎) Built in 2001, this private three-star hotel is definitely the best in town. It has streamlined contemporary furnishings, good facilities and a central location. Prices are lower October to April.

Hotel Moryak (☎ 324 14; www.port-feodosia.com; vul Lenina 8; s/d $10, with private bathroom $15/25) Many older Soviet-style hotels also exist. This one has decent rooms where there has been some attempt at refurbishment.

Dacha Stambul (☎ 300 82; pr Lenina 47) Serves standard Russian fare, but inside a 1911 Ottoman-style palace, built by a rich Tatar magnate.

Getting There & Away

Fredonia's train service is limited to Vladyslavovka (30 minutes, four daily) from where you can catch a train to Kerch (two hours); and to Moscow (22 to 26 hours, every other day) via Zaporizhzhya and Kharkiv.

The bus station is 2km north of the centre. Buses go to/from Simferopol (2½ hours, eight daily), Sudak (two hours, two daily) and Kerch (two hours, one daily).

Bus No 2 links the station with town. A bus goes twice daily to Koktebel (2uah, 35 minutes).

KERCH КЕРЧЬ

☎ 06561 / pop 157,000

At the eastern tip of the Crimean peninsula, Kerch is both an industrial port and military base. Its sights include the ruins of the ancient town of **Panticapaeum**, a history and archaeology museum, and some old **tombs** that have yielded fine ancient Greek art. There are six daily trains to/from Simferopol (seven hours). In the summer months, you might be able to catch a ferry to Russia, north to Temryuk (83km) or south to Anapa (96km).

Eastern Ukraine
Східна Україна

158

Eastern Ukraine is the business end of the country. While USSR still lived, this was the heart of the Soviet military-industrial complex and despite the unrestrained march of oligarchic capitalism that era still hasn't quite been consigned to history. Monolithic socialist realist monuments dominate the horizon, Lenin lives in myriad statues, and communist disdain for nature endures, as chimney stacks heartily bellow out smoke. It's just that these landmarks now happily coexist with neon signs, McDonald's restaurants, Benetton clothing stores and luxury goods, as cities such as Dnipropetrovsk, Donetsk and, to a lesser extent, Kharkiv appear a lot wealthier than their counterparts in the west or south.

Many of Ukraine's 'got-rich-quick' businessmen – as well as outright mafioso – are based in the region, and far fewer independent travellers venture this way than businesspeople. Indeed, as one cynical local joked to us in Dnipropetrovsk: 'What's there for people to do here? Go mountaineering? Swimming?…Or learn about criminality? Ha-ha-ha.'

However, it's an interesting detour for those looking for something different, plus a rich seam of history lies buried deep beneath the layers of money-making and industry. With the most famous band of Cossacks based at Zaporizhzhya in the 16th to 18th centuries – fighting off the Tatars to the south, Poles to the west and Russians to the north – the surrounding region was a crucible of Ukrainian nationalism. That's why many cruise ships now drop anchor in Zaporizhzhya and organised tours head for Poltava, the site of a famous battle.

Proud Ukrainian history aside, Russification following Moscow's 1775 rout of the Cossacks was so successful that many eastern Ukrainians still look north, even in the 21st century. There's a sizable ethnic Russian minority, Russian continues to be the dominant language and during the fraught election of a Western-leaning president in 2004, parts of the region even threatened to run home to Mother Russia.

HIGHLIGHTS

- Gaze on **social realist architecture** in Kharkiv's ploshcha Svobody (p161) or along Zaporizhzhya's prospekt Lenina (p166)

- Admire the candy-striped exterior of Kharkiv's **Blahoveshchensky Cathedral** (p161)

- Observe 'new' Ukrainian capitalism at work in **Dnipropetrovsk** (p164)

- See where Russia's Peter the Great defeated Sweden and its Cossack allies outside **Poltava** (p164)

- Revel in Cossack culture on **Khortytsya Island** (p166), Zaporizhzhya, home of the famous Zaporizhsky Cossacks

■ POPULATION: 18 MILLION	■ HIGHEST POINT: NOTHING OVER 500M

EASTERN UKRAINE

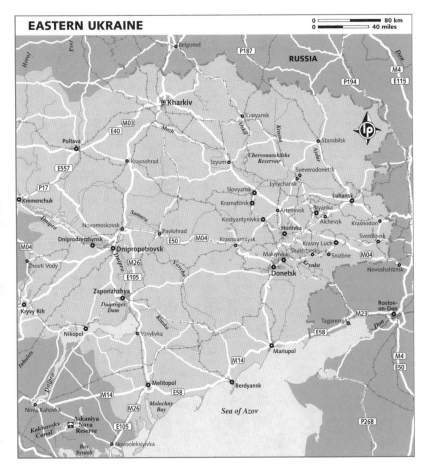

EASTERN UKRAINE

KHARKIV ХАРКІВ

☎ 057 (7-digit Nos), 0572 (6-digit Nos)
pop 1.6 million

If Dnipropetrovsk, Donetsk and Zapor-izhzhya are the strong-arm muscle of Ukrainian industry, then the more north-erly city of Kharkiv is its nerve centre and brain. It's a leafy university town that makes the unusual boast of being the birthplace of the Soviet nuclear industry. And it combines enormous, agoraphobia-inducing plazas – particularly its unfor-gettably enormous pl Svobody – with charming early-20th-century buildings on more compact streets. Plenty of parks soften the grey concrete tones and, with more 100,000 enrolled at the university,

there's a distinct student feel to Kharkiv's lively streets.

History

Modern Ukraine's second-largest city turned a young 350 in 2004, having been founded in 1654 as a Cossack outpost. Lying just 40km south from the Russian border it was quickly absorbed into the Russian sphere of influence in the next century.

Kharkiv (Kharkov in Russian) was the capital of Soviet Ukraine from 1917 to 1934, a period in which Ukrainian nation-alists and intelligentsia were repressed. The city was heavily damaged in WWII. As well as being a major research centre,

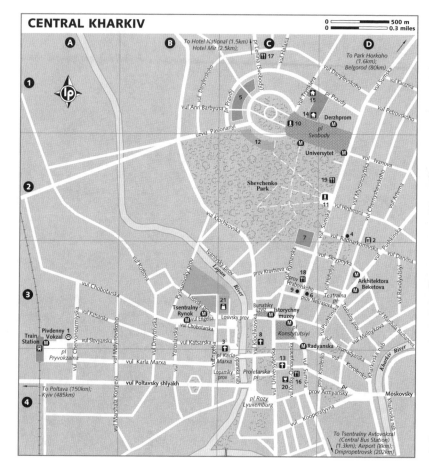

Kharkiv also manufactures tractors, turbines and engines.

Orientation

Central Kharkiv lies between three main squares. The southernmost of these squares is pl Rozy Lyuxemburg, with the Lopan River along its western end. Not far north of here is pl Konstytutsiyi (formerly pl Radyanskoyi Ukrainy). From here, vul Sumska (Sumskaya) heads north in the direction of Moscow, past pl Svobody. Nearby pr Lenina has a new street sign saying 'prospekt Svobody'. However, everybody and everything else – including metro exit signs – determinedly continue to refer to 'prospekt Lenina'.

Information

There's an exchange office, an ATM and an internet café in Kharkiv's main train station, and old maps of the city can be purchased from some stalls here. Vul Sumska is also full of banks, telephone centres and internet cafés. The **post office** (pl Pryvokzalna; ☺ mail counters 8am-7pm Mon-Sat, to 4pm Sun) also has a 24-hour telephone centre.

Sights

Walking is the best way to get to know Kharkiv and although the huge pl Svobody is Kharkiv's most unique sight, it creates a better impression to slowly walk through town and leave the square as the climax of your tour. If you're short of time, however, cut straight to the chase by going to metro Universytet.

TO PLOSHCHA KONSTYTUTSIYI

Start at the striking, red-and-cream striped **Blahoveshchensky Cathedral** (1881–1901) on pl Karla Marxa. Based on Istanbul's Hagia Sophia, the cathedral has a beautifully proportioned bell tower resembling a stick of candy. Cross the Lopan River behind the cathedral and head uphill to the gleaming domes of the **Pokrovska Church** (Intercession of the Virgin). As you do so, to your right you will also see the smaller **Uspensky (Assumption) Cathedral** with its landmark, 19th-century bell tower (89.5m tall). This church is now used only as a concert hall; ask your hotel about tickets.

The 1689 Pokrovska Church, on the other hand, can be visited, and looks in fine fettle after recent restorations. The main entrance to the monastery grounds surrounding the church is on pl Konstytutsiyi, beside the Kharkiv History Museum, which can easily be skipped. Opposite, in the centre of the square, is a large granite sculptural ensemble commemorating Kharkiv's designation as the first capital of Soviet Ukraine on 24 December 1917.

VULYTSYA SUMSKA

Cross the square to lively vul Sumska and head north. You'll soon pass the pretty **Shevchenko Ukrainian Drama Theatre** (vul Sumska 9) to your left, which is flanked by the busts of two writers, Gogol and Pushkin. Further on, you won't be able to miss the brutalist **Opera & Ballet Theatre** (vul Sumska 25). In the park opposite this theatre is the **Mirror Stream Fountain**, a landmark that newlyweds like to be photographed near.

Along vul Radnarkomivska (Sovnarkomovskaya), running along the northern edge of a park, is the **former KGB building**. It's the Department for Internal Affairs building on the corner of vul Myronosytska and has a bust of Felyx Edmundovych, a high-ranking KGB member, on one wall. Nearby is Kharkiv's famous **Art Museum** (vul Radnarkomivska 11; adult/child 2/1uah; ☼ 10am-5.30pm, to 4.30pm Mon, last entry half an hr before closing). Its principal claim to fame is as owner of one of many versions of Ilya Repin's *Zaporizhsky Cossacks Writing a Letter to the Turkish Sultan*, which is found in a room full of Repin paintings. However, the entire collection of romantic paintings is of a very high standard for Ukraine.

Further north on vul Sumska is the tall **statue of Taras Shevchenko**, of which Kharkivites are perhaps overly proud. Yes, it's big and it does portray the heroic poet surrounded by 16 peasants, Cossacks and other Ukrainians representing the national history. However, it's also rather brutalist and is only softened by the leafy **Shevchenko Park** behind.

PLOSHCHA SVOBODY

Keep heading up vul Sumska until you arrive in the enormous **ploshcha Svobody** (Freedom Square). Some locals declare this to be the largest in Europe, conveniently forgetting about Moscow's Red Square. At almost 750m long, however, there's no arguing that it's impressive.

Planned as an ensemble of Ukrainian government buildings when Kharkiv was the republican capital, it was built between 1925 and 1935. (Damaged during WWII, it was largely rebuilt by German POWs.) The late-1920s **House of State Industry** (Derzhprom)

EASTERN UKRAINE

KHARKIV METRO

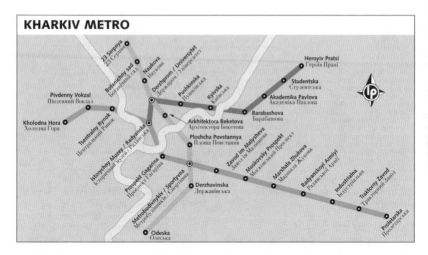

at its western end was the first Soviet sky-scraper – a geometric series of concrete and glass blocks and bridges. Its symmetry is now marred by the TV pylon on one tower. On the southern side of the square is the **university**, formerly the House of Planning, which displays classic Soviet aesthetics. The university and **Hotel Kharkiv**, on the opposite side of pl Svobody, date from the early 1930s.

Lenin still proudly stands in the midst of it all, his hand outstretched across the vast open space. In summer, celebrate the end of your walk by lolling on the nearby grass.

OTHER ATTRACTIONS

Like Moscow's, Kharkiv's **metro** is something of an attraction in its own right. It's not as opulent as the Russian capital's, but does feature high ceilings and space-age chandeliers. The nicest features are probably the stained glass portraits of the world's first man in space, Yuri Gargarin, above the stairs to the platforms at Prospekt Gargarina.

Even if you're not buying, the city's **central market** (vul Engelsa 33; M Tsentralny Rynok) is well worth a browse for its eclectic collection of everything from fur *shapok* (hats) to vegetables and used car parts.

About 2km to the north of pl Svobody, vul Sumska runs along **Horkoho Park**, where you'll find plenty of tree-lined paths, a funfair, cinema, summertime chairlift and children's locomotive, as well as hills for wintertime sledding.

Sleeping

All the following accept credit cards.

Hotel Mir (☎ 732 2330; fax 322 217; pr Lenina 27A; renovated/unrenovated r $45/20; P 🖳 ; M Botanichny Sad) Three kilometres north of pl Svobody, but easy to reach because of the metro station at its door, this friendly hotel has the nicest-looking rooms in town. Recently renovated, they have modern desks and bathrooms with mulberry-coloured towels and blue and white tiles. Which isn't to say the place doesn't have a few foibles, like scratchy seersucker sheets, occasionally noisy plumbing and an inedible breakfast.

Hotel Kharkiv (☎ 528 025; www.hotel.kharkov.com; M Universytet) Kharkiv's only central hotel still maintains a **'rich man's entrance'** (cnr vul Trynklera & pr Pravdy; s $50-60, d from $95) and a **'poor man's entrance'** (pl Svobody; unrenovated s/d with shared bathrooms $8/15). Staff in the latter section will only check in insistent Westerners. Others will be sent around the corner, where there's a sleek lobby below a time warp of lacquered wooden floors and 1930–50s furniture. The singles are quite spartan, but the doubles pleasant in a retro kind of way. Some of the suites even have modern decoration. The hotel serves a buffet breakfast and charges $15 extra to make a reservation. (That said, you'd only ever need book if arriving very late at night.)

Hotel National (☎ 702 1624, 330 8787; www.national .kharkiv.com; pr Lenina 21; s/d from $25/35; P 🖳 ; M Naukova) The in-between option, geographically speaking, this former Intourist hotel has various levels of rooms to suit different budgets. Take the metro to Naukova, then walk or take bus No 8 or 38 along pr Lenina.

Eating & Drinking

Yaske (☎ 759 8922; Danilyevskoho 19; mains 15-75uah; ☺ 8am-midnight) A see-and-be-seen glass box with a flattish golden dome on top, this sushi restaurant is understandably popular with Kharkiv's hip set, who often just come here for coffee and sumptuous desserts. If you want to fill up on miso soup, tempura and salads, however, you can do so for just over $10. It's on the corner of pr Lenina.

100 Pudov (☎ 587 530; vul Kvitky-Osnovyanenka 13; mains 10-45uah; ☺ 8am-last customer) This packs a lot of cool stuff into a small space, with a Nam June Paik–style chandelier of TVs and old radios, stamps from communist countries lacquered into the table tops and hookah pipes to smoke. Service is slow, however, so don't come here in a hurry.

ZanziBar (☎ 191 605; vul Sumska 11; mains 15-35uah) This hip but friendly café has a mix of zebra stripe and orange walls and staff dressed in leopard print. The casual food ranges from pizzas, lasagne and salads to seafood and meat. It's all good.

Stare Misto (vul Kvitky-Osnovyanenka) An old-school and touristy beer hall opposite 100 Pudov, which is still good for a drink.

Zhuly Buly (vul Sumska; dishes 3-4.50uah) Self-service cafeteria 'Once Upon a Time' only deserves a mention for its popularity among Kharkiv's student population. The staff are prone to raking over the vegetable buffet to try (unsuccessfully!) to make dishes look fresher. So if someone suggests meeting here, plan on just a beer.

Getting There & Away
AIR
Kharkiv airport is served by domestic and international flights (see p185 and p189). **AeroSvit Airlines** (☎ 195 370) has its office inside Hotel Kharkiv (entrance on pl Svobody).

BUS
Buses go to numerous destinations from the **central bus station** (tsentralny avtovokzal; ☎ 216 502; pr Gagarina 22; Ⓜ pr Gagarina). The most useful, however, are to Poltava (11uah, 2½ hours, at least eight a day), Dnipropetrovsk (18uah, 4½ hours, 20 a day) and Zaporizhzhya (24uah, 6½ hours, at least two a day).

TRAIN
The train station is on pl Pryvokzalna, 2km west of pl Rozy Lyuxemburg.

Although plenty of other trains pass through, there are three main services to Kyiv. The fast *Stolichny Express* (40uah to 65uah, six hours) runs early morning and late evening, plus there's an overnight service (45uah, eight hours). The daily *elektrychka* (8uah, 4½ hours) is the best option to Dnipropetrovsk (otherwise 30uah). There are a couple of daily services to Donetsk (45uah, seven hours), one to Odesa (40uah, 14 hours) and at least one to Simferopol (50uah, 16 to 17 hours, runs more frequently during summer).

Foreigners (even Russian-speaking ones) will usually be sent to the glassed-in service centre inside the train station to buy their tickets. Coming from the street, turn left from the main hall until you see the information counters. The centre is opposite these.

Getting Around
TO/FROM THE AIRPORT
The airport is 8km south of the centre, off pr Gagarina. Trolleybus No 5 from the pr Gagarina metro stop terminates at the airport. Bus No 119T runs between pr Lenina and the airport.

PUBLIC TRANSPORT
Tokens for the metro cost 50 kopecks. The Pivdenny Vokzal metro stop is in front of the train station.

POLTAVA ПОЛТАВА
☎ 0532 (6-digit Nos), 05322 (5-digit Nos)
pop 325,000
Given that they erected a prominent victory column and built a neoclassical plaza reminiscent of St Petersburg here, it is hard not to think the Russians were rubbing salt into an open Ukrainian wound in Poltava. Outside this pretty, quaint city on the Vorskla River, Peter the Great's army defeated the Ukrainian Cossacks under Ivan Mazepa and their Swedish allies in 1709, ending decades of dispute over the region and dashing hopes of an independent Cossack state (see p20). What's Poltava's revenge, having emerged from three centuries of Russian rule? In the middle of the Russophile east, it continues to speak the purest Ukrainian in the entire country.

Orientation & Information

The town lies between the two train stations, with Poltavska-Kyivska station 2km to its northwest and Poltava-Pivdenna 3km to its southeast.

Starting near Poltavska-Kyivska station, vul Zhovtneva heads southeast, through Kruhla pl, ending in maydan Soborny. The battle site is about 7km north of the centre.

Sights

The focal point is the circular plaza **Kruhla ploshcha** (Round Square), laid out in the early 19th century in an attempt to emulate the grand planning ideals of St Petersburg, particularly Palace Square. Eight streets radiate off the plaza, and in its centre is the **Iron Column of Glory**, topped by a golden eagle, erected on the 100th anniversary of Peter the Great's battle.

Southeast of Kruhla pl, vul Zhovtneva becomes a pedestrian precinct for a few blocks. Further down is the leafy Zhovtnevy Park, with the **Poltava Regional Museum** (Thu-Mon) along its southeastern edge, in front of a 1926 cubist Taras Shevchenko monument. The Art Nouveau building (1903–08) is ornamented with the ceramic crests of each district capital in the Poltava oblast. Inside are historic and ethnographic exhibits.

Overlooking the northeastern corner of the park is the **memorial cross to the Cossacks**. Bear east down vul Paryzhkoyi Komuny for one block to **Spaska Church** (1705) on the corner of vul Spaska. A block north (left), past the monument to Tsar Peter I, is the 1919 **Poltava Art Museum** (vul Spaska 11).

From the lookout point beside the museum, there is a good view of **Khrestovoz-dvyzhensky Monastery** (Elevation of the Cross), 3km northeast of the centre. The complex was built in the early 18th century in the Ukrainian baroque style and the main cathedral is one of only two in the country with seven cupolas, rather than five (the other is St Michael's Monastery in Kyiv, p56). To walk to the monastery (30 minutes) head east on vul Radyanska from Kruhla pl.

BATTLEFIELD

It's best to hire a taxi (15uah) to take you out to the battle site, 7km north, or ask your hotel. The battle was fought over a large area around what's now vul Zinkivska. The best starting point is the **Poltava Battle Museum**

(Shvedska mohyla 32; admission 5uah; 10am-5pm Tue-Sun) by the Peter the Great statue. Inside are displays concerning the battle including maps, paintings and military diagrams. Obviously glorifying Peter the Great's tremendous victory, there's nothing (beyond one paltry portrait) to document the Cossack forces under hetman Ivan Mazepa.

In front of the museum on a hill is a memorial cross to the Russian troops killed. Further down the road is a memorial cross to the 9000 Swedes who died in the battle.

Sleeping

Hotel Gallery (561 697; www.hotel.poltava.ua; vul Frunze 7; s/d $55/75) This is the best accommodation in town, built in 2000 and located midway between the two railway stations. However, there are only 25 rooms, so book.

Hotel Turyst (220 921; vul Myru 2; s/d $15/20) Some 500m west of Pivdenna train station, across the bridge and to the left, this unappetising Soviet-era hotel does have some remodelled rooms.

Getting There & Around

There are two train stations. Most services stop at Poltava-Pivdenna (south) including the daily direct train to Kyiv (30uah, seven hours) and 11 a day to Kharkiv (7uah, three to four hours). Two a day run to/from Odesa (13 hours). To get to the centre from the Poltava-Pivdenna train station, take trolleybus No 1, 2, 4, 6 or 11.

Crucially, however, the fast trains between Kyiv and Kharkiv stop at **Poltava-Kyivska station** (Stepana Kondratenka 12). Almost all the transport from this train station heads into town. Just check by asking 'do tsentr?'

DNIPROPETROVSK
ДНІПРОПЕТРОВСЬК
056 (7-digit Nos), 0562 (6-digit Nos)
pop 1.2 million

You don't have to be a rocket scientist to come to Dnipropetrovsk these days, but at one time you practically did. As the USSR's leading missile production base, it manufactured ICBMs (intercontinental ballistic missiles) and was closed to all outside the industry. However, that era is long past. Soon after Ukrainian independence the city gates opened, Europe's largest missile factory turned to making space hardware instead and its director, Leonid Kuchma, packed his bags and headed for Kyiv as national president.

Nowadays, local oligarchs have ensured that Dnipropetrovsk is one of the ritziest cities in Ukraine outside Kyiv. Its broad main thoroughfare, pr Karla Marxa, is awash with shops selling Swiss watches, Scandinavian furniture, French cosmetics, Italian fashion and more – all of which proves that shopping's the masses' new opiate.

Sights

Window shopping along tree-lined pr Karla Marxa – while watching the trams wend their way along the central, tree-lined strip – is one pleasant Dnipropetrovsk experience. Another is wandering along the riverfront, either at the eastern end of nab Lenina, near Monastyrsky Island, the site of the first human settlement here, or heading south down nab Pobedy.

Neoliths adorn the courtyard of the **History Museum** (☎ 463 422; pr Karla Marxa 16; adult/child 3/1.50uah; ☼ 10am-5pm Tue-Sun, last entry 4.15pm). Adjoining the museum is a **diorama**, an 840-sq-metre painted canvas featuring WWII. The terrace behind is lined with WWII anti-aircraft batteries, the centrepiece of which is a fighter plane. Its nose is aimed directly at the glistening gold spire and dome of **Preobrazhensky Cathedral** (Transfiguration of Our Saviour), a classical structure dating from 1830 to 1835, which languishes amid parkland.

Sleeping

Hotel Astoria (☎ /fax 442 304; pr Karla Marxa 66; standard/remodelled r $45/95) The handful of standard rooms at this central hotel offers the best midrange accommodation in town. They are old-fashioned, but large and clean. Book, because otherwise you'll pay over the odds for a remodelled *'polilyux'* room.

Hotel Dnipropetrovsk (☎ 455 327; fax 450 352; www.hoteldnepropetrovsk.dp.ua; nab Lenina 33; s/d from $40/60) About a 15-minute walk from the town's central square, this 11-storey concrete block on the waterfront is also a passable accommodation option. It's a typical old Soviet-style set-up.

Grand Hotel Ukraine (☎ 341 010; vul Korolenko 2; www.grand-hotel-ukraine.dp.ua; s/d from $120/175; ⚡ ▢) Grand by name, grand by nature, this is unquestionably *the* business hotel

in town, offering extensive conference facilities, a pampering fitness centre, business centre and modem points in rooms. It has a tendency towards formality, however, so if that makes you uncomfortable don't stay here.

Hotel Academy (☎ 370 0505; www.academya.dp.ua; pr Karla Marxa 20; s/d $100/125; ⚡ ▢) Some will find this small upscale hotel preferable to the Grand. Interesting historical paintings downstairs add character and staff are charming.

Hotel Astoria-Luxe (☎ 370 4270; s/d from $105/110) The modern rooms here are of a thoroughly Western standard, but you pay almost as much as at the Grand, and get less.

Hotel Central (☎ 450 347; pr Karla Marxa 50; s/d from $50/75) Although this is central and cheap, there's a strange set-up in some rooms, where you walk through the bathroom before coming to the sleeping area.

Two even cheaper hotels are **Sverdlovsk** (☎ 428 825; vul Sverdlova 6; s/d from $30/35) and **Sport** (☎ 320 932; vul Schorsa 4; s/d from $15).

Eating

Dnipropetrovsk is full of restaurants and bars, but the following two should cover most occasions.

Shamrock Irish Pub (☎ 362 335; pr Karla Marxa 41; mains 15-45uah; ☼ 10am-late) For a cheap casual feed, or a shot of vodka, beer or whisky, come to this quiet, newish venue. A warning, though: not everything on the menu will prove available. It stays open till 'the client's last breath'.

Reporter (☎ 337 575; cnr pr Karla Marxa & vul Barrykadnoy; mains 20-80uah; ☼ 7am-last customer) The neon penny-farthing bike on the neoclassical façade looks like something from a Western movie set. But, inside, Reporter caters to more refined tastes. The coffee shop, serving breakfasts, sushi and European fare, is popular with both 'biznezmen' and the city's beautiful people. (And it serves possibly the plumpest, tastiest homemade *varenyky* (dumplings) in the land.) Upstairs there's a restaurant while the pub downstairs also serves as a club.

Getting There & Away

AIR

Austrian Airlines flies from Vienna daily and Dniproavia has both domestic and international flights. Aerosvit flies from Kyiv (see p185).

BUS

The **bus station** (☎ 008, 778 4090; vul Kurchatova 10) is about a 10-minute walk west of the train station. Services include those to/from Donetsk (12uah, four to five hours, at least 10 daily) and Kharkiv (18uah, 4½ hours, 20 daily). 'Luxury' bus operators **Autolux** (☎ 371 0353; www.autolux.com.ua) and **Gunsel** (☎ 778 3935) operate services to Kyiv (50uah, seven to eight hours) and elsewhere from here.

TRAIN

From the **central train station** (☎ 005, 364 826; pr Karla Marxa 108) the fast *Stolichny Express* (40uah to 65uah, six hours) runs early morning and late evening, plus there are other services to Kyiv (10 hours). There are frequent services to Zaporizhzhya (25uah, two hours) and Donetsk (25uah, five hours), several daily services to Kharkiv (30uah, 4½ hours) and daily services to Odesa (50uah, 15 hours), Lviv (55-60uah, 22 hours) and Simferopol (40uah, 10¾ hours).

Getting Around

Dnipropetrovsk's metro is useless to the average visitor, as it runs west from the main train station, while the city lies east. Instead, trams are the best transport. Tram No 1 runs from the train station along the length of pr Karla Marxa, past most of the hotels listed. A taxi from the airport should cost between 20uah and 40uah, depending on your ability to negotiate with the driver.

ZAPORIZHZHYA ЗАПОРІЖЖЯ

☎ 0612 / pop 900,000

Zaporizhzhya (Beyond the Rapids) is a long streak of a city, concentrated along one 10km-long street. At the northeastern end lie the two main attractions: Khortytsya Island, the 16th-century base of the famous Zaporizhsky Cossacks, and Dniproges, a massive dam. The 40km stretch of difficult-to-navigate rapids in the Dnipro here, from which the city takes its name, was submerged in this dam in the 1930s and the resulting hydroelectricity was used to power massive industry.

Despite being not an especially charming destination, Zaporizhzhya's Cossack links

keep it firmly on the tourist map. And while it's still a little grimy, the only upside of economic downturn and factory closures is that the air quality is much improved. (Really, it used to be worse.)

Orientation

The main street, pr Lenina, stretches for 10km from Zaporizhzhya-1 train station at its southeastern end to pl Lenina overlooking the Dniproges Dam. Halfway down there's a centre of activity around pl Festyvalna, where you'll find both listed hotels. Three to four bus stops further northwest is bul Shevchenka. Khortytsya Island lies in the Dnipro, parallel to and 2km southwest of the Dniproges Dam wall.

Information

Just about every service you could need is found around pl Festyvalna, including the following. Ask at the Hotel Intourist-Zaporizhzhya for guided tours.

Post office (pr Lenina 133; ☒ 8am-7pm Mon-Sat, 9am-5pm Sun) With a bank, ATM and 24-hour telephone centre.

Privatbank/Western Union (pr Lenina 168; ☒ 9am-11pm)

Sights

KHORTYTSYA ISLAND

The Zaporizhska Sich on Khortytsya Island was the most important cradle of Ukrainian Cossackdom, where hetman (leader) Dmytro Baida united disparate groups of Cossacks in the construction of a *sich* (fort) in 1553–54. The island was perfect: strategically located below the Dnipro rapids and beyond the control of Polish or Russian authority. Any man could come to join the Cossack brotherhood, irrespective of social background, and like Galicia under self-rule in the 14th century (see p82) the *sich* is revered as a leading forerunner of an independent Ukraine.

At the height of its power the community numbered some 20,000 fighters, under the authority of one hetman. On the battlefield they were formidable opponents; off it formidable vodka drinkers. There was some code of discipline, however, and no women were allowed on Khortytsya. Even Russian empress Catherine the Great was prohibited from setting foot on the island and was reduced to spying it from a nearby rock. Some laughingly suggest that this, as well

LOSE THE BOWL CUT!

The Zaporizhsky Cossacks had a bit of a Samson fetish about their locks. Fully-fledged warriors sported *oseledtsi*, a long ponytail growing from the middle of an otherwise shaved head. Trainee Cossacks weren't allowed to grow their hair and during their seven-year apprenticeship had to resign themselves to having it cut *pid makitru* – aka in a bowl cut. Tests had to be passed to finally enter the Cossack ranks. It's fun to surmise that, as they furiously rowed upstream through the treacherous Dnipro rapids, trainees' desire to be rid of such a sartorial embarrassment as a bowl cut might have provided an extra incentive to succeed!

as the threat the Cossacks posed to Russian imperial ambitions, was why she had the *sich* destroyed in 1775.

Since 1965 the 2690-hectare island has been a reserve, although it's tough to imagine the Cossack revelry of the past with electrical cables and a massive bridge crossing over to the island, and the Dniproges Dam and industrial facilities in plain view. Nevertheless, you can visit the informative **Historical Museum of Zaporizhsky Cossacks** (admission 3uah; 10am-5pm Tue-Sun), which includes painted dioramas and numerous Cossack artefacts excavated from the island. Neoliths adorn its grounds, which sprawl across the island's rocky northern end. Other Cossack haunts on the island include the Cossacks' jetty, and the Hadyucha Peshchera (Snake Cave). Also here is the Chyorna Skala (Black Rock), where the Kyivan Rus King Svyatoslav was reportedly killed by the Pechenegs in 972.

As public transport no longer goes to the island, you have to get there on foot (see p168), by taxi or with a tour guide.

Cossack descendants frequently present shows of dancing, mock fights and horse-riding on the island in summer.

DNIPROGES DAM

Here's a quick quiz. What's missing from the following list? The Eiffel Tower, the Golden Gate Bridge, the Empire State Building, the Panama Canal, the Suez Canal, the Alaska Highway… Perhaps the Sydney Opera House? Nope. Apparently, for much of the past 50 years the seventh declared wonder of the modern world has been Zaporizhzhya's Dniproges Dam.

At 760m – two and a half times longer than the famous Hoover Dam – the wall of the USSR's first dam certainly represented a monumental engineering feat when constructed under US supervision in 1927–32. In some ways, it's still impressive, but it's not especially tall and you have to reflect that its concrete walls, stained by years of local pollution, are really rather less appealing than the Sydney Opera House. Little known in the West, it's hard to see the dam surviving as one of the 'New Seven Wonders' due to be announced in 2006.

ZAPORIZHZHYA OAK

West of the Dnipro River in the Verkhnya Khortytsya area is a 600- to 700-year-old oak from which you can dangle any Cossack legend you choose. Did Bohdan Khmelnytsky address his troops beneath it before they marched against the Poles in 1648? Or was this where the Cossacks wrote their insulting letter to the Turkish sultan as immortalised (or just imagined?) in Repin's painting? We may never know, but we can certainly admire the oak's girth of 6.5m. You'll find the tree down vul Hoholya off vul Istomina, reached by the very rare No 19 bus from pl Lenina, at the far northwestern end of pr Lenina near the dam. The tree's not in good health these days, so get there quick.

Sleeping

Hotel Intourist-Zaporizhzhya (330 554, 332 5564; www.intourist.com.ua; pr Lenina 135; economy s/d from $32/42, standard s/d from $55/65, business s/d from $75/85;) Having refashioned itself as the city's leading hotel, this huge establishment is now relatively service-orientated and friendly; even some of the maids speak good English. The 9th-floor 'business' rooms are luxurious, but the standard and economy rooms have been given a very minor facelift, too – mixing Ikea with retro.

Hotel Ukraina (346 673; www.ukraine.zp.ua; pr Lenina 162A; s/d $30/35;) Despite the enticing photos on the website, the rooms here are pretty standard ex-Soviet fare. They are, however, spotless.

UKRAINE'S CUTE CULT CAR

Move over Lada, there's another Soviet auto that's fondly joked about in the CIS today. It's the tiny, Fiat-like Zaporozhets, which never became as famous in the West as the Volkswagen or Trabant but which was designed as another sturdy, affordable 'people's car'. Millions were built between 1964 and 1994 in Zaporizhzhya and shipped across the Soviet Union.

Designed with air intakes along the sides to help cool the rear-mounted engine, the 'Zapor' was, if you amalgamate its various nicknames, a big-eared hunchback with constipation. It's quite sweet, really. While many older models survive, Korea's Daewoo has bought the Zaporizhzhya factory and it now churns out Tavrias.

Eating

Pizza Pau Vau (☎ 220 0476; vul Tsentralna 4; mains 10-40uah) The food here exceeds any expectations you might have based on the antiseptic, family-restaurant atmosphere. Pizzas are thick and tasty, while there's a good line in Ukrainian, Russian and Georgian staples.

O'Brien's Irish Bar (☎ 224 0385; pr Lenina 169; mains 20-140uah; ⏰ 10am-2am) Large but still cosy in the winter, this Irish pub serves good tucker and a wide range of beverages.

Just around the corner from O'Brien's is bul Shevchenka, which has a good assortment of restaurants. Zaporizhska Sich is a touristy restaurant on Khortytsya Island, open in summer.

Getting There & Away

Zaporizhzhya-1 train station (☎ 005, 512 296) is at the southeastern end of pr Lenina. From here, there are trains to/from Dnipropetrovsk (25uah, two hours), Kyiv (45uah to 55uah, 10 hours), Moscow (80uah to 90uah, 16 to 20 hours), Kharkiv (40uah, 4½ hours), Lviv (70uah, 27 hours), Odesa (40uah, 17 hours) and Simferopol (40uah, five hours).

The **bus station** (☎ 642 657; pr Lenina 22) is near Zaporizhzhya-1 train station. There are regular services to Dnipropetrovsk (eight to 10uah, 1½ to two hours) and Donetsk (12uah, 4½ hours). Arriving by bus from Dnipropetrovsk, you cross the Dniproges Dam, saving you the effort of making a special trip.

Getting Around

Most trolleybuses and *marshrutky* run the length of pr Lenina between Zaporizhzhya-1 train station and pl Lenina, but you can bank on No 3. One way to see the city's main sights is to get off the trolleybus at pl Lenina and take a long walk. Head across the wall of the Dniproges Dam, bear left (west) and left again onto the north, pedestrian bridge of Khortytsya Island to the Cossack Museum (about 5km).

DONETSK ДОНЕЦЬК
☎ 062 (7-digit Nos), 0622 (6-digit Nos)
pop 1.1 million

Making international headlines only with fatal mine collapses or explosions, or when it's threatening to secede from Ukraine, the capital of the coal-rich Donbas (Donetsky Basin) region sounds miserable. So it's a surprise to arrive in its Soviet environs to find that, despite the sci-fi sounding *terakony* (slag heaps) dotted around, it even won a Unesco award once for its relative cleanliness.

The secret is that, as in Dnipropetrovsk, local oligarchs have injected funds into the centre. Ukraine's richest man, Rinat Akhmetov, is based here and the talk of the town – apart from secession – is the new $200 million stadium he's building for Dynamo Kyiv's main rival, the Shakhtar (meaning miners) football team. The stadium is due to open in 2007.

That aside, there's almost nothing to lure the casual visitor, but if you've always wanted to visit a coal pit or salt mine, now's your chance.

History

Donetsk was originally called Yuzovka after Welshman John Hughes, who established the first metallurgical plant here in 1872 to exploit the region's coal. In 1924 the city was rechristened Stalino, and only in 1961 did it gain its current name. In true Full Monty style, it's twinned with Sheffield in the UK (since 1956).

After the collapse of the USSR, Donetsk found itself in a precarious situation. Many of its 40-odd mines were unprofitable, as well as unsafe, and miners had to fight closures in the 1990s. The then-regional governor, and later 2004 presidential candidate, Viktor Yanukovych intervened, arranging subsidies, raising wages and saving jobs – as well as winning himself a loyal electoral base. Plans for a more market-orientated, Western-looking economy with fewer subsidies have local miners worried about the future.

Orientation & Information

Vul Artema is 10km long and links the train station, at its northern end, with the centre. Central Donetsk is laid out in a Soviet grid system; most restaurants are clustered on bul Pushkina, the street running parallel (north–south) with Artema. Another block east is vul Universytetska. Bul Shevchenka crosses these three streets from east to west.

The website www.donguide.com has restaurant, hotel and shopping listings.

Sights & Activities

Business travellers will probably be occupied during the day, but might want to take in a performance at the **Opera & Ballet Theatre** (☎ 922 348; vul Artema 82) in the evening. Time between meetings can be filled with a visit to the **regional museum** (☎ 553 474; vul Cheluskintsiv 189A; admission 3uah; ☺ 10am-5pm Wed-Mon), which is largely a glorification of labour and mines. About 2km northeast of the centre, it can be reached by tram No 1 from bul Shevchenka.

Intours Donetsk (☎ 304 7192; info2@intours.donetsk .ua; vul Universytetska 48) inside the Hotel Druzhba organises tours of coal pits or down salt mines; contact them for individual prices.

Sleeping & Eating

All hotels listed are reasonably central.

Hotel Druzhba (☎ 337 3331; vul Universytetska 48; s/d from $35/40) Druzhba is a decent enough cheap hotel, of the ex-Soviet variety.

Hotel Dinamo (☎ 342 0385; vul Otechestvenna 10; s/d from $40) This modern midrange option is good for the independent consultant who's funding their own business trip or for the curious tourist – although the slightly old-fashioned furniture belies the newness of the hotel.

John Hughes (☎ 381 0848; vul Chelyuskintsiv 157; s/d from $80; P ✗ 🖳) For those who don't like the hubbub of large showy hotels, this is a small boutique option – which has a strangely German appearance.

Central Hotel (☎ 332 3332; www.central-hotel .com.ua; vul Artema 87; s/d from $75/115; P ✗ 🖳) A very corporate-orientated establishment, with plenty of business services and comfortable modern rooms.

Donbass Palace (☎ 343 4443; www.donbasspalace .com; vul Artema 80; r from $260; P ✗ 🖳 ✆) Not just Donetsk's leading hotel, but arguably the country's too, as it was the first to be asked to join an international luxury group. Come here if you're doing a little corporate entertaining and need to impress, or just want to enjoy, as the hotel puts it, 'the ambience of Monte Carlo in the heart of Donetsk' (cough).

Many visitors to Donetsk tend to dine in their hotels, but try **Shalom** (☎ 577 321; vul Artema 132) for Jewish fare, including vegetarian, **Arizona** (☎ 324 791; vul Universytetska 2) for steaks, **Zolotoy Dragon** (☎ 577 321; vul Universytetska 27A) for Chinese and **Alexander Hall** (☎ 332 2467; vul Stadionna 32A) for a blowout.

Getting There & Around

Donetsk airport (☎ 515 322) is north of the centre and has regular services from Kyiv (see p189).

Trains include an overnight service to Kyiv (50uah to 70uah, 12 hours), several trains a day from Dnipropetrovsk (25uah, five hours), and daily services to Odesa (45uah) via Zaporizhzhya (25uah).

Trolleybus No 2 links the train station with the centre; it runs the length of vul Artema.

Directory

CONTENTS

ACCOMMODATION

For a country where land travel costs pennies and overall eating out is relatively cheap, accommodation here is often wildly overpriced. This is particularly true in Kyiv and cities in eastern Ukraine, where decent hotel rooms usually start at $75 to $100. People have been praying for prices to drop to more realistic levels for some time, but this is unlikely to happen until the Ukrainian government makes tourism a priority.

It is only in the smaller towns that prices better reflect the standard of accommodation. Room prices in rural towns are as low as $20 to $30 a night, with rock-bottom prices plummeting to $10 in some places.

PRACTICALITIES

- Newspapers & Magazines: Ukraine's media might have had a big shake-up since, but at the time of writing the biggest-selling tabloid was *Fakti i Kommentarii* (controlled by Leonid Kuchma's son-in-law), followed by *Segodnya*. *Ukrayina Moloda* is the most respected pro-Western paper, although outsold by *Vecherniye Vesti* and the controversial *Silksi Visti*. *Den* is more centrist. In the capital, English speakers can read about news, politics and going out in the *Kyiv Post* (www.kyivpost.com) or enjoy entertainment tips in *What's On Kiev* (www.whatson-kiev.com).

- Radio & TV: Ukraine has six national TV channels, including the state-run UT1. Other leading channels include Inter, the independent 5 Kanal and Studio 1+1. M1 is the pop music channel, while the unbelievably popular Fashion TV is an endless parade of catwalk models – usually in lingerie. State-controlled radio channels include UR1. The BBC World Service (612 MW) and Radio Liberty (www.rferl.org; various rebroadcasters) also have services here.

- DVD & Video Systems: Ukraine uses SECAM L video, but some wealthier consumers have multisystem players and, in any case, DVDs are now widespread. In general, DVDs sold in Eastern Europe will be Region 2 DVDs, which mean that unless you have a multi-region DVD player, they will not play in North America (Region 1) or anywhere else where Region 2 is not the norm.

- Electricity: Electricity is 220 volts, 50Hz and most sockets take European continental plugs

- Weights & Measures: Ukraine uses the metric system.

While this guide quotes most other costs in the local currency, hryvnia (uah), accommodation prices are quoted in US dollars (or euros if that's what the hotel itself uses) to try to simplify the mental arithmetic. You will, however, be required to pay in hryvnia.

Camping

Camping in the wild is permitted in the Carpathian National Natural Park and parts of Crimea. Unless you're hiking through these areas, however, camping in Ukraine is not highly recommended. Most so-called camp sites are really former Soviet holiday camps, and slightly more formalised than most Western campers like. Facilities aren't brilliant, either. Lighting fires in national parks is officially forbidden, although everyone does.

Homestays

There are two types of homestay in Ukraine, both offering an opportunity to gain a fascinating insight into how people in Ukraine really live.

Firstly, people in Kyiv, Odesa and other large cities regularly stand outside train stations offering rooms for hire in their houses and flats. Look for older women, and occasionally men, touting signs reading 'кімнати' (*kimnaty*, Ukrainian) or 'комнати' (*komnaty*, Russian), meaning 'rooms'. You'll need to negotiate a price (50uah to 100uah or $10 to $20 is usual). Also try to find out what's involved; for example whether or not you have to share a bedroom with snoring grandpa or need to take an hour's bus ride to get there. Don't be too suspicious though. This can often be a refreshing alternative, with a great home-cooked meal thrown in.

Secondly, several tourism organisations offer more formal homestay programmes. Rural homestays are organised in the Carpathians by several groups. The leading player is the **Ivano-Frankivsk Green Rural Tourism Association** (http://members.aol.com/chornohora /index.htm); see p98 for more). Only a few householders in the program speak a foreign language and the accommodation is basic. All the same, we've had one good experience and heard further good reports.

A similar, if somewhat more bureaucratic scheme, exists in Crimea (www.greentour .crimea.ua).

The Russian organisation **Host Families Association** (HOFA; ☎/fax 812-275 1992; www.hofa.ru;

ul Tavricheskaya 5-25, St Petersburg) can also arrange homestays in Kyiv, Odesa, Lviv, Chernivtsi, Chernihiv, Yalta and many other Ukrainian towns.

Hostels

Hostels are an unfamiliar concept and the first have only just opened. Two that Westerners would really recognise as such are in Lviv (see p89), but one of these is seasonal.

Another proper hostel exists outside Balaklava (p144), but it has many drawbacks. So-called 'hostels' in Odesa and Uzhhorod are really budget hotels. Prices range from $4 to $20.

Hotels

Forget the system of rating hotels by one to five stars. Ukrainian hotels largely fall into two categories: stinky Soviet or stinkingly expensive. That's a slight exaggeration, but indisputably the country needs more good-value midrange accommodation. If its own citizens have enough money to avoid budget hotels, they generally want to show it by luxuriating in grand surrounds.

'Stinky Soviet' establishments have itchy blankets and bathrooms that look more suited to unmentionable medical procedures than having a wash. They might have problems supplying 24-hour hot water and often rely on city-controlled central heating, so you could find yourself freezing in early autumn before the local government turns on the heat. This guidebook tries to avoid such places, wherever possible.

Westerners will be unfamiliar with one particularly common type of Ukrainian hotel. These are the former Intourist establishments, offering a whole range of rooms from budget to luxury. They've usually renovated a few floors while others remain unreconstructed.

In these cases, hot water won't be a problem, and heating rarely, but the standard of the cheaper rooms might be poor. It's always worth asking to see a room before you take it, even a more expensive room. That's because sometimes a 'luxury' room is renovated and modern, and other times it's as bad as the cheap rooms, just larger. Correlations between price and quality are arbitrary in Ukraine; without a guidebook, it's all too easy to pay more for worse.

DIRECTORY

Hotels at the higher end of the market don't have hot-water or heating problems, and offer more double rooms with double beds (as opposed to twin beds or two singles pushed together).

Unless otherwise indicated, prices quoted include private bathroom and breakfast.

CHECKING IN

Checking in is a relatively relaxed procedure. You will always be asked to show your passport, so the receptionist can enter your details in a registration book. If asked to fill out a registration form yourself, you'll find it usually has some English on it; if not gesture politely for the receptionist to do it.

In return for payment, you're given a hotel card with your room number on it. Sometimes, you're also given your key. More usually, however, you will be required to take the hotel card to your floor lady *(dezhurna)* who will exchange it for the key. Whenever you leave the hotel, leave your key with the *dezhurna*.

Rental Accommodation

Apartments are a much more potent part of the accommodation mix in Ukraine than in other destinations. Even if you never usually think of renting one when abroad, you should consider it here. With so few midrange hotels, many locals and foreign expats living in the country have stepped in to fill the gap.

You can book an apartment for just one night if necessary. For longer stays, you not only have the benefit of being able to wash clothes and cook, you can save you up to 40% to 50% compared to a hotel. Apartments in Kyiv, for example, usually start at $40 for a downtown studio and $25 if you rent somewhere out of the centre.

There are some things to check for, though. Does the apartment have its own hot-water supply (the only guarantee of 24-hour supply)? Does it have its own central heating? Without the latter, you're waiting for the city government to turn on the heating in October and wishing it would turn the controls down in January.

Although many rented apartments are in a Soviet block with a concierge, it's also worth asking whether the entrance is well lit at night.

Train Stations

Many Ukrainian railway stations have a small 'hotel' of simple rooms designed for late-night arrivals or those departing early. While rudimentary, they might suffice for one night if you can't find anywhere else. Prices range from about $4 in small country towns to $20 for the much-better-than-average rooms at Kyiv's renovated train station (see p66). Of course, you hear the noise of passing trains.

Turbazy & Sanatoriums

Turbazy (tourbases) are a common form of accommodation in the Carpathian region. They are simple holiday resorts, sometimes with a series of cabins around a restaurant. Many remain unchanged since the Soviet era, but some new ones have been built in recent years. You'll find details of one or two, where relevant, in the Western Ukraine chapter.

Soviet-era sanatoriums – health resorts – speckle the Black Sea coastline in Odesa and Crimea. They don't really feature in this book, as they tend to require a week's stay at least. Many have become rather rundown, too, now no longer filled with groups of Soviet workers on organised holidays.

ACTIVITIES

In summer, the Crimea and Carpathian Mountains in western Ukraine are both extremely popular with hikers, climbers and mountain bikers. Both also attract winter skiers, but the reasonably priced Carpathians offer far better slopes. Ukraine's rivers, particularly the Dnipro, and seas make it a good place to go boating or take a cruise in summer. A handful of other activities is dotted around the countryside.

Boating

Boat trips down the Dnipro are a popular way for Kyivans to cool down in summer's searing heat. In Crimea, there are plenty of opportunities to rent a small boat with pilot who will sail you around the Black Sea coastal nooks and crannies. Both scheduled and chartered boats operate between May and mid-October.

The Centre for Green Tourism in Chernihiv organises kayaking tours with English-speaking guides (see p78).

Bungee Jumping

Crazy daredevils can bungee jump from one of most rickety bridges in the world (safety not guaranteed) in the breathtaking fortress town of Kamyanets-Podilsky (see p108).

Caving

Speleologists can embark on a three-hour extreme tour at the Marble Cave in Crimea (p153), or visit a series of karst caves in the Ternopil region, which includes the 200km-long Optimistic Cave (p111).

The catacombs which lie beneath Sevastopol (p140) and outside Odesa (p123) can also be explored. The former is more of an extreme tour, the latter easy for all.

Hiking

The Crimean landscape is arguably more spectacular, but you have a real sense of adventure and trailblazing in western Ukraine. Equipment and supplies are widely available. See the individual chapters for more details.

Ice Fishing & Swimming

Ice fishing is a national pastime for Ukrainian fishermen – usually vodka-fuelled – who sit for motionless hours next to a small hole drilled through the thick ice. Ice fishing is common on the Black Sea and on the country's many lakes.

People who like to make holes in the ice in winter and swim in the freezing water below are nicknamed 'walruses'. They're particularly common in the east of the country.

Mountain Biking

Mountain biking is a popular and fast-growing sport in Crimea, where the landscape is perfect for it (see www.mt.crimea .com). The Chornohora ridge in the Carpathians is a spectacular, if challenging, route (see www.lvivecotour.com).

Saunas

Cold winters and an historical lack of domestic plumbing helped make communal baths a national Ukrainian pastime.

Today many hotels have either a dry-heat Finnish sauna or a steamy Russian-style *banya* – or both. In the latter, it's common for people to pair up to beat each other's naked bodies with birch twigs, so the baths are divided into men's and women's

sections. Massages and the like are also commonly provided.

Skiing

A lack of low-cost flights means the Ukrainian section of the Carpathians isn't likely to become a major European skiing destination anytime soon, but it's already one of Eastern Europe's. If you're coming this way already, the passes, equipment rental and accommodation are reasonably priced. For more details see p99.

There is some skiing in Crimea, on Mt Ay-Petri or around the Marble Cave, but it is not as good.

BUSINESS HOURS

Official weekday working hours are 9am to 5pm or 10am to 6pm. Some banks close for the day at 4.30pm. Bigger shops, especially in Kyiv, tend to stay open later, until 8am or 9pm (Sunday closing is increasingly rare).

Most restaurants around the country are open from at least noon to 11pm, and times are not listed for individual eateries in this book unless they significantly diverge from these (ie where no times are listed for a restaurant, you can be sure they are open for at least lunch and dinner). Some cafeteria-style eateries and cafés open earlier, from 8am or 9am, and close at 6pm or 7pm.

Many places, especially government-run establishments, still close for lunch (1pm to 2pm or 2pm to 3pm). However, this is becoming slightly less common, especially in bigger cities.

Museum hours are typically from 9am to 5pm or 6pm, but they vary, and there are always one or two days a week when they're closed. In addition, museums usually close for cleaning sometime during the last week of each month. Some older restaurants, shops and hotel dining rooms also adhere to this system.

CHILDREN

If you're coming to Ukraine with kids it's best to limit yourselves to a short city break, probably to leafy, park-filled Kyiv. The country remains a fairly challenging destination to travel around and many parents would be unwilling to put their offspring on a not-particularly-roadworthy Ukrainian bus or *marshrutka* (see p190), or would worry about the dirty bathrooms in trains.

DIRECTORY

There are also practical difficulties with small children, from arranging bottled water to dealing with the bureaucracy with bored and tired toddlers in tow.

Ukrainians still tend to have children young, and local kids are generally very visible in public. There are many small playgrounds or 'fun fairs' in public parks and squares to cater to their whims. On the other hand, how appealing Ukrainian sightseeing attractions would be to Western children is another moot question. The most obvious option to recommend is the open-air folk architecture and life museum in Kyiv (p62).

For further information on family travel generally, see Lonely Planet's *Travel with Children* by Cathy Lanigan.

CLIMATE CHARTS

For more information on Ukraine's climate and the best time to visit, see p9.

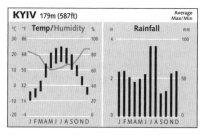

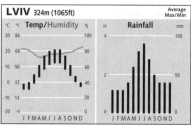

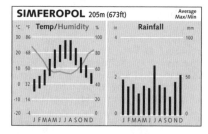

CUSTOMS

On arrival you must fill out an immigration card and possibly a *deklaratsiya* (customs declaration form). The obligatory immigration card has English explanations.

The official rule with the *deklaratsiya* is that you must fill it out if you are bringing in US$1000, 1000uah, or more.

This rule tends to be adhered to at Kyiv's Boryspil airport. So if you arrive with less than US$1000 etc here, you can usually go through the green channel without stopping to fill out a *deklaratsiya* (although you'll probably have to declare any local currency verbally). Otherwise, head through the red channel with a *deklaratsiya*.

At smaller international airports or land borders, however, you will most probably be asked to fill in a *deklaratsiya* whether or not you're carrying the threshold amount.

If in doubt – at Boryspil or elsewhere – it never hurts to fill out a *deklaratsiya* as a precaution. This form comes in English at Boryspil, but rarely anywhere else.

To start, you'll need to place a cross in the first of the three tick boxes at the top of the page if you're arriving, in the second box if you're leaving and in the third, if you're in transit.

Under Section 1, fill in your personal data. On the first line: surname, Christian and middle names. On the second line: country of residence, nationality and passport number. On the third: the country you have come from and your intended destination.

Under Section 2.1, tick the left-hand box if you have luggage with you and the right-hand box if not. If yes, write the number of pieces underneath. 2.2 asks the same questions in regards to luggage sent ahead, and so won't apply to most travellers.

Under Section 3, in the large box, fill in the money and valuables you are carrying (currency or item in the left-hand column, its value in figures in the middle, and its value in words on the right).

The tick-boxes 3.2 to 3.9 refer to prohibited items, including 3.2) weapons or ammunition 3.3) drugs 3.4) antiques 3.5) leaflets or printed matter 3.6) poisons 3.7) and 3.8) radioactive materials and 3.9) high-frequency radio devices. Tick 'no' in the right-hand column for each of these.

Tick-boxes 3.10 through to 3.12 refer to, respectively, goods to be taxed, goods to be imported/exported, and a vehicle.

Only fill in Section 4.1 if you're bringing in goods to sell or have prohibited items. 4.2 asks you to list the model, year, engine capacity, chassis number, body number and engine number of your vehicle.

Finally, sign and date the *deklaratsiya*.

If you do fill in a *deklaratsiya*, you will need to present it on leaving the country. If you lose it beforehand, contact your embassy. Everyone, with or without a *deklaratsiya*, gets a rude but perfunctory questioning about how much money they are carrying on the way out of the country.

What You Can Bring In

Ukrainian customs regulations are framed in typically bureaucratic jargon. You can bring in any item for personal use, as long as it isn't one 'that may cause damage to health or endanger people's or animals' life as well as cause damage to the environment'. This means no illegal drugs, weapons, ammunition, explosives, flora or fauna or radioactive material. Propaganda inciting war, genocide or racial hatred and any other propaganda flouting Ukraine's constitution is also forbidden, as are items breaching trademark or copyright. You will have to pay a duty on anything over: 1L of hard alcohol, 2L of wine, 10L of beer, 200 cigarettes, or – weirdly – 1kg of detergent.

What You Can Take Out

You're not allowed to take out antiques (including antique icons, books published before 1966, and furniture produced before 1945), works of art (fine or applied, such as handwoven carpets, rugs, folk art) or cultural/historical treasures (including archaeological and numismatic items, musical instruments) without special written permission. Write to the **Ministry of Culture** (☎ 044-226 2645, 226 2902; vul Ivana Franka 19, Kyiv). For the full, jargon-laden explanation, see www.ukraineinfo.us/consular.

Officially, you cannot take out more money than your customs form shows you came in with. You are now allowed to take out up to 1000uah. However, the previous limit was 85uah, so customs officers often ask to see your money before waving you through.

The duty-free limits for import (see preceding section) also apply for export. So go easy on the detergent shopping.

Finally, note that under international treaties, it is not permitted to take more than 250g of caviar out of Ukraine.

DANGERS & ANNOYANCES

Inherent bureaucracy and apathy are nasty hangovers from the Soviet Union that Ukraine has yet to shake off. Dumbstruck desk staff, blind waiters, paralysed shop assistants and the inevitable curtains being drawn shut after you've waited an hour in the ticket line – these are all little annoyances which, even if you approach an establishment armed with zero expectation, are still…darn annoying.

Annoyances that can be dangerous include: anti-Semitic and racist attitudes; open manholes in the street; driving at night on unlit, unmarked, potholed roads; zigzagging drivers; and those archaic gas water heaters (called *kolonky*) that refuse to ignite, then bang, you've got no eyebrows left.

Crime

Organised crime is big in Ukraine, but the *organisatoriya* leave tourists well alone and the worst that's likely to befall the average visitor is petty theft.

Received wisdom has it that Ukrainians can spot a foreigner at 100 paces (and if they have the slightest doubt, they'll ask you the time or for directions, just to check!). No matter how hard you try to blend in, you will stand out as a 'rich' Westerner. So use your common sense. Watch your wallet and belongings, particularly on public transport and in crowded situations. Don't flash your money, stay low-key in appearance and have more than one place on your body where you stash your cash. Avoid being alone at night in parks or secluded places.

Don't be too anxious, though, as Ukraine is usually as safe as most Western European countries. There have been rumours of credit card fraud in some upmarket restaurants in Kyiv, so you might prefer to pay cash in these. There are also some scams. Sometimes these are to do with large wads of cash being found within your view; just be alert, sceptical and ignore such things. Sometimes these are to do with bogus 'inspectors' on buses in Kyiv trying to fine you; ask to see identification before you open your wallet and never pay more than 10uah.

Reassuringly, though, the sort of organised robberies on trains that occur in other parts of Europe (including Russia) don't happen on domestic routes here, at least not yet. Keep your valuables with you at all times, of course, and travel 2nd class if you don't want to draw too much attention to yourself. However, no-one is likely to pour knock-out gas into your compartment while you sleep.

DISABLED TRAVELLERS
Even Kyiv, the best-equipped Ukrainian city, is not that friendly to people with disabilities. The rest of the country is worse. Uneven pavements, steep drops off curbs, holes in the road, lack of disabled access to public transport and very few wheelchair-accessible hotel rooms mean the only way to have an enjoyable time would be to come on a tour catering specifically for disabled travellers – and these don't exist.

EMBASSIES & CONSULATES
Ukrainian Embassies & Consulates
Where embassies and consulates have separate addresses in the capital, the address listed is for the consular section, where you obtain visas and visa information.

Australia Canberra (☎ 02-6230 5789; www.ukremb.info; Level 12, George Centre, 60 Marcus Clarke St)
Belarus Minsk (☎ 0172-283 1980; fax 0172-283 1990; vul Staravilenska 51)
Canada Ottawa (☎ 613-230 8015; www.ukremb.ca; 311 Metcalfe St, Ontario K2P lS3) Toronto (☎ 416-763 3114, fax 763 2323; 2120 Bloor St West, Ontario M6S IM8)
Czech Republic Prague (☎ 02-312 20 00; fax 312 43 66; Charles de Gaulla 29, Prague 6)
Estonia Tallinn (☎ 02-601 5835 for visas, ☎ 601 5815 for other enquiries; embukr@eol.ee; Lahe 6)
France Paris (☎ 01 43 06 07 37; fax 01 43 06 02 94; 21 ave de Saxe)
Germany Berlin (☎ 030-2888 7220; fax 2888 7219; Albrechtstrasse 56) Bonn (☎ 02228-94 1860; fax 94 1863; Rheinhohenweg 101, Remagen-Oberwinter) Munich (☎ 089-552 7370; fax 5527 3755; Oskar-von-Miller-Ring 33)
Hungary Budapest (☎ 1-422 4120; emb_hu@mfa.gov.ua; 77 Stefania St, Magyarorszag)
Japan Tokyo (☎ 3-3445 9229; www.ukremb-japan.gov.ua; 6-5-26, Kita-Shinagawa, Shinagawa-ku)
Ireland Dublin (☎ 01-668 5189; emb_ie@mfa.gov.ua; 16 Eglin Rd, Ballsbridge)

Israel Tel Aviv (☎ 23-602 1952; fax 23-604 6512; 50 Yirmiyahu)
Latvia Riga (☎ 783 2956; Elizabetes 2B)
Lithuania Vilnius (☎ 22-77 84 13; Kalvariju 159, 2600 Vilnius)
Moldova Chişinău (☎ 2-232 560/3; fax 232 562; Str Sfatul Tarii 55, 277004 Chişinău)
Netherlands Den Haag (☎ 070-362 60 95; fax 070-361 55 65; 26 Groot Hertoginnelaan)
Poland Warsaw (☎ 022-622 4797; Aleja Szucha 7) Kraków (☎ 012-656 23 36; fax 656 41 93; ul Krakówska 41, 31-066 Kraków) Gdansk (☎ 058-46 06 90; fax 46 07 07; ul Jaskowa Dolina 44, 80-246 Gdansk)
Romania Bucharest (☎ 01-201 69 86; fax 01-211 69 49; Calea Dorobantilor nr 16)
Russia Moscow (☎ 095-229 1079; fax 095-924 8469; Leontevsky pereulok 18)
Slovakia Bratislava (☎ 02-5920 2811; fax 02-5441 2651; Radvanska 35)
UK London (☎ 7727 6312; www.ukremb.org.uk; 78 Kensington Park Rd)
Turkey Ankara (☎ 440 5289, 442 1658, 441 5499; Sancak Mahallesi 206, Sokak No 17, 06550, Yildiz Cankaya) Istanbul (☎ 212-252 54 02; fax 252 54 03; Gumussuyu 9294)
USA Washington (☎ 202-333 7507/08/09; www.ukraineinfo.us; 3350 M St NW) New York (☎ 212-371 5690; 240 East 49th St) Chicago (☎ 312-642 4388; 10 East Huron St) San Francisco (☎ 413-398 0240; 530 Bush St, Suite 402, 94108)

Embassies & Consulates in Ukraine
The following are in Kyiv (☎ 044) unless otherwise noted. Call your embassy if you need emergency help. Consulates issue visas and can help their own citizens if there is no embassy.

Australia Honorary Consulate (Map pp50-1; ☎ /fax 235 7586; Apt 11, vul Kominternu 18; Ⓜ Vokzalna)
Belarus Embassy & Consulate (Map pp50-1; ☎ 537 5203; ukraine@belembassy.org; vul Mykhayla Kotsyubynskoho 3; Ⓜ Universytet)
Bulgaria Embassy & Consulate (Map pp50-1; ☎ 224 6164; vul Hospitalna 1; Ⓜ Palats Sportu) Odesa (Map pp120-1; ☎ 048-746 6553; vul Posmitnoho 9)
Canada Embassy & Consulate (Map pp50-1; ☎ 464 1144; www.kyiv.gc.ca; vul Yaroslaviv val 31; Ⓜ Zoloti Vorota)
Czech Republic Consulate (Map pp50-1; ☎ 238 2641; www.mzv.cz; vul Bohdana Khmelnytskoho 58; Ⓜ Universytet)
France Embassy & Consulate (Map pp50-1; ☎ 228 8728 for embassy assistance, 228 7369 for visas; www.amba france.kiev.ua; vul Reytarska 39; Ⓜ Zoloti Vorota)
Germany Embassy (Map pp50-1; ☎ 247 6800; www .german-embassy.kiev.ua in German; vul Bohdana

Khmelnytskoho 25; M Zoloti Vorota) Visa office (☎ 216 6794; vul Zolotoustivska 37-39)
Georgia Embassy & Consulate (Map pp50-1; ☎ 561 2696; vul Dmytrivska 46G) Odesa (Map pp120-1; ☎ 0482-22 00 75; fax 22 53 83; vul Lanzheronivska 21)
Hungary Embassy (Map pp50-1; ☎ 238 6381; fax 230 8004; www.hungaryemb.kiev.ua not in English; vul Reytarska 33; M Zoloti Vorota) Uzhhorod Consulate (☎ 671 994; vul Peremoha 92)
Japan Embassy & Consulate (Map pp50-1; ☎ 462 0020; www.ua.emb-japan.go.jp; prov Museyny 4; M Maydan Nezalezhnosti)
Lithuania Embassy (Map pp50-1; ☎ 254 0920; vul Buslivska 21; M Vydubychi)
Moldova Consulate (Map pp50-1; ☎ 290 7721; moldoukr@sovamua.com; vul Sichnevoho Povstannya 6; M Arsenalna)
Netherlands Embassy (Map pp50-1; ☎ 490 800; nlambkie@ukrpack.net; Kontraktova pl 7; M Kontraktova pl)
Poland Consulate (Map pp50-1; ☎ 234 9236; consulate@polska.com.ua; vul Bohdana Khmelnytskoho 60; M Universytet) Lviv (Map p84; ☎ 297 0861; konsulat@mail.lviv.ua; vul Ivana Franka 110)
Romania Embassy (Map pp50-1; ☎ 22 5261; romania@iptelecom.net.ua; vul Mykhayla Kotsyubynskoho 8; M Universytet) Odesa (Map pp120-1; ☎ 236 298; konsulro@tm.odessa.ua; vul Pastyora) Chernivtsi (Map p103; ☎ 540 900; konsulro@infocom.cv.ua; vul Holovna 14)
Russia Embassy (Map p48; ☎ 296 4504; embrus@ public.icyb.kiev.ua; vul Kutuzova 8; M Pecherska)
Slovakia Consulate (Map pp50-1; ☎ 234 0606; slovak@ i.kiev.ua; vul Chapayeva 4; M Zoloti Vorota) Uzhhorod (☎ 613 793; vul Lokoty 4)
Turkey Embassy (Map pp50-1; ☎ 294 9964; fax 295 6423; vul Arsenalna 18; M Pecherska) Odesa (Map pp120-1; ☎ 0482-347 241; vul Posmitnoho 8)
UK Embassy (Map pp50-1; ☎ 490 3600; www.brit emb-ukraine.net; vul Desyatynna 9) Consulate (Map pp50-1; ☎ 494 3400; Arytom Centre, vul Glybochytska 4)
USA Embassy (Map pp50-1; ☎ 490 0000 24hr emergency line; www.usemb.kiev.ua; vul Yuriya Kotsyubynskoho 10) Consulate (Map pp50-1; ☎ 490 4422; vul Mykoly Pymonenka 6)

FESTIVALS & EVENTS

Thousands of small cultural events and festivals are held throughout the country, many of them in celebration of the seasons and local folk traditions. Annual festivals include:

JANUARY
Feast of St Melania New Year's Eve, according to the old Julian calendar, falls on 13 January.

Epiphany Over the 18–19 January, the faithful celebrate the arrival of Christianity in Kyivan Rus. See p65 for details of the biggest celebration, in Kyiv.

APRIL
Humorina In Odesa, a one-day street carnival centred around humour, on the 1st of the month.

MAY
Kyiv Days A colourful spring celebration and festival in honour of the capital city; last weekend of May.

JULY
Ivan Kupalo A pagan celebration of midsummer (see the boxed text, p28).

AUGUST
Crimean Stars In Yalta, special events are scheduled throughout the month to celebrate Crimean history and culture.
Independence Day On the 24th, each city hosts festivals and parades with performances and special events.

OCTOBER
Kyiv International Music Festival In the first week of October hundreds of international composers and musicians perform at numerous venues.
Kyiv International Film Festival Molodist (www .molodist.com) A great time to check out new cinematic talent.

DECEMBER
New Year Gifts are placed under a traditional fir tree on the 31st, and special songs are sung. See out the old year with vodka and welcome in the new with champagne.

FOOD

In Kyiv, Dnipropetrovsk, Donetsk and Odesa, count on paying Western prices in restaurants. A full meal (not including drinks) typically costs $20 per person, although in an upscale place it can easily run to $50 or higher. However, lots of cafeterias mean it's possible to eat cheaply even in these more expensive cities. Away from these population centres, food becomes cheap – sometimes extremely cheap. In a typical country café, you can eat for less than $5. Street treats such as ice creams, pastries and cakes cost pennies.

GAY & LESBIAN TRAVELLERS

Homosexuality is legal in Ukraine, but few people are very 'out' here. Looking gay doesn't raise eyebrows – some straight men can look quite gay – nor do acquaintances mind it if they know you're queer. However,

DIRECTORY

you rarely, if ever, see displays of affection between two gay men or two lesbians on the street, and some locals warn it's likely to create hostility.

The biggest scene is in Kyiv, but Kharkiv and Odesa have one or two bars. Simeyz, in Crimea, is reportedly a gay mecca in August and early September.

HOLIDAYS

The main public holidays are:

New Year's Day (according to the new Georgian calendar) 1 January
Orthodox Christmas 7 January
New Year's Day (according to the old Julian calendar) 14 January
International Women's Day 8 March
Orthodox Easter (Paskha) April
Labour Day 1–2 May
Victory Day (1945) 9 May
Constitution Day 28 June
Independence Day (1991) 24 August
Great October Socialist Revolution Anniversary (1917) 7–8 November
Catholic Christmas 25 December

INSURANCE

It would be particularly foolhardy to travel to Ukraine without comprehensive insurance. Additionally, some foreign travellers are asked to prove they have valid medical insurance upon entering the country. Not all insurance is deemed acceptable and the rules are a little unclear on what's accepted and what's not. If they don't like your insurance, they will say you must buy a Ukrainian policy, which is cheap. Sample costs are: 12uah from one to five days, 62uah for 30 days.

The country has a reciprocal health agreement with the UK, so Britons will never be asked to prove they have insurance.

INTERNET ACCESS

Almost every Ukrainian town has at least one internet café. Some will be in or near the main telephone call centre or the post office. These are a quieter variant. Another category is the computer games centres with internet attached. These will be overrun with teenage boys trying to kill each other electronically.

Prices range from about 3uah in smaller cities to 10uah in Kyiv.

Usually when Internet Explorer (or any other browser) opens, the keyboard automatically produces English characters. If it doesn't, click on the language prompt (Ru/En) in the bottom right-hand corner of the screen. If no such prompt is visible, hit Ctrl+Shift to switch between the Cyrillic and Latin alphabets.

Internet service in Ukraine can be very intermittent, with networks and servers going down frequently. If an email address in this book doesn't work the first time, it's worth trying again the next day (or the next!).

LAUNDRY

Self-service laundries do not exist in Ukraine, but sending your clothes to the hotel laundry is pretty efficient. It usually costs 7uah to 35uah per item and can be turned around in a day – sometimes two hours if you're lucky. If that sounds too expensive, hand-wash clothes in the hotel sink. Most apartments for rent have a washing machine.

LEGAL MATTERS

You should carry your passport with you at all times; if stopped by the police you will be obliged to show it. However, ask to see ID first and know that they must return it immediately.

Have nothing to do with drugs or anything that might get you arrested. The penalties can be severe and the process before that labyrinthine. If the worst happens the US embassy in Kiev (http://web.usembassy.kiev.ua) maintains an online list of English-speaking lawyers.

MAPS
City Maps

UK travel bookshop **Stanfords** (☎ 020-7836 1321; www.stanfords.co.uk; 12-14 Long Acre, London WC2) sells a range of city maps, including Kyiv, Kharkiv, Lviv and Odesa. A limited number of city maps are available on the **Ukrainian Map Server** (www.infoukes.com/ua-maps), a free, online database.

In Ukraine, accurate city maps *(plan mista)* are available for all major cities.

Country Maps

Country maps are easy to find, both inside and outside the country. Gizimap produces *Ukraine: Moldova* (1:1,200,000) with a street map of Kyiv and an enlargement of Crimea, while IGN's *Ukraine* map (1:1,000,000) has street maps of Kyiv, Lviv, Odesa, Dnipropetrovsk, Donetsk and Kharkiv. Both are available online from **Stanfords** (☎ 020-7836 1321; www.stanfords.co.uk; 12-14 Long Acre, London WC2). **Freytag & Berndt** (www.freytagberndt.at in German) produces comprehensive *Ukraine: Moldova* (1:1,200,000) maps which can be ordered online. Stanfords also sell road atlases and a hiking map to the east Carpathians.

In Ukraine, keep an eye out for the excellent maps by **Topograficheskaya Karta** (☎ 044-274 6249, 274 6269; fax 274 6148). The series, based on former Soviet army mapping, covers the entire country in 286 maps (1:100,000). These are the most detailed maps available and useful to hikers (even though trails as such are not marked). The maps – printed in Russian only – cost less than $1.

MONEY

The Ukrainian hryvnia (frequently pronounced *gry*-vnya instead of the correct *hry*-vnya) is divided into 100 kopecks. Coins come in denominations of one, five, 10, 25 and 50 kopecks, plus one hryvnia. Notes come in one, two, five, 10, 20, 50 and 100 hryvnia.

In some places, particularly in Crimea, people quote prices in roubles instead of hryvnia. Don't be confused; it's just force of habit.

Officially, you can pay for only air tickets and foreign visas in US dollars. However, you will occasionally see dollars handed over, even by local citizens, in markets and expensive high-street shops. Some hotels and travel agencies will also let you pay in dollars, although they probably shouldn't. Your change will come in hryvnia.

The hryvnia is pegged to the US dollar currency at around 5.33, and has been stable since 1998. For other exchange rates see the inside front cover. It's virtually impossible to buy hryvnia before you get to Ukraine.

ATMs

Automated teller machines (ATMs) dot the landscape in Ukraine in all but the tiniest villages. Hence the best way to manage your money here is to simply take it out of your account in hryvnia. Cirrus, Plus, Visa and MasterCard/EuroCard are all recognised. Bankomats, as they are known locally, are also found in hotel lobbies, central post offices and Irish pubs, as well as on the street.

At Boryspil airport, there are several in the arrivals hall.

Your own bank will charge you a small fee for taking out foreign currency; check with it before leaving home. Some ATMs also distribute US dollars, should you need those towards the end of your trip.

Black Market

There is no real black market in currency visible to tourists. However, if you are approached to exchange money on the street, it's illegal.

Cash

US dollars and Russian roubles are the easiest currencies to exchange, followed by the euro. The British pound is hard to exchange, except in Kyiv and, to a lesser degree, Crimea. In western Ukraine, Polish zloty, Hungarian florints and Slovak crowns are widely accepted.

Whatever currency you bring, you should ensure that it is in fairly pristine condition. Banks and bureaus de change will not accept any old, tatty bills with rips or tears, or US dollar bills issued before 1990. Even a fold in a bill will prompt extra checks for counterfeiting.

Credit Cards & International Transfers

Aval Bank, UKR Exim Bank and Western Union/X-Change Points all make cash advances (in dollars or hryvnia) on major credit cards (around 3% commission). The procedure can be bureaucratic and confusing, however.

Credit cards are about as widely accepted by most upmarket hotels, restaurants and shops both in and outside the capital.

Western Union/X-Change Points will receive money wired from anywhere in the world.

Exchange Offices

Most hotels have an exchange office and there are numerous exchange kiosks (обмін валюти) scattered along main streets. The best thing is to wander around a bit comparing rates before choosing one.

Travellers Cheques

Travellers cheques should be avoided, or only be brought as a backup. It's relatively hard finding banks that will accept them

DIRECTORY

and the process is lengthy, occasionally involving trips to two different cashiers.

If you must use them, take Thomas Cook, American Express or Visa cheques in US dollars. Cheque-friendly establishments include branches of the nationwide chains Aval or UKR Exim Bank. Expect to pay 2% commission.

PHOTOGRAPHY

Western film is widely available in most cities and large towns, although colour slide and B&W film is hard to find. Film is expensive so bring a supply with you. The same applies to camera batteries (hard to find) and films/batteries for camcorders (nearly impossible to find). If using a digital camera check that you have enough memory to store your snaps – two 128 MB cards will probably be enough.

POST

Most main post offices (*poshta* or *poshtamt*) open from around 8am to 9pm (9am to 7pm on Saturday, closed Sunday). Smaller post offices close earlier and are not open on Saturday.

Outward mail is fairly reliable, but you should always send things *avia* (airmail). This takes about a week or less to Europe, and two to three weeks to America or Australia. Sending a postcard or a letter up to 20g costs 3uah to anywhere outside Ukraine. Postcards to international destinations must be sealed inside an envelope. Drop your stamped letters to destinations abroad in the post box marked за кордон. Take packages to the post office unwrapped, for their contents to be verified.

Express mail is faster, more reliable and more expensive, depending on weight. The state-run International Express Mail (EMS) is available at most main post offices; letters allegedly arrive anywhere within five days.

Incoming post is still unreliable. It's better to use email for everyday communications and a courier service if you need to take delivery of something important. DHL and FedEx have offices throughout Ukraine.

Addressing Mail

Traditionally, addresses were written in reverse order (eg Ukraina, Kyiv, 252091, vul Franko 26/8, kv 12, Yuri Orestovich Vesolovsky), but the continental European fashion (Yuri Orestovich Vesolovsky, vul Franko 26/8, kv 12, Kyiv 252091, Ukraina) is now common. The return address is written in smaller print in the top left-hand corner on the front of the envelope (not on the back).

When addressing outgoing mail, repeat the country destination in Cyrillic if you can. Incoming mail addressed in Cyrillic, rather than Latin, characters will reach its destination sooner. However, see the preceding section for the unreliability of this option.

SHOPPING

Ukraine's rich folk culture is renowned, but the most popular souvenir is its booze. Local vodka is cheap and frequently comes in attractively etched bottles. Top brands include Hetman, Ivanoff and Nemiroff. Wines and champagne are also produced locally, but you might want to exercise more caution here. Odesa champagne isn't really that palatable, although something like Krimsekt at 30uah ($6) might do the trick. Most Crimean wines are sweet sherries or madeiras. The dry-ish Cabernets produced by the Inkerman winery are an exception. See p175 for duty-free allowances.

If you're looking for nonconsumables, there are numerous souvenir markets in the major cities. Amongst other things, these sell embroidery *(vyshyvka)* in various forms, including long, narrow embroidered towels *(rushnyky)*, men's shirts *(sorochky)* and women's blouses *(bluza)*. Ceramics *(keramiky)* are another obvious choice. Sadly, most Ukrainian patterned eggs *(pysanky)* for sale are wooden imitations. You can, however, buy the real thing at the Museum of Ethnography, Arts & Crafts in Lviv (p91). Woven rugs *(kylymy)* are usually machine-made, too.

Several antique shops in Kyiv sell old hand-painted wooden icons – most of which are officially illegal to take out of the country (see p175).

SOLO TRAVELLERS

Independent travellers to Ukraine are a rarity and won't find the country geared to their needs. The lack of hostels means fewer opportunities to hook up with other travellers, although you will still chance across them in the Irish pubs and other expat hang-outs of larger cities like Kyiv, Lviv and Odesa.

However, some locals – especially those who speak a bit of English – like to talk to foreigners and will go out of their way to show you around. Furthermore, if you're moving around, rather than staying in one city, you'll never feel alone in Ukraine. Whether pressed against someone on a crowded long-distance bus seat or sharing a train compartment with them, they will want to chat. Even if neither of you speaks the other's language, they will make a valiant attempt. It's a good incentive to learn a little Ukrainian or Russian.

TELEPHONE

Ukrainian city codes are listed in this book under the relevant section heading. When calling Ukraine, the country code is ☎ 380. When dialling from abroad, drop the initial 0 of the city code (eg to call Kyiv from London dial ☎ 00 380 44).

As the Ukrainian telephone system moves from analogue to digital, many cities and towns now have two area codes. The longer one (say ☎ 0482 for Odesa) is used with the shorter old numbers. The shorter area code (say ☎ 048) just drops the last digit and will be used with longer new numbers.

For each city where this happens this guidebook lists both area codes, following them with the correct length (5, 6, or 7 digits) of the local number to be used. For example, under Ivano-Frankivsk, you will find the codes ☎ 0342 (6-digit numbers) and ☎ 03422 (5-digit numbers).

More than half a dozen town and cities have split codes like this.

Intercity & International Calls

Public phones on the streets are only for local calls. To make an intercity or international call you have to call from a private home or telephone office (the cheapest options), your hotel (the most expensive option) or from a Utel public card phone (the in-between option).

To make an intercity call from a private phone, dial ☎ 8, wait for a dial tone, then punch in the city code (including the initial 0) followed by the number. To call internationally, dial ☎ 8, wait, then punch in 10, followed by the country code, city code and number. If you can't dial directly, book a call through the international operator (☎ 079, ☎ 073) who will make the connection for you. Kyiv has some multilingual international operators (English ☎ 8-191, French ☎ 8-192, German ☎ 8-193, Spanish ☎ 8-195). They tend not to be very fluent.

Every city has a telephone office (many open 24 hours). To make an intercity *(mizhhorodny, mizhmisky)* or international *(mizhnarodny)* call, prepay the switchboard operator who will give you a metal tag imprinted with the number of the booth *(kabina)* you have been assigned. When the booth is available, dial the number you require, following the same system as from a private phone (see earlier). If there is a black button labelled 'ответ' (answer) on the booth phone, press it when the person you are calling responds; if you don't, you will be cut off. After your call, return to the switchboard operator who will give you a receipt plus, if necessary, change from your prepayment. In some telephone offices, the switchboard operator will dial the number for you, calling you to your assigned booth once the connection has been made.

Using a Utel card phone – located in some post offices and hotel lobbies – is the easiest way to make a national or international call. Chip cards in multiple denominations are sold in post offices and at hotel receptions. Instructions on how to make local, national and international calls are explained clearly in English in every Utel phone booth.

Local Calls

Local calls can be made from public phones on the street. In Kyiv, Lviv, Donetsk and other big cities, most of these phones require a phonecard, sold at post and telephone offices for just a few cents. Stupidly, phones in each city require a different type of card.

Mobile Phones

European GSM phones usually work in Ukraine, but check with your operator. Even when they say your phone will work, be aware that network coverage is patchy.

If you're going to be making a few calls, it's more economical to buy a local prepaid SIM card. They start at 37uah ($7) for a 'Uni' Sim Card from Golden Telecom. The main two network operators, Kyivstar and UMC also offer, respectively, a 50uah 'Ac&Base' pre-paid sim and 60uah 'Sim-Sim Club' card. All three cards are widely available from mobile phone shops, plus some hotel receptions and street kiosks.

Network coverage is quite widespread, often reaching up to the peaks of the Carpathian and Crimean Mountains. On the other hand, in urban areas, the network can irritatingly throw your phone offline frequently.

To dial a local mobile phone within Ukraine, you must always prefix it with an 8, as if calling another town. Common codes for mobiles include ☎ 050 and ☎ 067.

TIME

Ukraine is in one time zone – GMT plus two hours. During daylight saving from the first Sunday in April until the last Sunday in October, it is GMT plus three hours.

When it's noon in Kyiv, it is: 2am in San Francisco; 5am in New York; 10am in London; 11am in Paris, Warsaw, Prague and Budapest; noon in Minsk, Bucharest and Cairo; and 1pm in Moscow.

TOILETS

There's a Ukrainian saying: 'Where's the toilet? The toilet is everywhere!' When you see some of the public toilets you understand why. To be fair, only a few are really vile, stinky clogged holes with foot markers on either side, but when you encounter one you realise why people so often prefer to go behind a bush.

Where it's not possible to consult nature, pay toilets are the most bearable – although they will almost certainly be squat toilets. An attendant will demand 30 to 50 kopecks and proffer toilet paper in exchange. Public facilities in Crimea are generally much better than elsewhere in the country. The toilets at the Kyiv and Lviv railway stations are quite acceptable, too.

The bathrooms in trains themselves are another mucky subject. By the end of a journey, they are usually awash in liquid, but be consoled that it's usually nothing but water, splashed around from the tap.

Toilet paper in Ukraine is no longer so bad or so rare that you need to carry a major stash. That said, it's a good idea to always keep a little to hand.

A women's toilet *(tualet)* is marked with a upwards-facing triangle or ж *(zhinochy)*; men's are marked with a downwards facing triangle, ч or м *(cholovichy or muzhcheny)*.

TOURIST INFORMATION
Local Tourist Offices

Well-equipped tourist offices are virtually unknown in Ukraine, although this might change with the new government's focus on tourism. At the time of writing, only a few offices exist, in Lviv and Ivano-Frankivsk, and these were still finding their feet.

Therefore, you're largely thrown back on your own resourcefulness. Quiz the English-speaking staff who work in Ukraine's many Irish pubs (listed under Entertainment in regional chapters) or make contact with local expats. Even try asking the receptionist or service bureau in your hotel – although this might not always be useful.

Chance encounters and train journeys often yield interesting results. If you speak a little Ukrainian or Russian, or meet a local who speaks English, they will be very keen to fill you in on the undiscovered wonders of their country. It's not unheard of for them to spend a day just showing you around.

You could also approach a privately run travel agency instead.

Tourist Offices Abroad

Ukraine has no tourist offices abroad, and the information stocked by its consulates and embassies is very basic. Hopefully, in the post-Kuchma era, this will change. Meanwhile, foreign travel agencies specialising in Ukrainian travel (see p189) are helpful.

VISAS

One of the first publicly stated policies of the new Yushchenko government was to simplify Ukraine's tortuous visa regime. By the time you read this, it's possible EU citizens won't require a visa to enter the country, but check with your local embassy. At the time of writing, however, the only visitors to Ukraine exempted from visa requirements were citizens of Hungary, Lithuania, Mongolia, Poland and the CIS (excluding Turkmenistan). Visas must be obtained in advance.

According to the current rules, which might be subject to other changes, nationalities needing a visa must obtain one in advance.

To apply, you need to present to a Ukrainian consular office:

- a passport or other travel document, valid for at least one month beyond your intended departure from Ukraine;
- a completed visa application form;
- one/two passport-sized photo/s (varies in different countries).

Additionally, an invitation from a Ukrainian organisation could be needed, depending on your nationality and the type of visa that you require. See right for more details.

The application form can be obtained at any Ukrainian consulate or embassy (most will fax a form) or can be printed, for a fee, from their internet sites.

You can apply for a visa by post (usually taking 10 to 15 working days) or in person (three to 10 days). For an extra fee, consulates also offer express processing services (one to three days).

Types of Visa
Currently, there are several types of visa, but these might be streamlined, so check with your embassy.

BUSINESS & PRIVATE VISAS
A business visa can be single, double, or multiple entry. Sample fees are $55/80/200. A private visa allows visitors to enter Ukraine once or twice (single/double entry). Single-/double-entry prices are the same as for business visas.

TOURIST VISA
These are available for tourists as single- or double-entry visas. Sample single-/double-entry prices are $45/75.

TRANSIT VISA
A transit visa can be for a single or double entry and allows you to cross Ukraine by land when en route to a neighbouring country – from Romania to Russia for example. To apply, you need documented proof that you are only transiting and do not intend staying in Ukraine, eg a train/bus/boat ticket and visa for the country of destination.

Sample fees for a double-/multiple-entry visa are $30/110. Transit visas are not issued at any Ukrainian border.

OTHER VISAS
Other visas are issued for those from a Ukrainian background, students, sportspeople and, in some countries, missionaries; contact your nearest consular office for details.

Invitation Needed?
Business, private and tourist visas require an 'invitation' from a Ukrainian organisation. In the first two instances, this means a letter of invitation on official letterhead. For a tourist visa, it means confirmation of a hotel booking or a tourist voucher from a travel agency inside or outside Ukraine. The booking or tour need only apply for part of your stay in Ukraine.

Technically, exceptions are made for citizens of the US, Canada, Japan, Switzerland, Slovakia, Turkey and, if they still need visas, the EU. Nevertheless, the embassy might ask those applying for business or private visas to write on their application form the name of the person or the organisation inviting them. (Usually the consulate does not call the person or organisation named to check.) Additionally, for a business visa, the embassy might insist on a letter from the applicant's own company, explaining the purpose of their visit – which is almost as time consuming as arranging an invitation!

Tourists from the US, Canada, Japan, Switzerland, Slovakia, Turkey and, if they still need visas, the EU are technically entitled to a tourist visa simply by producing a return ticket. Some consulates, however, ask to see confirmation of a hotel booking as well.

Duration
Single- and double-entry visas are valid for six months for citizens of the US Canada, Japan, Switzerland, Slovakia, Turkey and, if they still need visas, the EU. For other nationalities, they run for three months. Multiple-entry visas last five years for US citizens, one year for others. Transit visas are valid for five days each entry.

Visa Extensions
Most visas (except multiple-entry business visas) can be extended for a maximum of two months at the **Department of Citizenship, Passport & Immigration** (☎ 044-224 9051; bul Tarasa Shevchenka 34, Kyiv; ⏰ 9am-5pm Mon-Fri). However, this bureaucratic ordeal is best avoided;

when applying for your visa, overestimate your intended length of stay.

WOMEN TRAVELLERS

Old-fashioned attitudes – so much for Soviet feminism! – still reign in Ukraine. Here, you're a *devushka* (miss or young lady) pretty well up until you become a babushka and retire – and that quaint quirk says it all. The upside is that security guards and police who might stop a male foreigner consider a woman harmless and usually let you pass. Hotel *dezhurny* and train conductors (usually women themselves) frequently take pity on you if you're alone and make an unusual effort to be nice.

The likelihood of being harassed is pretty slim. Unless they are extremely drunk, local men tend to be either wary of, or protective towards, foreign women. And young Ukrainian women dress to kill and deflect most sexual attention anyway. If you're very cautious, always travel 2nd-class on trains. Sharing the compartment with three others, rather than just one, means safety in numbers.

Most Western women will take a very dim view of the demimonde of 'dating agency' tourism in Ukraine between Western men and local women.

WORK

Most foreign workers in Ukraine are either part of large foreign joint-venture corporations such as Coca-Cola or Pac Tel, government workers, or part of some socially-oriented organisation, such as the US Peace Corps. The Ukrainian National Association (UNA) of America regularly sends volunteers to teach at universities, as does the Soros Foundation. Religious missionaries long ago descended on Ukraine in droves.

However, the freewheeling transient travellers common in other parts of Europe, who pick up seasonal work from place to place, really don't exist in Ukraine. Wages, unless you work for a foreign company, are minuscule and without the aid of some organisation or personal contact, the vast complications of setting yourself up are insurmountable.

Transport

CONTENTS

GETTING THERE & AWAY

Most people from Western Europe or further abroad will fly to Ukraine, most probably to Kyiv. However, if you're doing a grand tour across Europe, road and rail border posts are open between Ukraine and neighbouring countries.

ENTERING THE COUNTRY
Passport
Your passport must be valid for at least one month beyond your intended departure from Ukraine and stamped with a valid visa (see p182).

Other Documents
You will need to complete an immigration card and a customs declaration (see p174) on arrival in Ukraine. Both will be stamped on arrival and asked for on departure. Keep them safe. You might also need to show proof of medical insurance (see p178).

AIR
Airports & Airlines
Kyiv Boryspil airport (KBP; ☎ 044-296 76 09; www.airport-borispol.kiev.ua) is the country's main

> **THINGS CHANGE**
>
> The information in this chapter is particularly vulnerable to change. Check directly with the airline or a travel agent to make sure you understand how a fare (and ticket you may buy) works and be aware of the security requirements for international travel. The details given in this chapter should be regarded as pointers and not a substitute for your own careful, up-to-date research.

gateway, but airports at Dnipropetrovsk (DNK), Donetsk (DOK), Kharkiv (HRK), Lviv (LWO), and Odesa (ODS) also receive international flights. Simferopol (SIP) is well connected to Turkey and Israel during summer, and some charter services land there from Germany and the UK.

Ukraine's national airlines are **Ukraine International Airlines** (PS; ☎ 044-461 5656; www.ukraine-international.com) and **Aerosvit** (VV; ☎ 044-490 3490; www.aerosvit.com). The following airlines also fly to/from Ukraine:

Aeroflot (SU; ☎ 044-245 4881; www.aeroflot.com; Sheremetyevo-2, Moscow)

Air Baltic (BT; ☎ 044-238 2649; www.airbaltic.com; Riga)

Air France (AF; ☎ 044-464 1010; www.airfrance.com; Charles de Gaulle, Paris)

Austrian Airlines (OS; ☎ 044-230 0020; www.aua.com; Schwechat, Vienna)

British Airways (BA; ☎ 044-490-6060; www.ba.com; Heathrow, London)

Belavia (B2; ☎ 044-245 9407; www.belavia.by; Minsk-2, Minsk)

Crimea Air (OR; ☎ 0652-29-55-87, 044-249 0104; www.air.crimea.ua in Russian; Simferopol)

Delta Airlines (DL; ☎ 044-246 5656; www.delta.com; Hartsfield-Jackson, Atlanta, US)

Dniproavia (Z6; ☎ 0562-395 311; www.dniproavia.com; Dnipropetrovsk)

Egypt Air (MS; ☎ 044-228 2343; www.egyptair.com.eg; Cairo International)

Finnair (AY; ☎ 044-247 5777; www.finnair.com; Vantaa, Helsinki)

El Al (LY; ☎ 044-296 7696; www.elal.co.il; Ben Gurion, Tel Aviv)

Estonian Air (OV; ☎ 044-220 9853; www.estonian-air.ee; Tallinn)

KLM (KL; ☎ 044-490 2490; www.klm.com; Schiphol, Amsterdam)

LOT (LO; ☎ 044-246 5620; www.lot.com; Okecie/ Frederick Chopin, Warsaw)

Lufthansa (LH; ☎ 044-490 3800; www.lufthansa.com; Frankfurt International)

Malév (MA; ☎ 044-490 7342; www.malev.hu; Ferihegy 2, Budadpest)

Transaero (UN; ☎ 044-490 6565, 044-296 7913; www .transaero.ru/english; Domodedovo, Moscow)

Turkish Airlines (TK; ☎ 044-490 5933; www.turkish airlines.com; Atatürk Airport, Istanbul)

AUSTRALIA & NEW ZEALAND

Vienna is one of the most efficient transit hubs between Ukraine and Australia/New Zealand, although many travellers will choose London. Sample Sydney–Kyiv return fares in summer include A$3000 with Austrian Airlines via Vienna, and A$4350 with Qantas via London. With the latter option, it's cheaper to book a separate Sydney–London flight with Qantas, and the London–Kyiv leg with British Airways.

EUROPE

Ukraine International Airlines operates direct flights to Western European cities, while Aerosvit flies mainly to Eastern Europe, plus Greece and Sweden.

Ukraine International flies from Kyiv's main Boryspil airport at least daily to 13 destinations, including Amsterdam, Helsinki, London, Madrid, Paris, Rome, Vienna and Zurich. From Odesa it has a daily flight to Vienna, code-sharing with Austrian Airlines, whose own planes fly regularly between Vienna and Dnipropetrovsk, Kharkiv, Kyiv and Lviv. If changing flights in Vienna, allow yourself more than the minimum 30-minute transit time (see p91). Dniproavia operates some Ukraine International Airlines services from Dnipropetrovsk to Frankfurt-am Main, Germany.

There are daily flights from Kyiv to Eastern Europe, especially Budapest, Prague and Warsaw (with Aerosvit, LOT and Malév). Most major Western European carriers have regular (usually daily) flights to Kyiv Boryspil. Sample return fares are: London–Kyiv £255 (Ukraine Airlines or British Airways), Stockholm–Kyiv €225 (Aerosvit), and Vienna–Dnipropetrovsk €525 (Austrian Airlines). KLM sometimes has excellent fares (from €160) via Amsterdam.

RUSSIA, BELARUS, TRANSCAUCASIA & CENTRAL ASIA

There are daily flights from Moscow and St Petersburg to Kyiv (Aeroflot, Aerosvit or Transaero), as well as frequent Moscow flights to/from Dnipropetrovsk (Dniproavia), Odesa and Simferopol (Aeroflot or Transaero).

Belavia operates three flights a week between Kyiv and Minsk. Aerosvit flies to/from Kyiv and Ashkhabad (Turkmenistan) and Baku (Azerbaijan). From Simferopol Crimea Air flies to/from Tashkent and Samarkand (Uzbekistan) and Gyandsha (Azerbaijan).

Sample return fares are Moscow to Kyiv $240 with Transaero, or Moscow to Simferopol $180 with Aeroflot.

USA & CANADA

Aerosvit flies to Toronto (weekly) and New York JFK (three times a week). Toronto–Kyiv return fares in summer start at $720 and those from New York–Kyiv at $650.

Delta code-shares with Austrian Airlines from the US to Ukraine.

ELSEWHERE

To Kyiv there are at least four flights a week from Istanbul (Turkish Airlines and Dniproavia) and Tel Aviv (Aerosvit and El Al). Aerosvit and Eygptair each operate a weekly Cairo–Kyiv flight.

Aerosvit also flies from Kyiv to Dubai (three times weekly, business class only) and code-shares with El Al on flights from Tel Aviv to Dnipropetrovsk (twice weekly), Odesa (weekly) and Simferopol (twice weekly, April to October only).

Turkish Airlines flies from Istanbul to Odesa (four times a week) and Simferopol (four times a week).

Some sample return fares are: Tel Aviv–Dnipropetrovsk from $430 (with El Al/ Aerosvit) and Istanbul–Odesa $300 (with Turkish Airlines).

LAND
Border Crossings

Before leaving Ukraine, check that you have the correct visa for the country you're visiting next, particularly Belarus, Moldova or Russia. Purchasing a last-minute visa in Kyiv is not the cheapest option. You might need special medical insurance for Belarus.

Crossing the border on a train is straightforward but drawn-out, with several customs and ticket personnel scrutinising your papers.

When driving into Ukraine, always use official border stations to avoid complications. Foreigner drivers must have an International Driver's Permit and must sign a declaration that they will be leaving the country with the car by a given date (no more than two months later). You'll also need vehicle insurance valid for the former Soviet Union. Policies bought at the border often prove useless, so buy beforehand.

Belarus
BUS
In most cases, you're better going between Ukraine and Belarus by train or plane, although the Lviv–Brest bus service (40uah, nine hours, one or two a day) is a possible exception. It leaves from Lviv's bus station No 2.

CAR & MOTORCYCLE
Only two crossings are official. The M20 road north from Chernihiv to Homel crosses just north of the Ukrainian village of Novy Yarylovichy. The M14 road between Brest and Kovel crosses just southeast of the Belarus village of Makrany.

TRAIN
The main services are Kyiv–Minsk (100uah, 11 hours, daily), Kyiv–Brest (105uah, 14 hours, daily), Lviv–Minsk (100uah, 20 hours, every second day) and Lviv–Brest (65uah, 12 hours, every second day).

The faster Kyiv–Berlin train (670uah, 25½ hours) also passes through Brest (10 hours). Even to pass through Belarus you need a transit visa.

Hungary
BUS
One or two daily buses go from Uzhhorod to the Hungarian city of Nyíregyháza (26uah, three hours).

CAR & MOTORCYCLE
Only one frontier between Hungary and Ukraine is guaranteed to be open all year. Follow the E573 (M17) from Debrecen and Nyíregyháza, to near Chop.

TRAIN
Chop, 23km from Uzhhorod, is the international train junction for trains between Ukraine and Hungary. Because the two countries use different rail gauges, services running Kyiv–Budapest (500uah, 23 hours) and Lviv–Budapest (410uah, 12 hours) will have a long stop while the wheel-gauge is changed.

The daily 015 Kyiv–Budapest service continues to (or originates from) Belgrade, with connections to Zagreb three times a week.

Moldova
BUS
At least nine buses a day run between Odesa and Chişinău (15uah to 25uah, five to seven hours).

CAR & MOTORCYCLE
There are three crossings. The M21 heads northeast out of Chişinău, crossing the border frontier about 20km northeast of the Moldovan town of Duba, leading eventually to Kirovohrad in Ukraine.

The E581 (M14) crosses from the border town of Kuchurhan in Ukraine to Pervomaisc in Moldova, 30km from Tiraspol. The A272 crosses the Dnister River along the northern Moldovan border.

TRAIN
Trains to Chişinău depart from both Chernivtsi (65uah, 12 hours, every second day) and Odesa (15uah, five hours, three daily). Safeguard your possessions on these.

Poland
BUS
From Lviv's main bus station, there are buses to/from Warsaw (85uah, 11 hours, four daily), Kraków (75uah, two daily, nine to 10 hours), Przemyszl (30uah, three hours, 11 daily) and several other Polish cities. Long-distance buses between Lviv and the Czech Republic also cross through Poland.

CAR & MOTORCYCLE
There are several crossings, of which the easiest in terms of both distance and formalities is Shehyni on the E40 (A259) between Lviv and Przemyszl. Travelling Kyiv–Warsaw via Lutsk, you cross over the

TRANSPORT

border at the Buh River, before stopping in the Polish town of Okopy Nowe.

TRAIN

The Kyiv–Warsaw line (360uah, 17 to 18 hours, three times daily) passes through Rivne and Lutsk before entering Poland. The daily Kyiv–Berlin and Kyiv–Prague trains also passes through Poland.

There's a train every day passing through Lviv to Kraków (210uah, six to eight hours), from where you can change for Warsaw. There are additional direct services from Lviv to Warsaw (250uah, 15 to 18 hours) every second day. Note that some Polish trains – although not necessarily these – have recently become notorious for theft.

Romania

BUS

There's one bus a day from Chernivtsi to Suceava (30uah, four to five hours), leaving early morning. The short journey is drawn out by a lengthy border stop, as it's a popular cigarette smuggling route. You will have to change in Suceava and possibly even stay overnight before continuing to Brasov or Transylvania.

CAR & MOTORCYCLE

The E85 (A269) crosses from Romania 40km south of Chernivtsi, from Siret in Romania into Porubne on the Ukrainian side.

TRAIN

There's a daily Chernivtsi–Bucharest service (215uah, 11 hours).

Russia

BUS

There are weekly buses from Kharkiv across the border into Russia.

CAR & MOTORCYCLE

The main route between Kyiv and Moscow starts as the E93 (M20) north of Kyiv, but becomes the M3 when it branches off east some 50km south of Chernihiv.

Driving to the Caucasus, the border frontier point is on the E40 (M19) road crossing at the Ukrainian border village of Dovzhansky, about 150km east of Donetsk.

TRAIN

Most major Ukrainian cities have daily services to Moscow, all passing between either Kyiv or Kharkiv. There are up to nine trains a day between Kyiv and Moscow (130uah to 190uah, 15 hours), but only one from Kyiv to St Petersburg (175uah to 200uah, 26 hours). There's also a St Petersburg train, via Vilnius, from Lviv (205uah, 31 hours).

Many of the daily international trains between Ukraine and Western Europe either originate or terminate in Moscow.

Slovakia

BUS

One or two buses a day go from Uzhhorod to Košice (27uah, three hours) and Michalovce (13uah, two hours).

CAR & MOTORCYCLE

The E50 from Košice and Michalovce crosses at Vyšné Nemecké on the Slovak side to Uzhhorod in Ukraine, becoming the M17 in Ukraine. Expect long queues on weekends.

TRAIN

Chop is the international train junction for trains between Ukraine and Slovakia. Because the two countries use different rail gauges, services running Kyiv–Bratislava (380uah to 440uah, 30 hours) and Lviv–Bratislava (310uah, 19 hours) will have a long stop while the carriages' wheel-gauge is changed.

The 007 service between Kyiv and Bratislava runs five times a week, continuing on to (or originating in) Vienna twice a week. There are regular trains travelling between Košice and Prague.

SEA

Cruise ships are the main users of the ports at Odesa and Yalta, but some point-to-point boat services exist from Odesa to Istanbul (Turkey), Haifa (Israel), and Varna (Bulgaria).

Year-round there are two weekly services to Istanbul (from $110 one-way, based on two sharing, 36 hours) operated by two different companies. Those to Haifa (from $445 one-way, based on two sharing, 52 hours) leave once a month between March and November. Catamarans to Varna (from $50, nine to 11½ hours) leave weekly between the start of June and the end of August.

Contact Eugenia Travel in Odesa for tickets (p119).

You can double-check the latest schedules and prices for one of the boats to Istanbul online at **Ukrferry** (www.ukrferry.com).

TOURS
The following agencies provide package tours to Ukraine, as well as visa services and hotel bookings. Train tickets are much cheaper at Ukrainian railway stations than via agents.

Australia
Gateway Travel (☎ 02-9745 3333; www.russian -gateway.com.au; 48 The Boulevarde, Strathfield, NSW 2135) Offering many tours, including boat cruises down the Dnipro.

Canada & USA
Chumak Travel Agency (☎ 905-804 8826; www .ukrainetour.com; 2-3415 Dixie Rd, Suite 527, Mississauga, ON L4Y 4J6) Run by Ukrainians now based in Canada.
Meest Travel (☎ 416-236-7707, 1-800-210-727; fax 416-236-0447; 97 Six Point Rd, Toronto, ON, M8Z 2X3) This delivery and travel service has more than 400 representatives throughout Canada, the USA and Ukraine (and a sometimes less-than-cheerful phone manner).
RJ's Tours (☎ 780-415 5633, 1-877-353 5633 toll-free from western Canada; www.rjstours.shawbiz.ca; 11708, 135A St, Edmonton, Alberta T5M 1L5) Escorted tour groups.
Scope Travel (☎ 973-378 8998, 1 800-242 7267; www .scopetravel.com; 1605 Springfield Ave, Maplewood, NJ 07040) Everything from rafting down the Dnister River to climbing in the Carpathians or Crimea.

UK
Black Sea Crimea (☎ 020-8200 6834; www.blacksea -crimea.com) Small, but helpful southern Ukraine operator, with an informative and up-to-date website.
Intourist Travel (☎ 0870 112 1232; www.intouristuk .com; 7 Wellington Tce, London W2 4LW) One of the largest operators with former USSR contacts.
Regent Holidays (☎ 2117-921 1711; www.regent -holidays.co.uk; 15 St John St, Bristol BS1 2HR) A knowledgeable company.
Ukraine Travel (☎ 0161-652 5050; www.ukraine.co .uk; Falcon House, Victoria St, Chadderton OL9 0HB) The UK's leading Ukraine specialist, also known as Bob Sopel's, has everything you need, even Ukrainian football information.

GETTING AROUND
Ukraine's transport infrastructure is similar to that of the developing world, with a few Soviet legacies and some modern additions thrown in. The USSR left the country with a solid, if slow, rail service, while some airlines and coach companies are starting to buy new aeroplanes or vehicles. Land transport is cheap; you can go by train from one end of the country to another for less than $15.

AIR
In addition to the airports listed in the Getting There & Away section, Kyiv's **Zhulyany Airport** (IEV; ☎ 242 2308; www.airport.kiev.ua in Ukrainian) receives many domestic (and some international) flights. See the relevant sections for airports in Chernivtsi, Dnipropetrovsk, Donetsk, Ivano-Frankivsk, Kharkiv, Lviv, Odesa and Uzhhorod.

Airlines in Ukraine
Ukraine International Airlines and Aerosvit (see p185) own new aircraft and between them can book most internal flights. However, many services are operated by their domestic code-share partners, often using Soviet-era Antonov, Ilyushin and Yak aircraft. It's too complicated to deal with individual domestic carriers but, for reference, they and their IATA codes include Air Ukraine (6U), Dniproavia (Z6), Donbassaero (7D), Lviv Airlines (5V), Motor Sich (M9), Odesa Air (5K), Tavrey Airco (T6) and Ukraine Mediterranean Airlines (UF).

For domestic flight information call ☎ 056.

Tickets
Ukraine International Airlines and Aerosvit have offices in most cities, and the website of **Kiyavia Travel** (www.kiyavia.com) lists timetables, prices and aircraft used – all in English. Tickets can be booked with Kiyavia by email but must be collected in person.

Sample return fares include Simferopol–Kyiv ($210), Kyiv–Dnipropetrovsk ($305), Kyiv–Odesa ($165) and Lviv–Kyiv ($215).

BOAT
Crimean Trips
In summer, there is a catamaran service running between Odesa and Yalta, via Sevastopol

(from $35/75 single/return). Contact Eugenia Travel in Odesa for details (p119).

Dnipro River Trips

The Dnipro flows 1000km through Ukraine, from the northern border to the Black Sea, symbolically splitting the country in two.

River cruises plying its waters can be booked through many travel agencies, in Kyiv, Odesa or abroad, but the principal operator is **Chervona Ruta** (www.ruta-cruise.com). One-way or return cruises between Kyiv and Odesa stop in ports like Zaporizhzhya, Kherson and Sevastopol en route. One-way trips take 11 to 12 days and start at €1259 per person, based on two people sharing. Return journeys last 13 to 14 days and start at a cheaper €1179 per person, based on two sharing.

Passenger hydrofoil services are available between May and mid-October, but are limited. Ask travel agencies in Kyiv (p53).

BUS

Buses serve every city and small town, but are best for short trips (three hours or less) as conditions are not really comfortable. There's a very ad hoc feel to the experience, with buses continually coming and going, seemingly without rhyme or reason, and drivers sometimes decorating their buses with religious photos, curtains or plastic flowers.

Some Western-standard, 'luxury' coaches do ply major routes. The largest operator is **Autolux** (www.autolux.com.ua).

Bus stations are called *avtovokzal* or *avtostantsiya*. Some larger cities have several stations – one main, long-distance one and smaller stations serving local destinations.

Information

Reliable timetables are displayed near the ticket windows, but don't rely on the Soviet-era route maps. Destinations are usually signposted on platforms. There might be an information window (*dovidkove byuro;* довідкове бюро) charging 60 kopecks to 1uah per answer, but you can usually ask at any window for free.

Tickets

Tickets are sold at the bus station a few hours before departure and resemble shop-till receipts. Your destination and time of travel is clearly marked, as well as your seat number (*meest;* місц). Tickets from the bus station are only valid for one service. Having bought a ticket, you can't suddenly decide to take a later bus without paying again.

Unless the bus is full, you can always simply pay the driver, however. Indeed, if the bus is passing through tickets can only be bought from the driver.

CAR & MOTORCYCLE

We don't recommend driving in Ukraine. The roads are mostly terrible and there's a tacit, unofficial highway code that local drivers understand but which you probably never will. If you insist, drive carefully. Additionally, opt for the highest-octane petrol *(benzyn)* and pay before filling up. In winter, fill your windscreen cleaner with vodka to stop it from freezing.

Hire

Between them, **Avis** (www.avis.com), **Europcar** (www.europcar.com) and **Hertz** (www.hertz.com.ua) have locations in Kyiv (airport and downtown), Dnipropetrovsk, Donetsk, Kharkiv, Lviv, Odesa, Simferopol and Yalta. Rental starts at $55 a day (for a weekly hire). Check insurance and hire conditions carefully.

Road Rules

Drive on the right. Unless otherwise indicated, speed limits are 60km/h in towns, 90km/h on major roads and 110km/h on highways. Speed traps are common and traffic police often wave you down without obvious reason. Fines for speeding start at 40uah. Traditionally officers have been open to negotiation (meaning you pay less – 20uah – but don't get an official receipt). However, this might change in the new political era.

It's a criminal offence to drive after consuming alcohol or without wearing a seat belt – although everybody completely ignores the latter. Legally you must always carry a fire extinguisher, first-aid kit and warning triangle.

Road Types

There are four main categories of roads. The three main E/M highways traversing the country are the best, including the east–west E40 (M17) from Lviv to Kharkiv via Kyiv, and the E95 (M2) from Kharkiv to Simferopol. The E93 (M20) between Kyiv and Odesa has been under reconstruction to create a dual carriageway the entire distance. When it's finished, it will be a tollway. Unless it's finished, the route will still be chaos.

Main cities and large towns are linked by secondary roads that begin with the letter 'A'. Next are the shabbier roads that link small towns all over the country, which begin with the letter 'P'. Then there are hundreds of smaller unnumbered roads and tracks. Mostly, however, signs simply states the road's destination in Cyrillic. Bring a good map.

HITCHING

You simply can't hitchhike around Ukraine for free. Hitching a ride is common, but it's necessary to pay drivers for the privilege. Hitching is never entirely safe anywhere. However, given the prevalence of these unofficial or 'gypsy taxis' in Ukraine, it's reasonably safe to do so during the day, within big cities. Obviously, exercise common sense, particularly if you're a woman travelling solo.

You will need to speak the lingo to discuss your destination and price and it's easiest to get a ride where locals are flagging down cars. Put your hand up in the air, palm down.

LOCAL TRANSPORT

Ukrainian cities are navigable by trolleybus, tram, bus and – in Kyiv, Kharkiv and Dnipropetrovsk – metro. Urban public transportation systems are usually overworked and overcrowded. There's no room for being shy or squeamish – learn to assert yourself quickly.

Still, a ticket (*kvytok* or *bilyet*) is dirt cheap. A single bus/tram/trolleybus costs 50 to 60 kopecks. It's always simplest to pay the driver or conductor. Tickets have to be punched on board (or ripped by the conductor). Unclipped or untorn tickets warrant an on-the-spot fine, should you be caught.

For the metros you need a plastic token (*zheton*), sold at the counters inside the stations for 50 kopecks. Metros run from around 5.30am to midnight. Metro stations can have several names – one for each different line that passes through it.

Throughout, zippy *marshrutky* (minibuses) shadow most local bus routes. These *marshrutky* are unscheduled and simply

depart when full. A single ride usually costs 1uah to 2uah within a city (more for inter-city trips, depending on distance). Pass your money to the driver or to the passengers in front of you, who will pass it on. Any change will be returned the same way. When you want to alight call out '*ostanovityes pozhalusta!*' and the driver will stop.

TAXIS

Most taxis lack meters, and drivers double or triple their prices (or worse) when they hear your accent. There are several ways to deal with this. Ask your hotel to call for a quote. This doesn't always get you a truly local price, but it's never a total rip-off. Alternatively, haggle with drivers (you'll need some Ukrainian or Russian) and then bite the bullet. Even inflated prices are ultimately cheap for Westerners. Cabs in front of hotels and major train stations always charge a premium.

Published rates are roughly 5uah for the first 3km and 1.25uah for each kilometre thereafter. Be very happy if you're charged this. For day trips, it's worth trying to negotiate by the hour, but not with the few cabs that do have meters; they charge waiting time.

TOURS

Poor infrastructure along with difficult-to-negotiate bureaucracy means even the most independent travellers might find themselves hiring guides and going on organised day tours in Ukraine. Travel agencies are listed under Information in the relevant city sections.

TRAIN

Rail is the preferred form of transport in Ukraine. Trains are cheap and reliable – lateness is rare – although they're also very slow. Overnight services depart at dusk and arrive at their destination in time for breakfast.

Every train station (*zaliznychny vokzal* or just *vokzal*) has a left-luggage counter (камері сжову or камері зберігання) open 24 hours except for signposted short breaks. Pay when you deposit your luggage and retrieve it with the receipt or metal tag you are given.

Most railway personnel in Ukraine tend to be Russian-speaking. Train tickets are printed in Ukrainian and Russian.

TRANSPORT

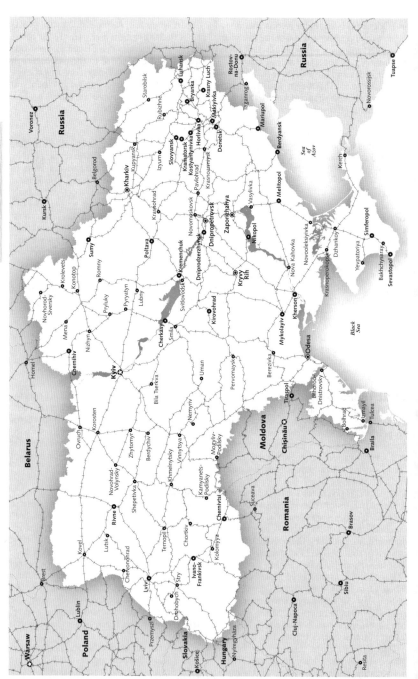

Classes & Types of Trains

Spalny vahon (SV) is a 1st-class couchette (sleeper) compartment for two people. This is perfect for couples but can be a little awkward if you're travelling alone. Your bed will already be made for you (there's a 6uah to 8uah charge for sheets) and SV toilets are much cleaner. Not all trains offer SV, which costs two to three times more than *kupe*.

Kupe or *kupeyny* is a 2nd-class sleeper compartment for four people. This is the most popular class – which books up fast on some routes – and also the safest and most fun. Sharing the compartment with two or three others is less awkward and there's safety in numbers. *Kupe* is about twice as costly as *platskart*. Unless otherwise noted, train prices quoted in this guidebook are for *kupe*. A sheet charge (usually 6uah to 8uah) is also levied in *kupe*.

Platskart is a 3rd-class sleeper. The entire train car is open (no separate compartments) with groups of four bunks in each alcove along with two others in the aisle. This is not really recommended for foreigners.

Zahalny vahon (*obshchiy* in Russian) means an upright, hard bench seat for the entire journey. This is only used over short distances.

All classes have assigned places with your carriage *(vahon)* and bunk *(mesto)* numbers printed on your ticket.

There are many types of trains, but the only important difference is between diesel-engined mainline services and electrified suburban trains or *elektrychka*. The latter will leave from a different part of the train station, set aside for local trains (*prymisky poyizd*, or *pryhorodny poyizd* in Russian).

Information

Sucking information out of surly, strictly Ukrainian- or Russian-speaking attendants in information booths (довідкове бюро) is a formidable task. Most charge 60 kopecks to 2uah for each oral/written response, although you'll escape these charges at smaller stations.

Schedules are posted on the wall – once you have mastered some basic words, they are simple to decipher (see the Language chapter, p203).

In Kyiv an updated and comprehensive train timetable is printed in the *Kyiv Business Directory*. At Kharkiv train station, you can buy pocket train timetables.

On the Journey

Each carriage has an attendant called a *providnik* (male) or *provodnitsa* (female), who collects your ticket, distributes sheets and makes morning wake-up calls. Most are helpful, providing cups of tea from their samovars throughout the journey (about 1uah).

It's *de rigueur* to change into sleeping wear in your carriage, so bring tracksuit bottoms, a comfortable top and thick-soled slippers or flip-flops (thongs). Your fellow passengers will happily leave the carriage while you change; just motion.

It's always been traditional to share food and drink with your fellow passengers. This is still common, although much less so than formerly. Dining cars rarely sell anything more than sandwiches, snacks and drinks.

Toilets are locked some 30 minutes either side of a station. Bring your own paper. Don't drink the water from the tap or even clean your teeth with it.

Tickets

Buying tickets at the train station is impossible without a smattering of Ukrainian or Russian. You will need to learn some basic phrases or point to the sentences in the back of this book (see p203).

Many cities have an advance ticket office in the centre. You will encounter the same linguistic wrangles here, but without being shoved by irate people waiting behind in line.

When buying train tickets you must show a passport (or give a name) for each ticket. This is to thwart the touts who once bought all the seats on popular routes and resold them at a premium.

TRANSPORT

Health

CONTENTS

BEFORE YOU GO

Ukraine's once excellent health service is now underresourced and ailing, so it's important to be prepared. Bring extra supplies of any medication you are taking and familiarise yourself with the Latin name if it's not on the label. In Ukraine this is often written in the Roman alphabet alongside any medicine's local name, and will therefore translate easily. Carry a spare pair of contact lenses and glasses if you need them. Although most Ukrainian hospitals now use disposable syringes, supplies can be short, so it doesn't hurt to bring your own, in a sterilised first-aid kit.

INSURANCE

Ukraine has reciprocal health care arrangements with some countries – the UK, for example – but these are only ever for emergency medical care, so make sure you have comprehensive medical and travel insurance. Strongly consider a policy that covers you for the worst possible scenario, such as an accident requiring an emergency flight home.

Citizens of countries that do not have a reciprocal health care agreement with Ukraine might be compelled to buy Ukrainian medical insurance at the border (see p178). Check with your local Ukrainian embassy (p176).

INTERNET RESOURCES

Before departing, travellers should check with their local public health service for information on current epidemic or health risks for travellers to Ukraine. The World Health Organisation's (WHO) publication *International Travel and Health* is revised annually and is available online at www .who.int/ith/. Other useful websites include www.mdtravelhealth.com (travel health recommendations for every country; updated daily), www.fitfortravel.scot.nhs.uk (general travel advice for the layperson), www.agecon cern.org.uk (advice on travel for the elderly) and www.mariestopes.org.uk (information on women's health and contraception).

VACCINATIONS

No jabs are mandatory to enter Ukraine, but it is recommended that your immunisations are current for diphtheria, polio, tetanus, hepatitis A and typhoid (the last two are given jointly). Those going hiking in summer should also consider shots against tick-borne encephalitis and/or rabies.

IN TRANSIT

DEEP VEIN THROMBOSIS (DVT)

Blood clots might form in the legs during plane flights, chiefly because of prolonged immobility. The longer the flight, the greater the risk. The chief symptom of DVT is swelling or pain of the calf, usually but not always on just one side. When a blood clot travels to the lungs, it might cause chest pain and difficulty breathing. Travellers with any of these symptoms should immediately seek medical attention.

To prevent the development of DVT on long flights, you should walk around the cabin, contract the leg muscles while sitting, drink plenty of fluids and avoid alcohol.

JET LAG & MOTION SICKNESS

To avoid jet lag (common when crossing more than five time zones) try to drink plenty of nonalcoholic fluids and eat light meals. Try to readjust your schedule for meals, sleep etc as soon as you board your flight, or even in the days before departure. Upon arrival, get exposure to natural sunlight.

Antihistamines such as dimenhydrinate (Dramamine) and meclizine (Antivert, Bonine) are usually the first choice for treating motion sickness. A herbal alternative is ginger.

IN UKRAINE

AVAILABILITY & COST OF HEALTH CARE

There are some Western-standard clinics in Kyiv, usually expensive. However, a shortage of cash in the post-Soviet era means equipment is often lacking or outdated in hospitals elsewhere. Doctors are usually well trained, but not all speak English. For serious complaints you should travel to a larger town or ask your embassy or consulate to recommend a hospital, clinic, doctor or dentist. Alternatively, the American embassy in Kyiv maintains an online list of hospitals and clinics with English speakers on the staff (http://web.usembassy.kiev.ua/amcit_medical_serv_eng.html). Most are in Kyiv, but there is one in Odesa and one in Donetsk.

INFECTIOUS DISEASES
Diphtheria
This bacterial infection of the throat, nose and tonsils is resurgent in parts of Eastern Europe, including Ukraine. The disease causes lesions in the infected area and in severe cases can cause swelling and fluid build-up in the neck. In many Western countries, diphtheria booster shots are recommended every 10 years. Travellers should ensure theirs is current before visiting Ukraine.

HIV & AIDS
Ukraine is the site of Europe's worst HIV epidemic. The country already has more than 10 times the number of HIV cases than equivalent Western European nations, and the virus is spreading faster here than elsewhere on the continent. WHO estimates that 360,000 people, or 1% of the adult population, are HIV positive. UNAIDS believes the true figure might be as high as 600,000. Infection rates have been doubling every year for the past three years.

While the epidemic was originally drug-driven, heterosexually transmitted infection is now on the increase, growing from 15% of cases to almost 40% between 1999 and 2004.

The worst-hit areas are Odesa and Mykolayiv.

The message should be clear: always practise safe sex.

Rabies
This is a potential concern considering the number of stray dogs running around in packs throughout Ukraine. If bitten by a homeless dog, seek medical attention immediately (most main hospitals will have a rabies clinic), but don't panic – while rabies is transmitted via the animal's saliva, the rabies virus is present in saliva only during the final stages of the disease in the animal, often only in the last week of the dog's life. It is therefore a relatively rarely transmitted disease. Still, do not take any chances and

seek medical attention. Any bite, scratch or even lick from an unknown animal should be cleaned immediately and thoroughly. Scrub with soap and running water, and then apply alcohol or iodine solution.

A rabies vaccination does exist, but it only reduces the level of treatment needed following a bite. Travellers vaccinated against rabies should still seek medical treatment if bitten.

Tick-borne Encephalitis

This is spread by tick bites. It is a serious infection of the brain and some medical practitioners advise vaccination for those planning to spend time hiking in the Carpathians or Crimea between April and August. The risk of getting bitten in Ukraine is quite low, however. So other clinics suggest prophylactic prevention – ie using DEET- and pyrethrin-based insect repellents to prevent tick bites – particularly for short-term visitors. In either case, check your body for ticks each evening.

Two doses of vaccine will give a year's protection, three doses up to three years'. However, many doctors' surgeries have to order the vaccine in advance and the shots need to be given at certain intervals for maximum protection. Therefore, if planning to have a series of shots, you should look at having the first injection about a month before departure.

Tuberculosis

As in many countries of the former Soviet Union, strains of drug-resistant tuberculosis (TB) have reached epidemic proportions in Ukraine. However, most travellers are really at very little risk of contracting this disease, because you need prolonged contact with an infected individual. Many West Europeans and Australians will have been vaccinated against some strains of TB in adolescence. This, and being in good health, is thought by some practitioners to increase your natural immunity against other strains too. American travellers, who won't usually have been immunised, might want to consider a TB vaccination if going into a high-risk situation. However, its efficacy is questionable when given in adulthood.

In any case, try to avoid spending a lot of time with someone with a persistent dry cough. If that proves to be unavoidable, it's a sensible precaution to get a TB test on your return home.

Typhoid & Hepatitis A

These diseases are spread through contaminated food (particularly shellfish) and water. Typhoid can cause septicaemia; hepatitis A causes liver inflammation and jaundice. Neither is usually fatal but recovery can be prolonged. Hepatitis A and typhoid immunisation is now routinely provided in a single vaccine. However, the first dose only lasts a year, after which you will need a booster to provide 10 years' coverage.

TRAVELLER'S DIARRHOEA

If you develop diarrhoea, be sure to drink plenty of fluids, preferably an oral rehydration solution (eg Dioralyte). A few loose stools don't require treatment, but if you start having more than four or five stools a day, you should start taking an antibiotic (usually a quinolone drug) and an antidiarrhoeal agent (such as loperamide), and seek medical treatment. Furthermore, if diarrhoea is bloody, persists for more than 72 hours or is accompanied by fever, shaking, chills or severe abdominal pain, you should also seek medical attention.

ENVIRONMENTAL HAZARDS
Chornobyl

The risk to short-term visitors thought to be is insignificant. Areas contaminated enough to present a health risk have been sealed off, and even if you visit the Chornobyl exclusion zone you are unlikely to be exposed to more radiation than during a transatlantic flight. Visiting the Chornobyl exclusion zone can be a moving experience, but you need to decide whether it's worth the risk (see p75 for more details).

However, some authorities have advised against swimming in the Dnipro around Kyiv, although that's a popular local pastime in summer. Portions of silt have been contaminated by radioactive particles flowing downstream.

The most absorptive foods are mushrooms and berries. These two staples of the Ukrainian diet should be avoided if they are from the woods around Chornobyl or if their origin is uncertain.

Hypothermia & Frostbite

Ukraine's harsh winters do present a risk of hypothermia, so be alert to the first warning signs, like chattering teeth and shivering, before loss of judgment and clumsiness set in. Unless rewarming occurs at this point, the sufferer deteriorates into apathy, confusion and coma. Prevent further heat loss by seeking shelter, warm dry clothing, hot sweet drinks and shared bodily warmth. Be aware that hypothermia can occur both because of a gradual loss of temperature over hours or following a sudden drop of temperature.

Frostbite is caused by freezing and subsequent damage to bodily extremities. It is dependent on wind-chill, temperature and length of exposure. Frostbite starts as frostnip (white, numb areas of skin) from which complete recovery is expected with rewarming. As frostbite develops, the skin blisters and then becomes black. Adequate clothing, staying dry, keeping well hydrated and ensuring adequate calorie intake best prevent frostbite. Treatment involves rapid rewarming.

Even on a hot summer's day in the mountains, the weather can change rapidly, particularly on the exposed ridges of Crimea. So always carry waterproof garments and warm layers, and inform others of your route.

Water

For foreigners in Ukraine, water straight from the tap is never safe to drink. You should at least boil or purify water (with filters, iodine or chlorine). However, an even safer solution is to drink bottled water, which is cheap and plentiful.

It's normally fine to clean your teeth in tap water, but on trains you shouldn't even do that. Take a bottle of water into the train bathroom with you.

When hiking, you're probably better off than in the cities. Mountain springs in the Carpathians and Crimea are safe to drink.

WOMEN'S HEALTH

Emotional stress, exhaustion and travelling through different time zones can all contribute to an upset in the menstrual pattern. If using oral contraceptives, remember some antibiotics, diarrhoea and vomiting can stop the pill from working and lead to the risk of pregnancy – remember to take condoms with you just in case. Time zones, gastrointestinal upsets and antibiotics do not affect injected contraception.

HEALTH

Language

CONTENTS

Ukrainian is the official language of Ukraine and is the first language of the great majority of the country's 49 million people.

Ukrainian belongs to the Slavic group of the Indo-European family of languages and is most closely related to Russian and Belarusian. Its recent development has been turbulent. The written form was banned by the tsars in the 19th century. In the 1920s the Soviets allowed the language to thrive in schools and publications, but Stalin's policy of 'Russification' meant that it was supplanted by Russian in the universities. Political factors were largely responsible for the development of what was regarded as 'proper' Ukrainian. The Ukrainian used in this language guide is the standard language spoken in the capital, Kyiv, and other major centres.

Ukrainian uses the Cyrillic alphabet (see p199), so called after St Cyril, the monk who is credited with inventing it in the 9th century to help spread Orthodox Christianity among the 'pagan' Slavs. The alphabet is easier to master than it may first appear, and with a bit of practice it will quickly become familiar to you.

Anyone visiting Ukraine who makes even a modest attempt to speak the language will be sure to receive a very warm welcome. By showing that you know some Ukrainian you are sharing in the adventure of freedom that the Ukrainian people themselves are now experiencing.

If you'd like a more comprehensive guide to the language, get a copy of Lonely Planet's *Ukrainian Phrasebook*. For information on food and Ukrainian terms that will be useful when dining, see p37.

PRONUNCIATION

Unlike English, where one letter may be pronounced in many different ways, each letter in Ukrainian usually stands for only one sound. Beware, however, of the letters that look like English ones, but in fact stand for quite different sounds.

The Soft Sign

The consonants д (**d**), з (**z**), л (**l**), н (**n**), с (**s**), т (**t**), and ц (**ts**) are sometimes rendered with a 'softened' pronunciation. A soft consonant is indicated in writing by the soft sign ь following it (represented in the transliterations with an apostrophe, eg **d'**). It is pronounced with the tongue closer to the palate than with its 'hard' counterpart, eg н/нь (**n/n'**) are pronounced like the 'n' in 'canoe' and the 'n' in 'sinew' respectively.

Word Stress

Where a word has two syllables or more, stressed syllables are written in italics in the transliterations.

ACCOMMODATION

Could you tell me where to find a ..., please?
ska-*zhit'*, bud' *la*-ska, de ...?
Скажіть, будь ласка, де ...?

  camping ground
  kem-pinh
  кемпінг

  guesthouse/youth hostel
  mo-lo-*dizh*-ny hur-*to*-zhy-tok
  молодіжний гуртожиток

  (cheap) hotel
  (de-*she*-vy) ho-*tel'*
  (дешевий) готель

What is the address?
ya-*ka* a-*dre*-sa?
Яка адреса?

THE UKRAINIAN CYRILLIC ALPHABET

Cyrillic	Roman	Pronunciation
А, а	a	as in 'father'
Б, б	b	as in 'but'
В, в	v	as in 'van' before a vowel
	w	as in 'wood' before a consonant or at the end of a syllable
Г, г	h	as in 'hat'
Ґ, ґ	g	as in 'good'
Д, д	d	as in 'dog'
Е, е	e	as in 'end'
Є, є	ye	as in 'yet'
Ж, ж	zh	as the 's' in 'measure'
З, з	z	as in 'zoo'
И, и	y	as in 'myrtle', but short
І, і	i	as in 'pit'
Ї, ї	yi	as in 'yip'
Й, й	y	as in 'yell'; almost always precedes or follows a vowel
К, к	k	as in 'kind'
Л, л	l	as in 'lamp'
М, м	m	as in 'mad'
Н, н	n	as in 'not'
О, о	o	as in 'pot', but with the jaws slightly more closed and the lips a little more pursed
П, п	p	as in 'pet'
Р, р	r	as a trilled 'r'
С, с	s	as in 'sing'
Т, т	t	as in 'ten'
У, у	u	as in 'put'
Ф, ф	f	as in 'fan'
Х, х	kh	as the 'ch' in the Scottish loch
Ц, ц	ts	as in 'bits'
Ч, ч	ch	as in 'chin'
Ш, ш	sh	as in 'shop'
Щ, щ	shch	as 'sh-ch' in 'fresh cheese'
Ю, ю	yu	as the 'y' in 'yell' followed by **u**
Я, я	ya	as in 'yard'
ь, ь	'	'soft sign' (see p198)

Could you write it down, please?
moh·lu·b *vy* za·py·*sa*·ty, bud' *la*·ska?
Могли б ви записати, будь ласка?

Do you have any rooms available?
u vas ye *vil'*·ni no·me·*ry*?
У вас є вільні номери?

I'd like (a) ...
ya kho·*chu* ...
Я хочу ...

bed
lizh·ko
ліжко

single room
no·mer na o·dno·*ho*
номер на одного

room
no·mer
номер

double-bed
lizh·ko na *dvokh*
ліжко на двох

twin room with two beds
dviy·*nuy no*·mer z dvo·*ma lizh*·ka·*my*
двійний номер з двома ліжками

room with a bathroom
no·mer z *van*·no·yu
номер з ванною

a shared dorm
mi·stse
місце

How much is it ...?
skil'·ky *ko*·shtu·ye no·*mer* ...?
Скільки коштує номер ...?

per night
za nich
за ніч

per person
za o·*so*·bu
за особу

May I see the room?
mo·zhna po·dy·*vy*·ty·sya na *no*·mer?
Можна подивитися на номер?

Where is the toilet/bathroom?
de tu·a·*let/van*·na?
Де туалет/ванна?

I'm leaving today.
ya vid·yiz·*zha*·yu syo·*ho*·dni
Я від'їжджаю сьогодні.

We're leaving today.
my vid·yiz·*zha*·mo syo·*ho*·dni
Ми від'їжджаємо сьогодні.

CONVERSATION & ESSENTIALS

Hello.
pry·vit (inf)/do·bry·den'!
Привіт/Добридень!

Goodbye.
do po·*ba*·chen·nya/do *zu*·stri·chi
До побачення/До зустрічі.

Please.
bud' *la*·ska/*pro*·shu
Будь ласка/Прошу.

Thank you.
dya·ku·yu
Дякую.

You're welcome.
do-*bro* po-*zha*-lu-va-ty   Добро пожаловати.
Yes.
tak   Так.
No.
ni   Ні.
Excuse me.
bud' *la*-ska, do-*zvol'*-te   Будь ласка, дозвольте
pro-*yty*   пройти.
I'm sorry.
pe-re-*pro*-shu-yu   Перепрошую.
What's your name?
yak vas zva-ty?   Як вас звати?
My name is ...
me-*ne* zva-ty ...   Мене звати ...
Where are you from?
zvid-ky vy?   Звідки ви?
I'm from ...
ya z ...   Я з ...
I (don't) like ...
me-*ni* (ne) po-*do*-   Мені (не) подобається ...
ba-yet'-sya ...
Just a minute.
khvy-*ly*-noch-ku   Хвилиночку.

DIRECTIONS
Where is ...?
de ...?   Де ...?
Go straight ahead.
i-*dit' prya*-mo   Ідіть прямо.
Turn left.
po-ver-*nit'* li-*vo*-ruch   Поверніть ліворуч.
Turn right.
po-ver-*nit'* pra-*vo*-ruch   Поверніть праворуч.
at the corner
na *ro*-zi   на розі
at the traffic lights
bi-lya svi-tlo-*fo*-ra   біля світлофора

behind   *zza*-du   ззаду
in front of   s-*pe*-re-du   спереду
far   da-*le*-ko   далеко
nearby   *blyz'*-ko   близько
near to   *bi*-lya   біля
opposite   pro-*ty*-*le*-zhny   протилежний
opposite to   na-*pro*-ty   напроти

beach   plyazh   пляж
bridge   mist   міст
cathedral   so-*bor*   собор
church   *tser*-kva   церква
island   *o*-striw   острів
lake   *o*-ze-ro   озеро
main square   may-*dan*   майдан
market   *ry*-nok   ринок

old city (town)   sta-*re mi*-sto   старе місто
palace   pa-*lats*   палац
sea   *mo*-re   море
square   *plo*-shcha   площа

HEALTH
I'm ill.
me-*ni* po-*ha*-no   Мені погано.
It hurts here.
u *me*-ne bo-*lyt'* tut   У мене болить тут.

I have ...
u *me*-ne ...   У мене ...
asthma
a-stma   астма
diabetes
di-a-*bet*   діабет
epilepsy
e-pi-*le*-psiya   епілепсія

I'm allergic to ...
u *me*-ne a-ler-*hi*-ya na...   У мене алергія на ...
antibiotics   an-ty-bi-o-ty-ky   антибіотики
penicillin   pe-*ni*-tsu-lin   пеніцилін
bees   *bdzho*-ly   бджоли
nuts   kho-*ri*-khy   горіхи
peanuts   ze-*mel*-ni   земельні
kho-*rikhy*   горіхи

aspirin
aspi-*run*   аспірин
condom
pre-ze-rva-*tyw*   презерватив
contraceptive
pro-ty-za-*chat*-tye-vy   протизачаттєвий
za-sib   засіб
diarrhoea
po-*nos*   понос

EMERGENCIES
Help!
   rya·*tuy*·te/do·po·mo·*zhit*!
   Рятуйте/Допоможіть!
There's been an accident!
   tam buw ne·*shcha*·sny vy·*padok*!
   Там був нещасний випадок!
I'm lost.
   ya za·blu·*kaw*/za·blu·*ka*·la (m/f)
   Я заблукав/заблукала.
Go away!
   i·*dy*/i·*dit'* (*zvid*·sy)! (inf/pol)
   Іди/Ідіть (звідси)!
Call a doctor!
   (*vy*·klych·te) *li*·ka·rya!
   (Викличте) лікаря!
Call the police!
   vy·kly·chit' mi·*li*·tsi·yu!
   Викличіть міліцію!

medicine
   li·ky (pl)   ліки
nausea
   to·*shno*·ta   тошнота
sunscreen (cream)
   krem vid *son*·tsya   крем від сонця
tampons
   tam·*po*·ny   тампони

LANGUAGE DIFFICULTIES
Do you speak English?
   vy roz·mow·*lya*·ye·te an·*hliys'*·ko·yu *mo*·vo·yu?
   Ви розмовляєте англійською мовою?
Does anyone here speak English?
   khto·*ne*·bud roz·mow·*lya*·ye an·*hliys'*koyu *mo*·vo·yu?
   Хто-небудь розмовляє англійською мовою?
How do you say ... in Ukranian?
   yak ska·*za*·tu ... po uk·ra·*yin*·sky?
   Як сказати ... по-українськи?
What does ... mean?
   shcho o·zna·*cha*·ye ...?
   Що означає ...?
I understand.
   ya ro·zu·*mi*·yu
   Я розумію.
I don't understand (you).
   ya (vas) ne ro·zu·*mi*·yu
   Я (вас) не розумію.
Please write it down.
   za·py·*shit* bud *las*·ka
   Запишіть будь ласка
Can you show me (on the map)?
   vy *mo*·zhe·te po·ka·*za*·ty (me·*ni*) na *kar*·ti?
   Ви можете показати (мені) на карті?

NUMBERS
0	nul'	нуль
1	o·*dyn*/o·*dna*/(m/f)	один/одна/
	o·*dne* (neut)	одне
2	dva/ (m & neut)	два/
	dvi (f)	дві
3	try	три
4	cho·*ty*·ry	чотири
5	pyat'	п'ять
6	shist'	шість
7	sim	сім
8	*vi*·sim	вісім
9	*de*·vyat'	дев'ять
10	*de*·syat'	десять
11	o·*dy*·na·tsyat'	одинадцять
12	dva·*na*·tsyat'	дванадцять
13	try·*na*·tsyat'	тринадцять
14	cho·tyr·*na*·tsyat'	чотирнадцять
15	pya·*tna*·tsyat'	п'ятнадцять
16	shi·*sna*·tsyat'	шістнадцять
17	si·*mna*·tsyat'	сімнадцять
20	*dva*·tsyat'	двадцять
21	*dva*·tsyat' o·*dyn*/	двадцять один/
	o·*dna*/o·*dne*	одна/одне
	(m/f/neut)	
30	*try*·tsyat'	тридцять
40	*so*·rok	сорок
50	pya·de·*syat*	п'ятдесят
60	shis·de·*syat*	шістдесят
70	sim·de·*syat*	сімдесят
80	vi·sim·de·*syat*	вісімдесят
90	*de*·vya·*no*·sto	дев'яносто
100	sto	сто
101	sto o·*dyn*	сто один
1000	*ty*·sya·cha	тисяча

PAPERWORK
name
   i·*mya*   ім'я
nationality
   na·tsi·o·*nal*·nist'   національність
date/place of birth
   da·ta/*mis*·tse   дата/місце
   na·*rod*·zhen·nya   народження
sex/gender
   rid   рід
passport
   pa·sport   паспорт
visa
   vi·za   віза

QUESTION WORDS
Who?	khto?	Хто?
What?	shcho?	Що?

What is it?	shcho tse?	Що це?
When?	ko·ly?	Коли?
Where?	de?	Де
Which?	ko·try? (m)	Котрий?
	ko·tra? (f)	Котра?
	ko·tre? (n)	Котре?
	ko·tri? (pl)	Котрі?
Why?	cho·mu?	Чому?
How?	yak?	Як?

SHOPPING & SERVICES

I'd like to buy ...
ya b kho·tiw/kho·ti·la ku·py·ty ... (m/f)
Я б хотів/хотіла купити ...

How much is it?
skil'·ky tse (vin/vo·na) ko·shtu·ye? (m/f)
Скільки це (він/вона) коштує?

I don't like it.
me·ni ne po·do·ba·yet'·sya
Мені не подобається.

May I look at it?
mo·zhna po·du·vu·tu·sya?
Можна подивитися?

I'm just looking.
ya ly·she dy·wlyu·sya
Я лише дивлюся.

It's cheap.
de·she·vo
Дешево.

It's too expensive.
tse nad·to do·ro·ho
Це надто дорого.

OK, I'll take it.
ha·razd, ya viz'·mu
Гаразд, я візьму.

Do you accept ...?
vy pry·ma·ye·te ...? Ви приймаєте ...?
  credit cards
  kre·dy·tni kar·tky кредитні картки
  travellers cheques
  man·driw·nu·ko·vi che·ky мандрівникові чеки

more
bil'·she більше
less
men·she меньше
smaller
tro·khy men·she трохи меньше
bigger
tro·khy bil'·she трохи більше

I'm looking for ...
ya shu·ka·yu ... Я шукаю ...
  a bank
  bank банк

the church
  tse·rkvu церкву
the city centre
tsentr (mi·sta) центр (міста)
the ... embassy
po·sol'·stvo ... посольство ...
the hospital
li·kar·nya лікарня
my hotel
  miy ho·tel' мій готель
the market
ry·nok ринок
the museum
mu·zey музей
the police station
mi·li·tsi·ya міліція
the post office
po·shta пошта
a public phone
te·le·fon·aw·to·mat телефонавтомат
a public toilet
za·hal·ny tu·a·let загальний туалет
the telephone centre
te·le·fon·ny tsentr телефонний центр
the tourist office
tu·ry·stych·ne byu·ro туристичне бюро

TIME & DATES

What time is it?
ko·tra ho·dy·na? Котра година?
It's (8) o'clock.
(vos'·ma) ho·dy·na (Восьма) година.
in the morning
wran·tsi вранці
in the afternoon
w·den' вдень
in the evening
u·ve·che·ri у вечері

When?	ko·ly?	Коли?
today	s'o·ho·dni	сьогодні
tomorrow	zaw·tra	завтра
yesterday	wcho·ra	вчора

Monday	po·ne·di·lok	понеділок
Tuesday	vi·wto·rok	вівторок
Wednesday	se·re·da	середа
Thursday	che·tver	четвер
Friday	pya·tny·tsya	п'ятниця
Saturday	su·bo·ta	субота
Sunday	ne·di·lya	неділя

January	si·chen'	січень
February	lyu·ty	лютий
March	be·re·zen'	березень
April	kvi·ten'	квітень

May	*tra*·ven′	травень
June	*che*·rven′	червень
July	*ly*·pen′	липень
August	*ser*·pen′	серпень
September	*ve*·re·sen′	вересень
October	*zhow*·ten′	жовтень
November	ly·sto·*pad*	листопад
December	*hru*·den′	грудень

TRANSPORT
Public Transport
What time does the ... leave?
ko·*ly* vid·pra·*wlya*·yet′·sya ...?
Коли відправляється ...?
What time does the ... arrive?
ko·*ly* ... pry·bu·*va*·ye?
Коли ... прибуває?

boat	pa·ro·*plaw*	пароплав
bus	aw·*to*·bus	автобус
plane	li·*tak*	літак
train	*po*·yizd	поїзд
tram	tram·*vay*	трамвай

I'd like a ...
ya b kho·*tiw*/kho·*ti*·la ... (m/f)
Я б хотів/хотіла ...
one·way ticket
kvy·*tok* v o·*dyn* bik
квиток в один бік
return ticket
zvo·*ro*·tny kvy·*tok*
зворотний квиток

I want to go to ...
me·*ni* tre·ba *yi*·kha·ty do ...
Мені треба їхати до ...
The train has been delayed.
po·yizd za·*piz*·nyu·yet·sya
Поїзд запізнюється.
The train has been cancelled.
po·yizd vid·*mi*·ne·no
Поїзд відмінено.

the first
per·shy/*per*·sha (m/f)   перший/перша
the last
o·*stan*·niy   останній
platform number
no·mer plat·*for*·mu   номер платформи
ticket office
kvyt·*ko*·vi *ka*·sy   квиткові каси
timetable
roz·klad   розклад
train station
(za·li·*znych*·ny) vog·*zal*   (залізничний) вокзал

You may come across the following when reading timetables (the first entry is Ukrainian, the second is Russian):

Departures
Відправлення   Отправление
Arrivals
Прибуття   Прибывать
daily
щоденно   ежедневно
on odd dates
парні   чётным дням
on even dates
непарні   нечётным дням

Private Transport
I'd like to hire a ...
ya *kho*·chu *vzya*·tu na pro·*kat* ...
Я хочу взяти на прокат ...
car
ma·*shy*·nu
машину
4WD
cho·ty·*ryokh* pry·vid·*nu* ma·*shy*·nu
чотирьох привідну машину
motorbike
mo·to·*tsykl*
мотоцикл
bicycle
ve·lo·sy·*ped*
велосипед

Is this the road to ...?
tse do·*ro*·ha do ...?
Це дорога до ...?
Where's the nearest service station?
de nay·*blyzh*·cha za·*praw*·ka?
Де найближча заправка?
Fill it up.
za·*pow*·nit′/za·*ly*·te
Заповніть/Залийте.
I'd like ... litres of petrol/gasoline.
da·yte, bud′ *la*·ska, ... *li*·triw ben·*zy*·nu
Дайте, будь ласка, ... літрів бензину.

diesel
di·zel
дізель
leaded petrol
ne·o·*chy*·shche·ny ben·*zyn*
неочищений бензин
unleaded petrol
o·*chy*·shche·ny ben·*zyn*
очищений бензин

(How long) Can I park here?
(yak *dov*·ho) ya *mo*·zhu pry·*par*·ku·*va*·tus tut?
(Як довго) я можу припаркуватись тут?

Where do I pay?
de pla·*ty*·ty?
Де платити?

We need a mechanic.
nam po·*tri*·ben me·*kha*·nik
Нам потрібен механік.

The car/motorbike has broken down at ...
ma·*shu*·na/mo·to·*tsykl* po·la·*maw*·sya na ...
Машина/мотоцикл поламався на ...

The car/motorbike won't start.
ma·*shu*·na/mo·to·*tsykl* ne za·*vo*·dut·sya
Машина/мотоцикл не заводиться

I've run out of petrol.
u *me*·ne za·kin·*chy*·wsya ben·*zyn*
У мене закінчився бензин.

I've had an accident.
ya po·*paw*/po·*pa*·la v ne·*shchas*·ny *vu*·pa·dok (m/f)
Я попав/попала в нещасний випадок.

TRAVEL WITH CHILDREN

Is there a/an ...?
chu *ye* tut ....?
Чи є тут ...?

I need a ...
me·*ni* po·*tri*·bno ...
Мені потрібно ...

  baby change room
  dy·*tya*·cha kim·*na*·ta
  дитяча кімната

  car baby seat
  du·*tya*·che sy·*din*·nya v ma·*shy*·ni
  дитяче сидіння в машині

  child-minding service
  du·*tya*·che ob·slu·*ho*·vu·van·*nya*
  дитяче обслуговування

  children's menu
  du·*tya*·che me·*nyu*
  дитяче меню

  (disposable) nappies/diapers
  (od·no·*ra*·zo·vi) pid·*huz*·ny·ky
  (одноразові) підгузники

  formula
  re·*tse*·it
  рецеіт

  (English-speaking) babysitter
  an·hlo·*mow*·na sy·*dil*·ka
  англомовна сиділка

  highchair
  du·*tya*·chy vy·*so*·ky sti·*lets*
  дитячий високий стілець

  potty
  du·*tya*·chy hor·*shok*
  дитячий горшок

  stroller
  lit·nya vid·*kry*·ta du·*tya*·cha ko·*lyas*·ka
  літня відкрита дитяча коляска

Do you mind if I breastfeed here?
tse ni·*cho*·ho yak·*shcho* ya po·kor·*mlyu* dy·*ty*·nu tut?
Це нічого, якщо я покормлю дитину тут?

Are children allowed?
di·tyam do·*zvo*·le·no?
Дітям дозволено?

Also available from Lonely Planet:
Ukrainian Phrasebook

LANGUAGE

Glossary

You may encounter some of the following terms and signs during your travels in Ukraine. See also the Language chapter (p198).

aeroport – airport
apteka – pharmacy
avia poshta – airmail
avtobus – bus
avtomat – automatic ticket machine
avtostantsiya, avtovokzal – bus station

babushka – literally grandmother, but used generally in Ukrainian society for all older women
bankomat – automated teller machine (ATM)
banush – Hutsul polentalike dish (wetter than *mammalyha*)
banya – bathhouse
benzyn – petrol
bez – without
biblioteka – library
bilyet (Russian) – ticket
biznesmen – literally, 'businessman', often used to mean a small-time operator on the fringe of the law
bluza – embroidered women's blouse
blyny – pancakes
bolshoy (Russian) – big
borshch – traditional Ukrainian soup, often made with beetroot, but comes in a huge number of varieties
boyar – high-ranking noble
bronya – reservation (of train seat, hotel room)
brynza – a crumbly cow's or goat's cheese tasting like feta
bulvar (bul) – boulevard
buterbrod – open sandwich

cholovichy, muzhcheny – men's toilet
cholovick (Ukrainian), **cheloveck** (Russian) – man (also person when taking about group numbers)
CIS – Commonwealth of Independent States; an alliance proclaimed in 1991 of independent states comprising the former USSR republics minus the three Baltic States. Ukraine is only a semimember having signed the alliance, but never ratified it in the national parliament.

dacha – country cottage, summer house
deklaratsiya – customs declaration
deshevy – cheap
devushka – young woman, miss (a common form of address to anyone not yet a *babushka*)

dezhurna – woman looking after a particular floor of a hotel
dim – house
dorohy – expensive
dvorets (Russian) – palace

elektrychka – electrified suburban train
etazh – floor (storey)

gallereya – gallery
gastronom – speciality food shop
gorod (Russian) – city, town
gosteenitsa (Russian) – hotel

haryachy – hot (but not of weather, see *zharky*)
hazeta – newspaper
hetman – Cossack leader
hora – mountain
hryvnia – Ukrainian currency

i, y, ta – and
ikra – caviar
imeni – 'named after'
inozemny – foreign
Intourist – old Soviet State Committee for Tourism, now privatised, split up and in competition with hundreds of other travel agencies

kabina – cabin, for making a phone call in a call centre
kamera skhovu (Ukrainian), **kamera khranenia** (Russian) – left-luggage office
karta – map
kobzar – minstrel-like bard
kozak – Cossack
kemping – camp site; often has small cabins as well as tent sites
kholodny – cold
kino – cinema
klyuch – key
knyga – book
kolhosp – collective farm
kolonka – archaic gas heater
kimnaty (Ukrainian), **komnaty** (Russian) – rooms, used to indicate rooms available for homestays
kimnaty vidpochynku (Ukrainian), **komnaty otdykha** (Russian) – resting rooms found at all major train stations and several smaller ones
kopeck – the smallest unit of Ukrainian currency
kordon – border
kruhlosutochno – around-the-clock

kulak – Stalinist name for a wealthier peasant
kupe – train compartment, most often used to refer to four-berth 2nd-class compartment or 2nd-class train ticket
kvartyra – flat, apartment
kvitantsiya – receipt
kvytok – ticket

lavra – senior monastery
likar – doctor
likarnya – hospital
litak – aeroplane
lyst – letter
lyux – a kind of hotel suite, with a sitting room in addition to bedroom and bathroom; a *poli-lyux* suite is the less spacious version

magazin – shop
maly (Ukrainian), **malenky** (Russian) – small
mammalyha – a Hutsul dish similar to polenta
marka – postage stamp or brand, trademark
marshrut – route
marshrutka, marshrutne taxi – minibus that runs along a fixed route
mashyna – car
matryoshka – set of painted wooden dolls within dolls
maydan – square
meest – seat number
militsiya – police
mist (Ukrainian), **most** (Russian) – bridge
miste (Ukrainian), **mesto** (Russian) – place, seat
misto – city, town
mizhhorodny, mizhmisky – intercity
mizhnarodny – international
more – sea
muzey – museum
muzhcheny, cholovichy – men's toilet

naberezhna (nab) – embankment
nomenklatura – literally, 'list of nominees'; the old government and Communist Party elite
novy – new

oblast – region, administrative district
organizatoriya – organised crime, encompassing everything from small-time rackets to big-time Mafia
ostanovka (Russian) – bus stop
ozero – lake

pamyatnyk – monument, statue
Paskha – Easter
pasport – passport
palats – palace
perepichky – frankfurters deep-fried in dough, fairground-style

perepustka – permit, pass
pereryv – break (when shops, ticket offices, restaurants etc close for an hour or two during the day; this always happens just as you arrive)
peshchera – cave
plan mista – city map
platskart – 3rd-class train sleeper compartment
ploshcha (pl) – square
plyazh – beach
poliklinika – medical centre
poli-lyux – less spacious version of a *lyux*, a kind of hotel suite with a sitting room in addition to the bedroom and bathroom. Equivalent to a semideluxe room, or junior suite.
polonyna – high-mountain pasture
polyana – glade, clearing
poshta, poshtamt – post office
posolstvo – embassy
posvidka – certificate
posylka – parcel
poyizd – train
prokat – rental
prospekt (pr) – avenue
provodnik (m), **provodnitsa** (f) – carriage attendant on a train
provulok (prov) – lane
prymisky vokzal – local train station (where *elektrychky* leave from)
pysanky – patterned eggs
pyvo – beer

rada – assembly, parliament
rakhunok – bill
rayon – region
restoran – restaurant
rekomendovany lyst – registered letter
remont, na remont – closed for repairs (a sign you see all too often)
richny vokzal – river station
rika – river
rizdvo – Christmas (see also *Svyata Vecherya*)
rushnyky – long embroidered towels
rynok – market

sad – garden/s
salo – pig fat
sanitarny den – literally, 'sanitary day'; the monthly day when some museums, shops, restaurants, hotel dining rooms etc still shut down for cleaning
selo – village
sich – Cossack fort or settlement
shchyot (Russian) – bill
shvudky poyizd – literally, fast train; a long-distance train
skhema transportu – transport map

snidanok – breakfast
snih – snow
sobor – cathedral
sontse – sun
sorochky – embroidered men's shirts
spalny vahon – 1st-class sleeping compartment on a train, with only two bunks
spusk (Russian) – descent, slope
stary – old
stolova – canteen/cafeteria, most commonly found in Crimea
Svyata Vecherya – Christmas Eve, Christmas eve dinner, an important part of the season's celebrations

taksofon – pay telephone
talon – bus ticket, coupon
teatr – theatre
teatralna kasa – theatre ticket office
telegrama – telegram
tramvay – tram
tryzub – Ukraine's trident symbol
tserka – church
TsUM (Tsentralny Univermag) – generic name of department store
tsyrk – circus (almost always with performing animals)
tualet – toilet
tudy i nazad (Ukrainian), **tuda i obratno** (Russian) – 'there and back', return ticket
turbaza – tourist camp

univermag, universalnyy magazin – department store
uzviz – descent, slope

vahon – train carriage
vanna – bath
varenyky – dumplings with a variety of possible fillings
velosyped – bicycle
velyky – big
voda – water
vodopad – waterfall
vokzal – station
vulytsya (vul) – street
vykhidny den – day off
vyshyvka – embroidery

z – with
zal – hall, room
zaliznychny vokzal – train station
zamok – castle, fortress
zamovlennya – reservation (of hotel room)
zapovidnyk – national park
zaproshuvaty – invitation
zavtrak (Russian) – breakfast
zharky – hot (weather)
zheton – token (for metro etc)
zhinochy – women's toilet
zlodiy – thief
zupynka – bus stop
zvorotny kvytok – return ticket

Behind the Scenes

THIS BOOK

This 1st edition of *Ukraine* was researched and written by Sarah Johnstone. This guide was commissioned in Lonely Planet's London office and produced in Melbourne.

THANKS from the Author

Sarah Johnstone The people I'm grateful to wouldn't fit into my allotted word space – which I think says something about the country. But there are several people I really must thank in writing. Above all, special thanks have to go to Slav at Lviv Ecotour for guiding, proofreading and general helpfulness above and beyond the call of duty.

Vitaliy (sorry for the late reply, but we were making revolution, you know?) Pavliuk in Kolomyya also deserves a mention for the info, directions and coffee, as does his mum Ira for her cooking. Ihor Brudny and Sergiy Sorokin in Yalta were also of great assistance.

Others who lent a hand include Cristina Teresa O'Keefe, Susan Waage, Peter Dickinson at *What's On Kiev*, Sergiy at Solo East Travel, MR (sorry!) Oleska Haiworonski, Yuriy Tatarchuk, Taras, Janna, Anastacia, Anna, Elena, Olena and Dima (best picnic ever) and Arsen and his granny.

Dyakuyu also to editor Imogen Bannister and cartographer/language coach Valentina Kremenchutskaya for unlimited patience and great emails.

Finally, thanks to neighbours Anna and Richard for watering the plants and the others holding the London fort.

CREDITS

Commissioning Editor Fiona Christie
Coordinating Editor Imogen Bannister
Coordinating Cartographer Valentina Kremenchutskaya
Coordinating Layout Designer Yvonne Bischofberger
Managing Cartographer Mark Griffiths
Assisting Editor Kyla Gillzan
Assisting Cartographer Simon Tillema
Cover Designer Candice Jacobus
Project Manager Celia Wood
Language Content Coordinator Quentin Frayne

Thanks to: Sally Darmody, Chris LeeAck

ACKNOWLEDGMENTS

Many thanks to the following for the use of their content:

Globe on back cover © Mountain High Maps 1993 Digital Wisdom, Inc.

SEND US YOUR FEEDBACK

We love to hear from travellers – your comments keep us on our toes and help make our books better. Our well-travelled team reads every word on what you loved or loathed about this book. Although we cannot reply individually to postal submissions, we always guarantee that your feedback goes straight to the appropriate authors, in time for the next edition. Each person who sends us information is thanked in the next edition – and the most useful submissions are rewarded with a free book. See the Behind the Scenes section.

To send us your updates – and find out about Lonely Planet events, newsletters and travel news – visit our award-winning website: **www.lonelyplanet.com/feedback**.

Note: We may edit, reproduce and incorporate your comments in Lonely Planet products such as guidebooks, websites and digital products, so let us know if you don't want your comments reproduced or your name acknowledged. For a copy of our privacy policy, go to www.lonelyplanet.com/privacy.

THE LONELY PLANET STORY

The story begins with a classic travel adventure: Tony and Maureen Wheeler's 1972 journey across Europe and Asia to Australia. There was no useful information about the overland trail then, so Tony and Maureen published the first Lonely Planet guidebook to meet a growing need.

From a kitchen table, Lonely Planet has grown to become the largest independent travel publisher in the world, with offices in Melbourne (Australia), Oakland (USA) and London (UK). Today Lonely Planet guidebooks cover the globe. There is an ever-growing list of books and information in a variety of media. Some things haven't changed. The main aim is still to make it possible for adventurous travellers to get out there – to explore and better understand the world.

At Lonely Planet we believe travellers can make a positive contribution to the countries they visit – if they respect their host communities and spend their money wisely. Every year 5% of company profit is donated to charities around the world.

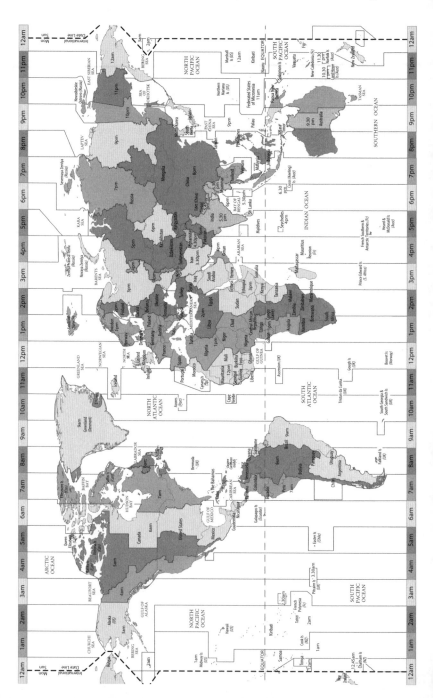

Index

000 Map pages
000 Location of colour photographs

INDEX

216

MAP LEGEND

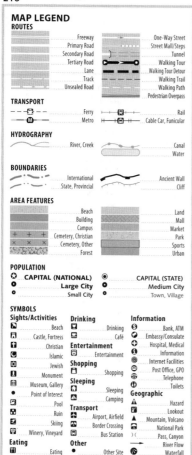

LONELY PLANET OFFICES

Australia
Head Office
Locked Bag 1, Footscray, Victoria 3011
☎ 03 8379 8000, fax 03 8379 8111
talk2us@lonelyplanet.com.au

USA
150 Linden St, Oakland, CA 94607
☎ 510 893 8555, toll free 800 275 8555
fax 510 893 8572, info@lonelyplanet.com

UK
72-82 Rosebery Ave,
Clerkenwell, London EC1R 4RW
☎ 020 7841 9000, fax 020 7841 9001
go@lonelyplanet.co.uk

Published by Lonely Planet Publications Pty Ltd
ABN 36 005 607 983